RAGE COMPANY

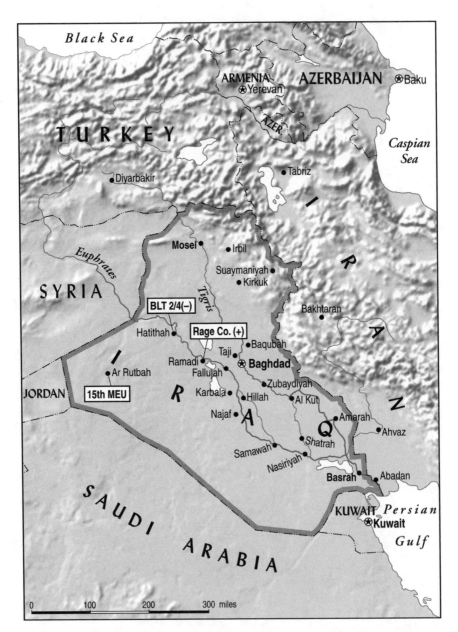

Iraq: The 15th Marine Expeditionary Unit in Anbar province 2006–2007

RAGE COMPANY

A Marine's Baptism by Fire

Thomas P. Daly

WILEY

John Wiley & Sons, Inc.

Published by John Wiley & Sons, Inc., Hoboken, New Jersey
Published simultaneously in Canada

Photo Credits: courtesy of Sergeant Martin Bustamante, 41, 42 (top), 125 (top), 266, 267; courtesy of Staff Sergeant Jerry Eagle, 275 (bottom), 276, 277; courtesy of Corporal Brian Holloway, 45 (bottom), 128 (bottom right), 270 (bottom), 271 (top and bottom left); courtesy of Lieutenant Richard Jahelka, 129 (top), 271 (bottom right); courtesy of Captain John Smith, 272 (top); courtesy of Lieutenant James Thomas, 129 (bottom), 130, 131, 132, 272 (bottom), 273, 274, 275 (top).

For general information about our other products and services, please contact our Customer Care Department within the United States at (800) 762-2974, outside the United States at (317) 572-3993 or fax (317) 572-4002.

Wiley also publishes its books in a variety of electronic formats. Some content that appears in print may not be available in electronic books. For more information about Wiley products, visit our web site at www.wiley.com.

Library of Congress Cataloging-in-Publication Data

Daly, Thomas P., date.
 Rage company : a Marine's baptism by fire / Thomas P. Daly.
  p. cm.
 Includes index.
 ISBN 978-0-470-44430-6 (cloth)
1. Operation Squeeze Play, Iraq, 2006. 2. Iraq War, 2003–Campaigns-Iraq–Ramadi. 3. Iraq War, 2003–Personal narratives, American. 4. Ramadi (Iraq)–History, Military–21st century. 5. Daly, Thomas P., 1982– I. Title.
 DS79.766.R36D35 2009
 956.704'4342-dc22

                                                                2009028777

Printed in the United States of America
10 9 8 7 6 5 4 3 2 1

*For lost friends
and fallen heroes.
May the world know of your sacrifice.*

Contents

Photo galleries start on pages 41, 125 and 266.

Foreword

Counterinsurgency theoreticians talk about winning hearts and minds; the practitioners—the grunts—in Ramadi focused on staying alive. When Lieutenant Thomas Daly arrived in late 2006, the U.S. battalion inside the city had mapped the location of eighty-three roadside bombs on the main streets. More bombs were planted each day than the Marine engineers could clear. No sensible patrol leader took the same route twice. No sane infantryman walked into the open. No convoy drove down a road that the engineers hadn't swept an hour earlier.

Insurgencies that are fought for the allegiance of the people are inherently local. Insurgencies are won or lost at the local level. "Rage"—the radio call sign of Daly's infantry company—vividly describes a local fight that illustrates hard truths and gets down to the nub of the matter: how do you break a tough insurgency? Daly's answer is: deploy tough troops who will persist year after year under grim conditions, absorbing and giving back blows, day after day, until a political and cultural dynamic grabs hold and changes the nature of the war.

Rage Company is a straightforward, honest account of what U.S. soldiers and Marines do when placed in a hostile urban area. Daly describes the valor and the selfishness, the heroics and the mistakes, the rushes to judgment and the regrets. His particular skill is his ability to suspend judgment and to present each wrenching combat decision from different points of view, empathizing with U.S. and Iraqi leaders even when he believed their snap decisions and impetuous commands were in error.

When Daly arrived in the fall of 2006, the United States was losing on the two critical fronts in Iraq. On the western front, concentrated around the province of Al Anbar, a U.S. Marine intelligence assessment reported that al Qaeda controlled the population. In Baghdad on the eastern front, a civil war was raging, and the Sunnis were being driven from their homes. Yet a year later, the tide of war was flowing in the coalition's favor.

What happened? According to one narrative that has achieved mythical status, in 2007 President Bush surged five brigades, imbued with counterinsurgency tactics that won the war. According to this view, the U.S. Army in 2007 finally grasped and implemented the four "pillars" of counterinsurgency: (1) provide the population with security, (2) give them services and jobs, (3) appoint honest government representatives, and (4) apply the rule of law. Given these four pillars, the population turned against the insurgents.

Most in the mainstream press subsequently subscribed to the "four pillars" explanation. But it's not what happened in Iraq. A combat veteran once wrote, "There is a vast difference in the perception of wartime events in histories and documents written later."[1] *Rage Company* tells how Ramadi turned around, from the viewpoint of a modest, sharp-eyed lieutenant who recounts the actual events, independent of theories.

Ramadi was the capital of Al Anbar, a Sunni province the size of North Carolina. During the war, Al Anbar was an economy of force operation, accounting for one-fifth of U.S. forces in Iraq and two-fifths of the casualties. A vast land occupied by truculent tribes, Al Anbar, according to the conventional wisdom, would be the last province to be pacified. The fractious Sunni tribes fostered several insurgent resistance groups, and by mid-2004, Al Qaeda in Iraq, or AQI, had emerged as the most ruthless. Composed mainly of tribal youths but led by outsiders, AQI summarily executed any sheikh who opposed its wishes and declared that its "emirate" would be ruled from Ramadi, a city of four hundred thousand, sixty miles northwest of Baghdad, along the banks

---

1. E. B. Sledge, *With the Old Breed: At Peleliu and Okinawa* (New York: Random House, 1981), p. 3.

of the Euphrates. In 2005, the arch terrorist Abu Musab al-Zarqawi preached in a mosque in the city and narrowly avoided capture twice. In early 2006, the sheikhs in Ramadi agreed that their followers could join the local police. Al Qaeda responded by murdering several sheikhs and killing more than fifty recruits.

So in September 2006, when a midlevel and rather obscure sheikh named Abu Risha Sattar urged the tribes around Ramadi to rebel against al Qaeda, he wasn't given much chance of succeeding. Things looked bleak in Al Anbar, while to the east, Baghdad was falling apart. In Washington, the press and the administration believed the war was lost. The first half of Daly's book graphically depicts why. He describes the frustration of undertaking patrol after patrol, all the while knowing the unseen enemy is watching every move of his Marines and deciding when and how to attack.

The rough rule of thumb was that every soldier or Marine in a line unit patrolled outside the wire at least once a day. Many units cycled between internal guard and maintenance duties and external patrols. In a rifle company, each squad conducted one dismounted or mounted six-hour patrol each day (or night). That was a heavy grind after three or four months. It was much harder for the soldiers with twelve- to fifteen-month rotations than for the Marines with seven to ten months.

Iraq was essentially a police war. We didn't do a good job of modifying military training and force structure to include police methods and measures. Soldiers aren't policemen—except when they are. In a U.S. city, about two policemen conduct detective work for every four police officers patrolling the streets. In Daly's battalion, nine soldiers performed the intelligence-gathering and detective tasks for five hundred infantrymen. Daly describes how frustrating it was to patrol.

In the second half of his book—about the winter of 2007—the tone of the book and the tide of the battle change. Local Sunnis commanded by former Iraqi army officers appeared at Daly's outpost, calling themselves "Thawar Al Anbar" and carrying notes of approval from a Marine battalion located outside the city. At first suspicious, Daly and the other beleaguered U.S. soldiers and Marines were quick to grasp the implication. Their greatest, most frustrating challenge was identifying the enemy hiding among the civilians outside the wire. Now Sunnis were offering to point them out. So vivid are Daly's descriptions that the reader can sense the tipping point and can anticipate that al Qaeda in

Iraq will strike back savagely. What a tale Daly tells! You won't read this
in textbook theories about counterinsurgency.

Gradually, the insurgents lost the initiative. Incidents of violence
in Al Anbar plummeted from more than 450 per month in late 2006
to fewer than 100 by mid-2007.[2] U.S. fatalities in Anbar fell from
43 percent of the total in 2006 to 17 percent in 2007.[3] From late 2006
onward, the coalition and Iraqi forces initiated a majority of the contacts
in Al Anbar.[4] The number of tips from the citizenry, who sensed that al
Qaeda was being driven out, skyrocketed, while Sunni recruits for the
police and the army (with assurances of assignment inside Al Anbar)
exceeded the number of openings.[5]

General David Petraeus and Lieutenant General Raymond Odierno
skillfully orchestrated the deployments of the U.S. surge forces. The
crucial precondition for success was that the Sunnis were predisposed to
greet the surge troops positively in 2007, which had not been the case
in 2004. Al Qaeda, resembling Robespierre's Terror in 1792, had killed
too many sheikhs, while empowering the criminal class and antagoniz-
ing the Sunni population. But the tribes weren't strong enough to push
out al Qaeda on their own. So they turned to the strongest tribe—the
U.S. military.

The U.S.-Sunni battlefield cooperation in Ramadi that Daly writes
about spread across Iraq. Petraeus, who took command of all forces in
Iraq in January 2007, used the "Awakening" as the lever to flip over
the war. In February 2007, he visited Ramadi and was impressed by
the thousands of tribal Sunnis joining what the American high command called "emergency response units." Petraeus authorized U.S.
commanders across Iraq to recruit similar irregular forces. Petraeus
and his operational deputy, Odierno, had already established U.S.
company-size outposts—identical to Daly's outpost in Ramadi—
throughout Baghdad and the surrounding belts of farmlands. By
2008, U.S. battalions were paying ninety thousand Iraqis, mostly
Sunnis, who had volunteered for neighborhood watch groups called

---

2. Jonathan Schroden, *Measures for Security in a Counterinsurgency* (Alexandria, VA:
Center for Naval Analyses, 2008), p. 10.

3. See icasualties.org. In 2006, there were 356 fatalities in Al Anbar, and 822 overall,
or 43 percent. In 2007, there were 163, and 904 overall, or 17 percent.

4. Schroden, *Measures for Security in a Counterinsurgency*, p. 12.

5. Ibid., p. 18.

the Sons of Iraq and who operated under the supervision of the U.S. outposts.

Ramadi, Baghdad, and a dozen other cities were taken back piece by piece, erecting barricades and fortifying police precincts. The greatest contribution of the tribal uprising—the Awakening—occurred outside the cities, by "draining the swamp." Thousands of kilometers of lush farmlands and dense undergrowth had enabled al Qaeda to rest and refit in safety. Once the tribes turned, those scattered hiding places of al Qaeda were eliminated.

The war in Iraq that had seemed a lost cause and a huge international embarrassment for the United States ended with reasonable stability and the gradual withdrawal of U.S. forces. America's mortal enemy—the al Qaeda organization that plunged the airplanes into the Twin Towers— suffered an enormous setback. Al Qaeda claimed to be fighting for the sake of the Sunnis. By the end of Daly's tour, al Qaeda was despised and hunted by those same Sunnis.

Daly does a terrific job of bringing the reader onto the urban battle-field and showing what happened that caused the turnaround and why. Without the perseverance, decency, and grit of U.S. soldiers and Marines, the Sunnis would not have turned against al Qaeda.

—Bing West
Former assistant secretary of defense for
International Security Affairs
in the Reagan administration

Acknowledgments

First, I would like to extend my sincere thanks to the countless Americans who have served in Ramadi. Regardless of your branch of service, military occupation, race, or gender, your sacrifice and perseverance in the face of a bold and determined enemy is a proud addition to our nation's history. With that in mind, I have tried to write as factually as possible regarding your daily existence in Ramadi. For any oversight on my part, I humbly apologize.

To the officers and Marines of Rage Company, you truly are magnificent bastards. May this book serve as a constant reminder of this fact. To Rage 6, your leadership enabled the Sunni Awakening.

T. X. Hammes, this book is the result of your introduction. Without it, *Rage Company* may never have been written. To my agent, E. J. McCarthy, your knowledge and skill are outdone only by your professionalism.

I'd also like to thank the staff at John Wiley & Sons, Inc., and in particular my editor, Stephen Power, for their support and belief in the potential of this story.

A special thanks to my father, who as a Marine officer set the bar very high. To my loving mother, brothers, and sisters, I am blessed to have your support.

Finally, I thank my wife. You were the light at the end of every firefight.

Maps

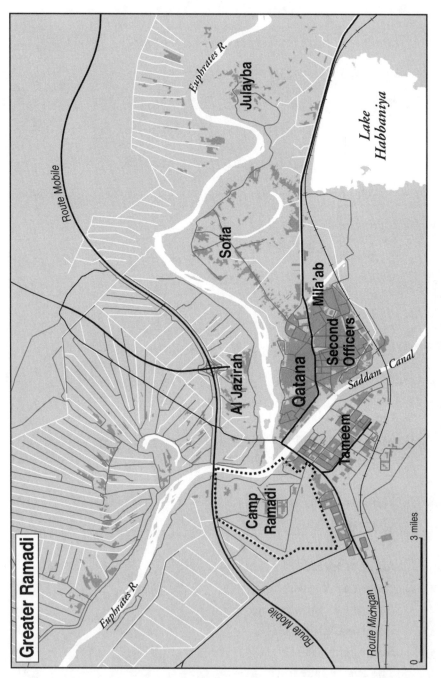

Greater Ramadi. The capital of Anbar Province, Ar Ramadi.

PART ONE

1st Battalion,
37th Armor

1

Becoming a Bandit: The Baptism

November 27, 2006

Lieutenant James Thomas walked out the front door of Combat Outpost (COP) Grant. Two concrete structures made up the American fortress in southern Ramadi. A few months earlier, two Iraqi families had called the structures home; now the buildings were covered in camouflage netting, sandbags, and reinforced wooden fighting positions. About three feet away, directly in front of the lieutenant, was a seven-foot wall of dark green sandbags. He briskly walked out from underneath the camouflage netting, following the wall as it snaked back to his left. The ground-level view of Ramadi confronted Lieutenant Thomas.

This was a city—a dense, quiet (for the moment) urban sprawl of structures. Block after block of small storefronts and houses occupied his vision. If you replaced the towering minarets and mosques with steeples and churches, Ramadi didn't look all that different from urban America. That is, assuming you could visualize what the city had looked like before undergoing years of conflict and neglect.

The neighborhood surrounding COP Grant was mostly residential, single-family homes. Three and a half years earlier, before the invasion, a hundred thousand people had lived in this southern part of Ramadi.

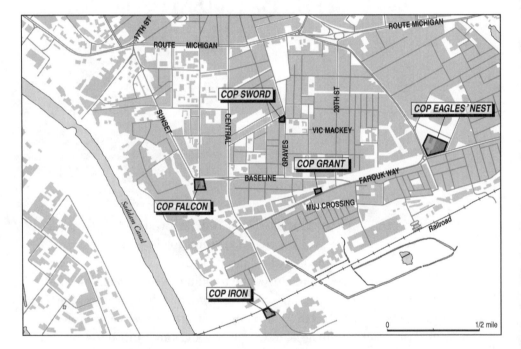

Area of Operations Bandit: 1-37 Armor's area of operations in southern Ramadi.

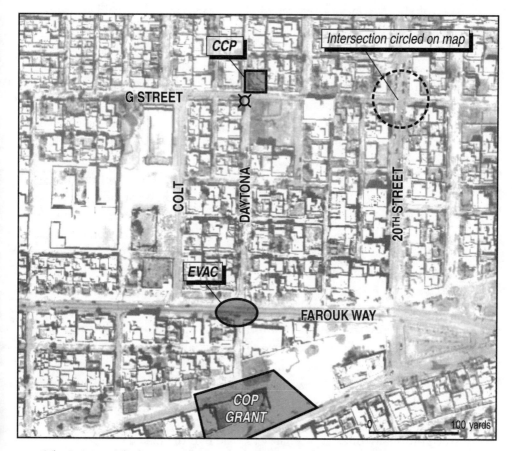

The Baptism: The location of events surrounding Combat Outpost Grant on November 27, 2006.

Now it appeared to be uninhabited. Most of the streets were covered in so much sand and dust that one might mistakenly assume they weren't paved.

The reinforced squad of Marines was already in formation, clearly visible to any observer. The nervousness of the first patrol was obvious. The purpose of the patrol was routine, nothing more than an orientation for the recently arrived Marine unit. If faces could tell a story, however, not many of the Marines were excited. Even the handful of soldiers who accompanied the Marines looked uncomfortable—and they had been here for months.

"Departing friendly lines," said Corporal Jesus Davila's voice in Lieutenant Thomas's left ear. The corporal was talking over the personal role radio (PRR), an unsecured intrasquad push-to-talk radio.

Lieutenant Thomas looked at his watch: 1547. It was the height of the day, and there hadn't been a gunfight yet. He stepped down into the dusty street, a one-foot drop. A Bradley fighting vehicle and an M1 Abrams tank were still in the COP's parking lot, both engines running. The vehicles were COP Grant's quick reaction force, on standby in case of an emergency. There was another Abrams tank 300 meters east down Farouk Way, the east-to-west-running street where COP Grant was located.

The squad's lead element, Lance Corporal Jason Heidbreder and an army sergeant, turned north and started to walk up Daytona Street. The men were 200 meters away from Lieutenant Thomas. Thomas stopped to adjust his gear and allow the formation to spread out. The red-and-white bandana under his Kevlar helmet was already soaking wet, and the thought of how nervous he appeared to his Marines must have crossed his racing mind. It was their first combat patrol. The dispersion was good, and the final element began to move. The dust in the street was probably a solid two inches deep on Farouk Way, but as the Marines turned onto Daytona, the asphalt was visible to the naked eye.

Lieutenant Thomas saw something out of the corner of his left eye. A dark black sedan, probably a BMW, was paralleling the formation on Colt, the adjacent street to the west. Although the lieutenant had seen vehicles being driven around the COP all day, this was different. The platoon commander for Rage Company, 2nd Platoon (Rage 2), maneuvered around the concrete barrier that prevented vehicular traffic from entering Farouk Way. His attention was precisely focused. The situation was heavily to the enemy's advantage.

The entire squad was on the same street, which limited its firepower to the front. On the flanks were two- and three-story homes, all surrounded by an exterior wall. Each had a two- to four-foot retaining wall on the roof, making every structure a small fortress to fight from. Every fifty yards there was also a narrow single lane, a path between houses, too small for a sedan to fit down, but a perfect spot for someone to shoot from and then quickly disappear out of view. The difficulty of winning in the urban landscape of Iraq was immediately clear to the religion major from the University of Rochester.

The formation now stretched about 250 meters along Daytona Street. The point element was coming up on the first four-way intersection they were supposed to cross. Heidbreder and the sergeant stopped to allow the rest of the first four-man fire team to catch up. They would provide security as the point element crossed. Lieutenant Thomas's eyes were fixated on the sergeant; something did not look right. The sergeant turned around to yell at the rest of the team to move faster. The concern on his face would soon become warranted. As the sergeant turned back to the front, a black sedan appeared at the far intersection. The sedan was less than 100 meters north of the point element. It looked like the same BMW the lieutenant had seen earlier.

"Rage 2 Actual, this is Dirty Beans, we got a . . ." Corporal Davila was on the PRR again.

Lance Corporal Heidbreder's weapon went to the ready. The black sedan slowly moved through the intersection. As soon as it left sight, it immediately went into reverse and reappeared. Lieutenant Thomas was already running, as Heidbreder began sighting in on the vehicle through his scope. The distinct sound of high-velocity 5.56mm projectiles filled the air. It was quickly followed by the chattering of dozens of rounds of 7.62mm.

Instinctively, Lieutenant Thomas focused in on the source of the noise, the BMW. The twenty-six-year-old New Yorker was sprinting now, his body propelled by adrenaline. He looked back at his Marine. Heidbreder was down. The lieutenant's ears were bombarded with sounds of pandemonium: on the left blared continual verbal traffic via the intrasquad radio, and on the right, the shouting of the combatants and the deafening din of gunfire going downrange. The black BMW sped off as the sergeant on point unloaded his entire magazine, almost thirty rounds, into the back windshield.

"Far right! CCP far right!" the young platoon commander shouted as he ran. His Marines knew that he was directing them to establish the casualty collection point in the far right building of the intersection. Heidbreder was struggling to get up. He couldn't. The sergeant on point dragged him to cover against a courtyard wall. Within seconds, Corporal Davila had dynamically breached the locked gate to the structure's courtyard, by using a small charge of plastic explosive. Inaccurate insurgent rifle fire filled the street. Lieutenant Thomas made it to his wounded Marine, kneeled next to him, and tried to analyze the wound's severity. Blood sprayed the lieutenant in the face. Heidbreder had been shot in the right side of the throat, and the semiconscious Marine was aware enough to recognize his platoon commander. "I'm sorry, sir. I'm sorry," said Heidbreder. The apologizing Marine was foremost in James Thomas's mind. He asked himself a single question: can I get Heidbreder out of here fast enough?

Hearing the gunfire, I walked from my half of the platoon's staging area in COP Grant and crossed over into the command building. I had to sidestep a soldier in full combat gear wearing workout shorts and a pair of sandals. Ten minutes earlier, Lieutenant Thomas had been briefing me on his squad-size patrol. We discussed the areas my patrol would hit following his. Rage 2 was graciously allowing me—the company Fire Support Team and Intelligence Cell leader— to command his Marines in combat. It was a subtle display of trust that weighed on my mind as I listened to our first firefight. Just then, Corporal Brian Holloway's hand slammed hard into the cinder-block wall next to the door. We were face-to-face, our noses only inches apart, but the sound of gunfire forced the twenty-one-year-old squad leader to shout, "Lieutenant Daly, they won't let us leave the building! The lieutenant is asking for the rest of the platoon to maneuver out down Farouk Way to the intersection of—"

Corporal Holloway continued speaking, but my train of thought was interrupted by one of the army captains who was in command at the COP.

He screamed into my ear, "You're not fuckin' going! I have one case-vac vehicle, and when it leaves, it leaves with the best medical care we have, our docs. This is my COP and I am telling you, you aren't going anywhere unless *I* say you can."

The professionalism of our earlier conversations was gone, the second casualty of this brief firefight. I turned to Corporal Holloway and said, "Get every Marine in your squad in this room!" I pointed to the foyer directly behind him. With its spiral staircase and ornate tiles on the walls, it was the most decadent staging room I had ever seen.

I looked back at the captain. I am sure he wanted to choke the life out of me. He knew there was only one reason to stage the unit, so I could brief them on the situation and leave to assist Lieutenant Thomas. Before he could act on his thoughts of strangulation, the combat operations center (COC) went deadly quiet as Lieutenant Thomas's voice came on the radio.

"Cobra Main, this is Rage 2 Actual. We have gone firm in building 146, patrol sector Juliet 8. We have one urgent surgical Medevac, gunshot wound to the throat. Requesting Medevac at our position."

The captain responded without hesitation. "Bullshit. We are not sending any of our vehicles down Daytona; those roads are not cleared and blocked by concrete barriers. Tell him he will have to 'man pack' the casualty back down to Farouk Way, where the casevac will link up with him." The radio operator relayed his intent to Rage 2 Actual, Lieutenant Thomas. The captain and I stared at each other. We both knew that an Abrams tank could roll right over a concrete barrier without a problem. And Lieutenant Thomas had just walked down Daytona—so what was too dangerous for the captain's tanks was safe enough for the dismounted Marines of Rage 2. I put on my Kevlar helmet and walked out of the COC, wondering whether he would have made the same call if one of his soldiers had been shot. The Marines were assembled. As the senior Marine, I had a decision to make.

Lieutenant Thomas threw the handset at his radio operator in disgust. Blood was beginning to pool on the courtyard floor, and he could hear one of the Marines screaming at the Iraqi family huddled inside to "shut the hell up." The family's loud sobs were intermingled with the distinct sound of oxygen and blood mixing in Heidbreder's throat as he lay unconscious. Doc Rodriguez looked up at the platoon commander, maintaining pressure on the torn arterial tissue.

"Less than an hour, sir." The navy corpsman was calm and somber.

Lieutenant Thomas jumped on the PRR. "Davila, we are man packing the casualty back the way we came to the intersection of

Daytona and Farouk Way. We need to move ASAP. Use a fire team to carry Heidbreder with a hasty litter, send two flankers with the litter team, lead and follow the litter with a team." Lieutenant Thomas released the push-to-talk button on his chest and looked down at Doc Rodriguez. Sweat was pouring out of the lieutenant. "Get him ready to move," he ordered.

On the roof, Corporal Davila was concerned. He had been to Ramadi before as a private first class back in 2004, and there was only one reason why the enemy was currently not engaging the patrol with small arms: they were moving closer. From his position he had limited observation to the west, and he knew the enemy was most likely going to exploit this by engaging the Marines as they left the relative safety of the home they occupied. The squad leader spotted a pile of two-by-fours in a corner and called up one of his fire team leaders. The team leader, Corporal William Bradford, took a knee next to him.

"Use these two-by-fours to get across to the roof of the house next door," said Corporal Davila. "I need you to cover the approach to the west so we don't get cornered in this house. The far side of that roof over there is slightly elevated above all the others around here so use that to your advantage. Take your sweet-ass time, too, and I will leave you." The team leader was moving before he finished. The thought of insurgents using the two-by-fours for the same purpose flashed in the squad leader's mind—why else would they be up here?

Davila got on the PRR. "Rage 2 Actual, this is Dirty Beans. I am putting a fire team on the roof of the home to our north to get a better field of fire to cover our movement out of here."

The lieutenant responded instantly. "Roger. I'll let you know when we are ready to move down here. We will start moving as soon as you displace from the roof."

Lieutenant Thomas began to account for each fire team in his mind. His attachments were already staging in the courtyard, and the first fire team was lifting Heidbreder as Thomas released the PRR.

A rocket-propelled grenade (RPG) streaked over the roof, and the sounds of gunfire again pierced the afternoon sky.

Corporal Bradford was on the PRR: "Muj three hundred fifty meters to the west on a rooftop. They just shot an RPG without—" The sound of his fire team's M249 SAW (squad automatic weapon) firing at the cyclic rate cut off the end of his transmission. A second RPG flew over the building. The urgent need to be decisive must have flashed in

Lieutenant Thomas's mind. They may have been there for only about five minutes, stabilizing the casualty, but the enemy was quickly maneuvering on the Marines' fixed position. The longer the patrol was stationary, the more precarious the situation would become.

"Davila, are you ready to displace?" asked Lieutenant Thomas.

"I am, sir," replied Davila.

Corporal Bradford launched two grenades from his M203 before he crawled back over the two-by-fours and onto Davila's roof. The team skipped down the stairs and through the Iraqi home, passing Lieutenant Thomas as they reached the courtyard. The first fire team was already out the gate. The squad anxiously moved out onto Daytona Street, with Corporal Davila and Lieutenant Thomas being the last two out. It was the same problem for the platoon commander, his entire unit spread down a single street.

Two Marines carried Heidbreder's unconscious body in a standard-issue poncho. The waterproof, camouflage material was the quickest improvised stretcher Doc Rodriguez could put together. As Lieutenant Thomas made it out into the intersection, a world of mayhem erupted. Numerous RPK and PKM machine gun positions opened up on the squad from multiple directions. Every man ran down the street toward Farouk Way.

The fire came perpendicular to the direction of their movement, and the Marines instinctively used the courtyard walls as cover. Lieutenant Thomas paused at the first alleyway he came upon. He watched as his men sprinted down the street, rounds skipping in the dust and debris. Then a burst of machine gun fire exploded over his head, slicing through shards of glass at the top of the wall. In slow motion, the green glass seemed to float past the lieutenant's face, glaring in the sunlight as it fell.

Down the street, Corporal Davila threw an M67 fragmentation grenade into a second-floor window. It was a hell of a throw. Then the stretcher team sprinted out into the open, exposing themselves to the alley directly in front of Lieutenant Thomas. Another burst of machine gun fire shot down the alley toward the Marines. They made it through, but Lieutenant Thomas noticed blood pouring out of Heidbreder, and the poncho that carried him was tearing apart under his weight.

The platoon commander unloaded his magazine as he went past the alley, trading inaccurate fire with the enemy machine gun position. Arriving at the improvised stretcher, he helped Doc Rodriguez apply pressure to the wound. The Marines resumed the mad dash toward Farouk Way, taking fire as they passed each alley. Two Marines carried Heidbreder, alternating between the different two-man buddy carries taught at boot camp. Doc Rodriguez continued to work on the wound as they moved between courtyard walls. Still 100 meters from the case-vac site, Lieutenant Thomas watched as the M113 ambulance pulled out into the intersection, waiting for Heidbreder. Corporal Davila was already there; he popped green smoke to obscure the vehicle and make it more difficult for the enemy to target. As Rage 2 sprinted, the air filled Lieutenant Thomas's lungs with gunfire smoke; yelling and screaming bombarded his ears. The platoon commander was oblivious to these distractions as he closed in on the vehicle. He allowed only one thought into his mind: get Heidbreder out of here.

One of the flankers went down just off to Lieutenant Thomas's right. The platoon commander could see the elation on the Marine's face as he got back up and realized he had only tripped and not been shot. Nearing the vehicle, Lieutenant Thomas saw the army first sergeant responsible for Medevacs coming out of COP Grant. The experienced soldier casually walked toward him on his left, indifferent to the bullets and ricochets dancing around his feet. The ramp to the vehicle was open, and the first sergeant helped Doc Rodriguez and Lieutenant Thomas place Heidbreder inside. Then he grabbed Lieutenant Thomas by his flak jacket. "Is any of this yours?" the first sergeant screamed over the .50 caliber machine guns blaring away around him. Lieutenant Thomas looked down and noticed that his entire torso was covered in Heidbreder's blood.

"No. Now get him out of here!" said the lieutenant. He took a knee behind a concrete barrier next to Corporal Davila. The two Marines began to engage multiple muzzle flashes as they waited for the convoy to move out. "Sir, we need to move!" Davila shouted at Lieutenant Thomas. The platoon commander ignored Davila, intent on engaging the enemy that had harassed him all the way to the Medevac site. Davila shouted again. Lieutenant Thomas turned to see his squad leader moving back to COP Grant. He also noticed that a humvee had pulled up right behind him, only a few feet away. The barrel of the vehicle's .50 caliber machine gun was directly above his head. Lieutenant Thomas immediately regretted ignoring his squad leader. The concussion of the machine gun opening fire knocked him flat on his back. He watched from the ground as the large-caliber bullets punished the origin of the muzzle flashes he had been engaging. Lieutenant Thomas got to his feet and quickly moved past the convoy, entering the confines of COP Grant. The inaugural running of what would be known as the "Daytona 500" was over.

I was still standing in the staging room of the command building. The rest of the platoon had formed in a small circle with all eyes fixed on me. Each pair was pleading with me to lead them out into the fire. The Marines knew one of us was down, and they wanted to get even.

Standing on my left was Lance Corporal Benjamin Eakin. Shaking and muttering that he was ready, he gazed toward the ceiling. Dust fell from every crack in the building as the MK-19 grenade launchers and other crew-served positions on the roof covered Rage 2's movement back into the COP. I had already decided not to move out of the COP, and the decision was killing me. It was my first day in Ramadi, on unfamiliar terrain, and I was in no position to coordinate a response to the insurgents' challenge. I had no support from the army leadership who owned the battle space. I barely knew the call signs of friendly units and would have spent half the time outside the wire staring at my map trying to figure out what building I was looking at. I knew that any initiative on my part would most likely end up costing us more casualties with little to show for it. I came to accept that on this particular mission we had been beaten by the jihadists. As the Marines accompanying Lieutenant Thomas began to filter back into the COP, I wondered how such a routine patrol had come to this.

As roommates at the University of Rochester, Lieutenant James Thomas and I had dreamed of this moment during our final two years. We prepared ourselves mentally and physically. We took Arabic courses at 0800 after two hours of physical training and drank a mixture of Kahlúa and black coffee to stay awake. We debated the war, protested Michael Moore's speech on campus, and skipped classes when something big was on the television news from Iraq. We were both exactly where we'd prepared ourselves to be, yet I had failed.

James Thomas was the last man of the patrol to walk back through the door. So much had changed in such a short period of time. I didn't know what to say. Our eyes met, and I knew there must have been a million things going through his mind. I had seen that face so many times before. It was tired and dreary, the exaggerated pick-me-up-because-I-am-down look. But I was dumbfounded. I let my best friend, covered in blood that dripped from his hands, walk right by me without saying a word. I even had to suck in my gut so he could squeeze past me in the hallway. I had control of half of his platoon, and I couldn't get them out the door. Now I couldn't even utter a single word. I never felt so low in my life. Welcome to Ramadi.

After five minutes, I finally mustered the intestinal fortitude to go talk to my friend James. I found him in the outhouse between the buildings, scrubbing the blood off his hands. He noticed me standing behind him.

"That was the first day-patrol the army has done since they established this COP a few months ago." James was scrubbing and talking at the same time.

"What?!" It was all I could think to say.

"Yeah, as I came back into the COP, one of their lieutenants told me that *this* was why they don't patrol during the day, ever." He held his hands up, showing the bright-red blood to emphasize his point.

"And the insurgents, they were waiting for us. They must have watched Rage 1 and Rage 4 head out on successive patrols. So the third time trucks carrying Marines arrived at another southern Ramadi COP, they knew what would follow—another patrol." James scrubbed harder.

I couldn't stop thinking about what had just happened. Our purpose on that patrol replayed itself in my mind. The company was dispersed to four different combat outposts in order to gain some familiarity with the area. On arrival at the COPs, each platoon would conduct a day-patrol, followed by another at night. Because we had only a limited number of vehicles to transport the platoons to the COPs, we were forced to conduct multiple trips from Camp Ramadi. Through the course of the morning the following happened: convoys went out, and, on arrival at a COP, a platoon of Marines dismounted, conducted hasty planning and preparations, then went out on a joint patrol with some soldiers from the respective COP. Well, by the time Rage 2 got to COP Grant, it was nearly 1500, and insurgents had watched two other platoons perform the previously stated plan.

With regard to the enemy, Lieutenant Thomas was absolutely right: we had set ourselves up. We were 100 percent predictable, and Heidbreder was the price we paid. The soldiers' apprehensiveness as we stepped off on the patrol began to make sense as well; it was their first day-patrol, too. The bastards might as well have been using us as their guinea pigs. I headed back into the command building and waltzed arrogantly into the COC.

"You still want to conduct—" said Cobra 6, the army commander. He was sitting with his feet propped up against the wall.

I didn't let him finish. "Yes, let's execute the night-patrol as soon as it is dark, and I want to head right into the area of the earlier firefight." I was shocked at the captain's response.

"You'll get one of my squads, eight soldiers. Do not bring more than fifteen out there. And come brief me on the route when you have it."

I nodded and headed back to our staging area in the far building. I found Lieutenant Thomas relaxing on the second floor, smoking cigarettes with Corporal Holloway.

We quickly discussed the plans for the upcoming patrol, and I got Lieutenant Thomas's blessing to take Holloway and one of his fire teams. I then went back to the command building to find Sergeant Arias, the army squad leader who would be on my patrol and the very same sergeant who was on point with Heidbreder earlier in the day. He had already been briefed on the patrol, and his boys were loading their assault packs with C4 and extra ammunition when I found him. He pulled out his strip map of the immediate area.

"Sir, I recommend we offset our approach a few blocks to the east." He pointed to the map, tracing the route as he spoke. "Then we will hit the cluster of six homes making up the block where the CCP was earlier today. We start at the northeast corner, and 146 will be the fourth house we hit. I have been to this block multiple times at night and each house has its own family living in it."

I was impressed with his unsolicited recommendation. The houses on the northern side of the block were slightly higher than the others in the area, and establishing ourselves there first made perfect sense.

"Roger-that, Sergeant. Have them downstairs at 1830." I looked around at each of his soldiers as I spoke, but not one of them looked up at me. The group was focused.

I walked down the spiral staircase, again amazed by the decorative Arabic script lining the tiles. I stopped in the COC and gave Cobra 6 a quick brief on the patrol's route. His demeanor told me that whatever I wanted to do would be approved. I spent five extra minutes staring at the situation map in the COC. A prominent intersection only 200 meters east of building 146 was circled in red.

"Sir, what's this intersection circled for?"

"That's where the insurgents would have ambushed our casevac if I sent 'em to pick up the casualty earlier."

I was puzzled.

Sensing it, the captain stood up and moved beside me. "The insurgent's wet dream is to cause a casualty, because then you, the injured dog, become predictable. Wounded, you choose the quickest way out, and at that point where casualty meets vehicle he is always waiting. He has already calculated where he wants to shoot you, so that you use his ambush site as the casevac location. Lieutenant, never take the easy path."

He was serious. I knew then that he had learned this lesson through immense pain. My earlier doubts about this man's judgment were instantly erased.

I headed back to the rest of the platoon and found a spot next to a snoring Lieutenant Thomas. I pulled out my own strip map and began to memorize the building numbers and the patrol sectors of every dominant structure that would affect my patrol. If we took fire from one, I wanted to be capable of coordinating a rapid response. I circled each intersection we would cross and added them up at the end. The number opened a pit the size of Texas in my stomach: twelve. We were moving a total of 700 meters, and I would go through twelve intersections. I slowly got up and tiptoed through a maze of sleeping Marines. I walked into the mess room and grabbed an O'Douls. No sooner had I taken it than I put it back. I jokingly reminded myself I didn't even like the taste of alcohol, and an O'Doul's was someone's attempt to replicate it without the actual kick. I'd be better off drinking a bottle of Pepto-Bismol. I returned to the corner in the wall next to the sleeping Lieutenant Thomas and stared at the ceiling for twenty minutes until I was ready. Then I headed back to the staging room in the command building.

Flak, Kevlar, side-SAPI's, drop pouch, bandolier with 162 rounds, AN-PRC 148 radio (the size of a large walkie-talkie), and PVS-14 night-vision goggles (NVGs). I touched each item as I mentally went through my own pre-mission checks. I grabbed my groin pad and crotch as I noticed Corporal Holloway staring at me, probably wondering what the hell I was doing.

"Made you look, fag," I said with a smile. He shook his head in amusement. The soldiers and the Marines were ready to go, and Sergeant Arias was heading out the door. Two-thirds of the way back in the formation, I followed the same path out of COP Grant that Lieutenant Thomas had taken a few hours earlier. It was a completely different world at night. Through my NVGs, everything seemed to tower over me. The formation moved down the thick dust of Farouk

Way and passed Graves, heading east. We were moving pretty quickly, but the pace wasn't too fast for us to notice our surroundings. I could tell Sergeant Arias had done this a few times before, and his squad knew what was and wasn't out of place in the random piles of debris that littered the street.

We approached the first intersection and halted. A flickering light illuminated the far side and would have revealed our shadows to distant observers as we passed. A soldier lifted a broken piece of the curb at his feet and nailed the light with a forty-yard throw. The elongated bulb shattered into a thousand different pieces. The soldier congratulated himself, and I began to rethink my decision to play soccer in high school.

We continued north on the side street, passing multiple parked cars with low-lying power lines drooping over the road. Although none of the wires actually ran to the vehicles, I fully anticipated that each one would explode as I walked past. We finally hit the target block of houses. The formation staged for entry on the northeast courtyard wall. I could hear Arias trying to pound his way through the locked gate without success. His voice came over the PRR: "Breaching in five . . ." The small charge of C4 blasted through the gate, giving the soldiers entry. My ears were still ringing as I went through the gate, and our presence was definitely known by the entire neighborhood. I came through the door to the sound of soldiers shouting, "All clear on two." Sergeant Arias stood in the foyer and said, "All clear, sir. The family is in that room on your left." He began to stage his soldiers for movement to the next house.

I grabbed the interpreter and entered the family room. The man of the house was about sixty years old, with gray hair and a well-trimmed mustache. His wife, daughter, and three grandchildren huddled in the corner, sharing a pile of blankets around a kerosene space heater. The interpreter began to go through the scripted list of questions I'd given him before we left. From my basic Arabic, I could discern that the old man answered each question with "No" or "I don't know what you are talking about." I felt insulted—this man had experienced 40mm grenades and .50 caliber machine gun rounds landing all around his home earlier that day, and now he denied even knowing about the firefight. I became more frustrated. Through his fear, the old man was telling me that the insurgents were the obvious power in the area. I had a limited amount of time. I jumped on the PRR and yelled, "Next house, go!" I staged in the courtyard, as Arias mechanically breached the gate this time.

The superbly quick clearing of the home repeated itself, as it would all night, only this time no one was home. I walked into the foyer, where Sergeant Arias greeted me again.

"They scattered, sir; they must have known we were coming." The sergeant pointed to the plates of half-eaten food on the floor. I looked over his shoulder and saw a brown leather jacket draped over the refrigerator in the corner of the room. I had seen a middle-aged man walking outside the COP in that jacket earlier in the day, before our first patrol. Added adrenaline was pumping through my body.

"Search it for two minutes; there has to be something here."

"Already on it, sir. Last time I was at this house, there were three middle-aged men living together. All three were teachers, surprisingly enough. Unfortunately, I couldn't find anything then, and I will be surprised if we do now." The soldiers searched for a few minutes in an extremely detailed but messy manner. They found nothing.

We moved on to the next house, which was occupied by another extended family. The man of the house refused to provide any information about the neighbors and again denied knowing anything about the earlier firefight only yards from his home. He even said he didn't know that Marines had been on his roof. Again I was frustrated.

Standing in the courtyard, I began to think there was no way in hell this city would ever get any better. Firefights like the one today were a daily occurrence, and the locals didn't seem to care anymore. The next house was building 146, the CCP. Sergeant Arias had no problems with the gate; it was already blown open. I sprinted down the sidewalk and into the confines of the courtyard. The driveway was smeared with a dark red bloodstain. Corporal Holloway's team of Marines picked up external security at the gate.

I moved in through the main door to the house. It was almost a replica of the previous four homes we had been in. The stark similarities between the houses reminded me of suburban America. Arias was pointing to the family room on the left as he directed his soldiers with verbal insults. His extended finger told me where the family was. As I entered the room, the man of the house, about thirty-five years old, with black hair and a dark complexion, immediately asked my interpreter to put his wife and three children in a separate room. As soon as they left, he began to speak candidly. After a solid minute of fast-paced conversation, the interpreter turned to me mid-sentence and asked, "Can he see the map you have, Lieutenant?"

I quickly pulled it out of my drop pouch. I placed it at the man's feet and kneeled on the floor. It was only a strip map and didn't show the distant sectors of the city, so I quickly oriented him to the confusing satellite imagery he was looking at. I pointed to the north and said, "Qatana," pointed to the east and said, "Mila'ab," and then pointed to his home and said, "*Casa.*" Realizing I had spoken Spanish, I laughed and the interpreter filled in the word I was looking for. The man grabbed my orange map pen out of my hand and began to circle intersections on the map. He was almost barking orders to the interpreter.

"He says you should place checkpoints at each circle he has drawn on the map and that if you give him back his Kalashnikov you took last time you were in his home, he will kill the insurgents next time they come near his house," the interpreter translated. The man continued to talk while the interpreter relayed the information. "About a week ago insurgents used a parked car near his home to snipe at COP Grant, and they often come into his house during the day to observe you at the base. The three men who live a few houses over moved in after the family who lives there moved to Syria a few months ago. He thinks they are terrorists."

Sergeant Arias interrupted the interpreter and told me, "We had a guy shot on the roof of the COP a week ago from this general direction. Luckily, it didn't penetrate his body armor."

I looked back at the Iraqi man and asked whether he had been in the army before the war. He smiled, revealing a few missing teeth, but said nothing in response.

The man's wife appeared at the far end of the room. She was crying. She began to speak quickly, all her words directed at her husband, who immediately stood up and waved at her to go away. The interpreter translated: "She wants us to leave right now and is upset for him talking to us. She says insurgents will know he spoke to us because we have stayed here so long, and they will come kill him. We must leave."

The woman was right—we could not stay any longer. As we prepared to move out of the house, the man grabbed me by the arm and said two words: *irhabi* and *Qatana.* He was telling me the terrorists lived in the Qatana sector of the city. We made it back to the COP without incident, and the following morning Rage 2 loaded up on its trucks and headed back to Camp Ramadi.

2

DETAINEE WATCH

November 28, 2006

The brigade conference room was smaller than I'd imagined. Centered in the room was a wooden desk that could comfortably fit twenty people around its frame. Another twenty or so seats lined the walls of the room. There was hardly enough space to squeeze between the seats at the table and those lining the wall. The interior decoration was, as in most places in Iraq, nonexistent. The far side of the room, opposite the end with the door, contained a white projection screen of average size. As the last few Marines entered the room, Major Mayberry, the brigade assistant operations officer, stood up from his chair. He removed the printer paper covering the projector bulb to reveal the motto of 1st Brigade, 1st Armor Division: "Ready First." It was the standard opening slide for all brigade briefs.

The officers and the staff of Rage Company sat at the table, while the squad leaders and those of lesser rank filled the exterior chairs. Only a week earlier, Captain John Smith and I had sat in this room for the first time, outlining all the required items for the company to the brigade. Now the entire company was here and ready to go. A sense of cautious optimism surrounded the fresh Marines, many still with thoughts of what had happened to Heidbreder in their minds.

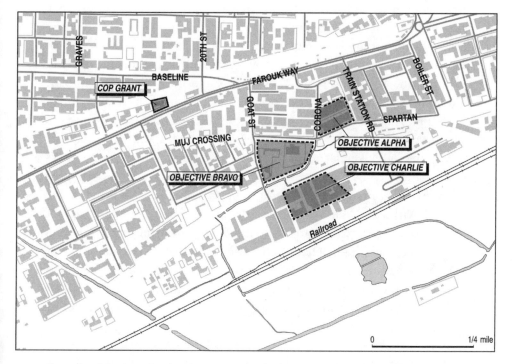

Operation Harrison Creek I: Rage Company's objective areas during Harrison Creek I.

Major Mayberry was the orator for the first of the day's half-dozen briefs. The pouch of tobacco and the Civil War–era pipe sitting in front of him complemented the Southern accent now heard by the Marines. "Operation Squeeze Play, gentlemen; this is the reason you are here. Roughly one month ago, the staff at Multi-National Forces-West [MNF-W] published the blueprint for this operation." The major proceeded to the next slide.

"The title of the operation encompasses its intent; the goal is to simultaneously squeeze al Qaeda out of the urban centers of Al Anbar Province. Once Al Qaeda is isolated in the rural villages, we believe that their grip over the Iraqi populace will falter, thus providing us the time and security to stand up Iraqi Security Forces [ISF]." He proceeded to the next slide, revealing the locations across Al Anbar Province that the 15th Marine Expeditionary Unit would surge into: Haditha, Rutbah, and Ramadi. The three cities formed a triangle on the map. Unlike the Sunni Triangle south of Baghdad, the interior of these three points was mostly desert. After a few moments of studying the slide, Captain James, the intelligence officer for 1st Battalion, 37th Armor (1–37 Armor) and a University of Florida graduate, began the intel portion of the brief. "Marines, it is a pleasure to be working with you. Before we carry on with the details of Operation Squeeze Play in Ramadi proper, I would like to capture the current nature of the insurgency for you."

I sat up straight in my chair. In my two and a half years as an officer of Marines, I had never been briefed on the actual elements that made up the insurgency. My perspective of Iraq had, to this point, been shaped by CNN, Internet surfing, some books I had read, and exaggerated war stories.

The reason for what I would call this lack of situational awareness is twofold. First, any report coming from the front is considered sensitive and therefore classified as "secret." On many occasions, it seems as if the words *al Qaeda* are all that is required to qualify a document for being "secret." This by itself is not the problem. Access to the secret network, Secret Internet Protocol Router (SIPR), is where issues arise. At Camp Pendleton, there is only one SIPR computer per battalion. It is always being used by the battalion commander, the intelligence section, and the rest of the staff. I had never even heard of SIPR until I arrived in Iraq and signed up for an account.

The second issue in training for the Iraq insurgency is the Corps's focus on maintaining its readiness to fight a Soviet-style war. During basic officer training, which lasted more than a year, I focused on learning how to counter the Russian art of war. This was during 2004, when Iraq's multifaceted insurgency was already under way. It was not until I left this schoolhouse environment that any thought of fighting a guerrilla force was seriously considered. Even then, the notion was that if you could assault an entrenched enemy position, you could handle a few Iraqis in black pajamas. We always discussed "knowing your enemy," but it never included anything more than pictures of an improvised explosive device (IED) attack. Tactical lessons from the War on Terror were not making it into the military's basic curriculum.

Captain James's brief began. "The original composition of the insurgency in the greater Ramadi area consisted of groups like 1920s Revolutionary Brigade, a national insurgent group characterized as Ba'athist. Within the Ramadi area, you will fight the Abdallah Ibn Al-Mubarak Brigade of this group, made up of former Fedayeen and Republican Guard officers." The screen displayed the titles of 1920s units and their locations. Next to Baghdad was Sa'd Ibn-Abi-Waqas Brigade, and the list continued with Fallujah, Haditha, and Haqlaniyah.

"Early in 2004, a shift occurred in the greater resistance movement. With the arrival of foreigners such as Abu Musab al-Zarqawi, the insurgent ideology became more Islamist in nature. This led to the birth of Al Qaeda in Iraq [AQI], and Zarqawi formed the Jama'at al-Tawhid wal-Jihad group [JTJ] to funnel average Iraqis into the organization's ranks. As the nationalist and Islamist groups originally had a mutually supporting role, their differences came to a head in January 2006 as Zarqawi attempted to force the numerous factions under the leadership of AQI. The result was a power struggle, with some nationalist groups choosing to follow Zarqawi and the newly created Mujahedeen Shura Council [MSC], but the majority of the nationalists opted out of this insurgent alliance. Most of these Ba'athists disagreed with AQI's horrific tactics against civilians and Shia, and this difference formed the basis of their resistance to joining AQI."

I began to think about just how powerful AQI must be in order to openly fight not only the coalition but other insurgents as well. The captain went to the next slide, showing Zarqawi's bloodied face, along with the circumstances of his death. "As you all know," Captain James said, "Abu Musab al-Zarqawi was killed by a U.S. air strike in June of this year. The death of this charismatic leader has emboldened the leaders of the Anbar tribes to question al Qaeda's authority to lead the insurgency, as evidenced by the creation of the Anbar Awakening movement, which has both a military and a political wing. Both elements of this Awakening movement are showing signs they may be willing to work with, not against, coalition forces." The Floridian went to the next slide, which showed the tribal breakdown of the brigade area of operations (AO). Friendly tribes were in green, while opposing ones were in red. There was twice as much red as green on the map.

"However, in September of this year al Qaeda and the military wing of the Awakening council, Thawar Al Anbar, fought each other in the streets of Ramadi. Thawar Al Anbar was initially successful, assassinating dozens of AQI terrorists while they prayed at a local mosque. However, we believe al Qaeda eventually solidified its control over the city. Those who would not join the newly formed al Qaeda caliphate, the Islamic State of Iraq (which would be the nation governed by the Mujahedeen Shura Council), were killed in dramatic fashion. They murdered doctors who worked at Ramadi General Hospital, Internet café owners with U.S. Web sites or e-mails to the United States were beheaded, and a flyer was posted at Al Anbar University with the names of the staff who had been targeted for assassination."

Captain James proceeded to the next slide, showing what I thought was a parade. "These events climaxed with the insurgent parade on October 18, where Ramadi was officially declared the capital of the Islamic State of Iraq. The parade was held here, in the mostly abandoned commercial district of the city referred to as *Qatana*."

No wonder the Iraqi I met the day before had said Qatana and Irhabi. The local populace had clearly heard about the parade. I stared at the PowerPoint slide and its detailed digital map with a new sense of purpose. This was the capital of the Sunni insurgency. Some of the buildings on the map were labeled "legal court of ISI" and "executive building of ISI." The executive building had been leveled by an air strike or some other type of combined arms attack.

The captain continued, describing how the insurgents lived in the Qatana and Mila'ab sectors of the city and moved during the day to the Second Officers and Al Andaloos districts to execute attacks. The following slide provided details and specific numbers of attacks for the month of October. The totals were staggering. From October 8 to October 14, coalition forces in Ramadi endured nineteen IED attacks, fifty-one small-arms fire attacks, twelve indirect fire attacks, twelve rocket-propelled grenade attacks, two hand grenade attacks, and two suicide vehicle–borne IED attacks, and found sixteen other IEDs. As the captain continued to describe subsequent weeks in his brief, the numbers only got worse. Ramadi was clearly the ultimate getaway during the fall season. With some of the Marines squirming in their chairs, Captain James gave us a ten-minute break.

I walked out to the smoke pit between the brigade Tactical Operations Center (TOC) and the headquarters building where the brief was being conducted. Lieutenant Thomas was smoking with the other platoon commanders and a few of the squad leaders. He offered me a smoke. Because I was a former runner, he knew what my answer would be.

"No, thanks," I said. "I appreciate my lungs and look forward to their good health for many years to come."

Rage 1, Lieutenant Cullen Shearburn, gave me a joking look of disgust. "Daly, there you go, thinking you're better than everyone else again." He placed his hand in between the second and third buttons of his blouse and imitated me turning down the smoke. While we had been sailing to Kuwait, Lieutenant Shearburn usually referred to me as "the Baron." It was an ironic nickname coming from him. He was by far the most pompous officer of the company. The Marines of Rage 1 loved him for it.

The group continued to smoke and joke until our ten minutes had elapsed. None of us dared to address the apprehension that was visible on our faces. We headed back into the building, and Corporal Holloway caught up to me, clearly wanting to say something.

"Sir, I saw you turn down Lieutenant Thomas when he offered you a cigarette."

I was kind of caught off guard by the seriousness of his voice. "Yeah?" I said.

"Well, I noticed you turned him down before Heidbreder got shot, too, but before we left on our night-patrol you smoked one with the lieutenant and nothing happened to us." Holloway was speaking quietly so no one else could hear his crazy implications.

"Look, Holloway, I don't believe in that crap," I said, pulling a quote from John Milton on him. "Luck is the residue of design."

His response was instantaneous. He had clearly planned it. "Then why do you never take that Saint Christopher medal off from around your neck? I know it rubs like hell every time you wear your flak."

I laughed and walked back into the conference room with the corporal, ignoring his pleas. Making myself comfortable in my executive-style chair, I noticed Holloway moving two fingers up to his mouth in an attempt to look like the Marlboro man. I shook my head.

Captain James pressed on. "Before I turn it back over to Major Mayberry, I would like to mention a few of the prominent insurgent personalities active in the area. The first is Mullah Qahttan." A picture of a thirty-year-old man popped up on the screen. "We believe that the former leader of JTJ in Ramadi has recently been promoted to an emir within AQI to coordinate efforts between Fallujah and Ramadi. His family is from southern Ramadi and his brother, Uthman, runs a large cell of fighters in their familial area, the Second Officers District." I analyzed the picture, noticing no visible characteristics of this man's truly horrific nature. Captain James continued, "Mullah Qahttan epitomizes the brutality of AQI. He has used an eleven-year-old Yemeni boy as a suicide bomber and a twelve-year-old to detonate five IEDs within the city, and he personally issues the orders and conducts the beheadings of local nationals for a multitude of 'crimes.' To capture the context of these crimes: his men abduct the children of the tribes associated with the Awakening and return their heads to their families in baskets."

As Captain James moved to the next slide, one of the Marines opened his mouth and said, "Sounds like an awesome dude . . ."

Again the screen showed another thirty-something Iraqi male. "Thamir Hamad Nahar is the man we believe replaced Mullah Qahttan as the head of JTJ within Ramadi. His credentials are much like those of his predecessor, and his family is also from the southern side of the city, in the insurgent safe haven of the Mila'ab. He has gained authority as a renowned explosives expert by building IEDs and coordinating mortar attacks. The leader of his own small insurgent group that coalesced with AQI, he has proved capable of facilitating the movement of foreign fighters into the AO and has used multiple local businesses to finance his campaigns. His merits have earned him a position as one of Zarqawi's lieutenants, and he now works directly for Mullah Qahttan. Thamir is known to travel with an estimated twenty-man security detail and frequents numerous AQI safe houses in the southern Ramadi area."

There were a few more slides showing insurgent tactics and techniques with IEDs or ambushes within the area of operations (AO). Then the captain looked at Major Mayberry and said, "Sir, I turn it back over to you."

A slide, blank except for the words OPERATION SQUEEZE PLAY, came onto the screen.

We all sat there, intently anticipating every word the major would utter. For two weeks, we had wondered how and where Rage Company would be employed. We all wanted to know where we were going, what kinds of missions we would execute, and, more specifically, how the insurgency was succeeding in Ramadi. We pored over any intel material we could find, wasting entire afternoons as we downloaded maps and briefs on the incredibly slow secure network onboard the USS *Dubuque*. Now we were finally seeing the details.

"Gentlemen," the major said, "this is a three-phase operation. The first will send you to southern Ramadi, where you will be attached to 1-37 Armor, the Bandits." The slide shown on the projector contained imagery of 1-37's entire AO. "The concept of operations for this phase is shown on the map. As you can see, each mission has its own color." Different sectors of the AO were highlighted, forming a backward L in the center of the city. "The intent here is to clear these areas, where coalition forces have not had a presence, in some cases, in over a year. As you can see from the backward L formed here [the major circled the area with a laser pointer], the intent is to push the enemy east and north to the center of the city." He proceeded to the next slide, glancing at his pipe and pausing to breathe in the aroma wafting from the pouch of tobacco next to it.

"The next phase will place you under operational control of 1st Battalion, 6th Marines. The intent during this phase is to clear the centrally located commercial sector of the city, the Qatana District." Every Marine had heard of this portion of the city; it was the most notorious and easiest to find information on when we surfed the secure network back on ship. Insurgent snipers in Qatana were extremely effective. Rumors of Chechens and other foreign fighters living in the district's abandoned structures made it our number one target.

"The desired end state is that we force the enemy to consolidate in the southeastern portion of the city, the Mila'ab District." Major Mayberry proceeded to the next slide, a view of the entire city, and circled the Mila'ab with his laser pointer. "We know the insurgent fighter will come and go as he pleases, so our success lies in finding his safe havens, his caches. If we have success finding these tactical caches of weapons, the insurgents will use the Mila'ab to regroup. This leads us to the final phase of the operation. Once we feel that the insurgents have consolidated, we will cordon off the entire Mila'ab—in most parts, literally making a wall out of concrete barriers and then conducting a thorough clear of the district."

The vision of intense urban combat and the idea of an assault on the scale of Fallujah from 2004 flashed through my mind. I am sure all of us in the room must have been thinking the same thing.

The major quickly demolished our dreams of an all-out kinetic assault. "However, your part in this third phase is not in the Mila'ab. We will be sending you east of the city to the rural suburbs of Sofia and Julayba. Here you will be confronted by the core of the AQI movement. We have long suspected the region of being the command and control center for both Ramadi and Fallujah, due to its geographic location between the cities. There has never been a permanent coalition presence here either. In the early summer of '06, a large contingent of AQI leaders fled Ramadi to this area. Your mission will be to prevent them from using this region as a safe haven while we take down the Mila'ab."

After another ten minutes of briefing, Major Mayberry proceeded to solicit questions from his audience, while occasionally glancing at his pipe. With no questions forthcoming, a short, stout lieutenant colonel stood up in the back of the room. He was probably five feet, four inches tall. With an outstretched arm, Major Mayberry gave the colonel the floor, which he wasted no time in taking. "Marines, I am Lieutenant Colonel V. J. Tedesco, Commanding Officer First Battalion, Thirty-seventh Armor, and as of now, you aren't Marines, you are Bandits!"

As quickly as he had taken the floor, he walked out of the room. The younger Marines took his comment as an insult, priding themselves on the title "Marine," but I knew what the lieutenant colonel meant: he would take care of us as if we were his own soldiers. I looked at the other lieutenants in Rage Company. We were nervous. The mission was on a scale beyond the likes of anything we had imagined. None of the officers had been to Ramadi before, but the Marines in the company who had, had plenty of experience on some of these streets and alleyways. Each experience usually had a casualty to go along with it. As I glanced over at Rage 4, Lieutenant Andrew Grubb, our eyes met. He winked and blew me a kiss.

We filed out of the room and made our way to the rest of the day's briefs. Rules of engagement (ROE), detainee processing, and mission planning for Operation Harrison Creek I filled the day. With the sun setting, we broke for chow. Immediately after this, I held a preparatory meeting for the intelligence cell. I directed both of my scouts, lance corporals

Joash Albin and Benjamin Eakin, to memorize the street names and the patrol sectors of southern Ramadi. We pored over every piece of reporting on the area. Names of cell leaders, distinguishing scars, locations of previous attacks, and an aerial view of the district repeatedly flashed in our minds. When Heidbreder was shot, we had all felt unprepared. Now we were making up for it.

With only about twenty hours until the mission, we were still producing strip maps for the platoons. Each squad leader would receive a specific map of the patrol sectors he would be clearing, as well as three-dimensional photos of the target buildings within his respective objective area. The photos had been taken by an aircraft the night before, courtesy of some special operations types. The materials, along with a list of potential insurgents to be found on the objective, would be distributed at that night's mission brief and rehearsal. We were going to end the day in true Marine Corps fashion, with the longest brief.

I was blindsided when Captain Smith, Rage 6, approached me before the mission brief and told me I would not be leaving the wire. He explained that he anticipated taking around twenty detainees and that I would be focused on their processing, rather than on the act of detention. I expressed my desire to execute the raid but was overruled. The captain was concerned with our knowledge of the proper administrative and questioning procedures. Based on our previous class regarding detainee processing, it would be an enormous task.

Each detainee would have a total of fourteen pages filled out on him. These individual packages contained sworn statements by coalition members, diagrams of the location of the detention site, a brief medical exam, and forms to accompany evidence and document the level of force used during detention, as well as personal information. If a detainee's paperwork was not in order, the regional detention facility would not prosecute the individual. Unfortunately, such events occurred on an almost daily basis and were an embarrassment to the unit that submitted the detainee. To highlight this fact, both Mullah Qahttan and Thamir had been detained earlier, and each had a photo of him in an orange jumpsuit on his briefing slide. In fact, it seemed like being detained by the Americans was necessary to be promoted within AQI. This was democracy at war.

I sat down for the mission brief with a bitter taste in my mouth. I hadn't become a Marine to do paperwork.

Marines and soldiers began to arrive. Chairs quickly disappeared in the thousand-square-foot room that was Rage Company's HQ on Camp

Ramadi. The room was built out of two-by-fours and plywood, while the walls were lined with huge maps of the city. Small pockets of dust added to the spartan atmosphere. The platoon commanders were among the last of the two dozen soldiers and Marines to arrive. Everyone was unusually quiet and serious.

The room was shaped like a giant rectangle, and the central third of the floor held a graphic representation of the objective area. Colored string marked roads; houses were wooden blocks, their corresponding building numbers written on top in black Sharpie. I grabbed my metal folding chair and moved to a spot with the rest of the headquarters platoon on the right side of the map. Lieutenant Thomas sat with the other platoon commanders on the opposite side.

Captain Smith began the brief. "Bandits, to start I want to make sure we have everyone and that each of you understands who you are working for." He pointed to some of the tankers to my left: "Task Force Cordon North, one section of Bradley fighting vehicles [BFVs] and a psychological operations team." The men nodded as their respective unit was mentioned. Captain Smith looked to his right, finding the next group. "Task Force Cordon South, one section of BFVs." He looked around again, finding the only "cool guy" in the room. "There will be one sniper team of SEALs in over-watch of objective Bravo. They will be a battalion asset. Finally, Pathfinder, you have EOD [explosive ordnance disposal] and a section of tanks attached." He then turned to each platoon and went down the list of its attachments: engineers, Iraqi army personnel, military working dogs. Two platoons had interpreters, and there was one human exploitation team (HET). Headquarters had an interpreter and Air Naval Gunfire Liaison Company (ANGLICO), which consisted of forward observers.

I was surprised by the ANGLICO observers' presence. I was Rage Company's forward observer; I had the sole responsibility for coordinating the use of combined arms assets. ANGLICO observers had only one purpose, and it was the same as mine. It finally dawned on me that they had taken my place. This was the reason I was stuck at the combat outpost. Without them, Captain Smith would have no choice but to take me on the raid. More important, I felt personally wronged. I had been replaced for our first varsity match.

Captain Smith pulled a laser pointer out of his right trouser pocket and said, "Orientation." I had heard that word so many times before during monotonous training exercises in which every Marine is taught through repetition. "This direction is north," he said, moving the laser in a north-south direction and emphasizing north with a much longer stroke. He pointed out COP Grant and each of the three company objectives: Alpha, Bravo, and Charlie.

The captain then moved on to the enemy situation. "Anti-Iraqi Forces [AIF] have established a safe haven in the southern portion of the Second Officer's District. The AIF use local mosques and schools as meeting places and cache sites and have established multiple safe houses. They have also established defensive IED belts as early warning and blocking obstacles. The AIF's most likely course of action would be to flee the area temporarily after the IEDs alert them and slow us down. Pathfinder's route clearance missions also provide a key indicator of an impending operation, so AIF may attempt to emplace hasty surface-laid IEDs to target our dismounted elements."

The brief dragged on. During training, the company officers (myself included) had hated the thoroughness of Captain Smith's briefs. It wasn't what he was saying; it was how slowly he said it. In agonizing detail, he went through the enemy's most likely course of action and most dangerous course of action, which were followed by the task force's mission, key tasks, end state, and the location of friendly forces. He briefly explained our mission statement: "No later than 2200 on 29 November 2006, Rage Company reinforced conducts near simultaneous raids on company objectives Alpha, Bravo, and Charlie in order to capture or kill high-value individuals."

Stopping to spit out some tobacco, Captain Smith moved on to his commander's intent and end state. Neither one produced anything unusual, but the concept of operations described the mission as succinctly as possible. "Pathfinder, along with its tank and Bradley escorts (the cordon force), will clear a casualty evacuation route through the objective area, setting the outer cordon as they clear. Once Pathfinder crosses the intersection of Corona and Muj Crossing, the platoons will depart COP Grant for their assault positions. Once in position, Rage 1 and Rage 2 conduct raids on objectives Alpha and Bravo, respectively, while Rage 4 provides overwatch and acts as a reserve. Once objective Bravo is cleared, Rage 2 moves to provide the internal cordon for Rage 4's raid of objective Charlie. Once all objectives' actions are complete, platoons will egress via separate routes back to COP Grant, where the detainee processing will begin."

He quickly moved into the tasks section of his brief, and the meticulous and detailed nature of Captain Smith shone center stage. "The

mission is broken into five phases." He announced, "Phase One," and
the representative from Pathfinder and the vehicle commanders of the
cordon force stood up and moved to the map for the walk-through of
Phase I.

The walk-through literally entailed the leaders of each element standing
on the terrain model. They would then move whatever toy soldier or car
represented their unit through the different parts of the mission. This
forced each leader to show everyone else what he was going to do and
where he would be located. The technique served as confirmation for
Captain Smith regarding the actions of his subordinates. After all, it was
our first mission with the army, and according to Marine Corps lore,
soldiers are only good for one thing: retreating.

I struggled to pay attention mostly because I knew the mission from
our own internal briefing but also because I was focused on my observer
rivals. Yes, they had more training, had been in country a lot longer, and
had better equipment than I did. I didn't care. Rage Company was my
company, and I looked at my fellow artillerymen with disgust. Bored
with the brief and jealous of the ANGLICO observers, I lost focus.

It would be another two hours before I left. The platoons were still
rehearsing on the terrain model when I walked out of the 1-37 Armor
headquarters. The battalion logo, a black diamond with a white skull
emblazoned over it, stared straight at me. Bandits. Insurgents were the
real bandits. Our missions were complex and required hours of rehearsal
and coordination to execute. I always considered banditry much more
opportunistic than that.

As I walked back to my tent with Albin and Eakin, I thought about
how many hours insurgents spent planning operations. How did they
communicate—or coordinate a response to our presence? They'd had no
more than half an hour to actually set up the Heidbreder ambush, and
they pulled it off in dramatic fashion. I began to think that the insurgent just might be more effective than I was in the urban environment.

The next evening we left for COP Grant under the cover of darkness.
The two structures that made up the COP were quickly overrun with
Marines. The floors in every open area were covered with weapons, gear,
machine guns, ammo, and snoring bodies. Heads rested against radios or
Kevlar helmets. Movement through a room required twenty seconds of
route planning. Our army hosts couldn't wait for the mission to start.

The arrival of twenty or so Iraqi army soldiers didn't help the situation. The Marines didn't exactly care to provide them with any space,

and the army had none left to give. So the Iraqi soldiers literally stood shoulder to shoulder in the corner of the command building's staging room. I was disgusted by our lack of hospitality. We were in an Iraqi's home, and every Marine was drinking Gatorade or stuffing his face with chow while the Iraqis were standing in the corner watching us. I walked back to the kitchen and grabbed a box of twenty-ounce Gatorades. I carried them into the room and made the Marines who were sitting on the floor move to create space. They grunted and jeered but within moments went back to resting uncomfortably on their gear.

I dropped the Gatorades at an Iraqi's feet and motioned them each to take one. They were surprised. One of them called over the interpreter and spoke to me through him. After they had introduced each other, the soldier said something to the interpreter that made the Arab American laugh. The interpreter looked at me, shaking his head. "Sir, I cannot tell you what he said."

I was confused. "Why not?" What could the Iraqi have possibly said? I had just brought him Gatorade and given them all space to sit down and relax. I was getting angry. "Tell me what he said." Everyone was listening now, most intently the Marines I had just evicted.

"Sir, he says you are cute," said the interpreter, who was laughing before he finished translating. The Marines around me erupted. Then the Iraqis, seeing the embarrassment on my face, all started saying no over and over.

The damage was done. I had been swallowed by the culture gap. I shook my head and pushed the box of Gatorades closer to the Iraqis with my foot. Then I turned around to face my hecklers. I had nothing. To their pleasure, I shrugged my shoulders and walked off. Everyone now had something to talk about before the mission.

An hour later, Pathfinder moved out on the clear portion of the raid. The cordon elements moved in trace. Once the areas surrounding objectives Alpha and Bravo were cleared for IEDs, the platoons were granted permission to move. One by one, they left. Everything was going smoothly. The company executive officer (XO) and I both sat in the command building's COC, listening to the radio. The duties of the XO, Lieutenant Craig Trotter, were about as mundane as my own. He was responsible for managing the raid and providing overall cognizance to the battalion, as well as to Captain Smith. With the CO out making decisions, the XO usually stayed behind and provided everyone else with information. His fear of never getting to leave the wire was even greater than mine.

At the moment, Lieutenant Trotter was struggling to get positive communications with each platoon. The farther away the platoons went from COP Grant, the more garbled their transmissions became. The intervening buildings obstructed the antennas of the platoon's man-packed radios. The lack of communications became the evening's first point of friction. As the clarity of transmissions decreased, voices grew exponentially louder. Radio handsets and antennas became weapons to beat a solution into the radio operators, who in turn smacked and pounded on the Vietnam-era radios. Such was the way of the XO, and somehow communications improved.

The night progressed. Rage 1 and Rage 2 reached their assault positions. Rage 4 set up in over-watch. One of the North Task Force tanks drove over the wall surrounding the school compound that was objective Bravo. Rage 2 flowed in through the gap, meeting no resistance. Rage 1 cleared objective Alpha faster than anyone had anticipated. Their orders were to detain any military-age male (MAM) located in their target buildings. The homes were apparently all occupied, as the XO and I were having a hard time keeping track of all the detainees. We had more than twenty.

Rage 2 began a detailed search of the compound and found a few caches that contained RPG rounds and some small-arms ammo. Corporal Davila's squad moved to hit objective Bravo's southernmost target building. It was about a 100-meter movement across open ground, by far the most dangerous part of the raid, because the squad would be exposed on both flanks. Seconds after they moved, machine gun fire echoed in the night. The XO informed battalion of the incident on the battalion net, while Captain Smith tried to get in contact with Corporal Davila on the company net. Davila wasn't answering; he was busy.

As quickly as the firefight began, it ended. Davila got on the radio and began to speak, but as he did, our communications went down again. It would be another fifteen minutes before we figured out there were no casualties. The COC was full of frustrated guys, and I walked outside to get some fresh air. The concept of a "raid" had nearly ended, as the platoons strongpointed around objective Bravo and continued the school compound's site exploitation. Battalion forced us to wait for EOD to show up and handle the small amounts of explosives in the caches before we could continue. The darkness quickly wasted away, and at 0330 Captain Smith aborted the raid on objective Charlie. All dismounted elements began moving back to COP Grant.

Unfortunately for the SEALs, they were the first ones to move back to the COP. No one bothered to inform the soldiers on the roof of COP Grant that the SEALs were even out there, let alone moving back. A short burst of machine gun fire from the roof began what would later be a heated argument. No one was injured. With confusion from the blue-on-blue incident still occupying the army command, Rage 1 reentered friendly lines, dragging their trail of detainees with them.

Albin and Eakin had set up the COP's gym to stage the detainees for processing. It wasn't an elaborate process; they simply moved free weights and benches to make room for the detained men to sit on the dusty floor. In the adjacent living room, the two dozen packets of paperwork were staged and waiting for the detainees' captors to fill out. One at a time, the blindfolded men made their way into the gym. It was somewhat comical. The blindfolds were a mix of sandbags, random pieces of cloth, or swimming goggles with the eyes blacked out. One Iraqi had his shirt pulled over his head because the cloth strip covering his eyes wasn't thick enough. About half of them were barefoot.

We searched each detainee as he came into the gym. Small pieces of evidence had been placed in a plastic bag draped around each detainee's neck. Written on the plastic in black marker were the patrol sector and the building number where the individual had been detained. Large pieces of evidence were carried back by the Marines and separated into black trash bags. We were rather surprised when the first few detainees still had all sorts of items in their pockets.

The first guy had white hair and was about fifty years old. We quickly named him Moneybags. Ten crisp one-hundred-dollar bills (U.S. currency) lined his pockets. He also had smaller denominations of Russian, Bulgarian, Syrian, Saudi Arabian, Jordanian, Kuwaiti, and Yemeni money. The Marines eyeballed the thousand dollars, and I wondered how much had really been on his person when he was detained. Following Moneybags was his son, who was probably in his late twenties or early thirties. He kept telling the interpreter that he was a propane salesman and not an insurgent. We named him Propane. The two large and tired men sat next to each other.

Detainees slowly filled the room, and the process continued for hours. Each detainee was photographed holding a piece of paper with his name on it and was thoroughly searched. There were twenty-two in all. A group of five twenty-something family members had the most evidence gathered against them. In their home, Rage 1 had found an AK-47, which by itself is legal, but there were also a 9mm pistol, an unusual amount of copper and miscellaneous wires, electrical cords, two European Union license plates from Sweden, two Motorola radios, premade IED initiation devices, and a small amount of propaganda. The next twelve hours would be spent trying to figure out what belonged to whom.

Albin, Eakin, and an intel soldier from 1-37 Armor began the paperwork. One of our corpsman and an army medic started the medical screening. I grabbed the tactical human-intelligence team (THT). We separated the Iraqis, based on the amount of intelligence and evidence gathered against each one. The first fourteen were guilty of nothing more than living in a target building. One guy had bullet holes all over the trunk of his black BMW, which was similar to the vehicle at the Heidbreder ambush. Then the group of suspected insurgents got better. Intel had multiple reports stating that Moneybags and Propane were the leaders of an IED cell responsible for the deaths of three American soldiers. Later we were told that two out of the family of five with all of the evidence had single-source reporting that stated they were members of a direct action cell.

This reporting was based on the names these detainees provided us. We typed the names into a Multi-National Corps Iraq computer network that pulled up all of the documents produced that contained those names. I was surprised that the Iraqis would give us their real names. In my mind, they were either foolish or simply used to the Americans not being able to overcome the language barrier.

Since I was not officially an intelligence officer (but was an artilleryman by trade), it was against the ROE for me to question any of the detainees. So I approached the THT leader, Sergeant Champion, who allowed me to sit in on each detainee's session of tactical questioning. We started with Beemer, the guy with the shot-up BMW. We used the bathroom for questioning. Sergeant Champion started easy on him: "What is your name?" The man answered between sobs. The sergeant asked, "Who is your local sheikh?"

The guy went hysterical, speaking faster than I could think. The interpreter relayed. "The Americans don't protect us. The Iraqi government doesn't help us. The criminals and terrorists will kill me because they will know I was arrested. Blah, blah."

The interpreter stopped translating and yelled at the man, who instantly went quiet. Sergeant Champion continued the questioning for another ten minutes, catching the guy in nothing more than a few small lies.

One of the Marines brought the detainee back into the gym. Champion turned to me and said, "We're going to let him go, sir." I nodded in agreement. There was no evidence against Beemer, and he wisely claimed that his car had been hit by stray gunfire. No matter how we might try, we could not prove otherwise. We decided to question the group of brothers and cousins next.

"Sir, I am only going to hold on to the two guys who have reporting on them. The other three will be released," said Sergeant Champion.

I was perplexed and asked, "Sergeant, we haven't even questioned them yet. What makes you so sure they are not insurgents?" I felt it was a valid question.

"We can say they are insurgents all we want, sir, but without evidence they will get released. It is better to save the time and effort and just release them here. If they get transferred to the ARDF [Ar Ramadi Regional Detention Facility] and are released, they will be reimbursed fourteen dollars for every day held. I wouldn't even bother with doing the paperwork on any of them except Moneybags, Propane, and these two brothers," said Champion.

I tried to conceal my frustration. Rage Company had gone nonstop for a day preparing for this mission. It was another twelve hours of getting to the COP and actually executing it. Now, about five hours into the paperwork, I was finding out that only four of the guys we had detained would be charged. I left the bathroom to Sergeant Champion and his interpreter. I couldn't stand to hear more Iraqis cry and whine about America or say they had never seen an insurgent.

I was now standing in the living room. Sleeping Marines covered every inch of floor space. Albin and Eakin were the only guys awake in the room; they were working on the twenty-two detainee packets. I told them to stop and said, "We're only filling out the detainee paperwork on Moneybags, Propane, and the two freaks in the bathroom."

They looked at me in disbelief; hours of wasted work sat on the table in front of them. Eakin spoke up. "I love you, too, sir."

I understood why they were frustrated, but I was more worried about the morale of the company. The Marines had risked their lives to bring us these detainees, and almost all of them were going to be released. Only a handful would even be questioned. I decided to inform Captain Smith about our progress.

I found Rage 6, Captain Smith, in the COC. He was speaking with Lieutenant Thomas and Corporal Davila regarding the raid's only contact with the enemy. Interested, I sat down. I was just in time. Davila said, "We moved out from behind the southern wall on the school compound. We moved quickly, and the enemy waited for the breach team to move up to the front door. My second team cordoned off the structure, while I banged on the door yelling for the occupants to open up. That's when we were engaged by heavy automatic fire. I thought it was coming from inside the house, so we set some C4 on the door to gain entry. We went in hot and quickly realized that the contact was coming from our left flank in the Papa 10. We didn't hit any of the civilians in the house, but the one MAM we detained did take a small piece of wood from the door in his right shoulder. The enemy ceased fire as soon as we gained entry to the home."

Captain Smith continued questioning Davila on why his squad had opened fire on civilians without positively identifying any hostile intent. He then told Lieutenant Thomas that Corporal Davila's squad would be sidelined while an investigation into the incident was conducted. Rage 6 explained that battalion was furious over the incident, and there had to be consequences for the squad's actions. The three men were visibly frustrated. None of them liked the situation. It was going to be a huge morale killer, and we all feared that the Marines would begin to second-guess themselves on the battlefield.

I waited until Davila left to update Captain Smith on the detainees. Rumors were already circulating that Beemer was the sniper who'd shot Heidbreder. Other rumors were more accurate, stating every detainee would be released. I didn't want to fuel the flames. Rage 6 coolly accepted the information and asked me to check in with him after we questioned Moneybags and Propane. Exhausted, he then went to find a place to sleep.

I returned to the gym. Marines were screaming at detainees to "shut up" and "stop talking." I found the injured guy, who needed nothing more than a large Band-Aid. The detainees were sleeping on one another. Blindfolded men were lying with their heads on their neighbors' crotches. Another man's head was dangerously placed between two men's rear ends while his feet almost touched another detainee's nose. The Marines who were guarding the detainees tried to spread them out, but the Iraqis didn't care. The exhausted men just wanted to sleep and stay warm.

Sergeant Champion was questioning Moneybags. I walked in for the tail end of the questioning. Champion was calm, while his interpreter looked like he was about to kill Moneybags. They wrapped up the questioning, and two Marines dragged the detainee back to the gym.

"How did it go?" I asked.

"He is dirty, sir. I think our reporting is right; this guy is the leader of the local IED cell in the Papa 8 and 10 patrol sectors. He claims to run a market, and that's why he has all the money. It's clearly a lie; the foreign currency usually represents the nationality of foreign fighters coming into the AO or different types of foreign weapons. He didn't give up any information, and he didn't care that we caught him in a few lies about his family and their occupations. Let's get Propane in here."

Two Marines brought in Moneybags's son. Champion proceeded with the usual basic questions and heard a description of a family that contradicted most of what Moneybags had said. Propane then proclaimed to be good friends with the mayor of Ramadi and said that if we called him, he would know who Propane was.

Champion took the opportunity to keep Propane in the dark regarding our knowledge of his nefarious activities. "You're right; a friend of the mayor is a friend of mine. We apologize for keeping you and your father here and thank you for your patience." He said it with a straight face.

I was less enthusiastic. I visualized pulling out my 9mm, flicking off the safety, and shooting the bastard in the head. The IED that had killed those three soldiers in Papa 10 was not only huge in terms of explosives, but it also contained numerous containers of propane gas. The accelerant ensured that if the soldiers somehow survived the blast, they would die in the ensuing fireball. Mr. Propane didn't sell the explosive gas simply for heating and cooking purposes; he was a death dealer.

As I finished my thought, Propane was taken back to the gym. Champion looked at me. "I have some word for you, sir. We are going to release Moneybags and Propane."

I sat down on the sink. "Why the hell would you do that?" There was a hint of anger in my voice.

"A few weeks ago the SEALs used their home as a sniping position," Champion replied. "They confiscated a satellite phone while they were there, and now we are going to give it back to them. Hopefully, they'll continue to use it and we will try to track down any senior leaders they are in contact with. It is coming down as a priority from the intelligence battalion commander."

I told the sergeant I understood. I immediately went to find Captain Smith, who was somehow awake in the COC. He looked like a zombie. "Sir, we have an issue," I told him and explained the scenario.

He buried his face in his hands and said, "Well, if intel battalion wants it to go down that way, we can't really argue with them."

I went back to the gym and thought about our first mission. It was about 1000 in the morning, and everyone was sleeping, detainees and guards alike. I looked at Moneybags and Propane. Three grieving families were about to lose an opportunity for justice. It was an unusual feeling, being so close to two men who were proud members of al Qaeda. They would be hailed as heroes who had suffered under American captivity. I tried to put them out of my mind. Only a picture of Beemer driving his car and shooting Heidbreder replaced them.

What a night. An hour later, the platoons started heading back to Camp Ramadi. After they all left, twenty of the detainees were released. I watched Moneybags and Propane walk away.

The next day signals intelligence intercepted a call: Moneybags had called his son in Syria to arrange transport out of Iraq. He never used the phone again. The two brothers we had brought to the ARDF were also released a few days later. That gave us a 100 percent release rate for Operation Harrison Creek I. Davila's squad was being investigated and sidelined. The rumor that Beemer had shot Heidbreder was considered fact by most of the Marines. They all eventually found out that he was released. We had been operational in Ramadi for three days, and everyone was pissed. What a night indeed.

A cache of weapons brought to COP Rage by the scouts. A white suicide vest lies innocently in the foreground.

Combat Outpost Falcon in southern Ramadi.

A Bradley fighting vehicle escorts a Rage Company convoy toward COP Falcon in southern Ramadi.

Rage 1, under fire, returns to COP Grant in two-man pairs.

Lieutenants Andrew Grubb and
James Thomas before Operation
Harrison Creek I.

Lance Corporal
Joash Albin catches
his breath during
Operation Windmill
Point.

The intelligence cell inside COP Falcon minutes before Operation Windmill Point.

Marines on the roof of COP Grant.

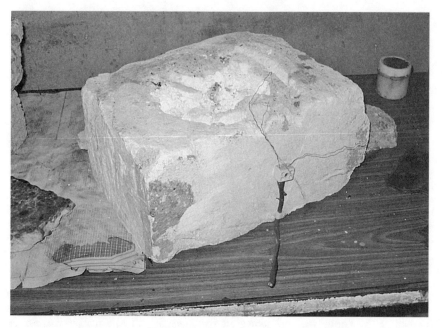

An IED in concrete disguised as a piece of a wall.

3

FORTRESS RAMADI

December 1, 2006

"Why the hell did you release Scrooge and Huey?" Captain James asked.[1]

The intel section at 1-37 had code names for its most wanted insurgents. Captain James was genuinely upset that the murderers of his friends had been set free. I was exhausted. It had been ten hours since I'd arrived back at Camp Ramadi, and I still hadn't gone to sleep. The last thing I wanted to do was talk about Moneybags and Propane.

Silence filled the air. I was unsure how to answer his question. "Sir, the THT guys made the call," I responded.

He had no clue what I was talking about. "Last time I checked, THT didn't take any detainees last night." The words implied sarcasm, but there wasn't any in Captain James's voice. More silence.

An army specialist from COP Grant came to my assistance. "They are trying to exploit their cell phone via signals intelligence," he said. We all glanced at one another, each man visibly frustrated. I finally opened my mouth and relayed the story of Moneybags and Propane to Captain James.

---

1. "Scrooge" was a nickname for Moneybags, and "Huey" was a nickname for Propane. The family was nicknamed after the characters in Disney's *DuckTales*, as Louie and Dewey were Moneybags's other two sons.

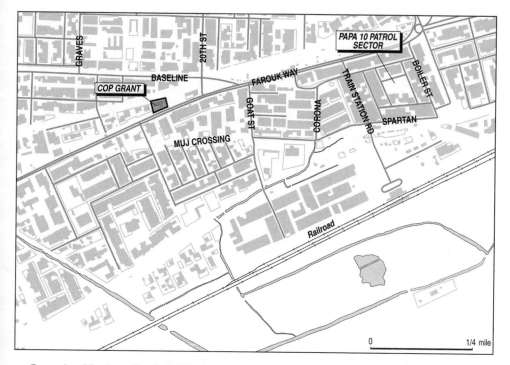

Operation Harrison Creek II: The Papa 10 patrol sector, one of Ramadi's most dangerous.

His response was short. "I got something for you, Lieutenant Daly." He turned and walked back to the intelligence sections office. I followed, expecting the worst.

The office consisted of two connecting rooms within the southern corner of 1–37's headquarters on Camp Ramadi. Each room was about three hundred square feet. The captain picked up a pile of rolled maps off his desk. "Thirty copies of the task force's area of operations." He paused for a moment. "I hear you are going to be walking in and out of the Papa 10 for Operation Harrison Creek II. A few words of advice; do not be there when the sun comes up." He handed the maps to me, and I found them much heavier than I anticipated. It was a lot of paper. They would be worth the weight. The production of strip maps was going to be exponentially quicker.

I stood waiting for the captain to rip me apart for releasing Moneybags and Propane. After a few awkward seconds, I realized he had only called me back for the maps. When I turned to walk out of his office, Captain James recognized that his point regarding the detainees hadn't hit home with me yet.

"Daly, when you take a detainee, he belongs to you. You, well, with the approval of Captain Smith, decide who gets released and who doesn't. Any detainee your Marines take belongs to Rage Company. Remember, the guy on the ground usually has the most information. You make the call. Consider yourself informed." Captain James spoke in a normal conversational tone. I took it as an example of the differences between the Corps and the Army.

Back at the Rage Company tent, everyone was asleep. I joined the club and slept for the better part of a day. When I awoke, the initial planning for Operation Harrison Creek II (HC2) was under way. I gathered the intel cell for the production of similar materials as those for HC1. Our work quickly became a discussion about the notoriety of the patrol sector we would be clearing. A few weeks earlier, SEALs had engaged in heavy fighting in the Papa 10. One SEAL lost his legs; another was killed. I later found out that Captain James was on the scene during some of these firefights.

The most important lesson from the SEALs' debriefs concerned the insurgents' manipulation of children. The enemy used these youngsters as combatants in an attempt to counter our small-kill teams (SKTs). The SKTs were six- or seven-man teams of snipers who infiltrated insurgent neighborhoods and established ambush positions on the upper floors of

Iraqi homes. Every day between 0700 and 0730, kids around the age of five or six would knock on the door of every house in the sector. They were searching for "Amriki." Each child was tasked with his own street. When the occupant answered the door, the child asked, "Can I come inside and play?" Whether they were allowed in or told to go away did not matter. The children judged the reactions of the occupants based on prior days' questioning. The children knew that if the Americans were upstairs, the owner would nervously tell them to go away.

An hour later, teenagers would show up to scope out any suspicious sites. These older kids had a much different task: find the Americans and cause a casualty. Their standard tactic was to throw grenades into homes potentially occupied by U.S. forces. Once the American position was confirmed, or when we were evacuating a casualty, the actual insurgents showed up. They tried to then inflict more damage using their standard weapons: RPGs, PKM or RPK machine guns, assorted sniper rifles, and a litany of small-arms weapons. It was a heartless but effective method of gathering real-time intelligence.

The methods showcased the insurgents' opportunistic nature. They sought to exploit everyone. Kindergarteners became reconnaissance men. Teenagers delivered accurate indirect fire in the form of hand grenades. Infantry maneuvered under the chaos of the grenade's detonation. The concept was standard military doctrine, but the soldiers implementing it were not your standard combatants.

One report had the Papa 10 as the unconfirmed home of Mullah Qahttan's immediate family. Based off the intel brief we received before HC1, Mullah Qahttan was one of the highest-ranking AQI leaders in Al Anbar Province. Flipping through the report, Albin wondered what Qahttan's mother was like and suggested we make a visit during HC2. I was skeptical that Mullah Qahttan or his family would be in the Papa 10. There were also five different reports stating that Mullah Qahttan had been killed in action. Each report wasn't worth the paper it was printed on. This poor intel highlighted the frustration of the cell's task: making sense of hundreds of pages of ridiculously formatted information. Almost half of the reports that Albin, Eakin, and I read were worthless. It drove Eakin so crazy that he began to sit in a wheelchair as if he were physically disabled. Albin scolded him. "That's bad luck, man. You sit in a wheelchair, you are gonna end up needing a wheelchair." Eakin stopped sitting in it, but not before I took a picture of him.

There was one piece of intel that we all paid particular attention to: a report that provided ten-digit grid coordinates inside the Papa 10 to the potential location of two insurgents responsible for a grenade attack on September 29, 2006, that killed a SEAL, Michael Monsoor, who would later be posthumously awarded the Medal of Honor for his actions. We made a note to ensure that the location would be meticulously searched.

I met up with Captain Smith, the XO, and the platoon commanders later that night. Rage 6 briefed his ideas on the concept of the mission, which was subsequently endorsed by the group. The plan was similar to HC1, but the methodology was slightly different. The Papa 10 consisted of two concentric squares. We referred to them as the outer and the inner square. At the center of the inner square was a small rectangle of open terrain. The ground was a historic point-of-origin (POO) site that the enemy used to fire mortars at COP Grant and the closer COP Eagles Nest. Our mission was straightforward: clear as much of the inner square of Papa 10 on the night of December 3 as possible. All elements were to return to friendly lines before sunrise.

To confuse the insurgents, Rage 1 would leave Camp Ramadi and set up first at COP Falcon. Using a few hours' separation, which we hoped would allow the enemy to focus on Rage 1 at COP Falcon, Rage 2 and Rage 4 would then depart for COP Grant. These locations were chosen to mask our objective. The most logical stepping point for HC2 was COP Eagles Nest. This COP was only 250 meters from the Papa 10, but we wanted to surprise the enemy by being less predictable. As with HC1, Pathfinder would be first onto the objective area, sweeping the roads for IEDs. They would depart Camp Ramadi at 1830. The cordon force would follow in the same convoy, setting up at the four corners of the outer square. Once the Papa 10 was swept, Pathfinder would continue on a diversionary route to the west.

At that point, Rage 1 would depart COP Falcon. When Rage 1 passed COP Grant, Rage 2 and Rage 4 would follow in trace. Each platoon would use the same route to get to the objective, following Farouk Way to the northwest corner of the Papa 10 patrol sector. The Papa 10 was next broken down into north-south running lanes. Captain Smith assigned each platoon a lane, and the platoons then gave each of their squads its own lane. When the elements finished clearing south, they would strongpoint—that is, take up a defensive position—on Papa 10's southern side. From there, they would wait until the order to move out of the objective area. Again, this is where our methods changed. HC1 was out and back to the same starting point. The egress for HC2 was heading south outside the city. We would cross over the old east-west railroad tracks and, using the berm as cover, walk 2,000 meters west to COP Iron, situated on the Saddam Canal. It was a much longer dismounted movement than HC1 had been.

Afterward, Captain Smith approached me. "Lieutenant Daly, I am going to be using ANGLICO again for this mission." He took a moment to gauge my reaction.

"That's fine, sir. How about I go on this one as the intel cell leader?" I had already explained to Captain Smith my previous conversation with Captain James. He was quiet, so I pressed harder. "I think it would greatly increase my effectiveness at filling out the detainee packets."

Rage 6 began to nod. "I think you're right. The last thing I want to do is take another twenty detainees and release them all. You can go with whichever platoon you want."

It was about time.

The next thirty-six hours were spent refining the plan and decompressing. We called our families and got haircuts. Captain Smith took three hours to brief the mission to the company staff and its attachments. I didn't have any trouble paying attention this time. The platoons took turns raiding the Camp Ramadi PX, rehearsing on the terrain model in the company headquarters, and watching movies on our one projector. The white walls of our tents made perfect movie screens. The mood was still soured, however, due to the investigation into Davila's squad. It wasn't much of an investigation. The squad was simply not allowed to execute the mission. They were on probation.

I knew Captain Smith didn't intend to charge Davila with any crime when he ordered the investigation. It was simply out of principle, to establish for the Marines what is and isn't acceptable on the battlefield. His reasoning was irrelevant to the Marines. Some of the officers were concerned that their men would be less aggressive and would hesitate on the battlefield. Most of the junior Marines felt betrayed. I was even upset about not leaving the wire for HC1. Confidence in our commander was quickly plummeting among the men. A rift among the officers was a likely next step.

In the early afternoon of December 2, I relaxed on my cot reading a few letters from home. The XO stormed into the tent. He went straight to Captain Smith, whose bunk was next to mine. "Guess who I just saw getting out of a hummer!" he said.

A few days earlier, Captain Smith had implemented a policy that officers were not allowed to drive vehicles. "If you are an officer, you will not drive a tactical vehicle," he had said. The decision was made after Lieutenant Thomas drove some of his Marines to Camp Ramadi's chow hall, avoiding the fifteen- to twenty-minute walk from tent city.

Captain Smith made the decision as a form of protection. If you aren't driving, you can't be responsible for any damages in an accident. The last thing Rage 6 wanted was to lose an officer to an investigation because he hit a pedestrian or crashed into something. At best, it was awkward for the rest of the officers, who would now have to ask one of their Marines to drive them around.

The XO looked back toward the entrance he'd come through and shouted. "Get the fuck in here!" Lieutenants Thomas, Shearburn, and Jahelka came into the tent.

Captain Smith put down his laptop and grabbed a spit bottle as he stood up. He looked down to the other side of the tent. "If you don't have a rocker on your collar, get out!" The junior Marines of headquarters platoon scurried out the other end of the tent. Rage 6 proceeded to give three of his platoon commanders the ass chewing I had expected from Captain James. I stayed on my cot, listening and thinking about how each individual would react to the incident. I understood both sides. Captain Smith needed to put his foot down. The lieutenants were professionally embarrassed, scolded in front of the men they led. All for what would seem a trivial matter. I lay back and started to read again, hoping neither side would take personal offense. Only time would tell.

December 3, 2006

It had rained for only about ten minutes, but somehow everything was caked in mud. The mud was an ominous sign, as more rain was in the forecast. Rage 1 had already left for COP Falcon. I had decided that I would execute HC2 with Rage 2. I found Corporal Holloway and his squad staged outside the headquarters tent, ready to go.

Holloway was smoking. "You know, sir, if you had smoked before the last op, Davila wouldn't be getting investigated. Seriously, sir, something is going to go wrong on every op until you smoke with Lieutenant Thomas before they begin." Holloway wasn't whispering anymore. The

Marines of his squad didn't even look like they thought what he was saying was crazy.

I wasn't going to budge. "For the last time, I do not smoke. And I will not be one of those combat smokers," I said.

Plenty of Marines had taken up smoking in-country. Somehow it calmed the nerves. The catchphrase for being one was *combat smoker*. I sat down with the squad and waited for time to pass. It eventually did.

The engines of Rage Company's seven-ton trucks and humvees roared to life. I climbed into the back of the personnel variant seven-ton. It was a massive vehicle. Wearing a full combat load made climbing the stairs an arduous task. Benches were placed in the center, allowing the Marines to face outboard and use the top of the three-foot armored wall as a firing stand for their weapons. The Marines dropped the canvas top of the truck's bed down over the sides, in an attempt to camouflage themselves from enemy snipers. It would also deflect any well-placed hand grenade throws.

The four idling seven-ton trucks and hummers drowned out all noise, except one: the high pitch of metal banging into metal randomly pierced the rumbling engines as Marines strategically placed gear on the back of their trucks. No one tried to speak over the ruckus. The last Marines of the squad struggled aboard, squeezing among one another and their gear. I had already made the trip to COP Grant multiple times at night; however, riding in the back of this truck on a daylight trip through Ramadi's streets seemed likely to produce the same outcome as our one day-patrol: a firefight. It didn't help that we were an IED's dream. With all of our gear and packs, we were trapped behind the armor that protected us. It was a perfect thought as we started to make our way toward Ogden Gate and Route Michigan.

We linked up with our BFV and tank escort just before leaving Camp Ramadi. The convoy stopped short of Ogden Gate. Weapons went condition one. The snap of charging handles slamming home was our way of punching the clock. It was time to earn some pay.

The convoy rolled forward, making a left onto Route Michigan and exiting the gate. Route Michigan was the main supply route through downtown Ramadi. It was repeatedly targeted by insurgent ambushes and IEDs. My side of the vehicle scanned into the industrial area adjacent to Camp Ramadi. The real threat was on the other side of the vehicle. A few hundred meters south of the road, the "Chinese" apartments were five or six stories high. Civilians still lived in them, and insurgents used the countless windows in the structures to engage coalition convoys along Route Michigan. They were also a great vantage point from which to observe all military traffic along the route. It was key terrain in the city. I bounced a few inches off the seat as we hit a pothole and made it onto the Saddam Bridge. I landed sideways on the seat, so I turned all the way around to see how the other Marines had taken the bump. I ended up getting a glimpse of the city I would never forget.

Driving over the Saddam Bridge and looking south showcased Ramadi's geographic importance. About a mile and half down the banks of the Saddam Canal, the city abruptly ended. Its streets and walled structures stopped like the ramparts of a medieval fortress. Sand replaced the insurgent stronghold and flowed down to the banks of what I first thought was a mirage: a lake in the middle of the desert. With the Euphrates River turning north and Lake Habbaniya blocking land movement to the south, there was only one direct route to Baghdad you could take without getting your feet wet: through Ramadi. For centuries, merchants had traveled along these paths through Sunni Anbar's first city. A lone highway runs west to Jordan; another snakes along the Euphrates north to Syria. Their intersection on the outskirts of Ramadi was the crossroads of the Sunni insurgency. That is, in the same sense that Quantico is the crossroads of the Corps. Everyone has been there once.

The column of vehicles crossed the bridge, moving through checkpoint 294. Directly to my front, where the Euphrates and Saddam Canal meet, was Camp Hurricane Point (HP). The former Ba'ath Party palace was now lined with fighting positions and observation posts. It was the headquarters for 1st Battalion, 6th Marines. The convoy veered to the right through the traffic circle outside HP's main gate. We were about 2,000 meters from checkpoint 295 along Route Michigan. In seconds, the buildings along the road began to resemble the remnants of a World War II battlefield. As we drove, there seemed to be one general rule: the larger the building, the more pockmarks and gaping wounds it would have.

We turned right at checkpoint 295, heading south on Sunset. The buildings seemed to close in on the road. One could almost touch the concrete walls by reaching out of the truck. The convoy rolled through COP Falcon and went directly south to Farouk Way. Making the left, it was only a few hundred meters to COP Grant. The convoy filled the COP's parking lot. I waited for a few mortar rounds to land. They never did.

The platoon dismounted and set up. With Rage 1 staging at COP Falcon, the living conditions at COP Grant for the next few hours were comfortable.

Most of the Marines slept to pass the time before the mission. At about 1945, no one was sleeping anymore. A huge explosion rocked the urban sprawl. Pathfinder had hit a massive IED at a notorious IED hot spot. None of the engineers were seriously wounded, though their vehicle was disabled. The mission would be delayed as we waited for another Pathfinder element to come out with a mine-resistant ambush-protected vehicle. The insurgents' string of IED belts was buying them time. Pathfinder would hit two more IEDs before we left the wire. Each one rocked COP Grant but strengthened our confidence in the mission. Every IED Pathfinder hit was one less we would find. The mine-resistant vehicles had the armor; we had small-arms protective inserts. The Marines in Rage Company owed their lives to the engineers of Pathfinder.

Just before midnight, we began our infiltration. I moved out of COP Grant with the lead squad of Rage 2. There was a bit of confusion because Rage 1 was not completely past the COP, and we had to halt in the middle of the road as they passed by us. We had messed up the order of movement, and our punishment was halting and kneeling in the middle of the road. The squad was stationary and exposed, occupying the outer sides of the road, while the last elements of Rage 1 flowed through us. I hated sitting still. There was too much time to think. I moved a few meters to a couple of concrete barriers and set up in the kneeling position behind one. It was a cold night, and not moving amplified the weather's effect.

Rage 2 began to move again. It was a straight shot down Farouk Way, and in the distance I could make out the flashing infrared (IR) strobes of an Abrams main battle tank and a more distant BFV. The Marines of Rage 1 were also less visible as their IR tape glistened in my NVGs. I focused on the immediate area. The road was surprisingly clean. It was also relatively safe. There was always an armored vehicle maintaining observation over the route, as it was a direct link between 1-37's COP Grant and 1-9 Infantry's COP Eagles Nest.

The column approached the tank. It was oriented south in the intersection. The 120mm cannon was facing down Train Station Road. The northern side of the T-intersection was open ground. It stretched a few hundred meters, and our only cover from that direction was two old market stalls. The stalls looked like a small garage that could hardly hold a compact car. The metallic front doors were blown open, and each stall was littered with debris.

I instantly appreciated the Abrams, because its roaring engine muffled every step I took. I crouched a few meters behind it and covered the Marine in front of me as he crossed Farouk Way. The houses on the perimeter of Papa 10 were exactly as they appeared on the map: one on top of the other, their exterior walls forming a defensive perimeter. I could see gaping holes in the roof's retaining walls, which undoubtedly had served as firing positions for previous engagements. We moved through the courtyard and into the first home. Within minutes, Rage 2 was oriented south and clearing its lane.

The squads poured into the first houses in their respective lanes. The platoon was most vulnerable during this initial clear phase of the mission. Understanding this, every squad quickly established its foothold. Marines aggressively moved through each room. Locked doors were quickly blasted open with a shotgun. There were at least a dozen shotgun blasts in the first five minutes of the clear, and the radio was full of call signs, followed by the words "Shotgun breeching!"

The first home was empty. With no one to question, I went straight to the roof. A fire team of Marines was already oriented into the heart of the patrol sector. The group covered the other squads in Rage 2 as they moved on to clear the second homes in their lanes. I took up a position next to the fire team's SAW gunner, scanning to the south with my scope. The enemy was out there. They had set off three defensive IEDs on Pathfinder, but would they stick around for the main event? I doubted it. Insurgents are survivalists. They were only going to fight if we could trap them. They had three hours to escape our cordon. It probably wasn't very difficult; a tank's armor is a better door than window.

The other squads took up positions on the second homes' roofs. They would now cover us as we cleared the next two houses, moving one ahead of them. This leapfrog concept ensured that we always had Marines manning the high ground.

We moved into the second house. It was occupied by two younger couples. Both were rounded up and placed in an upstairs bedroom. When I made it into the room, Sergeant Dimitrios Karras was questioning them. He was the closest thing to an interpreter the company had.

I immediately found the demeanor of the two men to be suspicious. I cross-checked each name on a master list of insurgents I had compiled. It was like playing Where's Waldo?, and I had never been good at that. What made it difficult was that I was unsure of how to properly spell their names. I quickly became frustrated. I was angry at myself for not paying more attention during my Arabic classes in college.

Each man we interrogated claimed to be a teacher. Right. There were so many great schools to attend in southern Ramadi. At the time, there wasn't a single one open. The men were too young to be former teachers, and I immediately thought the two were teaching something, but it wasn't educational. The one we found upstairs then admitted he didn't even live in the house. He appeared tired and depressed; his mannerisms shouted dejection. He was visiting his brother and had just come back from Saudi Arabia. I was in shock. Traveling at the time required protection from gangs of insurgents, unless you were one. Teaching in Saudi Arabia was as big an indicator as you could get. I called him "Wahhabi," and the man got very upset.

I directed the Marines to conduct a thorough search. Blankets and mattresses flew across the room. The women cried. Rage 6 gave us a few minutes to focus on the house. As usual, we found nothing. Now I had a decision to make. I walked out of the room to remove myself from the situation. There was no evidence against the guy. Should I detain him for going to Saudi Arabia? I couldn't. I thought about his getting paid for spending a few days at the ARDF. What a bureaucratic mess.

I went back into the room. The Marines had bagged and tagged him as a detainee. I looked at Corporal Holloway. "Leave him," I said. Holloway didn't question my call. He knew why I had walked out, and he also knew there was no evidence. I decided that our methods needed some serious reconfiguring. The insurgents had been playing this game for years. They knew better than to bring incriminating materials into their homes. We moved on.

I linked up with Lieutenant Thomas outside the house. The plan was evolving. Rage 2 was falling slightly behind the other platoons. To catch up, Rage 4 had cleared the homes across Hook Street, where we were supposed to go. This allowed us to skip the buildings opposite us and move down the no-name road where Pathfinder had hit the first major IED.

The squad move out of the courtyard and approached the intersection, only a few meters away. Lieutenant Thomas went around the corner with the first team. I sprinted across the street and instantly caught wind of a familiar smell: cordite. I followed the first team, finding the origin of the smell much closer than I'd anticipated. The blast hole for the IED was huge. Asphalt and chunks of concrete littered the road. It was a sobering sight. This was the spot, the same IED crater where the three soldiers had perished at the hands of Moneybags and Propane. I couldn't help but wonder if they had personally initiated the IED that hit Pathfinder here. Lieutenant Thomas jumped down into the smoldering hole. I ran up and looked at him. We had both been briefed on the fact that insurgents would hastily emplace victim-activated IEDs, which function like land mines, after Pathfinder came through. It was a smart attempt to counter the dismounted infantry that would follow.

I had a few choice words lined up for Lieutenant Thomas's actions, but in the presence of his Marines I held back. I was also shocked by the size of the crater. The platoon commander's head was level with my shins. "Rage FO, what do you think did this?" he said.

I laughed, finding it funny that he referred to me by my call sign. I didn't answer until after I helped him out of the crater. "Well, it's probably been used a few dozen times before." I shrugged, clueless as to the answer. "I have no idea. Smells good, though," I said.

He gave me a slight smile. "Say that to Pathfinder."

We turned the corner and found ourselves looking out over the central open terrain. It was much smaller than it appeared on the map. Holloway's squad made entry and began to clear the corner house. By the time I got inside, the family was isolated in a room and the building was clear. There was nothing suspicious.

As we prepared to move to the next house, Rage 6 came over the radio and asked me to move a few houses down to Rage 4's position. I reached the home within moments. It wasn't hard to find the room where the family was located. It was packed with six Marines questioning the three men living in the house. Two women and a cluster of kids cried in the room's opposing corners. On the floor was an AK with a few loaded magazines. An Iraqi police armband was draped over the weapon. A red flag went up in my mind. There was no way an Iraqi police (IP) officer lived in the Papa 10. IPs hadn't even had a presence in this area in more than a year, back when twenty or thirty of them had their throats slit in the street.

Captain Smith noticed that I was there. "Daly, try to figure this shit out," he said. He took the crowd with him, leaving one Marine to guard the group. The interpreter followed him out.

I grabbed the interpreter's arm and tried to get Rage 6's attention. "Six, you going to leave me the terp?" I said.

Captain Smith didn't even turn around. "No need; the old guy speaks English," he said.

This was going to be an interesting house. It took five minutes for me to get out of the dad that his son used to be an IP. The kid even had an ID card. The confusing part was why they kept the IP armband and ID card. They claimed to have burned the uniform, but they kept these items? I also found it abnormal that the mother continued to sob. Once an interrogator at the ARDF told me, "If you want to figure out an Arab, take note of his wife's behavior." Although I couldn't directly ask her questions or even look at her the wrong way, the reaction of the man's wife after the Heidbreder ambush confirmed the interrogator's advice.

I continued to grill the father with basic questions about the insurgents. His wife seemed to sob a little louder every time I said, "Irhabi." Something just didn't feel right about the group. Again, though, there was no evidence other than the items on the floor, none of which were illegal. There was nothing to detain the men for, and I stopped asking questions. As soon as I stopped, the father started.

The first question caught me off guard. "Are you an officer?" he asked. It was a pointed question. Why would this man care? I got the feeling that only an insurgent would want to know.

Partly intrigued and also being one of the only men in the room with a weapon, I answered truthfully. "Yes." The man was silent for a moment and then began to joke with his family in Arabic. I desperately wanted to know what they were saying, but there was only one interpreter and he wasn't here. The father was speaking only to his son, who was the IP. I got the feeling they were talking about how great it would be to kill me. I knew I was being slightly paranoid so I decided to leave. I wished the old man good health. The mother was still crying as I got up to leave the room. She didn't look at me the entire time. What was there to fear? I decided I was standing among a group of insurgents, but there was nothing I could do. No evidence. The squad moved on.

Outside the home was a company of Marines at work. Rage 4 and Rage 1 elements were clearing the exterior lanes. Rage Company's team of combat engineers was finishing up the sweep of the POO site, which turned up nothing. The squad I was with was now sprinting across the field to hit the far houses. As in HC1, we were running out of darkness.

The company staff went firm in a house on the southern side of the open field. Rage 6 began to coordinate our egress out of the objective area. To avoid putting on our own version of the Bataan Death March, we consolidated all of the detainees at our position. They totaled seven in all. None of the detainees were from any of the squads I traveled with.

The platoons continued to clear south. Rage 1 found an insurgent safe house with a mural of propaganda drawn on the wall. I had to give the *mujj* artist credit: he could draw. I moved up to the roof and watched a squad from Rage 1 clear two houses in six minutes. The guys were proficient. They were the only platoon to clear their entire lane. They also took the most detainees. Rage 1 was the main effort for a reason.

At 0455 the platoons went firm. Rage 1 left first, echeloning its squads out of the objective area. I was still with the headquarters element attached to Rage 4. We were waiting on a BFV to come pick up the detainees, so Rage 2 left next. The BFV took what seemed like an eternity to show up. When the ramp came down, there were already a few soldiers sitting in the back. Perfect. We needed transport and received a vehicle that was already almost full. It must have been all they had. When the soldiers realized who was getting thrown in with them, they were a little upset. Ramadi had no running water, and these Iraqis didn't smell good.

The first two squads from Rage 4 left the objective. Our numbers now totaled twenty Marines, a BFV, some soldiers, and seven detainees.

It was forty minutes to sunrise. I told myself it didn't really matter. It was 98 percent moonlight anyway, so it wasn't exactly dark. Lieutenant Grubb walked out of the house.

The BFV was full. The detainees were sitting and lying on top of one another, and there were two more to fit in. Lieutenant Grubb was ready to move. "Damn it, get those fuckers in there!" Grubb said. We had been standing in the courtyard long enough. There wasn't enough darkness left to keep track of, and we still had 2,000 meters to cover. What looked like a mosh pit was quickly forming in the back of the armored vehicle. I was interested to see whether Lieutenant Grubb could fit the last detainee in. He couldn't.

Rage 4 actually pulled out the last two detainees and shoved each one in the direction of a Marine. With each push, he muttered a word to the infantryman: "Escort." The Bradley raised its ramp and drove south to COP Iron. When it left, it seemed to take the darkness with it. Visibility with the naked eye increased every moment we stood there. I took off my NVGs and put them in my drop pouch. It was the first time I had felt defenseless on the mission.

Grubb walked next to me, taking a moment to rest against the wall I stood next to. I was ready to move and wondered where Captain Smith was. "Dude, we need to go; where's the boss?" I said.

Grubb exhaled heavily and said, "Talking to some hajjis or something." He got on the PRR and confirmed with Rage 4 Bravo that the platoon was accounted for and ready to step. Moments later, Captain Smith emerged from the house and we left.

The formation headed directly south, taking the shortest route to the old railroad tracks. I moved at the back of the dismounted column of Marines. Only Rage 4 Bravo and one other Marine were behind me. Directly in front of me were the two detainees and their escorts. It took only a few minutes for us to make it out of the eerily quiet city.

When we arrived at the berm, my bandolier came untied around my leg. I ended up having to hold the six twenty-seven-round magazines in place while I helped one of the escorts shove a blinded, flexi-cuffed, and barefoot detainee up the sandy hill. I'm sure Rage 4 Bravo was laughing deep inside, watching the three of us.

Once we were on the far side, the movement was long but simple— it was a straight shot. We did have to cross about 75 meters of ground that was nothing but jagged rocks. The barefoot detainee was having a hell of a night.

By the time we arrived at COP Iron, it was daylight. I immediately began to process the detainees. There was enough on each individual to warrant his going to the ARDF. After I finished all of the paperwork, however, and eighteen hours later back on Camp Ramadi, the ARDF decided to prosecute only one individual. They based their decision purely on the evidence provided. So be it.

After leaving the ARDF, I went to the dining facility on Camp Ramadi. I wanted to go to sleep, but my hunger pangs prevented it. When I got there, I loaded my plate with pizza, a burger, fries, and salad. I chose two lemon-lime Gatorades to drink. I found Captain James sitting at a table with some other 1-37 officers and joined them. I filled him in on the detainees. He had figured as much; none of the Iraqis were known terrorists.

While we were eating, a soldier came up to the table. "You guys hear? COP Eagles Nest just got hit by a coordinated suicide car bomb attack.

The insurgents suppressed the COP with heavy small-arms fire from the Papa 10."

I didn't say a word for the rest of the meal.

On the way back to my tent, I couldn't help but wonder if the guy from Saudi Arabia was the suicide bomber. Just about all the guys who conducted suicide attacks were foreign. It would have explained his dejected attitude. The guy was going to blow himself up the next day. I then wondered about the IP and his father. Were they talking about their plans after I told them I was an officer? I forced it out of my mind. Operation Windmill Point was only days away.

4

MASTER OF PUPPETS

December 7, 2006

It was a crisp, cool night as I checked my watch: 1730. Time was slowly going by, the pre-mission jitters were setting in, and we had just arrived at Combat Outpost Falcon. It was the night of December 7, 2006, and I was about to move out on Operation Windmill Point. Tonight's ordeal was a 7-kilometer foot movement through downtown Ramadi. The mission was to clear the Lima 2 patrol sector, roughly eight hundred buildings. It was our third and final mission as Bandits, and Captain James would be moving with us during the operation. He was shocked that nothing had been found in the Papa 10. This time he would see for himself.

I was walking out of the army COC aboard COP Falcon. The army captain in charge had just thrown out all of the Marines because we were eating too much of his food. It was a ridiculous situation; the COP had received extra food specifically for the Marines that day and now he was hoarding. I was infuriated, but the issue wasn't worth wasting time on. I headed toward a huge cinder-block structure with my team of scouts in trace. We were in a different world; arguing over food and listening to a distant firefight was becoming normal. I was coming to accept the city's state of affairs. Attacks across the AO continued unabated, and we had yet

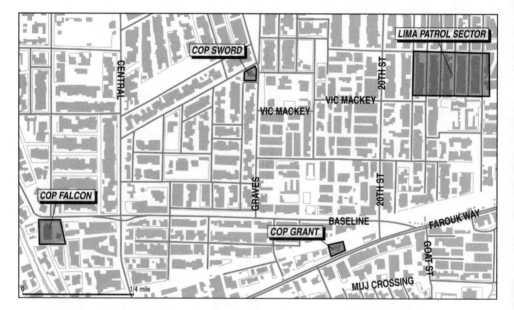

Operation Windmill Point: The dense urban terrain between Combat Outpost
Falcon and the Lima 2 patrol sector.

to confirm any enemy killed in action. Nearly all of the detainees we had taken on our previous two missions had already been released and were now living among the local population. None of this was shocking to us.

I came back to the mission at hand. American forces had not cleared any portion of Lima 2 in more than a year. The idea of walking through it wasn't sitting well with my mind. To make matters worse, today was a busy day. When an army convoy had driven near the area we were about to clear, it was attacked by an IED and a subsequent direct-fire ambush. The attack claimed the lives of two soldiers and one Marine (Major Megan McClung). I had met two of the fallen previously while I was on advance party to the brigade staff. The ambush turned into a sporadic firefight that raged until about 1700, allowing us to hear the last hour of hostilities because we had just arrived at the COP.

I entered the cinder-block structure. "Lieutenant Daly, sir," said Lance Corporal Albin.

"What?" I snapped back, still upset about being thrown out of the COC. "There's room for us in here."

Joash Albin was sitting inside a room built out of plywood and two-by-fours. Albin, standing about six feet tall, was everything I could ask of a Marine. He worked hard, had initiative, and was competent at his job. What he lacked in judgment, he made up for in his motivation and ability to listen to my lengthy lectures. Besides, judgment was my job. Lance Corporal Eakin and I were both standing in the doorway to the building. Like all buildings in Ramadi, it was made out of concrete and was literally empty except for the plywood rooms. There was a "toilet," a glorified hole in the ground, in the back of the building. The structure was partitioned by a concrete wall in the center. Rage 2 had moved into the left side of the building, leaving the right side, where Albin was, completely empty. The empty space was eventually supposed to be occupied by Rage 4, but for now it was a perfect place for us to hang out.

Lance Corporal Eakin went into the room and sat down against the wall. "Go ahead, Eakin, do what you do best and go to sleep," Albin said with a chuckle.

"Shut up, fag," Eakin retorted.

Benjamin Eakin was the team's radio operator. At five feet nine inches and thinner than many poor Iraqis, he was often the subject of Albin's and my jokes. To convince Eakin that he slept too much, Albin and I had resorted to taking pictures of him while he was asleep in random places. He was an average Marine and extremely loyal. In comparison to most radio operators I'd had in my short career as a forward observer (FO), he was the most knowledgeable. During our training for deployment, the radios of every other FO team went down during a live-fire exercise. Eakin single-handedly fixed the radios for the rest of the FO teams on the hill. Of course, our radio worked fine, and what confused all of the other lance corporal 0621s took Eakin five minutes to figure out. I challenged myself to transfer that technical knowledge into a vocabulary.

I sat down next to the two Marines. "Holy shit," I said, "this floor is cold as—"

Albin interrupted me. "Well, sir, if you had prepared properly, you would have put on some long johns." He stretched out on the concrete floor, relishing the moment that he could correct his boss. During our previous missions, I had told both Albin and Eakin not to wear any layers. With the men's adrenaline pumping, the added clothes usually led to profuse sweating. The temperature continued to drop as the days went by, however, and now hovered in the mid-thirties at night. With the bare floors and the concrete walls, sitting anywhere for more than five minutes left you freezing.

"Damn it, Albin, if I hear you say I told you so, I will non-req you," I said.[1] I pulled out my long john top, quickly dropped my gear, and put it on.

We sat around in that room for about two hours, doing anything we could to get warmer. During that time, I walked into the COC and acquired some food. I did so with pleasure. Time continued to inch along. At about 1930, we could hear the noise of the massive seven-ton trucks and the BFVs coming to the COP. Rage 4 was arriving. The mission was fairly complex. Over the course of the late afternoon, various elements of Rage Company would move into their staging positions at combat outposts Falcon and Grant. Each COP would receive two platoons, while the company commander and the headquarters element would go to COP Grant.

For this mission, Captain Smith had again decided to use an Air Naval Gunfire Liaison Team as his fire support element. This decision was essentially giving someone else my job yet again. I decided to attach my intel cell to Rage 2. We would basically be nothing more than an added fire team, commanded by a lieutenant. The company had a platoon of tanks and a platoon of BFVs attached; there would also be

---

1. Non-req is short for not-recommended. It prevents a Marine from being promoted to the next rank/grade.

a company from 1-37 clearing the patrol sector to the south. The routes we were using would again be cleared by Pathfinder, which would drop off the cordon force of BFVs and tanks as it went. The cordon force would be spread out over the entire 7-kilometer movement in an attempt to keep the whole route clear. I wasn't so sure. Once Pathfinder was done clearing the objective, Rage 2 and Rage 4, which were at COP Falcon, would step off. It was logical because those of us at COP Falcon had the farthest distance to travel. Rage 1 and Rage 3 would follow shortly after us and move along a different route. The platoons would follow the same tactics used in HC2, clearing designated lanes in a south to north direction.

Rage 4 filed into the building, and the three plywood rooms were quickly crammed with Marines and gear. In the corner, one of the corporals was explaining to another Marine how to use a shotgun. The infamous words "now all you have to do . . ." were no sooner uttered than there was a huge explosion. Instantly, dust and splinters of wood sprayed my face. I was dazed and confused. What seemed like an eternity was probably only a matter of seconds as people came to their senses. We sat in stunned silence. I brushed off my face, and the touch brought me back to reality.

I was amazed to see that all of the Marines standing in the corner were fine. In this room, no more than ten feet by ten feet, there were roughly thirteen Marines. A shotgun had just been fired and had ricocheted off the wall into the ceiling. Two Marines had literally been looking down at the weapon as dozens of pellets flew past their faces and into the wall. If the weapon had been leaning at any other angle, it would have deflected into the plywood and hit the Marines crammed into the room next to us.

"Albin, Eakin, you okay?" I said, breaking the silence.

"We're still here, sir," stated Albin.

I began to feel that I was working with a bunch of amateurs. Nothing shakes your confidence more than witnessing Marines, who have trained over and over again, nearly kill one another with such a blatant disregard for safety. In a dark room a noncommissioned officer was "teaching" another junior Marine how to handle a shotgun, and the junior kid just figured why not pull the trigger? The issue was not exclusive to Rage Company; it was Marine Corps–wide.

The standard rifleman's training focused on the organic weapons of a fire team: M16A4 or M4 rifle, M203 grenade launcher, and M249 light machine gun. Only a select few received basic training with the different types of shotguns available to Marines. Yet this didn't prevent the Corps from distributing dozens of the weapons to its infantry units before deployment. Rage Company's senior enlisted Marine, First Sergeant Eric Carlson, gave numerous classes on the operation of these shotguns, but with only days until movement into Iraq, muscle memory did not have time to set in. It wouldn't be the last incident involving the Marines of Rage Company and shotguns.

The gross negligence displayed here had added to the pre-mission jitters rattling my nerves. I wasn't sure whether it was the cold air that made me shiver or the thought of trusting these Marines with my life.

We heard more distant small-arms fire. Surprisingly, the next hour and a half went by quickly. With all of the action, we knew the enemy was going to play tonight. I walked over to the COC again and talked to Lieutenant Thomas about the shotgun incident. As we spoke, it came over the radio that Pathfinder was nearing the release point, meaning we would be clear to step off.

Rage 2 began to form up on the dusty road and oriented down Baseline Street. Baseline ran east-west through southern Ramadi, and we would move down it for about 2,000 meters. I went back to the building to get Albin and Eakin, who met me outside. "Gents, we are going to move with Corporal Holloway's squad. We will be directly behind his first fire team. Albin, you have point, followed by myself and then Eakin," I said.

"Roger, sir."

The sound of sporadic gunfire could be heard in the distance. As we formed up, it began to pick up in intensity. Measuring the distance of a firefight from one's position, especially in an urban environment, is rather tricky. It sounded like we were going to be in a hailstorm of fire as soon as we left COP Falcon. We began to step, and when I moved onto Baseline, still inside friendly lines, I could see bursts of tracers flying over rooftops about 1.5 kilometers away. Nothing like this had happened during HC1 or HC2. I punched the clock, sending my M4 to condition one. Tonight was going to be different.

There was complete silence as we began to move. The road was about two lanes wide in each direction, and the Marines maintained good dispersion with at least 5 meters between each man in a staggered column. We moved faster than usual, a direct result of the sounds of combat. The street was lined with small garages on either side, which had served as market stalls in a different lifetime.

I tightened my Kevlar helmet. The weight from my NVGs, which hung over my left eye, was forcing the helmet forward. I had literally tied the bandolier of ammunition magazines on my left thigh. It wasn't falling off tonight. On my right side hung a sustainment/drop pouch where I put spare batteries, my map, and a small notepad. On my body armor vest, I had another six magazines, a fragmentation grenade, a first aid kit, a butt pack with some chow, and a bottle of water. The vector and the dagger, a target location device and the essential tools of any forward observer, were slung over my left shoulder inside their carrying case. With a burden of right around one hundred pounds, I was carrying one of the lightest loads in the company. My M4 was at the alert. The moon was high, and vision with the naked eye was good out to roughly 150 meters.

There was another burst of tracer fire over the rooftops, and it quickly turned into a sustained firefight. I was now about 150 meters outside COP Falcon, and I was coming up on the first major intersection. Trash lay everywhere, all along the sidewalks. I swore that the electrical lines in Iraq ran external to the buildings. After years of neglect, they hung down over the fronts of the shops and homes. The wires always appeared to run randomly. To make matters worse, the most prevalent local method of initiating IEDs was with command wire.

Insurgents would run a wire from the IED to their hiding spot, detonate the IED as you walked or drove by, and take off. A few Marines carried wire cutters and cut every wire they came across.

I oriented down the intersection, walking sideways past a tire lying in the middle of the street. On the far side was a partially destroyed white sedan. The street was lined with concertina wire to prevent anyone from walking out onto the dusty asphalt and planting IEDs. I scanned the windows of a five-story building on the opposite side of the intersection. Without a PEQ-2, an infrared laser only visible with NVGs, I couldn't see inside the windows, but every few seconds another Marine would shine his in my direction. I nervously crept toward the structure. Captain James had given me a video of a substantial firefight that took place inside the building I was now looking at, no more than 25 meters away. We walked by without incident.

The platoon suddenly began to move onto a side road. For whatever reason, the point element recommended that we get off Baseline; there was probably a potential IED (PIED) in the street. After a 30-meter walk south, we turned east onto a much smaller one-lane road that ran parallel to Baseline. I was walking up on a four-way intersection when there was another blast of AK fire, followed by my first personal experience with an RPG. As it streaked across the sky directly above us, I took note of my surroundings. Between me and Baseline was one row of buildings. The fire and the RPG we had just received came from north of Baseline, and I could hear the loud rumbling of a huge engine. I peeked around the corner and saw an Abrams tank situated in the middle of Baseline just to my north. The tank was most likely the RPG's target. Corporal Holloway had already acted on the situation, and the squad was moving into the building on the far right side of the intersection. The first team moved in and began clearing.

Albin, Eakin, and I ran into the building behind the second team. The structure was surrounded by the usual exterior wall. Inside the wall was more of the same—a small courtyard, an outhouse, and a driveway. The home was situated about 5 meters back from the wall. It was the typical small fortress that formed the insurgents' urban jungle.

We made entry into the home, going first into the kitchen and then into the main living area. I was sweating profusely. "Sir, I am dropping my long johns," said Albin.

"Me, too," I said. "Make it quick, though; we will be moving here in a second." More Marines were coming into the house, and it soon became jam-packed with infantry grunts, an Iraqi family, and lots of rifles. Sporadic gunfire came from the east and the north.

"Nothing coming over the net about that fire, sir," Eakin said, knowing exactly what I was thinking.

"Don't worry about it," I said. "Switch over to Battalion every now and then when we go firm and see what's getting passed."

My thoughts came back to the immediate scenario, and after the previous experience with the shotgun at COP Falcon, my mind was screaming that the room was way too crowded. "Albin, Eakin, go outside to the courtyard," I ordered. "There are way too many people in here." I was still putting on my gear as they went out.

Corporal Holloway came up to me. "Sir, did you and my lieutenant smoke before this mission?" he asked.

For some reason I took a second to soak in the moment. Corporal Holloway was your usual all-American kid. He was athletic, not tall, not short, and had a genuine smile and confidence. I emphasized my response more than usual.

"I don't smoke," I replied.

"Sir, it's not too late," he said.

I walked away, shaking my head.

I headed outside and came across Eakin sitting in the kitchen. As a question went through my mind, Albin came through the door. Why was Eakin inside? I just told him and Albin to go out into the courtyard.

"Eakin, what the hell are you doing?!" screamed a visibly angry Albin.

"What?" replied Eakin.

"You left me out there by myself! Luckily, Cleveland was out there, or I would have been all alone in the street! You stupid, lazy . . . ," Albin continued on with the names.

"Albin, shut the hell up, and Eakin, we will talk later," I said, trying to quiet the two men. The last thing I wanted to do was deal with squabbling at that moment.

"We're moving!" bellowed Holloway.

"Holloway, I am putting my team behind your first fire team. Any objections?" I shouted back.

"None."

We headed out down the side street back to the intersection we had just crossed. The first team moved up just short of the tank. I was posted at the northeast corner, with Holloway crouched in between two crates and a break in the wall. Rage 4 walked by on Baseline, passing the tank. I knew from the operations order that this would mess up the order of movement into the objective area. Apparently, Rage 4 did not see any reason to move to the side road and had stayed on Baseline the whole time. We let the platoon pass and waited for a few minutes to get adequate separation.

A loud crackle of AK fire ripped through the air. It was close—deafeningly close. For the first time, I pulled my fragmentation grenade out of its pouch. I moved up to the corner and scanned for a target. I moved back to my previous position, and there was another two- to three-round burst. I could have sworn it came from the roof adjacent to us.

"Are you going to throw that?" asked one of the Marines on the corner of the four-way intersection.

"If I can figure out where the hell he is, yes," I said.

The question forced me to think about the risks involved in throwing the grenade. Since the source of fire was in an elevated position, I would be throwing from low to high, and gravity would send a poor throw right back at me. I was reminded by my conscience again that I had played soccer in high school, not football or baseball. Plus, maybe elements from another platoon were already clearing one of these homes. Although it was certainly AK fire—you can tell by the sound—I did not see any muzzle flashes, which meant that all I could observe was movement. The last thing I wanted to do was frag a group of friendlies or a family of Iraqis hiding out. As someone removed from the combat environment would put it, I did not have positive identification of a target or indication of hostile intent. I came to the realization that I was reacting to a confusing situation with poor judgment. I put the grenade back in its pouch. We waited a few minutes and continued to move.

Somehow, Holloway's squad was now in the lead of the platoon, and my team of "observers" was directly behind his point element. It took ten minutes for us to reach the intersection of Baseline and Graves. It was only a couple hundred meters south that Lance Corporal Heidbreder had been shot days earlier. After we turned, Graves Street would take us north toward another small army COP named Sword. It was one of the most isolated in all of Ramadi. As we neared Graves Street, a burst of tracers flew over the Bradley on the intersection. The sound of a distant raging firefight engulfed the city. As I watched the point team turn north on Graves, one thought went through my mind: fuck. I realized that for the first time I was thinking of saying a four-letter word for an actual reason and not just as a figure of speech.

Albin and Eakin were both on the left side of the road. I crossed directly in front of the Bradley, with the roar of its engine and my knowledge of its optics providing some comfort. Again the road was littered with debris, chopped-up portions of concrete, and wires running into every structure. The buildings were a mix of homes with courtyard walls and garage-style storefronts. The platoon came to a halt.

"Corpsman up!" shouted the team leader from the point element. It was repeated down the line.

"Eakin, what the hell is going on?" I yelled across the street.

"I'm not hearing anything, sir."

Holloway was moving up behind me. "The corpsman isn't for us, sir. He's for the soldiers at Sword," he said. The next day I was told that an insurgent had shined a high-powered flashlight at a soldier's position on Sword's roof, temporarily blinding him. This drew the soldier out from behind his ballistic glass to engage the enemy with his automatic weapon. The moment he did a sniper took his life. This trick was a standard insurgent tactic in Ramadi.

Our conversation was interrupted by a close firefight that replaced the distant echoes. "Sir, Fourth is in contact!" shouted Eakin. I signaled acknowledgment with my hand.

The platoon continued to go north on Graves. We were moving to another street, Vic Mackey, where we would proceed directly east. Then we would assume a position in our lane for the clearing portion of the mission. Rage 4 was already on Vic Mackey and heading east. I skipped over a pothole filled with water and moved through a T-intersection that opened up on my right. I looked up at the overhang and saw countless wires dangling. I ducked underneath and noticed a group of stacked crates on my right, and it happened. The deafening sound of medium machine gun fire ripped through the night. I saw the first tracer through my NVGs. I watched it land five feet in front of me to my left. As I instinctively spun, I watched another land even with me just on the edge of the sidewalk. It smacked the dusty pavement and screamed at roughly a forty-five-degree angle into the sky. I felt the thud of my body impacting the concrete wall behind those stacked crates, squarely on my right shoulder. I turned with my back to the wall and sent my M4 from safe to semi. There were now hundreds of rounds flying through the street, as every rifle behind me and ahead opened up. Since the streets were literally empty, there was nowhere for the Marines to get down; their best cover was their trigger finger and they all knew it. For about ten seconds I was in hell. I raised my M4 to cover the roofs on the far side of the street. I went to lift my rifle combat optic to my eye and was forced to push up my NVGs, taking away my night vision. A PEQ-2 laser pointer really would have been nice, and I cursed the Marine Corps' pride at doing so much with such a small budget.

"Cease fire!" Holloway shouted to his squad.

He peeked around the crates, as I scanned the far rooftops. "Sir, I thought—it looked like you were hit. Are you sure you're okay?" he said.

"Do you have a cigarette?" I asked.

Holloway laughed, and I felt like shit for being the only guy who actually had somewhere to take cover during the brief exchange of rifle fire. After a minute we were up and moving again. I walked about 5 meters to another T-intersection with almost the exact same setup as the last one. I was a few steps from kneeling down on the corner when I heard what sounded like the angriest group of bees I'd ever heard coming down the alley in front of me.

Thump, thump, thump.

I looked to the left and saw Albin head out into the intersection, seemingly oblivious to the rounds blasting all around him. "Get down!" I shouted, as I moved to the corner and posted down the alley. Whoever had just fired was gone.

"Albin! Get out of the fucking intersection!" I shouted like an upset parent. There was no response, only compliance. I turned around to check Eakin and make sure he hadn't been hit by a ricochet. "Eakin, pass up that we took contact to the east, one street over!" I went to pull out my map to read the street name, and more 7.62mm rounds pierced the air in the alley behind me. The Marines got down but could not identify where the shooter was. One rifleman stated the obvious: "We're taking fire!"

We stayed in the road for what seemed like an eternity. I was getting anxious. There were plenty of homes in the near vicinity where we could go firm and regroup. Instead we were sitting out in the open, waiting for something to happen. I needed a radio in my hands. I got Holloway's attention. "Holloway, how about we get in a house?" I said reluctantly. I was not in Rage 2's chain of command so I tried not to interfere with their tactics, but Lieutenant Thomas was somewhere behind me. As Captain James had said, I was the man on the ground, closest to the point of friction.

"Yes, sir!" Holloway directed his last team to move up and breach into a home on the western side of the street. We cleared the structure and moved onto the roof. Once we got our bearings and Rage 4's situation improved, we got ready to move.

Darting in and out of the streets was stressful after being stationary for fifteen minutes. The enemy was adept at placing surface-laid IEDs not only in the vicinity of dismounted patrols but literally on the doors or the gates to the compound they were clearing. It was an unwelcome surprise when the unit moved to the next building. Numerous 1-37 Armor units had come across this tactic, and, to be honest, I couldn't understand how it was possible until I actually cleared a building in southern Ramadi. Standing inside an Iraqi house with its courtyard walls is like being stuck in an armored vehicle. Who knows what is happening out in the street. We reached Vic Mackey, where Rage 4 had previously been engaged.

We turned east. Roughly 200 meters in front of us was a red chem-light in a small crater in the road. A red chem-light signaled a possible IED that should be avoided. The street was lined with homes on the south (my right), and to the north was some sort of school complex. A six-foot wall ran along the road on the north side. The wall was broken up in many places and was not continuous. Beyond the wall was an open field with larger one- and two-story structures. Although we had only 300 meters to move on the road, there was no easy way around the PIED.

We continued toward the chem-light. I constantly checked the north, ignoring the clutter of the residential area closer to me. I felt that if I was the enemy, I would set up in the larger buildings beyond the wall. They are most likely abandoned and filled with all kinds of potential firing positions. After we moved about 50 meters, I saw a spot where the wall cut north and formed a rectangular-shaped area where we could maintain cover and head into one of the school complexes, thus avoiding the red chem-light and the PIED. The first team saw the same thing and moved up to the wall. My team followed behind them.

"Bahhhhhh . . . bahhhhhhh!" There were goddamn sheep in a pen right next to me! I almost kicked one, thinking it was going to bite me. Sheep in a city; it was another culture gap. I checked out the immediate area and decided that nothing looked threatening. The squad moved up to the break in the wall, and we began to climb over. It was only about four or five feet high in the spot we went over.

"What a mission, sir." Eakin needed someone to talk to.

"How's that radio doing?" I asked.

"Wonderful; things seem to have quieted down for us on the net, but whoever that is still in contact out there, it sucks to be them." Eakin was referring to the distant firefight that continued to rage sporadically. The first team was over the wall.

I kneeled on the ground so that Eakin could step up on my other bent leg. He had a heavier load than I did. "Get over that wall, Eakin," I said.

We moved in complete silence over the wall into the school compound. The school was only one story high and had been built with four exterior structures centered on a courtyard. Dozens of dark windows stared at us as we followed the wall around the northern side. The area where we walked was covered in trash, and there was no avoiding it. I inadvertently crushed numerous cups and various plastic items. We came upon the school's eastern side, where the main gate was located. It was directly opposite the intersection where we wanted to be. We halted to allow the entire platoon to get in position to cross.

We were now looking at the Lima 2 patrol sector. Our lane was another 250 meters down the road. All three of the other platoons were already in the clear portion of the mission, but there was no sign of them. Only the infrared chem-lights that marked certain buildings as cleared had been left behind. The first team moved across the intersection. Albin and I were on the northern side of the street, with Eakin on the south. We had no sooner crossed when the point element halted us. There was another red chem-light. Kneeling on the sidewalk, I looked back at Holloway and saw Albin on the corner. I thought I heard the sound of a classical ring tone.

"Shit! What the—it's a cell phone or something!" A screaming Albin broke noise discipline as he shouted, stood up, and stared into a market stall.

"We need to get out of here!" said Holloway.

I looked at the jamming device on his back. "Holloway, is your Warlock Blue on?" I asked. I got up and ran as fast as I could down the block. I was running straight toward the red chem-light. It was no longer the primary threat.

"Yes, sir!" he answered, then shouted to the point element to move faster.

The area we were operating in had an active remote-control IED element. There was an insurgent team capable of employing IEDs that were detonated from a distance with garage door openers, cell phones, and Seneao base-station phones, to name a few devices. The Warlock Blue was designed to jam the receivers in the immediate area we were in. Although it didn't project a lot of power and only covered certain frequencies, the fact that a cell phone had been set off within a few meters of it disturbed me; I wondered how much the damn thing had cost. We pushed a few teams into a couple of the buildings to try to flush out the possible triggerman as the rest of the platoon moved up. No one suspicious was found.

We finally arrived at our lane.

The first house was occupied by a large family. They were petrified of us. The scene of us bursting into the home was being repeated by eleven other squads executing the same mission. The sounds of that night's previous firefights had changed to the clamoring of Marines ripping down doors. We were no longer concerned with noise discipline; everyone knew where we were. I went straight to the room containing the family. My goal was to question every MAM I came across during the clear phase.

In this particular house, there were two MAMs sleeping under blankets with the other eight members of the family. I pulled the red-and-yellow blanket off the closest MAM's face and told the interpreter to start with that one. The young Iraqi's eyes were the size of watermelons. The interpreter began to question him, but he merely stared into my face with no response. I gave him a mean, quizzical expression. I pulled flexi-cuffs out of my drop pouch and grabbed the young man's right hand. It was a poor attempt to get the kid to say something through fear. Apparently, fear worked only for the insurgents. The young man began to cry. The mother in the room was now shouting at the interpreter. She was obviously pleading with us to leave him alone.

The interpreter began to laugh. "Sir, he is what you call, uh, stupid?" We looked at each other with confused expressions. The interpreter was still searching for the correct English term, and I was still primarily focused on the people in the room.

Corporal Holloway spelled it out for me. "Congratulations, sir, you just tried to detain a mentally challenged Iraqi." The Marines in the room were laughing now, and the story of Lieutenant Daly taking down the retard spread throughout the house as if Britney Spears had been photographed without her underwear again.

I photographed the family, and the squad staged to move to the next house. As I stepped out into the courtyard, the crisp December air cooled my mind. I felt like such an ass, and I wasn't exactly looking forward to the exaggerated story I was going to hear all day at Camp Ramadi tomorrow. I reminded myself that forty minutes earlier, I had narrowly escaped death. I followed behind Albin as he sprinted through the courtyard gate and 10 meters down the street to the next home.

As I moved up the driveway, a Marine was pounding away on a locked shed door in order to search its contents. The sound of metal banging on metal was like fingernails on a chalkboard. On entering the home, I found Holloway separating the men from the women and children. The Marines had found an AK-47 and four loaded magazines in the kitchen. The man of the house was legally allowed to have all of the items, but we decided to test his hands for gunpowder residue anyway. The test came back negative. On the roof the Marines found what appeared to be spider holes and firing positions knocked out of the concrete on the retaining wall. I photographed the potential hasty fighting positions and hurried back downstairs. The other two squads in Rage 2 were moving faster than we were, and we needed to pick up the pace.

To increase our speed, I cut out two of the four questions I had given the interpreter to ask each MAM.

The remaining clear portion of the mission was rather simple. The process of searching homes and questioning residents continued for another hour and a half. It was nearly impossible for me to distinguish insurgent from civilian based on the few questions we asked as we entered each house. Unless the insurgents were keeping IEDs in their bedrooms, searching their homes was pointless. In order for them to maintain the average of five IEDs a day, they had to be keeping them somewhere. We needed to hit the Qatana. Being a mostly abandoned commercial district, it was the only logical place for a large cache of explosives.

When we hit the drop-dead time, we finished the house we were clearing and moved back down to Vic Mackey. As in the insertion, the platoons offset their movements back and we used slightly different routes. Instead of heading back to COP Falcon, every platoon was directed to go to COP Grant in order to make our trip back to Camp Ramadi easier.

As we proceeded south along a side road, I heard what sounded like music. The column of Marines in front of me came to a halt. I took a knee, leaning against a courtyard wall opposite Albin and Eakin. They did the same on the far side of the street. Right after we halted, we began to move again. I got up slowly, trying to be as quiet as possible. I wanted to avoid another incident of being the Marine picked out as the target by a machine gunner. I heard the music again. It was very faint, but I could make out the words "Master! Master!" in English. I was immediately freaked out, and as the sounds got louder there was no mistaking them: it was American rock. Unfortunately, I had never heard the song "Master of Puppets" by Metallica before. I was pretty sure the guy in front of me hadn't either because I could see him visibly shaking. After about a minute of fear, I realized how much of a blessing the blaring music was.

As we got closer, I could have literally shouted across the street, and no one would have heard except the Marines with me. It was like being at a concert, only everybody had rifles. The psychological operations team for 1-37 Armor was masking our movement back to COP Grant. I never felt more like a badass, scanning rooftops and windows as dark turned to light with that song in the background. It was surreal.

Rage Company made it back to COP Grant at 0555 without a shot being fired during the egress. After a brief look at the detainees taken by the other elements, eight in all, I took a quick nap. By 0830, I was on a seven-ton escorting the detainees to Camp Ramadi for processing. My tour as a Bandit was over. Our inability to defeat al Qaeda was apparent.

PART TWO

1st Battalion, 6th Marines

5

ENTERING QATANA

December 16, 2006

The front door was solid wood and heavy. I had a difficult time opening it. While the structure and the architecture itself were uniquely Middle Eastern, the door reminded me of a posh estate in America's Northeast. Lined with concrete barriers and reinforced fighting positions, the exterior of the compound bore a sole reminder of its former affluence: the door I was now opening. Camp Hurricane Point was a Marine base, the headquarters for 1st Battalion, 6th Marines, located where the Saddam Canal and the Euphrates River meet. Situated on the northwest corner of downtown Ramadi, Hurricane Point was a former Ba'ath Party palace and symbol of the Saddam regime. Now it was an American fortress. The company staff had traveled to the camp to receive the order for the next mission: Operation Hue City.

The five senior Marines of Rage Company—Captain John Smith, Lieutenant Craig Trotter, First Sergeant Eric Carlson, Gunnery Sergeant Edward Bishop, and I—sat around a large T-shaped table. Our four platoons remained at Camp Ramadi, anxiously awaiting the details of the second phase of Operation Squeeze Play that would be relayed on our return.

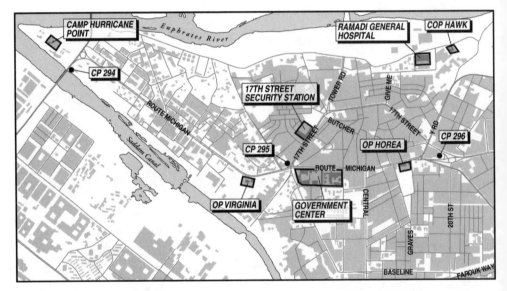

Area of Operations Tarheel: 1/6 Marines area of operations in central Ramadi.

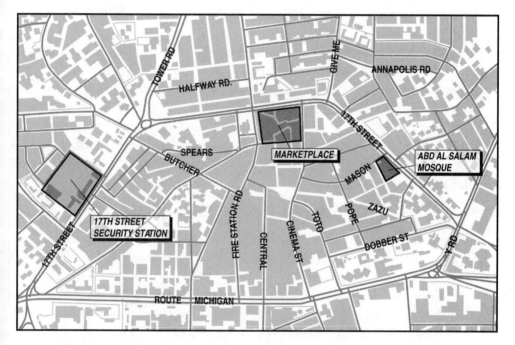

The Qatana: Before the war Qatana was Ramadi's commerical hub. When Rage Company entered, it was the capital of the insurgents' Islamic State of Iraq.

The battalion commander and the operations officer for 1/6 personally briefed us on the first of what would become many incursions into Qatana. The two men were the only other individuals in the room, and I quickly noticed the differences in their personalities. The battalion commander, a lieutenant colonel, was short at five-seven and had graying hair and a stocky frame. He silently sat at the table, his eyes scanning the Rage staff and undoubtedly forming opinions of us in the same manner that I now judged him.

The operations officer was the complete opposite. This youthful major was always talking. His jet-black hair provided a direct contrast to the lieutenant colonel's graying status. It also highlighted the significant difference between the two men: experience.

I sat back and listened to the brief. This first mission, Operation Hue City, was going to be conducted after a daytime movement to Combat Outpost Firecracker. Firecracker was a company-size COP situated on the western fringe of Qatana that would become Rage Company's base of operations. We would spend one night and the next day preparing for the mission and conducting coordination with Alpha (Apache) and Charlie (Comanche) 1/6. Once we arrived at COP Firecracker, Lieutenant Grubb's platoon would attach to Comanche for the duration of the operation.

Beginning on the second night at the COP, we would clear east, directly behind a Pathfinder element on the southern side of Racetrack Street. Charlie would clear the northern side, and Alpha would be on our southern flank. For the mission, Alpha was going to be represented by one platoon of Marines, rather than by the entire company. They would bring less than 20 percent of the manpower in Rage Company into the fight.

The purpose of the mission was to clear about 1.5 kilometers east down Racetrack and secure Charlie Company's new home, Combat Outpost Qatana. It was briefed that the mission would most likely take only one night. If there was a delay, we would execute the remainder of the clear the following night. Somewhere in the brief, the operations officer (OPSO) mentioned that there was an uncorroborated intel report saying that the future COP might be rigged with explosives. To counter this, 1/6 was going to send in a team of bomb-sniffing dogs before they occupied the structure. If it was booby-trapped, then Comanche's secondary and tertiary buildings to use were across the street.

I was relieved when I found out we wouldn't be going into the potentially rigged building.

The entire brief lasted about thirty minutes. The operations officer for 1/6 did not go into detail about what would happen after we seized the COP. He also used key Marine Corps phrases such as, "I don't know how it is in your battalion, but here in 1/6 we . . ." I was immediately unimpressed by his condescending mannerisms. To say the least, it wasn't anywhere close to the good reception we received from 1-37 Armor.

After a round of questions, which weren't thoroughly answered, Captain Smith asked the 1/6 battalion commander why the request made by the Navy SEALs to take part in the operation had been rejected.

While working with 1-37 Armor, the SEALs had been in support of our raids. They mentioned that they were never allowed to operate in 1/6's area of operations. So Captain Smith, who had a background in the force reconnaissance community, decided that he would try to help his fellow operators, telling them to make a formal request to support Operation Hue City. The SEALs followed his advice, and the offer was turned down.

From his facial expressions, I could tell that 1/6's battalion commander was clueless about the request. He had no idea what Captain Smith was talking about. Not until he was asked by the battalion commander did the operations officer take the opportunity to confess that he had been responsible. "Sir, we don't need their assistance. They are honestly more of a hassle to deal with than they are an asset," he said.

That was the first time I had ever heard someone refer to Navy SEALs as a hassle.

Following the brief, I went to visit the battalion intelligence section. I personally knew one of the lieutenants. We had attended Officer Candidate School together in the summer of 2003, and he knew my twin brother from college. A prior Marine sergeant and around six feet tall, Lieutenant Jason Mann was also one of the smartest guys I knew. His strong reputation followed him everywhere he went. As a candidate, he more than earned his place as our company honor graduate. For good reason, I was interested in hearing his valuable opinion about Qatana and the insurgents operating in the area.

I bumped into Jason as I walked past the combat operations center. We exchanged a man-hug, nothing more than a handshake and a back tap. I followed him into the intelligence workspace. For the first time, I was going to view the products of a Marine battalion's intelligence section. I wondered how their methods differed from 1-37 Armor's.

At no time during our predeployment workup did 2/4, Rage's parent battalion, have a fully staffed intelligence section. In training, the products they produced—intelligence summaries, and so on—were nothing of note, not because of a lack of competence but because of a lack of manpower. When I first met Captain James at 1-37, I was blown away by the depth and scope of the intelligence he had access to. It was above and beyond what I had expected.

We walked into a room with a twenty-foot ceiling that contained numerous desks. Maps were strewn about the floor and pinned to the walls. Lieutenant Mann moved to the closest desk on my right. He picked up a stack of small maps, each containing three or four laminated pages bound together by a small D-ring, the contents of which were thorough.

Each page was a map of one objective. Some objectives had multiple target buildings, others only one. On the reverse side of the page were a picture and a description of the high-value individuals who might be located at the target. There was also a three-dimensional image of the target building, with entrances and exits highlighted, as well as details about what the location was used for. I opened my assault pack and started to drop the laminated pages in, counting them as I went.

Jason Mann had essentially done my work for me. Unlike the stack of intel reports that 1-37 Armor gave us to sift through, Jason was giving me the information that mattered to the Marines on the ground. Instead of spending hours scanning through piles of information, Albin, Eakin, and I would do nothing more than hand out the packages. After that, we would have a free night aboard Camp Ramadi.

"So, what did you think of the brief?" Jason asked me.

"It was ambitious. That was a lot of territory to cover in one night," I casually replied. I thought about mentioning the SEAL conversation but held back, not knowing the rest of the audience.

The other person in the room, a captain sitting at his desk, joined the conversation. "We have been trying to get the battalion to action some of these targets for over a month," he said. "Others like the amusement park, VBIED [vehicle-borne IED] factory, sniper alley: they have been targets since the battalion got in country. We just can't convince the operations officer to hit the damn places." The captain was pointing to a map on the wall of roughly fifty targets within Qatana. He gestured toward some of the places as he spoke. I was struck by the fact that he said "convince the operations officer" and not the battalion commander.

"I guess we will hit them for you." I felt awkward as soon as I had finished the sentence. It came across as an insinuation that 1/6 wasn't doing their job. The last thing I wanted to do was burn bridges with the intel section. I changed the subject. "Jason, what is the deal with these buildings they are going to use as the new COP?" I asked, breaking the uncomfortable pause in the conversation. The issue of the booby-trapped buildings was still very real in my mind.

"You don't want to know," Jason replied. "Let's just say that some of our local sources are speculating that the primary, secondary, and tertiary build sites for COP Qatana are now giant mines awaiting our arrival."

I was in disbelief. The OPSO had failed to mention that the secondary and tertiary buildings were potentially bombs. I didn't mention this to Jason, not wanting to fan the preexisting distrust among the various battalion sections.

The XO, Lieutenant Trotter, poked his head through the door and looked around the room. His eyes stopped searching when he found me, and I wondered whether I had done something wrong.

"Daly, hurry up!" he barked. "You won't believe who is here."

The XO was gone before I could ask him what he was talking about. I stuffed the last of the intel packages into my pack and followed him out, telling Jason I would see him around.

Catching up to the XO in the hallway, I pondered who could generate such interest. "Who is it?" I finally asked, matching him stride for stride.

A smile spread over Trotter's face. "Oliver North. Captain Smith is going to give him shit for announcing our deployment in country while we were still on the information blackout."

Back in mid-November, Mr. North had announced the deployment of the 15th Marine Expeditionary Unit (MEU) into Al Anbar Province. He had also detailed the assets and the troop strength of the MEU. Then he listed potential cities we would be deployed to. Captain Smith and I watched his announcement on Fox News from the brigade headquarters. The MEU was still cut off from contact with the outside world, and our families thought we were in Kuwait. My family found out I was going into Iraq not from me but from Oliver North. I'm sure al Qaeda's leadership learned of our presence the same way.

The entire company staff was on the move to the colonel-turned-journalist's room. We got to the space, which was so small it had likely been used as a closet in the Saddam era. Ollie was sitting at a desk, probably filing a story, while his two cameramen relaxed on their bunk beds. The civilians looked exhausted. Captain Smith introduced himself as a company commander with the 15th MEU. He wasted no time in getting to the point.

"Sir, why did you tell the insurgents we were coming?" he asked.

"What do you mean?" Mr. North said.

Captain Smith explained how we were on an information blackout when North had made his announcement on Fox News. I got the feeling from the colonel's mannerisms that someone had mentioned this to him before.

"The pentagon released it," North said. "I wouldn't have said anything unless they had released it to the press."

First Sergeant Carlson, who was the tallest man in the confined space, shook his bald head over and over in disgust. "Bullshit." It was all the large man uttered. The rest of us just stared at the colonel.

Not in a friendly way.

Oliver North was visibly taken aback. Captain Smith tried to calm the group. "Well, sir, you know what this means," he said.

There was a pause while questioning eyes glared at one another.

"You have to take pictures and sign autographs with each one of us," Captain Smith said with a slight smile. Gunnery Sergeant Bishop, our logistics chief, had come up with the plan to make North as uncomfortable as possible before we walked in. It worked.

"I would be delighted," replied a relieved Oliver North.

The next thirty minutes were spent posing for photos as if we were standing with a celebrity. The entire time, I waited for Oliver North to hurry us along so he could get some sleep. He never did.

Back at Camp Ramadi, Captain Smith briefed the highlights of Operation Hue City to the platoon commanders. The intent of the mission was to open a secure route to COP Qatana, seize the building to be used as the COP, and then clear the surrounding areas beyond the structure. Racetrack Street was the most direct route to the new COP and was the focus of the operation. The mission would use Pathfinder and dismounted Marines as mutually supporting elements.

As Pathfinder cleared down Racetrack, they would be providing the dismounted units with a safe casualty evacuation route and quick access to armored vehicles or tanks. By clearing the structures directly behind Pathfinder, the dismounted Marines would force any IED triggermen or RPG teams, who usually harassed Pathfinder, to rethink sticking around. With such a large force of Marines moving through the night, the insurgents would likely rely on their defensive IEDs and withdraw from the objective area.

Captain Smith outlined the lane that was assigned to the company to clear. He instructed the group that all unit leaders, squad leader and above, must label every PIED on their maps. Rage 6 was ordering us to do this because he knew we didn't take most of the reporting seriously. Almost every intersection had a PIED. Annotating each one resulted in your map's being covered in an excessive amount of ink—not to mention that we were going through the intersections regardless.

What I did not realize at the time was that the issue of so many PIEDs was the first hint of the truth in the 1/6 intel officer's statement regarding the battalion's inability to act on its intelligence. Many of the PIEDs had been reported more than six months earlier. The majority were between three and six months old. Only a handful had less than a month since their initial reporting. Looking at the map led to one thought: there were not enough Marines in Ramadi. The battalion was therefore not able to vet its local sources of information because its combat power was stretched to the limit. Such a lack of intelligence would have a serious effect on Operation Hue City.

After reviewing the mission with the company staff, I headed to Camp Ramadi's gym to relieve some stress. Many of the Marines said good things about the quality of the equipment, and I figured my body could use the exercise. After all, I hadn't worked out in a month. When I got there, I found out that the warehouse-style building, a ten-minute walk from my tent, was more than a gym. It was a movie theater, an arcade, and an indoor basketball court. Chess sets and board games lined the shelves. Soldiers and Marines were slaughtering one another playing Halo 2 and Gears of War for the Xbox 360, as if their everyday lives weren't exciting enough.

I skipped the modern entertainment and opted for a treadmill. A few miles later, I found myself playing basketball with some Marines from the company against a group of National Guardsmen. Even with the not-so-agile Joash Albin, we made short work of the larger and quickly winded soldiers. Over the course of the game, I came to pity the armed citizens. Their entire existence was spent driving convoys to the vast reaches of Al Anbar's desert. Since IEDs were the number one threat everywhere, the Marines of our company swore their lives to one truth: better to walk than drive. Unfortunately for the guardsmen, they did not have the choice to walk.

I played three consecutive games on the court and headed back to my tent. I ran the half mile in near pitch-black conditions. A bitter cold attacked my sweat. Two distant explosions and machine gun fire echoed over the city. I jogged past the Ar Ramadi Regional Detention Facility, the barbed wire atop its sand-filled HESCO barriers barely illuminated by the moon. I turned into our parking lot after passing the ARDF. Rage Company's dozen M1114 humvees and three seven-ton trucks were neatly aligned, awaiting the next morning's convoy that would take us to Qatana. The sentry watching over them greeted me as I went past.

After entering the large white headquarters tent, I grabbed a pair of sandals, toilet paper, a towel, and some clean clothes. I headed straight for the shower trailer. Unfortunately, I forgot my shampoo. I had no idea it was the last time I would shower and use an actual toilet for twenty-five days.

The column of seven-ton trucks and uparmored humvees followed the same route along Michigan through Ramadi's war-torn streets that we had taken to COP Falcon for Harrison Creek II. The only difference was our heading north at checkpoint 295 onto Racetrack, rather than turning south along Sunset.

The sight of Qatana from checkpoint 295 highlighted the intensity of modern urban combat. At the checkpoint's northeast corner lay a pile of rubble that stretched for at least a quarter mile east along Michigan. Weeks earlier, coalition forces had leveled the structures because they were repeatedly being used by insurgents to engage Ramadi's government center, which was on the south side of the street.

The mayor of the city had drawn up plans to one day turn the area into a park and a monument. At the moment it sounded like a fool's dream.

It was only a few hundred meters up Racetrack to our new home. After several moments of staring into destroyed buildings, the convoy made a left and pulled into COP Firecracker, slowly inching its way through the narrow gate. The COP itself had been built in a massive school compound. The large structure that was the main barracks and the living space for the COP, as well as five of the barren surrounding buildings, had been a school before the war. Combat had transformed these places of academia and development into symbols of conflict.

A wide, open courtyard was centrally located among the structures. It was lined with towering concrete barriers, isolating it from the rest of the city and allowing us to use it as a parking lot. A recent downpour had turned this secure area into a giant pit of mud, chunks of which sprayed up around the vehicles as they pulled into a dispersed formation and occupied the vast space.

We spread the vehicles out as much as possible. Only a few days earlier, a Marine had been killed from an incoming mortar round in this parking lot. The platoons quickly dismounted their trucks and hurried through the mud into COP Firecracker. I jumped down off the back of a seven-ton and followed suit.

The mud clung to my feet. I saw a Marine carrying a boot in his hand while he hopped toward the building. After a few jumps, he gave up and ran, exposing his naked toes to the muck. The empty boot was so filled with mud that he probably had made the right choice. I continued to slosh through the mess, without losing my boots, and eventually made it to the small doorway into the COP.

A group of Marines congregated around the entrance, stomping and kicking their boots against a litany of objects. It was a vain attempt to remove the mud that had caked onto their feet. I thought about skipping the pointless endeavor, but a staff noncommissioned officer (SNCO) from 1/6 was inside checking the cleanliness of the Marines' boots. Men with too much mud were being sent back out to stomp some more.

I didn't see the point. With our nearly four hundred feet, we were kicking against the same sandbags, wall, and wooden planks to remove the persistent dirt. The end result, regardless of how long we stomped, was a trail of muck up the COP's wide staircase to the third floor. Nobody had to ask where to go; mud pointed the way.

The interior of the COP itself was empty, except that every window and thin exterior wall was lined with sandbags. Not a single item hung on the walls. There was no furniture. The floor plan on every level was exactly the same. The centrally placed front and back doors opened into the staircase, which spiraled all the way to the roof. A central hallway, stretching about 250 meters, split the four-story building along its length. There were opposing rooms on either side. At the end of these hallways were larger open rooms that served special functions. The second floor, north end, was the chow hall. The third floor, south end, was the bathroom.

There was no plumbing.

In the bathroom, a single urinal stood in the center of the room, elevated on what I considered a stage. With a line of squirming onlookers behind you, you could watch your urine as it traveled through plastic tubing that ran at a downward angle to a hole in the wall. The tube continued out of the structure and over the exterior wall of the small, unoccupied building next door. The owner of which had probably fled to Syria and was in for an unpleasant smell when the war was over.

The toilets were even better. Nothing more than five plastic chairs, each lined with a small green garbage bag in the center, would contain the bowel movements of two hundred Marines. You did your business in the bag, wrapped it up, and stuffed it into a separate green ziplock bag. On the way out of the bathroom, you tossed this semi-sealed container, known as a Wag-Bag, into a garbage can. Every few days a group of unfortunate Marines would burn the COP's trash, Wag-Bags included.

For living arrangements, Captain Smith had chosen a small hundred-square-foot room. From the top of the stairs on the third floor, it was the first door on your left.

It wasn't much of a door. There were no hinges. You literally slid the plywood out of your way to go in and out. It was considered a luxury, though. No other room on the third floor had an actual door. Inside the room's sea-green walls, laced with Arabic graffiti, the same five men who were at the photo op with Oliver North had placed their military-issued cots. The two enlisted men took the left side of the room, while the three officers went to the right. Somebody had set up a Christmas tree in the middle.

Once all of the platoons had arrived and were settled, the staff and the officers of Rage and Apache 1/6 gathered to discuss Operation Hue City.

We met in the COP's chow hall. A layer of sandbags lined a few former windows. Only one or two small rays of light breached the green bags and shone into the room. A large flat-screen TV adorned the wall on the left. Next to it was a white microwave. On the right side of the room, a lone table was set up to serve food. Hastily built wooden shelves were stocked with a few loafs of bread and the inseparable duo of peanut butter and jelly. The rest of the room was filled with picnic tables and a standard cafeteria-style table with built-in chairs. Fifty men could sit comfortably.

Seats quickly disappeared as Marines from the two infantry units showed up for the brief. Some of the squad leaders ended up standing as the brief began. Alpha's commander, Apache 6, started first. The Marine outlined his platoon's lane, which would be on our southern flank. After going over their route, he highlighted each of the targets his men would action. When he was done, he took questions from the group, most of which came from his Marines.

Next, it was Captain Smith's turn. He got up and followed in the exact same format that Apache 6 had. Before I knew it, the mission was briefed and everyone turned to chow. I instantly regretted not asking more pointed questions at Hurricane Point days earlier. Tactically, our two units had done minimal coordination. We had simply told each other what we were going to do. There was no discussion of standard operating procedures or any warnings for insurgent trends. The basis of a working relationship was never established. Introductions between members of our two staffs never occurred.

I sat at a picnic table wondering whether anyone in the room knew what would happen once Comanche seized their COP. Were we going back to Camp Ramadi? Clearing the rest of Qatana? The realization that the gaps in the plan rested at the battalion level dawned on me. The battalion staff had whisked us out of Hurricane Point for good reason.

The intent of the mission was for Comanche to seize the new COP that would become their home; however, Rage and Alpha were tasked with clearing south of Racetrack. These tactical tasks were slightly contradictory: one was to control a specific building, while the other entailed the searching of five hundred. Unlike the previous missions with 1-37, there was no specific objective area. Instead, there were targets to search along the route that we would clear. I was concerned with the lack of specificity in our task.

For a moment, I almost realized what Operation Hue City would become. Tactically, the infantry units would execute the mission as ordered, but at the operational level the battalion was going to find itself reactionary. There was no plan for what would happen after the seizing of COP Qatana. Hindsight is, of course, 20/20, and at that moment I dismissed my own concerns, thinking I wasn't seeing the bigger picture. Time would prove otherwise.

I leaned in close to the small flame emitted by the silver Zippo that Lieutenant Thomas held. Corporal Holloway did the same next to me. Simultaneously, our cigarettes caught. The flame went out and the enclosed room turned pitch-black, except for the dozen burning shredded rolls of tobacco already hanging from our lips.

The three of us sat down. "I'm glad you could join us, Tom," said James Thomas. I didn't respond. Instead, I awaited Holloway's voice.

"Twenty minutes from staging, and Lieutenant Daly is purposely smoking with Lieutenant Thomas. Only good can come of this, gentlemen," said the corporal, satisfied that I had given in to his demands of smoking before the mission for luck. After nearly being shot in the Lima 2, I welcomed his idea of a pre-mission ritual. The three of us finished smoking and went to get our gear.

Forty minutes later bodies shivered, awaiting the word to step off. Lieutenant Richard Jahelka and the Marines of Rage 3 congregated at the front door to COP Firecracker. Rage 2 and Rage 1 had already stepped off to clear the company's assigned lane. Now we were waiting for them to establish themselves on the eastern side of the Racetrack, inside Qatana. The company was going to move with two platoons forward, clearing the lane. Rage 3 and the headquarters element would fall in trace, acting as a reserve.

The lobby for COP Firecracker was packed with anxious warriors. Most of the Marines conversed in hushed voices. The only ones who shouted were the squad leaders, double-checking that their men had brought extra C4, linked 5.56mm ammo for the SAW, or an incendiary grenade.

"Tarheel, this is Rage 6, my last platoon is departing COP Firecracker time now, over," said Captain Smith on the battalion net.

The first few Marines moved out of the building. I waited impatiently for my turn to follow them. Once I was outside, the frigid air amplified the effect of my fear for what awaited. Even though I had urinated moments earlier, my bladder seemed full. I repeatedly fidgeted, not just to keep my near-stationary body warm but also as an outlet for my anxiety.

Immediately after leaving the building, we went condition one: round in the chamber. The single column of Marines snaked its way through a maze of concrete barriers and sandbagged positions that made up COP Firecracker's perimeter. I passed a guard tower manned by Apache Marines. One of the sentries wished us luck.

"Death to the hajji," he said.

A Marine in front of me pumped his fist in acknowledgment. Just before we made it to the end of the perimeter, we stopped. The column got backed up as Marines waited at the gate for the men in front of them to get proper dispersion. My bladder was about to explode. I gave in to its urges, still unsure whether it was a mental fixation or if I really did have to go again. I was surprised when, after I moved toward a concrete barrier, the urine flowed freely. I wasn't the only one who required such relief. Three other Marines joined me in marking the concrete barrier at the COP's northeast corner.

Eventually, Albin walked out into the street and began to scan his right flank. I paused and waited for him to get about 3 meters in front of me. On my left, a small strand of barbed wire, which served as the door for the five-foot-wide gate, ran at a forty-five-degree angle away from me. Three waist-high concrete barriers served as the entrance's serpentine, spread out over roughly 50 meters to my direct front.

I started to walk.

The formation was crossing Racetrack immediately after exiting the serpentine. As I crossed the street, I scanned north. An Abrams tank was 200 meters away on the far side of a five-way intersection. A destroyed five-floor apartment building towered over it on the southeast corner. Dozens of dark windows in the war-torn structure faced outward in every direction, a perfect vantage point for the enemy and a dangerous trap for us. With the building's one-level height advantage over COP Firecracker, insurgents had used it to stage dozens of attacks against the COP's Apache defenders during the previous three weeks. A handful of Marines had been wounded or killed by insurgent snipers operating out of the windows I now stared into.

An explosion shook the ground. Startled, I realized that the flash of light in my NVGs had originated beyond the apartment building and slightly to the right. Pathfinder had either hit or found an IED. I crossed Racetrack, following the two dozen Marines ahead of me onto Finney Street. The neighborhood opposite COP Firecracker was exclusively residential. The small one- and two-story homes were similar in appearance to those that surrounded COP Grant.

The column of Marines turned north onto an unnamed side street. Breaking from the plan, individual squads began to enter and clear homes. Instead of moving all the way to our first phase line, Fire Station Road, we were halting our advance, probably to wait for Pathfinder to collect itself from the earlier blast.

I randomly entered a house in downtown Ramadi. It was the usual layout. The owner, who was about fifty years old, was speaking with

Captain Smith in the foyer. I headed back to the room where the rest of the family had stayed. Mud covered the carpets, tracked inside by the twenty Marines who had just barged through the front door. A strong scent of kerosene wafted through the hallway. At the door to the family room, the company's one interpreter, Marlo, was chatting with some of the home's occupants. A Marine stood guard next to him.

I asked Marlo to apologize to the owner, who still stood in the foyer, for the mud caked on his carpets. When he walked away, I looked into the room. A dozen frightened sets of eyes stared back at me. Most of them belonged to young children.

I took off my helmet, revealing my human face, which had been masked by NVGs and a radio handset. Two elementary school–age girls exchanged smiles with me. They were every bit as cute and expressive as American children. The only difference was that these girls lived in one of the most dangerous places on earth. For three years, machine gun fire, IEDs, ambushes, air strikes, and constant scenes of death had surrounded their home. At the age of eight or nine, they had witnessed more of life's horrors than Stephen King could fit into some pointless book. Yet they were still here, living in Qatana.

I removed my camera from a drop pouch and waved at the group, telling them to "say cheese." The girls waved back in glee. The teenage boys waved at me to go away. I took the picture and moved out of the doorway. I was quickly replaced by a few Marines, who offered candy to the children in the crowded room.

As I moved from room to room, my mind was full of thoughts. I also took note of everything we had disrupted. Furniture was randomly rearranged. Mud seemed to find its way onto everything. The observations led to a broader perspective. Young, aggressive Marines had come into this house, shouting, with weapons at the ready. They had systematically cleared each room and secured all of the entrances and the exits. In the darkness of the night and blinded by the high-powered Surefire incandescent lamps of the Marines, the Iraqis had been forced into a single room, barely lit by a kerosene space heater. Laden with body armor, NVGs, shoulder-fired rockets, and a litany of miscellaneous gear, the Marines resembled something from outer space more than human beings. The family had good reason to be frightened.

I took a seat on a plush green couch and looked at the floor. We, the alien invaders, were going to provide this family with nothing more than the dirt caked on their carpets. Not security or hope; just fear and mud.

I found the headquarters element in a living room off the foyer. Some of the guys were asleep on a couch, huddled together for warmth. I took a seat next to Eakin, who was acting as the battalion radio operator for the mission, instead of fulfilling his usual position as my personal radioman. Even my purpose had changed. Instead of focusing solely on detainees, I was also the nominal leader of the headquarters element. The concept was intended to allow Captain Smith to focus on directing the company, rather than on the ten Marines who accompanied him on every mission. Looking at the group, I understood why he had asked me to perform the task. Half of the Marines were asleep.

Their slumber was interrupted by a shouting Eakin. He had just received a transmission from Tarheel that cleared us to resume our advance, and he was now notifying Rage 6. I staged the headquarters element and followed a squad from Rage 3 out into the street. The formation carried onward into the Qatana darkness, heading toward Fire Station Road. Rage 1 and Rage 2 would be waiting for us there. Once we established an over-watch position of the sniper alley and the marketplace, the two platoons would begin a detailed search.

To avoid a prominent intersection, the formation turned into the backyard of what had once been a large family compound. The expanse stretched for about six city lots. I climbed over knee-high rubble that had once been the exterior wall and stared into the back of a large home. Initially, I was impressed with its grandeur. Then I scanned its many windows, anticipating a hidden enemy. The Marines ahead of me snaked in a single file line through the yard. Trash was everywhere. I assumed that the family had fled during the war, and their former neighbors now used the empty space as a garbage dump. We maneuvered through the debris and came out on the far side.

Standing in the dark street, Eakin received new orders from Tarheel on the battalion net. We were being directed to halt. Pathfinder had found a larger IED and was attempting to disarm it. The battalion had decided to exercise caution and was telling us to get inside a structure.

The two lead platoons took up positions on Fire Station Road. They were now waiting for us to establish the over-watch in order to continue the advance. It became a small point of friction. With the order to halt, even though there were a hundred buildings between the IED and us, Rage 3 and the headquarters element were falling behind in the mission. Once we were given the green light to continue movement, Rage 1 and Rage 2 would be stuck waiting for our arrival. In the first three hours of the mission, our lead units had moved less than 500 meters. There was no way we would have enough darkness to clear the full 1.5 kilometers.

Relaxing in another Iraqi's living room with a dozen Marines, I interrupted the usual jokes and banter of bored men. "Eakin, relay to battalion: Rage 1 and Rage 2 have reached Fire Station Road," I said.

He looked at me quizzically. "I already told them that, sir," replied the sleepy lance corporal.

"Just do it," I said. I hoped that by our reminding battalion of our forward units, they would realize that we should be allowed to move.

Eakin keyed the handset and slaughtered what I had told him to say. "Tarheel COC, this is Rage, Rage lead trace Seventeen Old Railroad Station Road, over," he said.

The young Marine was clearly bored and tired. The other Marines in the room laughed hysterically. One inadvertently burned himself with his cigarette. I snatched the handset and sent the transmission myself. The entire room was now chiding Eakin, so I brought him outside, where it was cold. "Wake up and get focused," I told him.

I turned around and walked back into the house. I bumped into Captain Smith on the way in. As we came face-to-face, an F/A-18 screeched low across the Qatana skyline. His radio operator dove to the ground next to us, expecting some sort of incoming mortar fire.

"I think the communications guys are scared tonight," I said to Captain Smith.

An hour later, Pathfinder had disarmed the IED and was ready to continue moving. It was more than enough time for insurgents to hastily emplace surface-laid IEDs. Instead of continuing through the urban terrain, Captain Smith directed the platoon to move north to Racetrack. Pathfinder was now clearing the Give Me–Racetrack intersection and was a few hundred meters ahead of us. To make up lost ground, the formation got on the now cleared portion of Racetrack and headed to the intersection with Fire Station Road.

I was walking down the same road that hundreds of insurgents had held a parade on two months earlier. I recognized each of the buildings from the video that 1-37 had given me of the event. They had pulled it off a jihadist Web site.

After turning onto Fire Station, we went firm in the large school complex. The massive two-story structure was empty. The walls of every cinder-block room were barren. Two basketball courts were in the central courtyard. A squad from Rage 3 cleared the second floor and positioned itself on the roof. Rage 1 and Rage 2 both began the clear of the Islamic State of Iraq (ISI) compound opposite Fire Station Road. Rage 1 was prosecuting the old marketplace, while Rage 2 hit the insurgent sniper range.

Minutes later, the Marines' search bore fruit. The radio crackled, "Rage 6, this is Rage 2 Actual, we have discovered a small cache of rifles and grenades. How copy, over?" said Lieutenant Thomas.

The response was short: "Solid copy."

The intel on the insurgent sniper range in the marketplace's alleyways was confirmed by the contents of Rage 2's cache. Unlike most insurgent AK variant weapons, the rifles in the cache were all scoped. The insurgents were perfecting their marksmanship skills less than 500 meters from COP Firecracker. Leaving weapons in the street was also evidence of the truth behind Lieutenant Mann's concerns. The insurgents had not been expecting us to prosecute targets within Qatana. They were accustomed to the less direct approach from 1/6.

I moved up to the roof to get a better view of the objective area. I found four Marines scanning the skyline, waiting for an insurgent to show himself. I leaned against the cold wall with the fire team leader. Unexpectedly, a string of five successive blasts ripped into the street below. Each one was small, nothing more than a breaching charge of C4. The few glass windows that were still intact shattered downstairs. Profanity-laced tirades were audible from the roof—like those of us perched above, the Marines occupying the rooms below hadn't known the blast was coming. Rage 6 was the most upset. I could hear him yelling at Rage 1, who was across the street. He berated his platoon commander to such an extent that his voice was noticeably strained afterward.

I headed down from the roof and back to the first floor. Apache 6 came on the company net, requesting the nature of the explosions. They didn't like the answer. "Controlled detonations by Rage 1, over," said Captain Smith. Rage 6 asked for Rage 1 Actual, Lieutenant Shearburn, to come to his position. The two men argued over whether Rage 1 had given advance warning before the blasts, intended to gain entry to the locked portions of the marketplace. The conversation ended awkwardly.

Rage 1 Actual looked at Rage 6; something was coming over the PRR in his ear. "Sir, we got something," said Lieutenant Shearburn.

The two men left to link up with the squad that found what could only be described as an insurgent armory. After blowing down a locked market stall door, the Marines of Rage 1 had found every tool known to be used by Iraqi insurgents. The cache contained all the things you would expect an insurgent to have. It was huge.

Moments later, Rage 2 found another cache in the alleyway. The hide site contained a grenade and a sniper rifle. We spent the next two hours consolidating all of the items in one place. It would make the destruction of the assorted insurgent materials much easier for EOD. I watched Lieutenant Thomas and a few of his Marines, who were carrying the weapons they had found, walk down Fire Station toward Rage 1. They turned down an alley and disappeared into the shadows.

Five minutes later, a solitary figure emerged from the alley. The Marine recognized me standing in the school's double-door entrance.

"Daly, you need to see this. Come on," said James Thomas. I followed him south down Fire Station to the same point his shadow had originated from. The massive dome of Qatana's central mosque dominated the horizon about 200 meters away. An ornate minaret stood behind it. I thought about the fact that I was walking the streets of Ramadi with only one other American. It happened to be my college roommate.

We approached two Marines standing outside a market stall door. Farther down the street, a squad was searching and clearing more of the marketplace. All of the structures were a single story.

I ducked my head as I went through the small door. I was immediately standing among two dozen Marines who were sifting through every type of Soviet-style weapon I could think of. The tools of war were being stockpiled by category. Assault rifles, sniper rifles, machine guns, rocket launchers, and matching ammunition were spread about the room.

In the far corner, our public affairs Marine was videotaping the find. He stood over garbage bags full of plastic explosives. Next to him, one of the Marines shined his flashlight against the wall. The light revealed a half-dozen bloodstains below a row of grotesque hooks. This was how al Qaeda controlled the population.

Farther down the wall, a few shelves held cases of small-arms ammunition. I moved about the room, stepping on several garbage bags that overflowed with copper wire. Next to them lay four blue Iraqi police vests with their corresponding ballistic plates placed on top of them. In the center, next to the growing pile of weapons, were multiple metal stands that served as stabilizing rifle platforms or support for homemade rocket launchers.

I looked back toward the entrance. Two Marines, each carrying 122mm artillery rounds, were straining to put the shells on the floor. When one of the Marines almost dropped a round, I took note of all of the explosives in the room. Our company commander, four of his lieutenants, and three SNCOs were in the same place. If something exploded, the company would have been almost leaderless. I ignored the thought.

Standing among the piles of insurgent materials, Lieutenant Shearburn and Captain Smith began to discuss how to continue the advance. Shearburn's squads were supposed to be progressing on the clear. With such a large find, however, the Marines were busy consolidating and compiling a list of the cache contents. Captain Smith decided to send two of Rage 3's squads past Rage 1 and have them search the area around the ISI's executive compound.

I decided to head back to Rage 3's over-watch position. I shared the 100-meter walk with Sergeant Martin Bustamante, the public affairs Marine who had videotaped the cache. On our way, we passed a group of EOD engineers looking for the cache site. I left Bustamante at the school and led the lost EOD team to Rage 1. When we entered the market stall, the EOD engineers were horrified. They immediately told Captain Smith that we, as in anyone other than EOD, were not allowed to move any explosive material from its original position.

Captain Smith responded by noting that we had our own combat engineers who were supervising the effort. His reply led to a bitter exchange. EOD did not consider our engineers to be versed enough to spot insurgent trickery; for example, IEDs could be left in the open for us to find, but as we remove them the real IED will be set off. They also quoted the ROE as stating that only EOD could touch any sort of cache, regardless of its size. If we found a solitary weapon, they expected us to secure the site, radio for EOD, and then wait while they removed it. With such an approach, the city of Ramadi would never be cleared.

Captain Smith gave up on the conversation. He left Staff Sergeant Jerry Eagle, our senior combat engineer, to handle the issue. Rage 6 and the rest of the headquarters Marines at the cache site went back to the school. I went with them. As we walked through the door, Rage 3 said on the radio that they had found a new cache. Lieutenant Jahelka described a room with ten barrels of Iraqi currency, artillery rounds, and miscellaneous IED-making materials.

I took a seat on the school's concrete hallway floor. Outside, Marines were ferrying weapons and ammunition to EOD's vehicles. The items that were in good-enough condition would be given to the Iraqi army for use. The rest were going to be detonated in place by EOD. There would be two explosions: one for Rage 1 and 2's caches and another for Rage 3's. They were going to be large blasts. The combined weight of both caches was a few thousand pounds of explosives.

Captain Smith began to pull each of his platoons back to the school we were in. The complex was a solid structure, and, unlike many of the surrounding buildings, its foundation had not been significantly damaged by the war. Plus, Shearburn had already blown out all of the remaining glass windows. It was the best position to seek shelter in for the coming explosions.

Hours passed before EOD was ready to detonate the charges. Eakin notified battalion, which subsequently ordered all units to acknowledge that they were under the protection of cover. Once given the green light, the EOD technician gave a five-minute warning to the first and larger blast. The grotesque hooks and bloodstained walls I had seen were about to be blown hundreds of feet into the Qatana sky.

Two minutes . . .

One minute . . .

At forty-five seconds, the Marine at the door freaked out. "Who is that?!" he shouted over and over. Captain Smith ran to his side. I moved to a window in an adjoining room.

It was the worst possible sight. A squad of our Marines was walking down the alley where the cache was located. Only a few hundred feet separated them and the impending explosion.

"Run, damn it! Run!" screamed Captain Smith, who was now outside the school, waving at his men. His strained voice cracked with each shout, giving in to its overuse that evening.

Every member of the exposed squad began to sprint as he realized what was about to happen.

Eakin's lone voice cried out, "Thirty seconds!"

It was repeated by a hundred men, urging their comrades to move faster.

At fifteen, the first fire team had almost reached the school. The last had just turned onto Fire Station Road, nearly a hundred meters away.

They were each carrying a full combat load, and I didn't think they were going to make it. At ten seconds, I moved back out into the hallway.

The entire company was now echoing the EOD technician's countdown, second by second. Some of the stationary Marines were already scolding the members of the squad who were now under cover.

I stared at the door. As we said, "One!" the delay in the radio transmission caught up to us. Between the flash of light and the audible sound of the explosion, the last man from the squad and Captain Smith ran through the door. Their heads hung waist level as they slid behind the wall next to the entrance.

The concussion of the blast shook my inner being. Looking out the window, I watched the fireball and the subsequent mushroom cloud from a detonation that had just shaken the whole of Ramadi. I thought about the young children I had met earlier that night. I wondered whether this was the largest blast they had ever heard.

After confirming that everyone was, in fact, under cover, the EOD technician set another, less eventful, ten-minute countdown. Once the explosion had come and gone, we began to prepare for our movement back to COP Firecracker. Only three hours of darkness remained, not enough to restart the clear.

One at a time, the platoons left the school. Rage 1 went first, moving the 100 meters north to Racetrack, which they would follow back to the COP. After Lieutenant Thomas and Rage 2, I left with the headquarters element. As I exited the school and walked onto Fire Station, the city's minarets began to announce the morning's call to prayer. The devout prayers, which I did not understand, made for a highly emotive experience.

Turning onto Racetrack, I looked east. Six or seven vehicles were outside the future COP Qatana, with countless Marines moving in and out of the structure. Comanche was fortifying their new home. The double-column formation slowly moved down the road, each man listening to the singing of a dozen Muslim clerics.

With two large blasts, the seizing of what could only be described as an insurgent armory and bank, Rage Company had just destroyed the capital of al Qaeda's Islamic caliphate. Reassured by our success, I entered the confines of COP Firecracker. Twenty minutes later, asleep on my cot, I was unaware that Lieutenant Grubb, Rage 4 Actual, was about to endure the insurgents' response.

6

Demons of Hurricane Point

December 19, 2006

Lieutenant Andrew Grubb was looking at Racetrack from a south-facing window in the second floor of Ramadi's former Ministry of Oil building. The three-story structure was a perfect vantage point for Rage 4's platoon commander to observe the construction of COP Qatana through his NVGs. The dark street below contained a dozen small puddles from a light rain that ended the day. A tank and two seven-ton trucks full of sandbags stood over the reflective water. Grubb nervously watched the Marines of Comanche Company move in and out of the building that 1/6's intelligence section had warned was rigged to explode. The fact that combat engineers had swept the building with bomb-sniffing dogs was of no comfort.

A group of four Marines carrying sandbags struggled past an Iraqi policeman smoking at the structure's exterior gate. The policeman was a product of America's attempt to put an Iraqi face on the war. At the time, it wasn't a successful enterprise; there were fewer than twenty Iraqi police officers in the heart of the city.

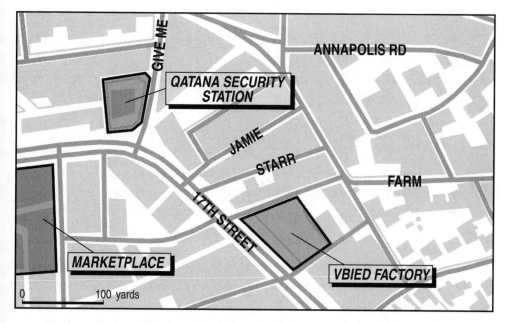

Northeast Qatana: The planned location of Commanche's Qatana Security Station.

The noise of dozens of Marines working to fortify the structure, seized earlier that night, punctuated the darkness. The Marines were racing to build sandbagged fighting positions that would protect them during the next day. Each man knew the enemy would focus their efforts against the most vulnerable target in the area. At that particular moment, they were the most vulnerable.

An explosion ripped through the exterior wall a few meters from the gate. A bomb hidden in the wall had been detonated by an unseen observer. Shouts and screams of pain replaced the earlier sounds of productive manual labor. Marines ran out of the structure to assist their wounded comrades. Lieutenant Grubb hastily scanned the windows and the doorways of the intersection's surrounding buildings. The enemy had to be close. If the insurgents had detonated the device with command wire, they were probably across the street, limited by the small amount of copper wire available. The same was true for a remote-controlled initiation device. The insurgents would have had to overpower the electronic countermeasures on each of the vehicles in the intersection. Either way, the triggerman was still within range of a well-aimed shot from a Marine's rifle.

Grubb grabbed the handset from his radio operator. A nervous voice came over the net. "Get out! There are fucking mortar rounds in the floor! Everyone get out!" The Marine gave no call sign to identify himself. It didn't matter, though; every Marine obeyed his command. Dozens of the exhausted men ran out onto the street. Some congregated near the Abrams tank posted at the intersection of Give Me and Racetrack. Others stood in the middle of the road, unsure of what to do or where to go.

"Rage 4, this is Comanche 6, we are abandoning the COP and moving to your position, over," said the Charlie Company commander. His voice contained an even mix of fear and anger. Grubb acknowledged his temporary boss, whom he had only met days earlier.

Rage 4 looked over at the dark structure. The second- and third-floor windows were already sandbagged. A couple of pieces of ballistic glass were still visible. Most of the Marines in the street were empty-handed. Nearly all of the materials they had brought into the building had been left behind. Grubb had an ominous thought. The enemy had just secured their own COP without firing a single shot. They hadn't even filled or carried any of the thousands of sandbags fortifying the structure.

The platoon commander thought about his own building. If the insurgents had set up mines next door, they probably were going to do it here, too. The Ministry of Oil structure was twice the size of the neighboring COP. The enemy could be setting the Marines up for an even larger explosion.

Grubb got on his PRR. "Squad leaders, check this damn place. Look for any loose tiles on the floor or new plaster on the walls. Cut any random electrical wires," he said.

Chaos ensued in Rage 4's position. Confused Marines from Comanche poured into the building. Squad and team leaders were shouting over one another to get accountability for all of their gear and personnel. Lieutenant Grubb met up with Comanche 6 near the centrally placed stairwell on the second floor. The captain was trying to find new structures to position his forces in. The short and stocky Grubb stood there, patiently awaiting orders. He looked on as Comanche 6 was having trouble making out the exact numbers for each building with his red-lensed flashlight. Then a Marine behind the two officers leaned against the wall with his right hand. Unexpectedly, the wall gave way, and three 120mm mortar rounds fell onto the floor.

The chaos of COP Qatana repeated itself in the Ministry of Oil building. Shouts of "Get the fuck out!" rang through the air. Nearly a hundred confused and disoriented Marines congregated on Racetrack. As Grubb made it out of the dark, dank building, someone from Comanche was trying to take charge. He attempted to get accountability by ordering the Marines into formation on the exposed street.

Grubb was horrified. Only a few hours earlier, Rage 1 had discovered the largest cache ever in downtown Ramadi. The stash of weapons contained numerous RPGs and medium machine guns. The enemy was clearly capable of taking advantage of a hundred Marines standing next to one another in columns. Grubb refused to expose his Marines to such an unnecessary risk. The platoon commander pulled out his map and found the closest structure large enough to house his platoon.

"Staff Sergeant Williamson, we're going to building 17, Golf 3 patrol sector. Head north on Fire Station Road, and it is the first major building on your left," he said over the PRR. The lieutenant did not wait to ask or inform Comanche 6 of his decision—he took action.

Staff Sergeant Scott Williamson, the same staff sergeant who had watched me struggle over the berm and the railroad tracks during the Papa 10, took control of the platoon. He was on his fifth or sixth deployment and had spent a couple of years in Iraq, in a war that was slightly more than three years old. The man had more combat experience than training. Describing him as a veteran would be a disservice.

It would ignore the true impact this one man had on not only the platoon but the entire company.

With the Marines of Comanche in formation on Racetrack, trying to figure out how many pieces of bulletproof glass and antitank rockets they had left inside COP Qatana, Rage 4 moved down the street and cleared building 17. Staff Sergeant Williamson obtained accountability for every piece of gear and Marine on the way. The night was ending, and so was the Marines' grip on the initiative. The insurgents would now dictate the terms of the next day's battle.

In the following early-morning hours, the rest of the officers and staff of Rage Company huddled around the picnic tables in COP Firecracker's chow hall. A prolonged firefight echoed over the Qatana skyline as insurgents engaged Rage 4 and elements of Comanche with accurate small-arms fire. The response from the Marines was usually a twenty- to thirty-round burst from a machine gun.

Captain Smith laid out a map of Qatana on the table. He updated us on the night's previous action, including the four wounded Marines and the abandoning of COP Qatana. The group sat, awaiting the nature of our countermove.

The assistant intelligence officer for 1/6, Jason Mann, was also at the table. He had expressed an interest in going on a mission with Rage Company, so I made the necessary coordination. The previous night's events were difficult for him. He was the guy who had received the intelligence, from multiple sources, stating that the string of large structures around the intersection of Give Me and Racetrack was rigged to explode. Armed with this information, he had argued against the chosen site as the COP's location. He was overruled. The battalion had decided that the terrain was too advantageous and must be taken. They were absolutely right, and it was this commanding nature of the new COP's location that foreshadowed our desire to eventually use it.

For me, it was another glimpse into the insurgents' minds. In the same sense that we had been predictable in the planning of the patrol that led to the Heidbreder ambush, 1/6 was telegraphing their future operations at the battalion level. The battalion had already seized the dominating structures on the western side of Qatana. They were used to construct COP Firecracker.

The insurgents had anticipated this strategy to continue and therefore booby-trapped the large structures on the eastern side of Qatana. Lieutenant Mann's intel sources had stated that five structures, all of which were more than three stories high, in the vicinity of the Give Me and Racetrack intersection were booby-trapped. The enemy was clearly thinking ahead, and their success in understanding our thought processes had bought them valuable time.

Captain Smith pointed out the positions of Rage 4 and Comanche units on the map. Each unit was set up in a defensive position around the abandoned COP Qatana. All forces were located west and south of the old construction site. "Gentlemen, the new site for COP Qatana is this area south of the Give Me–Racetrack intersection," said Captain Smith. He circled the terrain on the map. The larger structure in the compound had a circular hole in the roof. I immediately recognized it as the executive building of the ISI from Major Mayberry's in-brief, which, although it had taken place only a few weeks earlier, was already a distant memory. I was struck by the symbolism: the capital of the Islamic State of Iraq was now going to be a combat outpost.

Rage 1, Lieutenant Shearburn, spoke while Rage 6 was circling with his map pen. "Sir, that is insane. Those buildings are all one-story tall. Each of the structures across the street towers over the new construction site, and while those larger buildings are all mined or booby-trapped, the insurgents will still use them," he said, trying to maintain a conversational tone. I think we all generally agreed with what Rage 1 Actual was saying, but Captain Smith was visibly annoyed that he had been interrupted.

"Let me finish, Lieutenant. Tonight we are going to clear the areas northeast of the new COP's location, minus the larger, mined structures. The platoons' specific lanes stretch along the streets Jamie, Starr, and the no-name parallel road south of Starr. We will search the suspected VBIED factory along the no-name road and then evacuate the local populace on these streets to Farm. Then 1/6 is going to drop an undetermined amount of ordnance on the new site for the COP. Over the course of the next few nights, engineers will level the ground and begin constructing from the bottom up. Now I'll take your questions."

At first, no one knew what to say. Then the questions started to fly. How long was this going to take? What did they plan on building the COP out of? Why not level the buildings that were rigged to explode? These were all legitimate questions, none of which Captain Smith had any real answers for. It was a predicament only a leader would find himself in.

Rage 6 was torn. As our commander, he had to express confidence in the mission, but it was plain to see, through his frustration in answering our questions, that our reservations were the same as his. He silenced the crowd, ending the inquiries. "Gentlemen, we take this one mission at a time," he said. "We know what to do tonight. After this mission, expect to relieve Comanche and Rage 4 out in sector while the COP is built. Remember, this isn't going to be our COP, so do not concern yourselves with its composition. We are here to see it gets built."

The entire scenario was making me uneasy. It was the first time I seriously thought the operational situation was to the enemy's advantage. As an officer in the military, I understood that the enemy might, on occasion, have the upper hand tactically. That is to say, he may ambush us or have some other tricks that temporarily give him a better position; however, these tactical scenarios could be overcome through intellect in the application of our superior firepower. In our current situation, the enemy was forcing us to make poor decisions. I was not particularly impressed with 1/6's plan to overcome these rigged buildings, and I was unsure whether there was a good alternative. The psychological effect of the insurgents' shaping of the battlefield was taking its toll. The nerves would be worse than usual.

One hour later, we finished the planning for that night's raid of the VBIED factory. Rage 1 and Rage 3 would clear Jamie, Starr, and the objective. Rage 2 was going to establish itself on the south and west sides of Racetrack in an over-watch position. After hashing out the details and deconflicting lanes for the platoons, a group of the lieutenants and the staff headed down to the COC on the first floor. We were interested in the latest on Rage 4 and Comanche's situation.

It wasn't pretty.

On arriving at the COC, we quickly found out that an RPG had torn into a hummer at the Give Me–Racetrack intersection. One Marine was killed in the blast. Others were wounded. When I first heard this, I was confused. I had only ever seen tanks manning that position during our previous missions. I came to discover that as soon as it was light outside, humvees had taken the place of the tanks. It immediately struck me as an absurd tactical decision.

Somebody within 1/6 had decided that the tanks would occupy the observation posts at night because they had better night-vision optics, while the thin-skinned hummers would take over during the day. Apparently, nobody had told 1/6 that insurgents did not have NVGs. In my humble opinion, whatever NVGs the hummers had at night put them at a significant tactical advantage over the enemy. Instead, 1/6 was parking the lightly armored vehicles on city streets, surrounded by four- and five-story buildings, and leaving them there all day long. They might as well have been in formation.

I noticed that the battalion commander was in the room. He had clearly placed himself at the point of friction, trying to make himself as informed as possible for any future decisions regarding the COP. I got the feeling the command had been caught off guard when the bomb went off the night before. They had doubted their own intel sources and were now regretting it.

An officer from Apache began to update the colonel, while the officers from Rage huddled around a television screen. Lance Corporal Albin was flying the Wasp unmanned-aerial vehicle (UAV) over the VBIED factory, as well as over the rest of our objective area, for the raid. After about five minutes, the UAV was running out of battery. Albin flew it back toward Hurricane Point, where the battalion tactical operations center took control of its frequency.

I walked over to the XO for Apache and asked him when the next UAV was going up. He looked at his watch and said another hour. The rest of the lieutenants headed back upstairs to brief their Marines, while I stuck around to ask Albin about the capabilities of the UAV. After a few minutes, we both left the COC, but as I was going out the door, the XO for Apache stopped me. He was waiting for me in the hallway.

"Hey, Marine. When you address me, you call me sir, especially when the colonel—" The Apache XO had an arrogant tone. I lost it.

"And who the fuck are you?" I interrupted, continuing on a profanity-laced rant. "I'm First Lieutenant Daly; last time I checked, that's the same fucking rank as you!"

The Apache XO tried to calm me down. It worked, and in a sense he was right: I wasn't wearing my rank insignia. I didn't care, though. I considered his line of thought one of garrison duty, deserving no place on the battlefield. He was too concerned with what the colonel might think of him, instead of worrying about the welfare and employment of his Marines. Now was the time for solving problems, not for stroking egos.

I eventually apologized to the guy and continued on toward the stairwell. That's when I noticed a wide-eyed Albin staring at me. I was instantly disgusted with myself, knowing that I had been in the wrong. I told Albin to shut up before he said a word. It was the only time I would lose my temper with another officer in a combat environment. Luckily for me, we were the same rank. Albin and I headed up the stairwell and started to prep our gear in silence. The initial success of Operation Hue City was clearly over.

The exchanging of small-arms fire continued through the afternoon. Every building housing Marines in the Qatana was engaged at some point. The rooftop positions on COP Firecracker were the last to take fire. For the Marines of 1/6, it was a normal day. The insurgents were usually very active in the daylight because most American units did not patrol or execute raids without the cover of darkness. Ramadi was that dangerous.

As the night drew close, a damp cold enveloped the COP. The temperature dropped into the low forties. I briefed the headquarters Marines on the raid. The senior enlisted was Sergeant Bustamante, who was our public affairs expert. Instead of carrying extra ammo in his assault pack, he had an NVG-capable video camera. For this raid, he was going to document whatever we found at the VBIED factory. The company staged on the stairwell as soon as darkness set in.

The headquarters element moved between the second and third squads of Lieutenant Jahelka's Rage 3, which was the middle platoon in the order of movement. Rage 1 was out in front, while Rage 2 followed. The insertion route of the mission was dangerously similar to the first two raids of Operation Hue City. We left COP Firecracker, heading north on Racetrack. The destroyed apartment complex at the five-way intersection just outside the COP was scarier than the first time I walked past it. I recognized all of the debris as we passed the structures, however, which gave my mind some comfort because I found everything where it was supposed to be.

The formation maintained about 3-meter dispersion between each Marine. As we went through the intersection with Fire Station Road, I could make out the infrared strobes from Rage 4 flashing on the roof of building 17. We moved past the market on my right and then the Ministry of Oil building on the left. I was surprised when we made it through the Give Me–Racetrack intersection without any of the buildings exploding.

We passed Jamie and Starr, where Rage 1 had already begun to clear their lane. A squad from Rage 3 also went down Starr, clearing the southern side. The headquarters element followed Sergeant Clinton

Ahlquist's squad onto the no-name road where the VBIED factory was located. We hit the first house on the left. There weren't any houses on the right, only the wall surrounding the VBIED factory, which was bordered by an empty lot.

Ahlquist's Marines stormed into the house. The lights were still on. Food was spread out on the living room floor and in the kitchen sink. The occupants of the home had left in a hurry.

The fact that the people who lived here had left in such a manner circumstantially confirmed a piece of intelligence Lieutenant Mann had received on the house. A few months earlier, a convoy from 1/6 had made a wrong turn at checkpoint 296. The vehicles hung a left at the first Y in the road, instead of veering to the right, and ended up on Racetrack. At the time, U.S. forces did not maintain any sort of presence in the area, and Racetrack was laden with a defensive belt of IEDs.

When a humvee in the convoy struck a massive IED, the turret gunner was thrown more than 100 meters from the vehicle. In the ensuing chaos, a group of three Iraqi men, said to be brothers, dragged the body onto this no-name street. They hid the fallen Marine under some trash in the empty lot next to the VBIED factory. According to the source, the three brothers lived in this house. The report was already partially confirmed because the massive search launched by 1/6 to find the body discovered it on this street immediately after the attack.

Marines began to tear the house apart, looking for any sort of contraband. I headed to the roof with Captain Smith, Lieutenant Jahelka, and Sergeant Ahlquist to observe the VBIED factory and come up with a plan on how to prosecute it. We were extremely wary of defensive IEDs or any sort of booby traps. Our plan to counter the threat was simple. First, we would fire shoulder-launched multipurpose assault weapon (SMAW) antitank rockets into the buildings, in order to set off or disrupt any larger explosives awaiting our arrival. Then we would fire into the open courtyard 40mm grenades from the M32 street-sweeper, an automatic grenade launcher carried by Rage 3's platoon sergeant, Staff Sergeant Michael Crippen.

I headed back downstairs. Marines were sifting through everything. Furniture was being moved and rugs were pulled up off the floor. Boots stomped on the tiles, as the Marines tried to find hollow spots where an underground compartment might be. I moved through the home's central hallway, past the busy Marines, in search of the headquarters element. I found them sitting on a couple of couches in the living room and quickly joined the group.

Ahlquist positioned a small security detail on the roof. He carefully placed the team of Marines outside the back-blast area of the SMAW's firing positions. In a booming voice, he shouted down the stairwell for SMAW team one to get on the roof. I noticed Bustamante sitting on the couch with Eakin and immediately sent him up to take video of the fireworks.

The sounds of 9mm tracer rounds served as advance warning for the incoming rockets. The tracers are fired by the Marine holding the rocket and are used to verify that he is aiming at the target the spotter wants destroyed.

The thundering blast of the rocket being fired shook the house. SMAW team one was aiming at the correct building.

After SMAW team two traded places with SMAW team one, the same process repeated itself. Following the second rocket shot, we could hear the building it hit collapse. At least we didn't have to search it.

Next, the wily Staff Sergeant Crippen, who insisted on carrying the street-sweeper, headed up to the roof. He fired off four of the 40mm grenades into the compound. There wasn't a single secondary explosion from any of the blasts. As Ahlquist moved his Marines down off the roof, I began to doubt whether the compound was in fact a VBIED factory.

Captain Smith directed me to keep the headquarters element inside the house. A team from Ahlquist's squad remained with us to help provide security. Ahlquist led the rest of his squad to a predesignated breach site along the northern side of the VBIED factory's wall. Instead of walking through the compound's main gate, we would use our team of combat engineers to blow a hole in the exterior wall. It was less likely to be booby-trapped.

I took Bustamante back up to the roof to keep videotaping. The engineers blew down the wall and immediately found unexploded ordnance. Mortar and artillery rounds were inside tires and buried under standard household trash: garbage bags, plastic and Styrofoam cups and plates, and discarded debris. A small ditch contained an assortment of automatic rifles. After a few minutes of listening to the radio, I headed over to see for myself. Staff Sergeant Jerry Eagle, our senior combat engineer, was walking about carrying artillery rounds half his size. A large pile of explosives quickly formed. More stuff for EOD to blow up.

I headed back to the headquarters element. Eakin was monitoring the radio. He informed me that while I was gone, another squad from Rage

3 had discovered a room full of fire extinguishers. When I didn't seem all that impressed or concerned, Eakin qualified his initial statement with, "Sir, each one of the extinguishers is hooked up to det cord or something."

He suddenly had my attention. I remembered that one of the platoons had found a pile of empty fire extinguishers during the Papa 10. It seemed that making bombs out of the benign red cylinders was suddenly an insurgent trend. We sent a team of Marines with Staff Sergeant Eagle to the intersection of Starr and Farm Road to assess the home-made bombs.

It took about an hour for EOD to show up. The group of technicians was petrified that we had moved the large amount of ordnance. As they had during the destruction of our previous cache, they accused us of violating the rules of engagement and endangering our Marines by letting them touch the explosives. The EOD technicians truly believed that only they were allowed to touch something that was potentially dangerous. Our combat engineers soon grew annoyed with the criticisms of EOD.

With the night dragging on and EOD trying to decide where and how to detonate the pile of explosives, 1/6 canceled the leveling of the new COP site by a combined-arms attack. Again, our own success at finding the enemy's tools had prevented us from achieving the primary mission. There simply was not enough darkness left to evacuate the surrounding homes and then destroy the structures along Racetrack. So the entire company exited the area along the same route it had come. I walked past all of the same structures and debris back to COP Firecracker. With a squad from Rage Company for security, EOD stayed behind to detonate the stockpile from the VBIED factory where it was. The explosion was smaller than our previous experience but impressive nonetheless. Loud noises were always good for morale, so long as you were responsible for them.

When we arrived back at the COP, most of the Marines went straight to sleep. Before the officers hit the rack, Captain Smith informed us that 1/6 was sending us out on the same mission the next night. We would use the same route to get there. The platoons would have the same lanes. Everything was literally the same as we had just done.

I felt sick to my stomach. After my first day in downtown Ramadi, I had become deathly afraid of being predictable. Now I was ordered to be predictable. Not a single Marine was happy about the mission, but we all knew that COP Qatana had to be built. The mission came first, and the next night was going to be déjà vu.

The following day began with the usual harassing fire from the insurgents. As soon as a light drizzle developed around midday, the fighting stopped. For the Ramadi insurgent, fifty degrees and wet was too cold. I was surprised that our elusive opponent was willing to relinquish the initiative while he was dictating the terms of the fight. Rage Company enjoyed a dinner of peanut butter and jelly sandwiches without a shot fired in anger.

As we had done the night before, we stepped off when darkness set in. The insertion to the objective area went by smoothly. We passed the same debris, the same flashing infrared strobes. The platoons filed into their assigned lanes. The three brothers' home was still empty. The same food littered the kitchen and the floor. Nothing had changed.

The neighboring house had an entire extended family living in it. After we spent about five minutes of searching this second house, the déjà vu quickly ended. It came over the net that a Marine from Rage 3 was wounded. I snatched the handset from Eakin and listened to the conversation between Captain Smith and Lieutenant Jahelka.

The injury was a shotgun blast to the foot. It had happened when one of the squads was gaining entry to a home. A breach team had used a shotgun to open a locked door. As the entry team went by, the lance corporal with the shotgun tried to force his weapon into a makeshift sling on his back. The safety for the shotgun got caught on his gear and became disengaged. The trigger was stuck on this same gear, and the weapon went off as the entry team passed by. The pellets blasted into another lance corporal's foot. A dangerous trend with shotguns was forming.

Captain Smith coordinated a vehicle from COP Firecracker to come pick up the wounded Marine.

After handling the incident, the platoons continued to evict the local population. Rage 1 was searching for a suitable site to move the locals to that was east of Farm Street. While on this part of the mission, a squad from Rage 1 discovered a house they described as a torture chamber. The only furniture in the building consisted of two iron bed frames. Hooks hung from the ceiling, and electrical wiring was strewn about the floor. Countless bloodstains marked the walls. Captain Smith sent the interpreter to the squad, ordering him to question the local populace about the residence. One family told him that it was where the ISI carried out the judgments of its legal court.

Back on no-name road, we continued clearing east. We entered the third house, which turned out to be a multi-building compound. The squad had the extended family from the previous home in tow. When I went through the third house's gate, I was immediately greeted by three small residences. Each one faced inward to the common courtyard that I stood in.

The Marines simultaneously cleared each of the small homes, two of which were empty. I directed the headquarters element to put the neighboring extended family in the empty house on the left to keep the families separated. If the neighbors were going to give up dirt on one another, they certainly wouldn't do it knowing that the others could hear them.

I headed into the central home, which contained the owners of the compound. Again, it was an extended family. The man of the house pleaded with us in English to go away. We all stood around kind of staring at one another until the interpreter made it back from Rage 1's position. Marlo, the interpreter, immediately went to work on the group. He asked questions to multiple people at once. Then he started to focus on one of the teenage boys. I couldn't understand anything they were saying, but I still tried to listen closely. Curious, I tapped Marlo on the shoulder. "What are you talking about?" I asked him. The Shia Iraqi said he was simply asking the same questions I had given him for the last mission.

The interpreter spit out another question at the boy, then nonchalantly turned back to me. "The building back at the intersection is a bomb," he said. Even though I figured as much, I asked him to be more specific about the building's location. The boy responded to Marlo by saying that it was the big apartment building on the corner of this no-name road and Racetrack. The teenager had watched insurgents place explosives in it only a few days earlier.

I looked at my map. The structure that the kid was referring to was not one of the originally rigged buildings. I left the room to update Captain Smith, who was with Rage 1, on the new information. Marlo continued to question the family. About ten minutes later, with the Marines still searching the compound, we were told over the radio to halt the clear. There was no explanation besides "Hold your current position." So we sat there. In a matter of minutes, our sweat became colder than ice. Bones and teeth chattered in the cold, and the stationary Marines began to wonder what was going on. An hour passed by, then another. The lull in the mission became an opportunity for the Iraqi family to share their kerosene heater with us. A couple of Marines and Iraqis even shared a blanket. I got the feeling we were falling into a false sense of security.

Finally, we got word over the radio. The mission was being aborted. All units were to return to base. Captain Smith directed Rage 2 to leave first, followed by Rage 1. I walked out to the front gate and watched the squads from Rage 1 move past us. Captain Smith used it as an opportunity to link back up with Rage 3, meeting me at the gate. After a few minutes we began to move, but when the point element reached the intersection with Racetrack, we stopped. Somebody said that we were waiting for adequate dispersion, but whatever the reason, we were halted directly beneath the apartment complex that we had just been told was recently mined. I tried to conceal my frustration at the carelessness of the situation.

The battalion had canceled the mission because they felt that the area was too dangerous. Too many buildings were booby-trapped. Now we, the units in this dangerous area, were kneeling underneath the overhang of the rigged structure. Staring into the darkness of an empty window, I was very aware of the twisted irony in the event. To have us kneeling under the building that was rigged to explode was not the battalion commander's intent.

It was another example of the psychological effect of being stationary while exposed. There was too much time to think. You became aware of the urban environment's countless concealed positions. Knowing that you couldn't cover them all at once led to irrational thoughts. I looked around and wondered whether the relaxed Marines, some of them leaning against the rigged building, knew where they were.

A couple of agonizing minutes went by, and we stepped off. It was the usual route back: following Racetrack. We approached the intersection with Give Me. A tank was stationed there, its barrel oriented north down the side street. I turned back to maintain a visual reference on Captain Smith and noticed that he had halted and was shining his PEQ-2 laser into the mined structure on the northeast side of the intersection. It was the same building that the RPG had been fired from the day before. I got Albin's attention and halted the headquarters element.

I jogged back to Captain Smith. "Sir, what are you looking at?" I asked. The rest of the column was stopped behind us.

"There is something in there, Lieutenant Daly. I can't tell what it is," he said.

I was really not in the mood for standing around. Giving in to my anxiety, I tried to coax Rage 6 into leaving, saying, "Sir, the building is mined. Let's just head back to the COP." It was an attempt at coercion that I soon regretted.

The captain's response was adamant. "Daly, a fucking Marine died from an RPG that was shot from this building. If that's an RPG in there, we are going to get it!" he shouted.

A couple of Marines from the squad behind us came up to see what was going on. I took a few steps back, grabbed Eakin by the collar, and told him to get the rest of the headquarters element over to the far side of the intersection, where Albin was standing. I wanted to keep the formation moving and reduce the number of bodies standing around the building. I headed back to Captain Smith, who was trying to pry open the sheet-metal door to the former market stall he was staring into. The tallest Marine in Rage Company, Lance Corporal Adam Duvall, was helping him. Duvall was one of the most capable junior Marines in the company, full of initiative and a desire to do something. He was best known for declaring everything hajji "un-American." At the moment, he was asking Rage 6 whether he wanted him to rip off the door. In his ridiculous Southern twang, Duvall kept saying, "Just tell me, sir, an' I'll rip 'er off."

Duvall suddenly identified what Captain Smith was looking at. He said it was a discarded engine block that was in rough condition—probably the aftermath of an IED blast. Captain Smith kept trying to get a better look at the shadowy hulk of debris, but the sheet-metal door was in his way. He eventually gave up and walked down off the curb, toward me in the street. I knew by his demeanor that Rage 6 was frustrated. We all were. No matter what we did, in a couple of hours the sun would come up and insurgents would own this part of Qatana. To an extent, I had come to accept this fact. It was the reason my sole desire was to head back to COP Firecracker as quickly as possible.

Captain Smith took my former position at the front of the headquarters element, and I ended up being third to last. Only Eakin and Bustamante were behind me.

We continued our movement, and I noticed that the squad from Rage 3 behind us had halted. They were increasing the dispersion between our two groups. It was the same walk back, scanning the same windows and rooftops, only in opposite order. The column moved at a snail's pace.

We made it to the five-way intersection, best characterized as a traffic circle, just outside the COP. Moments later, I walked into the serpentine. I was two steps beyond the first waist-level concrete barrier, and a machine gun exploded behind me. Instead of running into the protection of the COP, only twenty feet away, I turned around to face the threat. Dozens of red tracers flew through the sky. Eakin stood motionless ten feet away, staring into the darkness. Through my NVGs, I could make out Duvall and the other members of his squad sprinting toward the COP. Some of them were firing their weapons; one of the Marines went down.

I shouted at Eakin to hand me the radio's handset. There was no response; he was frozen. Sergeant Bustamante ran past us and into the COP. I screamed Eakin's name, trying to shout over the machine gun still spitting out dozens of rounds. No response. I began to add four-letter words to my shouts while I ran toward him. He turned around as I reached for him with my right arm. "Get the fuck in the COP!" I shouted directly into his face. The young man's eyes were wide with fear, but his mind was back in reality. He sprinted into the COP.

The Marines from the squad behind us made it to the serpentine, and the shooting ceased. Duvall went by first, shouting to me as he passed. "It was that damn tank there, on the corner, sir! He's doing all the shootin'," he said.

I waited for the last guy, which was, of course, Staff Sergeant Crippen. I told him I'd seen one of his Marines go down inside the traffic circle. He laughed when we got behind the ten-foot concrete wall that was the COP's perimeter. "I know you did, sir, because it was me. I stepped in a sewer hole, and my legs are soaked with shit." We walked through the maze of concrete barriers and concertina wire, entering the four-story building that was our home.

I thought about going straight to bed, but I was too curious about the new plan. I was also interested to hear what the tank had been shooting at. I went directly to the COC to find out. Captain Smith was already there. I could hear the tanks, call sign Warlord, giving the battle-damage assessment over the radio. Two-man RPG team killed in action, right on. I thought about my previous idea of using hummers to man the positions at night. There was no way a Marine with NVGs would have spotted the RPG team. Using the tanks for their optics had just prevented our first serious casualty. It was a reminder to me that military tactics is an art, not a science. There is no set answer for battlefield problems, only principles to help you make up your mind.

Rage 6 then went over to the battalion net and tried to get in contact with Tarheel 3, 1/6's operations officer. I stuck around to see what word was getting passed. I had to wait until Captain Smith was off the net to ask him about the conversation. The radio he was using wasn't hooked up to a speaker box. I positioned myself between him and the door. When he finished, he walked right up to me and said, "It's Christmas in Qatana!" then left the COC.

I stood next to the blank television monitor for a moment, my questions unanswered. I headed upstairs to the third floor and sat down on my cot. Trying to sleep was impossible. It was the first time I had ever wanted Christmas to simply come and go. I had no thoughts of gifts, only death. The pressing questions mingled in my mind. There was one that would not go away. How long was Operation Hue City going to take? Over the last few days, Gunny Bishop had convoyed all of our gear, including some comfort items, out to COP Firecracker. Every Marine was keenly aware that January 11, 2007, was the scheduled last day of combat operations for Rage Company. In order to make it back to the ships by the end of January, we would have to start packing by that date.

I made up my mind that our deployment would be extended. Operation Squeeze Play was already behind schedule, and there was no way we were going home until it was completed.

Albin came into the room. He had picked up an antenna for the Wasp UAV so that we could control it from our own position while out in sector. The excited Marine showed me what looked like a PlayStation portable but was actually the video screen for the UAV. From the comfort of an Iraqi's home, we would be able to watch the UAV's live feed. I felt like a kid with a new toy. It was Christmas after all. Tired, I jokingly asked Albin whether he would scratch my back. He said no.

After Albin left, I started to think about 1/6 and their collective indecisive nature. There wasn't a single part of the operation they had planned that I was impressed with. The missions and the routes we used were predictable. For the first time, I seriously thought about how my wife's life would change if I was killed in Qatana. An indescribable fear gripped my mind. It became an internal demon I had to wrestle with, then and there. I closed my eyes and let the fear consume me.

That entire night I dreamed about my own death. I must have watched myself die a hundred times. There were IED blasts, sniper shots, friendly fire, machine guns, improvised rockets, mortar rounds, and vehicles running me over. Sometimes I died alone; on other occasions, my friends joined me. I slept through the entire night. When I awoke, my misery was over. This visual reference for the unspeakable had dulled the edge of fear's blade. While fear was still there, I had accepted that death might be my destiny. In doing so, anxiety had become a part of my being.

Now, with a new sense of purpose, I was ready to celebrate Christmas.

The northwest corner of checkpoint 295 on the southwestern edge of Qatana. Before November 2006 this intersection and beyond was controlled by al Qaeda.

From right to left, Lance Corporal Joash Albin, Lance Corporal Benjamin Eakin, and Lieutenant Thomas Daly on the roof of building 17 following a firefight.

Lieutenant Thomas Daly
waking up on Christmas
morning 2006.

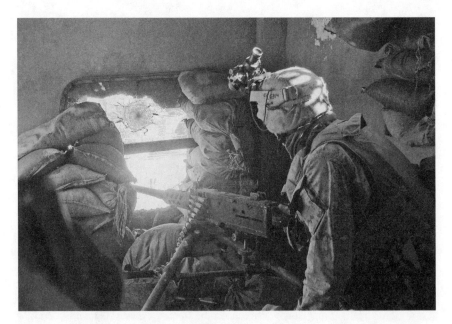

The sniper shot that nearly killed Lance Corporal Cooke on Christmas Day.

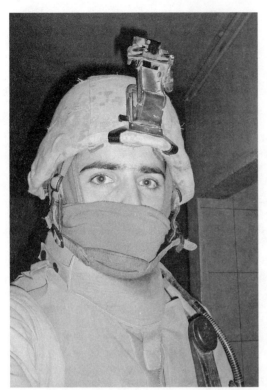

Lieutenant Thomas Daly
freezing in Qatana.

Rage Company's intelligence cell and one of the company's interpreters, Marlo (third
from left), in Qatana.

127

Lieutenant Thomas Daly minutes before the clearing of the VBIED factory in Qatana.

Lieutenant Thomas Daly inside COP Firecracker with a makeshift insurgent sniper rifle.

Corporal Brian Holloway in Qatana.

A group of fire extinguishers reconfigured as IEDs in Qatana.

Lieutenant James Thomas smokes inside his platoon's combat operations center in building 17, Qatana.

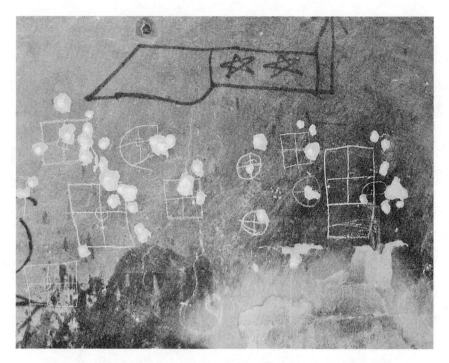

A rudimentary insurgent target range found on the streets of Qatana.

Corporal Jesus Davila in Qatana.

First Sergeant Eric Carlson in Qatana.

Captain John Smith in building 17, northern Qatana.

IED found by Sergeant Adam Sempert a few hundred meters from building 17.

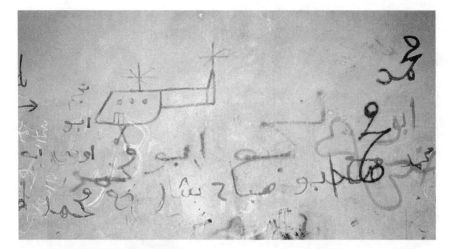

Insurgent graffiti and accompanying instructions on how to target U.S. helicopters found on the streets of Qatana.

7

THE BATTLE
OF CHRISTMAS DAY

December 21, 2006

First Sergeant Carlson was furious. He looked at the significant action report, then held it up in the air. The piece of paper crumpled in his hand.

"Sir, this is bullshit," he declared. "Look at this: the bastards claim 1/6 found the cache! There isn't a single mention of Rage Company in this damn report. Why would they do that? Taking credit for what we found! Lejeune pricks." He left the room, vowing to change the official wording in the report.

I picked up the wrinkled paper off his cot and read it:

G3WNCO—At 190215C DEC 06, 1/6 discovered a weapons cache IVO (38S LC ———), in N Ramadi. 1/6 searched Bldg # Sect. H-# IVO (38S LC ———) and the surrounding areas and discovered the following items: (1) IRL, (7) grenades (1: 36mm MK-1 and 1: F1 Russian), (20) 60mm mortars, (2) 82mm mortars, (3) 105mm mortars, (5) 120mm mortars, (160) 160 mm mortars,

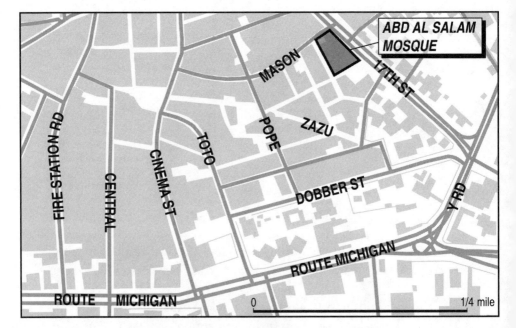

Operation Hue City II: The area to be cleared during the second half of Operation Hue City.

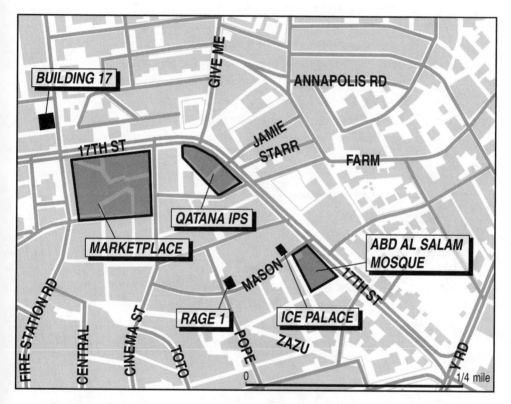

The Battle of Christmas Day: Significant locations during the fighting on Christmas Day, 2006.

(12) arty fuses, (1) M17 US Arty round, (18) RPG rockets (2x-PG9, 14x PG7, 2x PG 7S-3), (1) hollowed out missile, (2) video cameras, (30) cassette tapes, Misc propaganda, (1) IED pressure plate IED, IED making materials, (10) barrels of Iraqi currency, (15) acetylene tanks, (1) canister of propellant, (8) RPG, (2) RPG sights, (14) masks, (4) Draganovs, (1) GS 31 rifle, (1) MI Garand, (2) 60mm mortar systems w/ sights, (4) PKMs, (1) H&K G3, (4) chest harnesses, (2) level IV bullet proof vests with plates and POLICE on the front, (37) AK Mags, (3) sniper rifle mags, (3) black outfits, (2) license plates (Al Anbar), (1) handcuffs, (51) rounds of 5.56mm US linked ammo, (6500) rounds of 7.62mm, (2) Senao base stations, 300ft of copper wire, (4) 14 ga. Shotgun shells, (10) 60mm shotgun shells, (8) propellant sticks, (19) AK-47s, (8) PKCs, Misc 9v, 12v, and 24v batteries, IRL material, (30) electrical caps, Remote firing devices, 10 ft of Det cord, 20lbs of various explosives, 25 lbs of various propellants, (2) 2.5in launcher, (2) rifle grenades, (3) 85mm APHET, (1) AT mine (type 72), (1) 122mm projectile and (3) 130 mm projectiles. The items and munitions were removed to Hurricane Point for inventory, exploitation, and disposal by EOD. No casualties or damages reported.

The fact that Rage Company had been left out of the opening line was deliberate. All significant action reports state the company that was involved in the event. This was the first one I had seen that left the company out. Gunnery Sergeant Bishop leaned up in his cot, yawning and stretching his extremities in his usual morning routine. "Who would be responsible for that, sir?"

It was a good question. There was only one group that filled out the reports: the battalion operations section. "Tarheel S3 Gunny, the OPSO," I said. "It was probably the S3 officer himself who typed it up. I couldn't see a lance corporal doing something like that."

I lay back down on my cot in COP Firecracker. I wasn't really concerned that we'd been left out of the report; my mind was wrapped around what I was going to be doing that night.

Half an hour later, the company was in the chow hall. Captain Smith was briefing the follow-up to our original push into Qatana.

The battalion was still unsure of what building to use as the new COP Qatana. To buy themselves time, as well as move the focus of the fighting away from the Give Me–Racetrack intersection, we were going to clear the southeastern side of Qatana. It was essentially finishing the clear that had originally been scheduled to take one night.

Following the brief, which went rather quickly, seeing that we were continuing an already planned mission, a few unexpected visitors came into the room. The commanding officers of the 15th MEU and the 2nd Battalion, 4th Marines, were both in town to visit Rage Company. Sort of a morale and welfare check during the Christmas season. I was surprised that both men would leave their own areas of operation to come visit us (the MEU was a few hundred miles west in Rutbah, and 2/4 was just as far, only north in Haditha).

The battalion commander, Lieutenant Colonel Jim Glynn, gave the first pep talk. It was pretty good. When he turned it over to the MEU commander, I was relieved. Every so often, Lieutenant Colonel Glynn spoke too long or said something the Marines did not understand. This time, though, it was the usually impeccable MEU commander who said something that went over the Marines' heads.

The colonel started off well, but as he wrapped it up, he mentioned something that would stick in my mind for the next few days. "Gentlemen, you have worked hard and you deserve some time off. Multi-National Forces-West has mandated that all units do the bare minimum on Christmas. That is, no patrols, no missions. The Corps does not want to be informing families of tragedy around this holiday. As we are in AO Bull-Rush [15th MEU] and AO Bastard [2/4], I am sure the brigade leadership will comply with the order," he said, continuing on with the MEU's accomplishments to date.

The faces of two hundred puzzled Marines revealed that for the first time, lance corporals and sergeants knew something that a colonel did not: we *would* be fighting on Christmas. The result of such knowledge ensured that morale remained low. The realization that we would be the only unit fighting in all of Al Anbar Province during the holiday season sank in. Whether it was true didn't matter; it was the perception that entered each Marine's mind.

The insertion to southeast Qatana was a dismounted movement along Racetrack all the way to the eastern side of Qatana. We walked through the five-way, Fire Station–Racetrack, and Give Me–Racetrack intersections. Our shadows passed Jamie, Starr, and the VBIED factory on the left. We headed toward the Abd-al Sala'am mosque and then turned off on the road south of it.

Passing the mosque, I scanned its minaret and windows for a few seconds too long. When I turned back to spot Captain Smith and ensure proper dispersion, I saw that he had halted. Through my NVGs, it appeared that he was looking at his boots, and I assumed he was going to tie his bootlaces. I scanned a few more buildings and continued to follow Lance Corporal Albin, the headquarters point man. Then I turned around and saw that Captain Smith was not moving. Instead, he was kicking around at an object in the street's dusty, broken asphalt.

I flashed the IR strobe in my NVGs to try to get him to keep moving. It was the wrong thing to do. I should have told Albin to halt. When I rotated around seconds later, Albin was gone. He had turned the corner after the mosque's compound wall and entered the clearing lane for Rage 2.

I sprinted after him and negotiated the turn's sharp angle with the path of a wide arc. I stopped in my tracks. I was staring at a Y-intersection. The compound walls surrounding the homes prevented me from seeing more than ten feet down each road.

Albin was gone. I slowly crept out into the intersection, gripping my M4 rifle, the power of which inspires men to do just about anything. I looked down the left fork in the road first; it was the direction Albin was not supposed to go. The street was empty.

I spun around and saw Albin staring at me from a few feet away. "It's about time, sir. I thought you left me," he said. Albin remained kneeling on the corner while I ran the 50 meters back to Racetrack and directed Captain Smith to our position. Then we moved to the first house and began to follow Rage 2 while they cleared their lane.

The first home was the nicest I had ever entered in Ramadi. Vaulted twenty-foot ceilings complemented each room. A center portion of the house had even higher ceilings and was finished off with its own small dome. A mahogany desk and bookcases were expertly paired with beautiful rugs. The house did have one drawback, however. The owner was recklessly selling boxes of toy rifles at the local market, the same market where Rage 1 found their massive cache and the insurgents practiced their marksmanship. The toys weren't your usual cap-gun or red-capped rifles. They were life-size depictions of actual weapons, something that could easily result in the deaths of innocent children.

The Marines destroyed the plastic weapons and carried on the clear.

After about three blocks, as the clear proceeded south and closer to Michigan, the company began to enter an area where all of the residences were empty. The families had moved out long ago, most likely due to the violence that had plagued Michigan for the last three years.

Lieutenant Shearburn and Rage 1 immediately made a startling find in the area. The walls surrounding the houses were laced with graffiti. Marlo, our interpreter, was with Rage 1 and identified what could only be described as directions. He informed us that the walls literally stated, "To avoid American sniper at cemetery go."

As their movement progressed, the interpreter found more and more of the directions, each of which provided the follower with safe passage away from the fighting positions of OP Horea, a Marine observation post 200 to 300 meters south on Michigan, located next to Ramadi's downtown cemetery.

The formation of three platoons clearing abreast continued toward Fire Station Road. Two hours of clearing empty houses became hours of clearing empty commercial buildings. The three- and four-story office buildings were barren, just as empty as the homes we had cleared.

While searching the bottom floor of a large structure, Holloway's squad, which I was with, couldn't find any stairs leading to the upper floors. We headed back out to the street and found a boarded-up door. Sheets of plywood were nailed across the frame in an obvious attempt to prevent entry. We ripped them down. The men awkwardly climbed over the shattered pieces of wood and up the narrow stairs. The two thousand square feet of office space was utterly empty, nothing but dust. We took the opportunity to take a break, sitting on the dirty floor.

"Rage 6, this is Rage 1, I have a controlled det in two minutes, over," said Lieutenant Shearburn over the radio.

Captain Smith was upset. "I never approved that," he said to Shearburn.

After the blast, Captain Smith ordered Shearburn to leave his platoon and come to our position. We all knew what it meant: Shearburn was going to get scolded. Captain Smith waited for him on the stairs. When Shearburn showed up, Rage 6 berated him for all of Ramadi to hear. It was an awkward scenario; Captain Smith stood at the top of the stairs screaming down at his lieutenant. Broken chunks of plywood separated the two men. After the yelling, Shearburn went back to his platoon, and the company continued with its mission.

We moved quickly and were ahead of schedule. Instead of heading back to COP Firecracker early, we crossed over Fire Station Road and continued clearing. Holloway's squad finally entered a commercial building with something in it. Well, in at least one of the rooms, anyway.

The ten-foot-by-ten-foot space was filled with cardboard boxes. They were stacked all along the walls, reaching about six or seven feet high. I pulled on the one closest to me and started to pry it open. Holloway was doing the same, only his were no longer taped shut. Someone had already opened them.

"I got lamps over here, sir," he said.

I tugged harder, ripping the piece of cardboard completely off the box. "Interesting. Lamp shades for me," I said.

There were dozens of boxes exactly like mine, while only a few were similar to Holloway's. I looked back out into the hallway and recognized what could pass as a storefront. This was probably once a legitimate business, but the lack of parity in numbers of similar boxes was a trademark of the insurgency. The white electrical cords from lamps were among the cords of choice for detonating IEDs in the area. This was most likely where it all came from. Somewhere in the vast Ramadi sprawl, there was a house full of nothing but lamps, all of which were missing their power cords. If anyone ever found that building, they would have been standing inside an IED factory.

The squad was setting up in a defensive posture in the building, clearing the rest of the structure's rooms. The other rooms in the building were like most of those around it, completely empty. Eakin sat on the floor, listening to the radio.

"Rage 3, controlled det in ten seconds!" shouted Eakin. Holloway directed his squad to get away from the door and the windows. Rage 3 was across the street from us.

Eakin began to count down the seconds.

When he got to one, a thunderous explosion ripped into our building. The walls shook. Glass shattered. Looking into the hallway, the entrance to the building, I watched a cloud of dust carrying shattered glass from the door blow over a kneeling Marine. Shouts of profanity came from every room. I ran over to the Marine in the hallway, expecting to find chunks of glass stuck in his arms or legs.

As I got to him, the Marine stood up, said, "That was cool," and walked over to the door to check out the aftermath of the explosion. He was fine, and so was everyone else in the squad. We finished clearing the structure and staged outside.

The squad from Rage 3 that had just blown us up was in the street as well. The Marines exchanged insults, and I noticed that an entire wall was missing from the first floor of the building that Rage 3 had destroyed. It was a three-story structure, and I couldn't help but think that it was now going to fall on me.

The squad moved down Fire Station Road and eventually hit Michigan, the main supply route through Ramadi. All elements of the company were now moving toward this historic IED hot spot. It was the most dangerous part of the night.

The closer our double-column formation got to the intersection, the more gaping holes and pockmarks the buildings contained.

At the intersection Lieutenant Thomas was rummaging through four-foot-tall weeds in a ditch, cutting away the double and triple strands of concertina wire that prevented civilians from entering the road. His boots sloshed around in a few inches of stagnant water. Once the wire was cut, Rage 2 moved onto Michigan. Headquarters followed behind them.

We drew closer to the government center. It was cold enough outside that I could see my own breath. I was petrified. The four- and five-story buildings on either side of the road towered over the dismounted column of Marines in front of me. My mind was struck in a serious dilemma. If I took my eyes away from the ground, I might step on an IED. If I didn't scan the windows above, I risked being engaged by an enemy combatant.

I resigned myself to doing the opposite of the Marine in front.

The street was covered in a small layer of mud and dust. The resulting picture in my NVGs was a textured surface. Clean asphalt looked like gaping holes, while the mud was wavy lines. Everything was suspicious, and each step was painful. Fifty meters could have been 500. Ten seconds was a lifetime.

We drew closer and closer to the government center until we finally entered its serpentine, a maze of concrete barriers erected to prevent vehicles from driving through at a high rate of speed. Once through the serpentine, we stayed on the exterior side of the compound's defensive barriers. The squad was exposed only on the right flank. I scanned the city blocks of rubble that made up the area north of the government center.

My left foot touched the ground. It made contact with a small metallic object that instantly gave in to my weight. I was certain I had stepped on a pressure-plate IED, and I glued my foot to the ground. I turned around to see what Albin was doing behind me. He was scanning the same rubble I had been looking at and didn't see that I had halted. Hoping that no one was looking, I jumped off the potential bomb. With all of my gear, I didn't go very far. To add to the embarrassing experience, the inertia of my body armor and its weight carried me forward. I subsequently stumbled into the soft, wet dirt.

Lying in the mud, I thought, At least there wasn't an explosion . . .

I quickly got up and heard a few chuckles from Albin. "What the hell was that?" he quietly asked, catching up to me.

"Fear," I said. I was always amazed by my own reactions to battlefield paranoia. Every infantryman fights his own personal battle against the fog of war, the unknown. Clearly, I didn't always win.

Eakin was shaking me. I opened my eyes, realizing I had fallen asleep against the white concrete wall. It was the morning of Christmas Eve, and I was in an abandoned Iraqi apartment building. I stood halfway up, still wearing my flak jacket and Kevlar helmet, M4 rifle slung across my chest. Every muscle in my body ached. They had been stuck under the weight of my gear for almost fifteen hours. My butt was frozen, having been exposed to the bare tile floor. There was no warm eggnog. No midnight mass to look forward to. Only Eakin, showing off the picture he had just taken of me waking up. He'd had the audacity to take the photo with my camera.

I threw a piece of gum into my mouth and collected myself. My breath was visible as I slowly chewed the rock-hard stick of sugar. Captain Smith's radio operator, Corporal Robert Craig, was monitoring the radio next to a kerosene heater ten feet away. I headed toward the warmth, moving through a cluster of Marines sleeping under large hajji blankets. "Where did we get this stuff, Craig?" I asked in a hushed tone, referring to the blankets and the kerosene heater.

"One of the squads went out on a comfort patrol and found an Iraqi willing to sell it all," he said, speaking through a balaclava. Condensation formed around his lips. I wondered how much truth was in the statement. Had the man wanted to sell it or did we force him?

The previous night, Rage Company had executed a relief in place with Comanche. In doing so, we had assumed their mission: secure, by observation or other means, the new COP's construction site. The platoon of Marines I was with was exhausted. After occupying the building, they had spent the evening moving a few thousand sandbags and pieces of ballistic glass into the apartment complex. We were building a temporary COP until the new one was finished. Everyone knew the project would consume weeks; construction hadn't even begun.

A map of the Qatana was taped to the wall behind Corporal Craig. I moved closer to it and noticed something written along the bottom: WELCOME TO THE ICE PALACE. I smiled, thinking of how fitting the name was. This tiny room on the third floor was Rage Company's new COC. The headquarters element was colocated with Rage 3, which manned the Ice Palace's six fighting positions. Rage 2 took over Rage 4's position at building 17, and Rage 1 set up a defensive position in the five-story apartment building 200 meters away at the northeast corner of Thornton and Pope streets.

Headquarters and Rage 3's initial position was a large apartment building on the southern side of the Give Me–Racetrack intersection. Walking toward the building the night before, I had noticed that the larger mined structures along Racetrack were more open and dominated the skyline. Captain Smith had seen the same thing. After seizing it, we did a thorough analysis of our ability to fight from the structure.

Rage 6 decided to pick a new location. He moved Rage 3 south to Thornton and assumed a position inside another large apartment complex with a better layout to defend. The new structure overlooked the construction site, and 1/6 gave us permission to switch positions. From the Thornton-Racetrack intersection, it was the third structure west, on the north side. Its new name was the Ice Palace.

Across from the Ice Palace, in a walled compound that stretched all the way to Racetrack, was a team of Navy SEALs. The special forces sailors were attached to Rage Company for the mission, a direct result of Captain Smith's repeated requests to get them in on the action in Qatana. The frogmen also brought a lot to the table: they had their own unmanned aircraft, usually a Predator drone, which was more sophisticated than the Wasp UAV we employed. In addition, the SEALs used large-caliber sniper rifles and more complex radios capable of reaching a broader range of frequencies. The fundamental difference between Rage

Company and the SEALs, however, had nothing to do with their large budget, which provided them with all of these aforementioned toys. It had to do with the ROE and was the factor that contributed to regular units', such as 1/6's, desire to avoid the highly skilled instruments of war.

Navy SEALs were not subject to the standard ROE.

They could shoot whomever they wanted, whenever they wanted. This reasoning was based on their highly intensive selection and training process, as well as on the amount of money spent on each man to get him to such a proficient state. In a sense, the military was looking for a return on its investment, by removing the standard government over-sight. You could refer to it as the Pentagon's version of laissez-faire.

This inherently uncontrollable nature of the frogmen and their spec-ops brethren was to blame for 1/6's previous decision not to allow them inside Qatana. No matter what the SEALs did, they would answer to a separate chain of command. The leadership of 1/6 had no authority to punish or take corrective action against them. It was a situation that most military leaders, and middle management, had nightmares about: a subordinate who could tell you no and get away with it. I was about to experience such a scenario firsthand.

I stared at the map with Lieutenant Jahelka, listening to Captain Smith's plan for the evening. My fingers were freezing inside their thin Nomex gloves. I could barely take notes. Our conversation was inter-rupted by five or six muffled gunshots. I didn't recognize the weapon at first, but Captain Smith, being the former spec-ops type, instantly identified the sound as a suppressed rifle. Only the SEALs had suppressed weapons.

Rage 6 turned around, snatching the radio handset from Corporal Craig. He waited a few moments for the SEALs to report what was going on. They never did. Our commander broke the silence. "Frogman 6, this is Rage 6, what is the nature of your contact, over," asked Captain Smith. There was still no answer, only another short burst of suppressed rifle fire. "Frogman 6, Rage 6, what are you shooting at, over." Captain Smith was getting annoyed now, frustrated that he was being ignored by the same guys he had vouched for.

Finally, someone responded. "Rage 6, this is Frogman, we are engaging Iraqis, over," said the voice. The Marines in the room let out a few short laughs. Captain Smith gave the handset back to Craig, saying, "They wonder why no one wants to work with them."

The SEALs made no attempt to explain their actions, let alone build our situational awareness about the threat perceived from their position. An hour passed. Then a hail of suppressed rifle fire erupted for about ten seconds. Captain Smith immediately reported the incident to 1/6 before getting word from the SEALs as to the nature of the contact. After speaking with the SEALs, we learned that they were opening fire on a group of Iraqis coming too close to their position. We relayed the vague statement to battalion, who in turn asked whether the SEALs had taken fire or observed hostile intent (meaning that the Iraqis were armed). Battalion also asked for a battle damage assessment (BDA).

The SEALs' answer to both questions was no, and there was no BDA.

I immediately understood the attitude of 1/6's operations officer during the brief for Hue City. Engaging unarmed Iraqis because they were close to your position did not fall within the standard ROE. The Marines of Rage Company would have been investigated for such an incident.

Thirty minutes later, Tarheel 3, 1/6's operations officer, was on the battalion net. He was furious and directed his ire at Rage 6. "Rage 6, Tarheel 3, there is a teenage boy at Ramadi General Hospital with a GSW [gunshot wound] to the abdomen. He claims he was shot by coalition forces near the intersection of Pope and Manson. The boy was wearing a red sweater with blue jeans. My understanding is you had no BDA for your previous engagement. Is that accurate, over," he said. Captain Smith told Tarheel 3 to stand by. He asked the same question of Frogman 6 over the company net. The SEAL's reply was maybe.

The answer served as an accelerant to the fire burning within Tarheel 3. His anger spewed over the net toward Rage 6. I thought he was being unprofessional.

While the SEALs may not have been the most talkative bunch on the radio, I knew they were not randomly targeting civilians, as Tarheel seemed to suggest. These men were veterans of the Papa 10. They invented the use of small-kill teams. In one twenty-four-hour period, a SEAL sniper team had killed more than twenty insurgents.

The SEALs' story wasn't all success, however. Over time, the enemy brutally adapted to their methods. The frogmen watched eleven-year-olds innocently walk up to their position, only to throw hand grenades at them. Children scouted their locations. Few Americans bore the brunt of the fighting in Ramadi as they had. If they were shooting, there was a reason. According to the ROE, they didn't have to explain themselves to 1/6, so they didn't.

Throughout the day of Christmas Eve, the Marines manned their fighting positions. None of the platoons ventured outside. Although the Ice Palace was not shot at, Rage 1 and Rage 2 both took numerous rounds of small-arms fire over the course of the day. The insurgents were testing the Marines' positions, trying to figure out what terrain was covered by them. If the insurgents were successful at mapping out our sectors of fire, they would undoubtedly devise a plan capable of engaging us without facing an immediate response. With this knowledge, they could easily overwhelm our static positions. If they did so, it would force us to occupy the roof to engage them, bringing us out from behind our ballistic glass. It was the same concept as the flashlight trick from the Lima 2.

I spent most of the day observing the city with the Vector 21b from each fighting position. On the fourth floor and in the late afternoon, I spotted a group of three middle-aged men smoking. The trio stood near the intersection of Playground and the no-name alley that connected it to Farm Road. After I watched them for a few moments, a pattern began to develop. Two of the men blatantly stared at the Ice Palace, while the third, with his back to me, turned his head every few seconds. My instincts told me the group was up to no good. I seriously considered shooting at them. The thought never developed into action. Since they didn't have weapons, I would have been violating the ROE. I pointed them out to the Marine manning the .50cal machine gun and headed down to the COC on the third floor.

A few hours after dark, Gunny Bishop brought a convoy to the intersection of Thornton and Racetrack. The primary purpose was to bring more sandbags, but he also had a few heated vats of chow. The warm chicken fingers, French fries, egg rolls, and bland noodles were good for morale. We were all thinking about how quiet the day had been, and I was sure it wasn't luck. Everyone knew the insurgents had their own Christmas gift for us.

From the enemy's point of view, attacking us on such a holiday was a necessity. They had to remind the locals who was in control. The easiest way to do so was with the sound of gunfire and explosions. Without an effective information network, the rumor on the street was the only source of news. Insurgents could spin it however they wanted.

Sometimes they didn't have to.

The day after the Heidbreder ambush, an insurgent blogger posted the details of their small victory online. Without any sort of local media, this version of the event was the only option for the citizens. I was first enraged when I read the translation of the article. Those were the early days; every incident elicited an emotional response.

Once I convinced myself I had made the right decision in not taking Holloway's squad out of COP Grant, I put the blogger in context. It was nothing more than the Ramadi news cycle, which the insurgents updated almost daily. It was also a reminder that the enemy understood how to win in Ramadi: control the population.

The temperature dropped. After finishing the dinner of assorted finger foods, I hit the rack. Eakin, Bustamante, and I all huddled under the same blanket. I slept with my flak jacket wrapped around me. Before falling asleep, I thought about the MEU commander's speech a few days earlier. I found it amusing that he'd told us that MNF-West was issuing a directive to essentially not fight on Christmas. Yet here we were, sleeping on the floor of an abandoned building in the heart of the insurgency's capital. To the insurgent, there was nothing more provocative.

That night I pulled a four-hour radio watch, staring at my time-piece as Christmas officially arrived. The only excitement was listening to the brigade's engineers trying to level the ground for the new COP. Apparently they had found some large-caliber mortar rounds while bulldozing half a dozen buildings. It made for some good radio traffic.

When I switched out with Lieutenant Jahelka, Corporal Matthew Conley's 2nd squad relieved the SEALs across the street. The frogmen then moved to a position at the intersection of Farm Road and the no-name street the VBIED factory was on. It was an attempt to counter the insurgents' previous day of reconnaissance. The Ice Palace's north-east flank had a lone .50cal machine gun covering it, and the insurgents would have certainly noticed this basic fact. If the enemy, the trio of men I had spotted, figured out the weapon's dead space, they would be able to mass their firepower on the lone position.

We wanted to put them back at square one. With a quick study of the map, Rage 6 determined that denying the insurgents movement along Farm Road took away their easiest insertion route on the exposed flank. The only question after that was deciding who would take up a position in the area.

When Captain Smith presented the SEALs with the mission, they jumped at the opportunity. It would allow them to operate independently but still under the protection of the .50cal machine gun. The frogmen also had the assets to succeed on their own.

I went back to sleep thinking about Christmas. I dreamed about one gift: the one the insurgents were going to give me when the sun came up. Waking the next morning was the same cold routine as the previous day's experience. With about twenty minutes to sunrise, everyone was getting ready for the big day.

Albin put the Wasp's antenna on the roof, and Eakin helped run the cable to the video screen in our small COC. After everything was hooked up, we turned it on to make sure it was operational. The three of us huddled over the tiny screen. I made a joke about how the morning had a Christmas feel to it, setting up the new piece of gear and all. Albin reminded me that it wasn't new; he had to carry the extra thirty pounds of antenna, cable, and batteries out here.

Disappointed with his lack of holiday spirit, I grabbed my camera and took a short video of our Christmas morning. One day, I chided him, his family would want to know what he did for Christmas 2006.

Walking around the third floor and videotaping, I realized that the street below us was flooded. I knew it had rained a little overnight, but there were literally five inches of standing water surrounding the Ice Palace. I came to find out that the engineers who had been working on the new COP ruptured the city's water main after I went to bed. The entire Give Me–Racetrack intersection was underwater, exacerbating the usual small puddles that were the by-product of the slightest drizzle.

At around 1000, 1/6 flew the Wasp out to our position. Albin took control of the aircraft when it came within range of our antenna. As it drew closer, the buzzing of the UAV's motor was audible from inside the Ice Palace. It sounded like a lawn mower hovering overhead. I wondered whether the sound would keep the insurgents indoors for the day. I already knew the answer: not a chance.

I was surprised by the clarity of the picture on the Wasp's video screen. During training, I had experimented with other UAVs, but they were generally useless. Nothing on their small screens was discernable. The Wasp was different. With the well-placed antenna, we received a clear top-down view of Ramadi from a couple hundred feet up. I watched Albin fly a circular pattern around each platoon. The streets were generally empty, except for a large group of children playing soccer about 500 meters to the south of the Ice Palace. The fact that I could differentiate between child, teenager, and adult on the screen was a capability unique to the Wasp.

With the Wasp running low on battery, Albin flew it back to Hurricane Point. The sound of the flying lawn mower was gone. In retrospect, it was the signal for the enemy to occupy their assault positions.

Rage 2 was hit first, taking sporadic sniper fire from the abandoned COP's location. Rage 2 responded with medium machine gun fire from a 240G. Its 7.62mm rounds raked the northern second-floor windows, ripping through the dark green sandbags the insurgents hid behind. The same sandbags Comanche had placed in the white structure days earlier.

For the insurgents, this northwestern side of the building was the most protected. Even the Abrams tank, less than 50 meters away, could not directly engage that portion of the structure. The tank could see only the south- and eastern-facing walls. At that moment, I knew the insurgents had successfully mapped our fighting positions.

From the Ice Palace, only one fighting position covered the COP. The position had no crew-served weapon, only a Marine with an M16. We had placed our crew-serves where we thought we were most vulnerable, on the east and west flanks. We assumed that the Abrams outside the abandoned COP was more than an equivalent of a crew-serve. Now the enemy was exploiting our assumption.

A loud blast ripped through the Ice Palace. The Marine manning the post that overlooked the abandoned COP was thrown backward, nearly falling down the stairs he stood above. I ran out of the COC and to his position. I looked out his small window to see dirty brown smoke billowing 20 meters away. An RPG had detonated on the exterior wall of the small building north of us. The angle of the impact had blown the debris into the wall of the Ice Palace. The RPG shot came from our direct north: the abandoned COP.

Rage 6 got on the radio next. "Warlord, this is Rage 6, we just took an RPG shot from the abandoned COP. Can you ID the—" His transmission was interrupted by Lieutenant Thomas, who shouted, "Break, break, break! Rage 6, this is Rage 2, we just took another sniper shot from the COP. Requesting tank main gun, over."

Moments later, Tarheel approved Rage 2 to use the tank's 120mm cannon.

Bustamante videotaped from the Ice Palace.

Warlord fired from 15 meters away, directly into the second floor of the building. Dust and debris blew out of the open windows. The concussion shook Bustamante's camera. There was one problem. The tank was firing from the southern side, and its blasts were not impacting the northern corner where Rage 2 was taking fire from.

Another sniper shot hit the side of Rage 2's building. It was followed by a few shots at Rage 1. At some point, the Wasp showed up again. The arrival of the flying lawn mower temporarily ended the chaos that was developing. Captain Smith, Lieutenant Jahelka, and I all huddled around Albin and the small video screen he held. With three officers watching, he flew the UAV around each platoon, starting with Rage 1.

As he progressed, our frustration built; there were no insurgents running through the streets on the video feed. The enemy, knowing the UAV was overhead, was going to wait it out. They understood the concept of battery life, and they patiently waited. During the UAV's flight, we saw a few suspicious vehicles, nothing more. Again, Albin flew the Wasp back to Hurricane Point.

Everyone was tense. Rage 2 took another sniper shot from the same position in the abandoned COP. We responded with a tank main gun round. With our attention focused to the north, Corporal Conley's squad across the street was tested next.

Three teenage boys walked down an east-west alley toward Conley's compound. On the roof was Lance Corporal Ezekiel Aranez, who painfully watched the boys casually walk closer to his position. Two of the young men held hands.

The previous day, in the same alley, was where the SEALs had shot the teenager for walking toward them in such a manner. Now, in accordance with ROE, Aranez watched. It wasn't the first time teenagers had walked toward him that day, but it would be the last.

The boys walked so close to Aranez that the exterior wall on the roof blocked his view of them. The three had come to the intersection with the north-south alley that bordered Conley's compound and ran north to the Ice Palace. Aranez knew that the alley was covered by a fighting position in the Ice Palace. He didn't know the Marine there was not at the ready. His weapon was leaning against the wall next to him.

This simple mistake allowed two of the teenagers to remove hand grenades from their pockets without consequence.

The Marine at the Ice Palace reached for his weapon.

Aranez saw only the first grenade. It sailed over the roof's exterior wall and bounced off his chest, landing at his feet. Merry Christmas, Aranez.

The second grenade hit the top of the wall and fell back toward the trio of Iraqis, who were now 50 meters down the east-west alley and out of sight of the Ice Palace's fighting position.

The Marine at the Ice Palace watched the grenade in the street explode. As it did, Aranez desperately dove for cover. For whatever reason, the grenade that had hit him in the chest did not detonate. Lying on the dusty concrete roof, Aranez stared at the circular object he had thought was going to kill him. Instead he was alive, spared by luck or some higher power. Merry Christmas, Aranez.

In the Ice Palace, those of us in the COC were putting together what had just happened. After the grenade throws, the insurgents had backed off, or so I thought. What they were really doing was waiting. They thought they had just caused a casualty at Conley's compound. Now they were waiting for the convoy to come pick up the injured Marine. Surely, they planned to ambush us as soon as we exposed ourselves to take the casualty to the Medevac vehicle. They finally figured out that no one was hurt when the convoy never came.

The insurgents began to harass Rage 1 and Rage 2 with more small-arms fire. Rage 2 fired another tank main gun round into the abandoned COP. Again the Wasp flew overhead, and a lull in the shooting developed. We circled over Rage 1 and the Ice Palace first. There was civilian activity, or what appeared to be, to our south. All of the civilians were males. They seemed to wander aimlessly. I figured they were following the directions written on the walls we had seen during Hue City II.

A little farther south, and in the same spot as the previous day, was a group of two dozen kids playing soccer. We watched them for a few moments. A black vehicle pulled into the middle of the group. Three adult males wearing mostly black got out of the car. The kids stopped playing soccer and stood motionless, looking at the men. A conversation that we obviously could not hear was taking place. After a few moments, the men got back into the car and drove away. With the children dispersing, Albin followed the black car's progress with the Wasp.

I looked at Captain Smith; he, too, was watching the screen. What had the men told the children? Stop playing soccer; there is going to be an attack? Were they recruiting fighters or a suicide bomber? Something was going on, but we were almost powerless to stop it. Captain Smith turned away, probably to update his platoon commanders. He never got to the point where he actually made a transmission on the radio.

I continued to watch the screen. The black car crossed over Racetrack, heading east, 150 meters north of checkpoint 296. It made a left at the intersection where I had spotted the three men smoking fewer than twenty-four hours earlier.

That's when I saw it.

A man in black pajamas with an RPG on his shoulder sprinted across the street. "RPG! RPG!" I shouted, telling Albin to take a picture; it was a unique capability of the Wasp. He took the picture but wasn't quick enough to catch the guy going across the street. Rage 6 got on the net and asked battalion whether they had seen the man sprint across the street on their monitor. They had not.

We stared at the map. The RPG gunner was only 400 meters from our position. As we stared at the map, a blast smacked the wall above us. My first thought was that the RPG had taken out the .50cal position.

"Holy shit! Holy shit!" a Marine above was screaming. I sprinted up the stairs. At the top I froze, not in horror but in sheer amazement. An RPG had not hit the building; a sniper round had. The large-caliber bullet had smacked directly into the ballistic glass that Lance Corporal Cooke, who manned the .50cal and was the source of the screaming, sat behind. Inches from his face was the spiderwebbed glass containing fragments of the bullet. The shot was perfectly aligned with his head. I must have been in a similar state to Eakin's only a few days earlier because Lieutenant Jahelka sprinted past me to reach his shocked Marine.

The lieutenant leaned beside the now-useless glass; another round would have gone straight through it. "Man that fucking .50cal, Cooke!" Jahelka was taking control. He scanned the distant horizon, lining up the angle of the bullet's impact with the only two-story structure dead ahead of the position. It was only about 200 meters away. He analyzed the building through his rifle combat optic. "Movement! Second floor!" shouted the platoon commander. Cooke sighted in on the position, awaiting the word to open fire.

"PID! Give him a burst!" Jahelka had spotted the weapon the insurgent was using, and the thundering recoil of the large-caliber machine gun rocked the Ice Palace.

I skipped down the stairs and back into the COC. Albin had the Wasp hovering over the black car. It was parked outside the front door of the home Cooke was now blasting with the .50cal machine gun. Captain Smith got on the radio and requested a guided multiple launch rocket (GMLR).

GMLRs were the most accurate weapon in our inventory. The flying telephone pole carried a significant punch, and the enemy never saw it coming. The weapon could be fired from more than 300 kilometers away and still maintain a high degree of accuracy, the degree of which is obviously classified. An observer didn't simply request for a GMLR to be used; he specified which part of the building he wanted to destroy. It was the power of pinpoint target location. Observers refer to it as a mensurated grid (three-dimensional target location).

Being an artilleryman, I had made it my purpose in life to observe the use of this weapon. It would be a unique experience for me; my unit was transitioning from cannon to rocket artillery on its return to Camp Pendleton. It would be *sweet* if I could say I spotted for one in combat. To ensure that I got my wish, I repeatedly rambled off the capabilities of the GMLR to Captain Smith.

The weapon system sold itself. It was more accurate and all-weather, and it had a quicker time to impact than air. On average, it took slightly more than twenty minutes from the time that contact with the enemy was initiated to the impact of an aerially delivered munition. If the GMLR's use was approved, the building would have been gone in five minutes or less. The best part was that you could be standing 100 meters from the impact and walk away without a scratch. The top-down angle of attack blew all of the structure's debris straight up into the air and usually left the building standing while completely destroying its interior.

The bandits of 1-37 had a video of a GMLR striking a large structure on Broadway outside COP Falcon. An insurgent who had been on the roof at the time could be seen falling back down to earth moments after the dust cloud cleared. To great fanfare, the video was widely circulated among the population of Camp Ramadi. With such a natural PR campaign, this accurate form of rocket artillery was the precision guided munition of choice for the coalition. I knew Captain Smith was sold.

Unfortunately, the battalion's response to our request was no. They denied it because we weren't taking continuous fire from the insurgents. I thought it was a foolish rationale; how do you define continuous fire when you are engaging snipers? The insurgents were clearly used to 1/6's not-so-aggressive tactics. We had been taking sniper fire all day, but it wasn't continuous enough to rate the GMLR. If Cooke had been killed by that sniper's bullet, we would have leveled the building. Because he was still alive, however, we would allow the enemy to escape.

We fired another burst from the .50cal into the structure. With the black car still sitting outside, the Wasp left for Hurricane Point. When the UAV came back, the car was gone.

Later in the afternoon, a single shot was fired from Rage 1's position. Lieutenant Shearburn's voice came over the radio and stated that Corporal Dustin Anderson had just scored Rage Company's first confirmed enemy killed in action (KIA). The platoon commander reported that the insurgent had attempted to sprint out of the four- or five-story building that Rage 1 had received fire from earlier in the day. An alert Corporal Anderson shot him only a few steps outside the door.

With most of the Marines in the room smiling or cursing the recently deceased hajji, Captain Smith asked Lieutenant Shearburn whether the man was armed. The cheering stopped as we waited for Shearburn's answer: no. Captain Smith ordered his lieutenant to take out a squad when it was dark and search the body.

As soon as the cover of darkness set in, Rage 1 went out to search the body of our first confirmed kill. The Marines maintained observation of the deceased man until the end of the day, in order to ensure the body was not booby-trapped. It took them less than five minutes to make it to the fallen man. Seconds later, they confirmed that he was an insurgent.

"Rage 6, this is Rage 1 Actual, confirm KIA as enemy. Two grenades on his person; recommend we BIP, over," said Lieutenant Shearburn.

Inside a small metal container that the twenty-something Iraqi had been carrying were two hand grenades. Captain Smith approved the request to blow the items in place (BIP). Staff Sergeant Eagle detonated the fragmentary devices, and Rage 1 headed back to their position.

I was ready to zone out and reflect on past festive Christmas holidays. All day the enemy had desperately tried to cause a casualty, without success. I noticed Captain Smith staring at the map, debating our next move. The day wasn't over yet. Rage 1 came over the net. Lieutenant Shearburn was requesting to execute a raid south into the region they had been taking fire from during the day.

Captain Smith liked the idea. With the insurgents recovering from the day's activities, we would go on the offense. Rage 1 proposed to take two of his squads and raid the structures in the vicinity of the Pope-Zazu intersection. They would also search the large commercial buildings they had taken fire from closer to their location.

It was a dangerous raid. None of the roads in the objective area had been cleared by Pathfinder. There was no way to know whether any of the buildings had been mined. Shearburn would not be deterred, however. There was one concept the officers of Rage Company all agreed with: the best defense was a good offense.

Rage 1 stepped off on the raid. Within moments of arriving at Pope and Zazu, they discovered a network of fighting positions on the roofs of the area's abandoned buildings. The exterior walls all had spider holes broken into their sides, each of which was oriented toward Rage 1 or the Ice Palace. Most of the fighting positions still had empty 7.62 shell casings around them, evidence of their use during the day.

The most interesting part of Shearburn's find was the connectivity between the fortified structures. Holes had been knocked out of the structures' adjoining walls. The same style of two-by-fours that we had found on my first patrol littered the roofs of the buildings. None of the homes were occupied. Either the insurgents had kicked everyone out, or the occupants had left long ago.

Rage 1 began to demolish the fighting positions. For hours into the night, the Marines used sledgehammers, plastic explosives, and incendiary grenades to dismantle the network. When Shearburn ran out of C4, he conveniently found an insurgent stash of plastic explosives to continue his demolition with. It was a successful raid.

The next day saw almost no enemy activity. Whether it was the raid executed by Rage 1 or the insurgents simply taking some time off did not matter. We were regaining the initiative, and that night we looked to keep it that way.

Captain Smith studied the map all afternoon. He had already ruled out heading south that night, fearing defensive IEDs laid by the insurgents to prevent another successful expedition. Rage 6 decided that going south was too predictable, so he looked to the north. The intersection of Annapolis and Farm Road contained half a dozen target buildings within 200 meters. I informed him that 1/6 had never actioned any of the targets. Americans hadn't been in the area in half a year.

We debated the purpose and the risks of the mission. There had to be a defensive belt of IEDs in the area; Pathfinder had never cleared the roads before. It became the one precondition for the operation. Pathfinder had to clear our insertion route to the target homes. Captain Smith got on the net and made the request to Tarheel. They put us on standby while they relayed the request to brigade.

Waiting in the Ice Palace, Captain Smith hashed out the details with Rage 2 and Rage 3. Rage 2 would take two squads, while Rage 3 brought one into the raid. We used the intersection to deconflict the targets. Rage 3 would hit the targets west, and Rage 2 got the east. Captain Smith was also taking out the headquarters element. He wanted to establish the forward COC in building 11, Golf 6. The three-story house overlooked the Annapolis-Farm intersection and appeared to be a commanding structure on the map.

Tarheel came back with their answer: yes. Pathfinder was going to break off its planned route and begin to clear our designated streets within thirty minutes. We prepared our gear.

I did not smoke with Holloway or James Thomas before the mission.

On the first floor of the Ice Palace, the Marines of Sergeant Ahlquist's squad waited for the word to step off. The floor was completely open and empty. The lone object of mention was a wall of sandbags with a Marine standing behind it. He covered the Ice Palace's only entrance.

We left the Ice Palace in silence. The sound of boots sloshing through three inches of water was the only noise we made. I scanned the alleyways around Conley's compound as we went past. There was a sense of determination in my mind that I had not felt before. Maybe it was a reaction to being shot at all day on Christmas. Regardless of the reason, Christmas's feeling of defenselessness was gone, replaced by the adrenaline of action. The damp cold attacking my wet legs was of no consequence. Unlike previous nights, there was no fear of death, no anxiety of hidden enemies, only an acute sense of awareness.

This inner voice directed my rifle from window to window and down every alley. I walked past houses but saw fighting positions. A young boy stood in the front doorway to a house 50 meters away. I sighted in on the target. I had become engrossed in my environment and was having an emotionally withdrawn response. I welcomed its calming effect.

The squad turned north onto Racetrack. We followed the familiar street to Give Me and passed the stationary tank on the corner. Its roaring engine was a reminder of the vehicle's awesome power. Captain Smith informed Rage 2 of our location. The intersection was the release point for Rage 2, meaning that they would now step off from building 17 en route to the objective area.

Less than 30 meters up Give Me, we turned off onto a small alley that led to the five-way intersection of Annapolis and Farm. The alley was flanked by six-foot walls on either side. The Marines' silhouettes quietly followed behind them in the moonlight.

The first team halted at the end of the alleyway. Ahlquist moved up and assessed the intersection. I leaned against the six-foot wall, letting it hold the weight of my body armor for a few moments. My back was to the target house, the one that would become our forward COC. Ahlquist spoke to his first team leader. With the nod of the leader's head, the first team sprinted out and breached the gate 20 meters to the left. The rest of the squad followed. Headquarters brought up the rear.

The front door of the house opened to a small living area. Two elegant bookshelves stood in the far left corner. I headed straight back toward the barely visible staircase at the far side of the house. I quickly moved through the kitchen and another living area. The four Marines from the first team stacked at the bottom of the stairs and began to move up. I fell in behind them and helped clear the top two floors. Once they were cleared, the five of us took up positions on the roof, looking down into the intersection we had just moved through.

I sat down behind the roof's wall and pulled the Vector 21b out of its tan carrying case. I quickly attached the NVG mount and began to scan the windows and the buildings on the opposite side of the intersection.

No movement.

A large house on the opposite corner was perfectly oriented over the worn traffic circle below me. A single streetlight was lit on the northern side where Farm and Annapolis met. The light revealed the far half of the intersection, precisely where Rage 2 was headed. I remembered how 1-37 had taken out all of the lights at the far sides of intersections they had crossed.

I thought about shooting the bulb, but before I did, the first squad from Rage 2 showed up. Firing at the bulb now would have caused massive confusion, so I decided against it. The first fire team began to move out into the intersection. The Marine next to me sighted in on the far house with his SAW, anticipating where the enemy might be. I did a quick scan of the far side with the Vector again: nothing. I then scanned down on Rage 2; the first team was now in the dim light given off by the small bulb.

I recognized Lieutenant Thomas as he walked behind his first team. Next was his radio operator (RO); the small antenna was barely visible outside of his assault pack. The enemy was waiting for this sign of command and control. No sooner had the antenna appeared than we heard a shrieking blast.

I instantly dropped down behind the wall. The blast was right next to the radio operator. I had to force myself to look back up over the wall, fearing the worst. "Shoot the fucking light!" I shouted to the rifleman next to me. He and a Marine down below took the shot before I finished my sentence. One of them hit it.

I started to scan the far houses, looking for any movement. It was pointless; the still dissipating smoke rendered the Vector useless. I couldn't see through to the other side. Instead, I turned my attention to directly beneath me. The nature of the chaos below made it clear that someone was injured.

Two small successive blasts ripped into the darkness. The sudden light washed out my NVGs. I ducked back down behind the wall. In the moment that I paused, my fear returned. I had just watched my college roommate get blown up. It wasn't the fear of my own death that brought me out of my confused state; it was the fear of his. In the second that I leaned against that wall, I thought about our uncommon friendship. I remembered that I had convinced him to request this unit. Now I thought he was gone. What would I tell his mom and dad? Sorry I didn't shoot out that lightbulb? Anger overcame me. I was no longer emotionally withdrawn.

I popped back up over the wall. Smoke still lingered twenty feet away. I could hear Corporal Davila and Lieutenant Trotter shouting orders. Then James Thomas sprinted through the intersection, heading toward the building I was in. I thought I might be seeing things. The sound of his voice shouting into his PRR confirmed that he was real. I headed down into the house, praying that my indecision regarding the light-bulb hadn't killed his RO.

I stopped on the second floor, where Captain Smith was. Knowing James, I could imagine only one thing going through his mind; update Rage 6 on Rage 2's status. I was right. He sprinted past every Marine in the house, shouting at each one, "Where's Rage 6?" He kept asking, unable to hear each Marine's response. The lieutenant's ears were still ringing from the blast.

He went up the stairs and spotted Rage 6. He took a knee. "Sir, remote-control IED blast fifteen meters from my RO and me. Only casualty is my RO. He took a small pellet to the foot." James's speech was interrupted by three or four quick, shallow breaths, his pale skin whiter than usual. "We got lucky, sir; they put the IED in a storm drain. The blast went straight up into the air."

The two men started to coordinate the evacuation of the casualty. I headed back to the roof.

One of Rage 2's squads evacuated Lance Corporal Charles Norris, the wounded RO. Sergeant Ahlquist began his search of the two target houses he was supposed to hit. Eventually, Rage 2 hit their four targets as well. Nothing of note was found. When the squads finished prosecuting their targets, we headed back to the Ice Palace. The next day we conducted a relief in place with Comanche.

Rage Company headed back to COP Firecracker.

Inside the comfort of the COP's COC, we did a quick debrief of the battle of Christmas with the staff. While we reviewed the last few days' events, I noticed some army captains hanging out in the Marine base. I hadn't seen them before and wondered what their purpose was.

Tired after the debrief, I walked upstairs. Mud was caked along each step. The smell of soft, wet dirt emanated from the concrete slabs. When I got to the third floor, I was taken aback. Two dozen soldiers were sprawled out in our common area at the top of the stairs. These guys were obviously the reason that two captains were hanging out in the COC.

I was curious as to who they were. I spotted Albin talking to a few of them in the far right corner. We made eye contact, and I motioned for him to follow me. I went into the staff room and sat down on my cot. Albin came through the doorway seconds later.

"Who are those soldiers out there?" I asked.

He said they were the Brigade Reconnaissance Team and were like snipers or something. Apparently, one of their sergeants first class told Albin they had been sent here because we couldn't handle it.

I laughed at the foolishness of the soldier's comment, adding, "I hope they are as good as they claim to be."

The next day everyone would find out they weren't.

8

A Dysfunctional Family

December 29, 2006

I sat by myself carefully buttering a slice of white bread. An open, clear plastic bottle of water was on the table in front of me, its blue cap resting on my left thumb. Eating alone was my punishment for sleeping in. The other officers had already eaten breakfast, but I didn't mind the time to myself. That night the few days of rest we'd had at COP Firecracker was coming to an end. The mission was another relief in place with Comanche, the same purpose as our previous time out. Hopefully, we would come back relatively unscathed, as on our last trip.

I took a bite of the bread and tasted hand sanitizer rather than the small amount of butter. My solitude was interrupted by Lance Corporal Eakin. He sat down across from me. "Sir, did you see the BRT guys leave?" he asked.

I didn't know what he was talking about. Eakin informed me that all of the counter-sniper soldiers had walked out of the COP with a full combat load about ten minutes ago. I didn't know what to think. Were they going to occupy a position in broad daylight?

I got up from the table and headed toward the stairwell. Going down, I saw Apache 6 walking in the hallway; he was yelling at his watch officer while heading toward the COC. "Who gave them permission to leave?" he shouted. The lieutenant met his commander within earshot of the stairs. I listened to their conversation.

"Tell them to get the hell back here!" said Apache 6.

"We can't, sir; we think they forgot to get the new crypto before they left," replied the lieutenant. Crypto was the material that encoded our radio's hop set, or the specific set of frequencies that the radios hopped along. It is what prevents the enemy from seeing what frequencies you are using. Standard procedures were to change the crypto weekly and whenever a radio was lost.

A Marine poked his head out of the COC farther down the hall and said, "We got 'em, sir; the battalion radio still had the old crypto on it." He headed back into the room when he finished speaking. The lieutenant and Apache 6 hustled into the COC behind him. I stayed outside the door, keeping out of the annoyed 1/6 Marines' way.

Listening to their conversations, I heard that the BRT soldiers had taken a KIA. It was a gunshot wound to the head. Only a few minutes after they had set up in an abandoned building, an insurgent sniper inflicted the casualty. It was a poor showing for the soldiers. They didn't have a single piece of ballistic glass. No sandbags to hide behind. The result wasn't a surprise. It was the same rookie mistake we had made with the Heidbreder ambush, moving out in the light of day without a specific purpose. This time, though, the result was the death of an American.

I thought about Albin's previous conversation with one of their senior enlisted soldiers. The BRT considered themselves "counter-snipers," yet they walked to their position along Racetrack in the middle of the day. They didn't have a single thing to protect themselves when they got to their positions. There wasn't even a radio check before they left, let alone permission to move out.

The young soldiers were in over their heads, and it cost an American his life. After sustaining the casualty, they ran back to COP Firecracker, carrying the lifeless body.

I was surprised the insurgents had let them. The enemy I had encountered in Qatana was always ready to hit you when you were most vulnerable. For a moment I wondered whether the insurgents felt pity for the naive soldiers and allowed them to run away. I knew this couldn't be true, however; al Qaeda was renowned for its brutality, and I was simply accustomed to the insurgents' ability to exploit every situation. It was the first time I saw the enemy incapable of inflicting maximum damage.

The soldiers returned to the COP. I watched them fall in on their cots. None of them spoke. It was a sobering moment, the same sense of loss I had felt after the Heidbreder ambush. Only this time I wasn't as attached to the men who had suffered the setback.

Their two captains came up the stairs. The group had a short discussion. At the end, they packed up their gear and left. The brigade was pulling them out. At least, that's what their captains said. I figured 1/6 had told the brigade they didn't want them. I assumed that if they had done it to the SEALs, they wouldn't hesitate to do it to the BRT.

With the soldiers of the BRT leaving the COP, the Marines of Rage Company packed their gear for their next stint in Qatana. Before we left the company staff, Rage 6 in particular became obsessed with the theme song to the movie *Team America: World Police*. It was a catchy tune, and the chorus of "America, fuck yeah!" took the place of "Good morning" and "Good afternoon" as we passed one another in the dank hallways of COP Firecracker. False motivation was high; morale was low.

The company staged in the stairwell, as it usually did when it got dark. Rage 2 left first for building 17, followed by Rage 1, which headed to their position at the corner of Thornton and Pope. The platoons were occupying the same positions as on Christmas Day. Ten minutes after Rage 1 left, the headquarters element and Rage 3 headed for the Ice Palace.

Progressing north and east down Racetrack, our column formation was properly dispersed on either side of the road. We moved at a slow walk, trying to observe our surroundings. When we began to pass Fire Station Road, a platoon of Comanche Marines turned the corner, heading north. Rage 1 must have finished the turnover with the 1/6 Marines, who were now on their way back to COP Firecracker.

The unusual aspect of the group was their method of movement. The Marines were running in a single column with maybe forty inches between each man. All of their PEQ-2 lasers were shining into the ground at their feet, which was also the general orientation of their heads.

The sight of thirty Marines running back to chest, oblivious to their surroundings, caught me off guard. One IED, RPG, or machine gun burst could have inflicted multiple casualties in a matter of seconds. It was one of the worst tactical methods I had seen. Their platoon commander should have been fired; it looked like he was leading a collection of schoolgirls, rather than the world's most efficient infantrymen.

Our column moved onward and arrived at the Racetrack–Give Me intersection. A large convoy of engineers and heavy equipment vehicles was parked in the street. Ten- to fifteen-foot-tall concrete barriers surrounded the future COP Qatana. The concrete perimeter was almost complete, and inside the confines of the wall the ground was leveled. A few containers that looked like something off the back of a tractor-trailer were stacked randomly in the muddy dirt. COP Qatana was starting to resemble a defensible position.

The formation moved past the busy engineers and eventually to the intersection with Thornton. We turned onto the side street, splashing through the small remnants of the flood that had engulfed the area around Christmas. After entering the Ice Palace, I headed straight to the third floor and our COC. The room was almost exactly as we had left it: barren. I dropped my assault pack on the hard, cold floor and checked on each fighting position with Lieutenant Jahelka. Comanche 6 left after doing his turnover with Rage 6. We were back in Qatana, and I was not excited.

The next morning, downtown Ramadi awoke to the sounds of a sporadic firefight. Half a mile to our south, the Marines of 1/6 who protected the provincial government center were busy. The standard insurgent sniper fire was harassing their static positions. Although the Marines had not sustained any casualties, we heard over the radio that their request for a GMLR was approved. Less than a week earlier and during the fighting on Christmas Day, our request in a similar situation had been denied; now an organic 1/6 unit was in the same predicament and being approved.

I moved to a south-facing window with Albin and Eakin to observe the impact. The targeted building had five or six floors and was on the intersection of Fire Station and Michigan. We were about 600 meters away. In the moments preceding the explosion, there was no audible gunfire. I wondered how Tarheel had defined "continuous fire" in this specific instance. I was still dwelling on the fact that they had been approved for the use of a GMLR when we had not.

The small group of Marines huddled around the same ballistic glass window that had failed to protect Lance Corporal Aranez when two grenades were thrown at his position. Instead of the frustration of that past moment, we smiled and giggled like kids at a summer movie.

Seconds later the rocket struck. A cloud of dark smoke and debris shot straight up in the air, almost forming a mushroom cloud. The impressive sight was followed by an intense concussion that shook the Ice Palace.

A couple of Marines cheered. Albin turned to me and said, "America, fuck yeah!" I smiled and finished the tune's chorus with him, but in my mind his words brought about a moment of reservation. It wasn't until I witnessed this example of American firepower that I began to think about our purpose. Had we brought anything more than destruction and chaos to this city? This was a huge building that we had just obliterated in one moment. I knew the structure was abandoned—elements of Rage Company had cleared it during Hue City II—but hundreds of people called that home a few years ago.

It was my forty-eighth day in Ramadi, and I had never even considered how the locals viewed me, an American. This wasn't out of ignorance but because I convinced myself that such a thought would force me to second-guess myself in moments when decisiveness was required. Now I was looking out at a city America had destroyed. I realized that when the war was over, no one would remember the lone sniper who was in that building. They would remember that America had destroyed their home. Ramadi was a public relations nightmare.

Watching the debris from the GMLR's explosion fall back down to earth, I forced those thoughts from my mind. I harshly told myself that the self-preservation of my fellow Americans was worth more than some Iraqis' home. After all, this was a war.

I'm not sure I bought into my own rationale.

I looked out at the horizon of ruined buildings. The sun was still rising. I tried to find a place in the Ice Palace where I could sit in its warmth. It was a futile effort, so I ended up sharing a blanket with our interpreter, Marlo. Not long after I finally started to warm up under the heavy cotton material, insurgents began to fire at Rage 1's position 200 meters away. It was the same four-story building that Rage 1 had consistently taken fire from during our last stay in Qatana.

After a few exchanges, the firing ceased. A welcome calm overtook our area of Qatana. Albin pulled out his bayonet. The Marine began to inscribe "America" into the white concrete wall of the COC. Captain Smith was listening to the radio and singing the verses he could remember from Team America's theme song. When Albin finished scratching out "America," he continued underneath with "fuck yeah!" Once he was finally done, he turned around and started to sing in unison with Captain Smith. I nodded in approval from underneath a red blanket. False motivation was better than no motivation.

Our session of boredom was quickly ended. Three large explosions shook the ground. Rage 2 came over the net and reported that three large-caliber mortar rounds had impacted around their position. I was surprised when the explosions were not followed up with any small-arms rounds. I wondered why the enemy wouldn't use the potentially devastating indirect-fire asset in conjunction with direct-fire weapons. It seemed like a waste of three good mortar rounds. There were no casualties.

About an hour later, Rage 2 was engaged with a few shots of sniper fire. Instead of the shots coming from the abandoned COP site, they were fired from the south. The building the insurgents were using was located almost directly between the structures that Rage 2 and Rage 1 occupied. The enemy was trying to get us to fire at one another. The shooting ended without consequence.

The day's fighting was over.

We didn't plan any large raids that night, but Rage 2 did send out Corporal Davila's squad on an SKT mission two blocks north of building 17. During the day, we spotted a large number of locals congregating on that street and figured we would have a surprise for them that night if they tried to maneuver on building 17.

At the Ice Palace, Captain Smith decided to shift the headquarters element to Rage 2's position at building 17. During our previous days at COP Firecracker, Lieutenant Thomas had bragged about the comfort and warmth of his abandoned five-story Iraqi apartment complex that was pockmarked with the scars of war. The Marines of his platoon told stories of a basement full of every different type of soda imaginable, and most returned to COP Firecracker with two-liter bottles of RC cola and Pepsi.

Whether Captain Smith was tired of constantly being cold and wanted to check out this mythical place or simply wanted to let Lieutenant Jahelka run his platoon without his presence did not matter. I was leaving the Ice Palace for a location where two fireplaces roared heat into the air and the Marines wore dresses, sipping on sugar water while they fought. Of course, this was based on speculation, but soon I would see for myself.

We packed up our gear, including the Wasp UAV, and staged on the first floor. On top of my assault pack was a rolled red hajji blanket that drooped down so far, it almost touched the ground. Just about all of the headquarters Marines carried their own blankets, concerned that building 17 wouldn't have any for us when we got there.

Before we left, Tarheel requested Rage 6 on the net and asked him to link up with Comanche 6 near the Racetrack–Give Me intersection. Comanche's commander wanted to scope out the position we had initially seized during our first stay in Qatana. He was concerned that the building would look directly into his future COP and was considering using it as an observation post to deny its use to the enemy.

Rage 6 accepted the task. We left the Ice Palace moments later and headed the 300 meters to the building. Standing along Racetrack with the moon shining down made me realize how vulnerable we were. There wasn't the usual squad of infantrymen for security, only headquarters. Two of the seven Marines carried large radios and stared aimlessly at the ground. Albin had the thirty-pound UAV in his pack and wasn't very mobile. Bustamante carried a camera, a tripod, and other public affairs–type equipment, and Captain Smith was on the radio trying to get Comanche on the net.

The only person besides Albin and me who was capable of providing security was the interpreter, Marlo. What I knew and he didn't was that his AK-47 was loaded with fake 7.62mm bullets. Instead of firing a projectile at the enemy when he pulled the trigger, his gun was designed so that the bullets would melt the weapon's barrel, rendering it useless.

We really did trust our Iraqi counterparts.

I always wondered how many interpreters had tried to kill their American friends to get us to resort to such betrayal. I thought about telling Marlo, then and there, that he might as well throw stones at the insurgents. I figured it would be better than his trying to do something heroic, only to discover what we had done.

Directly across the street were the VBIED factory and the home of the three brothers we had raided a week before. There were no American positions in that direction now, and the insurgents were most likely observing our progress on the new COP. I wondered whether they would attack us.

A few hundred meters down Racetrack was the Abd-al Sala'am mosque, where Mullah Qahttan preached. It was the same place where a meeting between a Zarqawi lieutenant and a 1920s Revolutionary Brigade leader in December 2005 had resulted in a bitter street battle between the two insurgent groups. Now I stood in that same street with five Americans and an Iraqi. Much had changed since 2005.

The noises of the engineers building COP Qatana calmed my mind. The cacophony drowned out my thoughts of our surroundings.

The few anxious moments passed, and Comanche showed up. Captain Smith discussed his thoughts on the building with his fellow company commander, while we congregated in a small group around the two men. There were now twenty Marines in the area that we had previously occupied. I had anticipated feeling more secure when Comanche arrived, but I was only more paranoid. The group of Marines broke noise and light discipline, shouting to one another and shining their Surefire incandescent lamps at random objects. A few of them smoked.

Where did these guys think they were? Recruits at boot camp were more capable than this group of Marines. I scolded Eakin for taking a puff on someone's cigarette. The corrective action was really intended to get Captain Smith's attention. It worked; he heard my voice and looked around. Seeing the mess of stationary men, he directed me to get the group ready to go. I was relieved.

I was ready to die for my country, but I didn't intend for it to happen because of another's stupidity.

We headed toward the working engineers, and Comanche went the opposite direction, doing their own reconnaissance of the area surrounding the future COP.

When we made it through the Racetrack–Give Me intersection, I turned around to see that Captain Smith had halted the formation ten feet behind me. I turned back to the front and got Albin's attention to halt. Jogging back to Rage 6, I figured out why we were stopped. One body was missing. Marlo had walked off with Comanche or was lost. I kicked myself, knowing that it was my responsibility to ensure that everyone was aware of what was going on. When I had told Marlo to get ready to move, he probably didn't realize we were headed in a different direction than the other Marines. So when people started to move, he went with them. I felt horrible; not only did Marlo have fake bullets, but I had left him behind.

In seconds, Captain Smith confirmed with Comanche that our interpreter was with them. We kneeled next to the Ministry of Oil building, waiting for a team of Comanche Marines to bring Marlo back to us.

Down the street I spotted a Marine from Rage 2, waiting for us at the intersection of Fire Station and Racetrack. I walked the 150 meters over to him and recognized that it was Corporal Bradford.

"What's up, sir? You guys waiting for something to happen?" he asked.

"No, I lost the interpreter," I replied. "It will be a few minutes." Bradford smiled and informed the rest of Rage 2 about the delay via his PRR. Eventually, Marlo made it back to our small group, and we headed to building 17.

I followed Bradford north on Fire Station. He went in a straight line to a massive three-floor building on the left. It was a strong defensive position, isolated by streets on all sides. The open space limited the enemy's ability to close on the building. Lieutenant Thomas met us at the only entrance, a narrow stairwell that could barely fit a large man. At the top of the stairs a Marine was posted in a plastic lawn chair: the gatekeeper. Once inside the building, you were on the second-floor balcony, over-looking a central courtyard.

Below, I could hear a couple of Marines rummaging through what I thought was trash. Then I heard what they were talking about, "Dude, where is that hajji stuff in the green bottles?" said one of the men.

"I don't know; just grab one of these Pepsis, man. I didn't bring my flashlight, and it's creepy as fuck down here in the dark," replied the other.

I looked at James Thomas. "It's true?!" I asked in astonishment.

He smiled at me and said, "Would I lie to you?"

We headed up the next staircase, only a few yards from the first, and went to the third floor. On the eastern side of the building, Lieutenant Thomas had set up his own COC. I followed him and Captain Smith into the small room.

Unexpected heat blasted me in the face as I went in. The room was filled with smoke and a thick aroma of kerosene. On the far wall was a duct-taped map of Qatana. Two chairs and a couple of sleeping bags were arranged around a centrally located kerosene heater. A few radios lined the wall facing the courtyard, their antennas reaching up through a cracked window that provided visibility of the inner portions of the building. Staff Sergeant Tyson Hall, Rage 2's platoon sergeant, sat next to the map on his sleeping bag. A hajji cigarette was lit in his hand. The professional Marine stood and greeted the group as we entered.

Lieutenant Thomas quickly briefed Captain Smith on Davila's SKT patrol and the defenses of the position. Outside the structure was a maze of trip-flares and other hastily emplaced early-warning devices. Each of the four corners of the building had a machine gun position, two on the third floor and two on the second. A five-foot retaining wall surrounded the roof, providing substantial cover for Marines to assist the static positions in responding to an insurgent attack.

After the orientation by Lieutenant Thomas, Captain Smith dropped his pack on the floor, declaring, "I know where I am crashing tonight." His radio operator set up the battalion net in the room, and the headquarters element was officially stationary.

I went down to the second floor to check out my new sleeping arrangement. Sergeant Peter Kastner, Rage 2's third squad leader, had set up a room directly under the COC with small mats and a few blankets. When I arrived, Albin and Eakin had already stocked the small space with a dozen bottles of Pepsi products. There were enough blankets for me not to care that there was no kerosene heater.

Before I went to bed, I walked across the hallway to go to the bathroom. The standard hole in the floor was overflowing with urine. A staunch smell of piss emanated from the tile floor. It was complemented by the scent of shit. Behind me was a black garbage bag filled to the top with Wag-Bags. Sergeant Kastner heard me commenting on the situation from his sleeping bag. "Use the empty soda bottle against the wall, sir!" he shouted to me. I found the Pepsi bottle he was referring to and made my deposit. I went to sleep dreaming about the revolutionary invention of indoor plumbing.

I woke the next morning to the sun shining down on my face. Our window was perfectly positioned for a natural wake-up call. I headed up to the COC and made sure nothing significant had happened during my period of rest. Captain Smith was in a zombielike state. I could tell he hadn't slept at all in the few hours I was out. I went back downstairs to get the Vector and my bandolier of ammunition. I wanted to check out each fighting position and get a general idea of where the insurgents had consistently been engaging Rage 2 from.

On my way down to the room, I heard a ruckus coming from one of the apartments on the far side of the second floor. I headed over to check out the commotion. When I opened the door, I was in shock. The apartment was fully furnished, and Marines were everywhere. They were lying on a couch and two stacked mattresses. One was prancing around in a ladies' nightgown. In the kitchen Corporal Davila was cooking eggs on a stove. My jaw was hanging down to my knees.

Davila turned and saw me in the doorway. I pointed at his crossdressing Marine. "Don't mind him, sir; he's good for morale!" stated the squad leader. I walked toward Davila, who offered me some scrambled eggs. I turned him down; there was no way I could impose on such a rare commodity.

Hearing my refusal, one of the Marines spoke to me over the ruckus in the living room. "Sir, we already had some and we're about to go on post; live it up!" he said.

Again, I refused. Davila explained to me that during the previous night's SKT, he had paid the Iraqi whose home they were in for a large quantity of eggs. Now they were celebrating life before manning their posts.

I took a seat on the couch and watched the tomfoolery. After a few moments I couldn't hold it in any longer. "You know, Rage 3 is freezing their asses off five hundred meters from here while you all have a fairy prancing around your furnished apartment, stuffing your faces with scrambled eggs," I scolded.

The Marines quickly responded to my jealousy with their greatest asset—sarcasm. "Those poor bastards!" said one. Another was more direct and asked, "Don't you wish you were in Rage 2, sir?" I laughed at the group. Then I ate some of the best scrambled eggs ever made.

When I was done, I headed back to the room and prepared to go to each fighting position. Before I headed out, I went to our pleasant bathroom to fill my own Wag-Bag. Eggs go through me quickly. I shut the wooden door behind me, isolating myself in the stench. Halfway through my unpleasant experience, Eakin walked in. He caught a glimpse of his lieutenant I am sure he will never forget. Squatting and holding the green bag up to my freezing ass, I asked him if I could help him with something. He quickly left the room.

Minutes later, I headed to the first fighting position. It was on the second floor and was the south-facing window that insurgents had shot at the day before. I could make out the building that Rage 1 was in on the left side of the horizon. Corporal Davila was at the position, checking on his Marines. He gave me a quick rundown on the structure used by the hajjis. It was about 350 meters away and had three visible floors. The first floor was not visible, blocked by the sprawl of single-level structures surrounding it.

The top floor was similar to the top of the Ice Palace. It was a small, roughly five-hundred-square-foot room that opened up to the roof. Through the Vector, it looked like a plywood table, and sandbags were set up inside the large picture window that stared at us.

The insurgent sniper position was plainly visible.

Davila walked away to go check on the rest of his Marines. He hadn't made it out of the room when I shouted at him, "Davila, get on the 240!" referring to the unmanned machine gun on my right. I had scanned down one floor and was staring into the first window from the left. A black garbage bag that had been covering the window was now blowing from a slight breeze. Behind the garbage bag was the side profile of an Iraqi's black hair, dark skin, and black shirt. He was staring out of another window, in the direction of Rage 1 and the Ice Palace. A rifle leaned against the wall next to him.

For the first time I was staring at my enemy. Blood rushed through my body, pumping a heightened sense of awareness to my extremities. I turned back to see Davila stationary a few feet from me. "Serious?" he asked.

"Unless you want him to get away!" I responded. The veteran Marine quickly manned the 240G medium machine gun. I shouted in an authoritative tone, almost as if bullets were already flying, "The same building you just briefed me on! Second floor from the top, first window in on the left; fire when ready!"

A burst of machine gun fire ripped toward the building. The Iraqi immediately ducked out of view. "One meter down! One meter down!" I corrected Davila's tight burst based off the tracer round. I directed another three or four bursts at the window and gave him the command to cease fire. I continued to scan the building's windows, waiting for the Iraqi to poke his head out. I turned around to see a group of Marines videotaping. I gave one of the Marines the Vector and instructed him to maintain observation on the building. Then I went to find Lieutenant Thomas.

I met him on the balcony. I started to recount what had happened, but he cut me short. One of the Marines who had been manning the position before I got there had already explained it to him.

"I am going to put a rocket into that sniper position on the roof," he said.

I nodded in agreement. "I doubt that we hit him with the machine gun," I said. "He ducked for cover after the initial burst. He's probably watching us from behind the sandbags up there." Even if the insurgent wasn't on the top floor, destroying the visible firing platform was worthy of the rocket itself. The enemy was clearly using the building.

A groggy Captain Smith showed up moments later. He had just fallen asleep before we opened fire, and now I was keeping him up.

I brought him over to the position and explained the situation to him. He subsequently approved Lieutenant Thomas's plan to hit the position with a shoulder-fired rocket. It was going to be a tough shot, right about the max effective range of a SMAW. Corporal Bradford was up for the task, though. He quickly readied his team.

The 240G and a squad of Marines on the roof opened fire on the building, suppressing any would-be insurgents while Bradford lined up his shot.

I watched from the same position that I had directed Davila's fire from. As Davila had been before him, the Marine manning the 240G was incredibly accurate with his fire. The impacts of his rounds raked the window he aimed at. A small flash of light came from the target. I figured it was an M203 grenade exploding, but it was followed by another smaller flash and a loud smack in the side of our building.

Was the insurgent shooting back?

The intensity of our rifle fire picked up. Bradford fired the rocket. The round fell significantly short of the target, hitting the roof of a single-level structure between our opposing fighting positions. A flock of pigeons flew through the cloud of white smoke given off by the explosion.

There was another flash from the target.

I watched our exchange of gunfire in amazement. The deafening sounds and sight of our overwhelming rifle fire led me to shout in excitement. The sniper had moved to exactly where I thought he would.

Lieutenant Thomas shouted, "Cease firing!" over the ruckus. The Marines on the roof couldn't hear him, and a tank along Racetrack had identified where we were aiming. The Abrams was now firing its coax machine gun at the west-facing side of the building. I watched some of its rounds impact into a telephone pole. Chunks of wood flew through the air.

We eventually ceased our firing and began to analyze the enemy position. The sandbags and the sniper platform remained. Without the impact of the rocket, we had done nothing but sling thousands of rounds at the enemy. "Bradford, get another rocket ready," Lieutenant Thomas said over the PRR.

"I got it this time, sir. I underestimated the effect of the distance on the rocket's trajectory," replied the Marine.

James Thomas decided that the next rocket shot was worthy of motivational music. From his stereo, the sounds of Ozzy Osbourne's "War Pigs" reverberated throughout the apartment complex.

Captain Smith ordered the tank on Racetrack not to fire unless we requested it. He also limited the number of Marines firing in suppression and did not allow any machine guns to open up unless we took fire. Rage 6 was controlling the chaos that was our previous engagement. This time everyone would cease fire when told to do so.

Lieutenant Thomas began the suppression with a single shot from his rifle. A dozen of his Marines followed suit and began to suppress the target. Bradford took the second SMAW shot. The rocket slammed into the building maybe a foot above the large window. It was almost a direct hit. A cloud of smoke and debris blew out of the room. The dark brown color of the cloud indicated that a large amount of dirt was present, probably from the sandbagged fighting position.

The Marines ceased firing, and we analyzed the target yet again. To my surprise, the wooden firing platform was still standing, exactly as it had been before the rocket. Captain Smith quickly directed another rocket to be fired at the room. The same course of events repeated itself, only this time Bradford put the rocket directly through the window. The shot probably impacted the wooden stand itself. I guess the third time really is a charm.

After the third rocket shot, we went back to our normal state of readiness. To calm the Marines, the music changed from rock to Kelly Clarkson's "Since You Been Gone." I grabbed Albin and Eakin and brought them up onto the roof. I told the two Marines that I wanted to document the first time they ever fired at a living person in anger. The three of us posed for a picture that Sergeant Bustamante took. Hundreds of shell casings littered the ground at our feet.

The rest of the day went by without incident. The insurgents did not fire a single shot at us following the decimation of their firing position. I wondered whether we had disrupted the enemy to the point where his plans for the day were ruined.

After the evening call to prayer, I headed into the COC. Rage 2 Actual and Rage 6 were discussing the night's events. Sergeant Sempert, the assistant squad leader for our detachment of combat engineers, was sitting in the corner. He was about to be tasked with taking down numerous palm trees that prevented clear sectors of fire for a few of the building's machine gun positions. Lieutenant Thomas's main concern was a suicide VBIED attack. He wanted a straight shot along each road that approached the building.

I sat down next to Sempert and asked him how many games of poker he fit in during the day. "Not enough" was his answer. The Marines, myself included, respected the young sergeant. He had proved himself to be a courageous and tactically savvy Marine during the Heidbreder ambush and other firefights. His expertise with explosives was unmatched, except for maybe by that of his boss, Staff Sergeant Eagle.

The best part about Sergeant Sempert: he was addicted to poker. I will say that the Marine had one hell of a poker face. One night I watched him knock Lieutenant Shearburn out of three games in a row. When he lost, however, everyone knew it. You could hear his shouts from Camp Ramadi's coffee shop all the way to tent city during a game. It made for some good times between missions.

While we sat, Tarheel came over the net and informed Rage 6 of an Apache raid in our sector. The Marines from COP Firecracker were going to head north along Fire Station, passing by our position, and hit a cluster of target buildings about 300 meters from us. They were going to step off in twenty minutes.

Lieutenant Thomas and Captain Smith quickly finished their planning and decided to execute a squad-size patrol of the immediate area around building 17. After the Marines from Apache went by our position, Sergeant Sempert and Lieutenant Thomas, with a security detachment, headed out to set up the explosive charges that would knock out the palm trees.

We didn't want to detonate any of the charges until the Marines from Apache were gone, so the squad-size patrol began to search some of the buildings adjacent to us while we waited.

Directly across the street to our south, the Marines entered the first building. It was no more than twenty steps away. In moments, the Marines found a cache of large-caliber mortar rounds. I left building 17 with Sergeant Bustamante in tow to check out the find. By the time I got there, the Marines had laid out all of the rounds in neatly aligned rows. I quickly looked them over. It was a mix of 120mm and 82mm rounds, the standard insurgent calibers. Rage 6 informed Tarheel of the find, and EOD was dispatched to pick up the cache.

After a few minutes and some photos, I headed back to the COC. I stopped in the street and watched as the Marines from Apache went past, moving south along Fire Station. It was the same thing as Comanche: a tightly packed group of men all looking at the ground.

They were almost all out of sight when the last man looked over and saw me watching them. He lifted his rifle and pointed it directly at me.

"Hey, Marine, get out of the street, I almost shot you!" he shouted at me.

I was furious. Did the idiot not know he was walking past a platoon-size friendly position? I didn't exactly look like the enemy in my full-body armor and Kevlar helmet. Not to mention the glowing infrared chem-light in my trouser pocket.

I leaned over and pulled the glowing stick out of my pocket. I shook it vigorously at the 1/6 Marine. I wanted to shout back and contemplated throwing the chem-light at the ignorant bastard. Somehow my professionalism prevailed. I walked back into building 17 and headed up to the COC.

Sergeant Sempert was ready to start blowing up palm trees. I watched from the various fighting positions as the massive trees were cut down by small explosions. It was an entertaining night, counting down to the actual explosion and watching the blasts shake the ground. It wasn't quite as exciting as the party going on in Times Square that evening, but it was a night I wasn't going to forget. It was the first time someone had pointed a loaded rifle at me.

Once the destruction of the palm trees was complete, I met James Thomas in the COC. He dropped his body armor and gear and took a seat on his sleeping bag next to the radio. I gave him my camera so he could watch the videos I had taken of Sempert's work. While he was watching, Corporal Holloway, the acting sergeant of the guard, asked Lieutenant Thomas why he had played Kelly Clarkson during the day's engagement.

I leaned forward in my chair, angling in the general direction of Corporal Holloway. "You mean you have never heard the story of Captain Chontosh and Kelly Clarkson?" I sarcastically asked Holloway. In an attempt to build suspense, I snapped my head back toward Lieutenant Thomas.

"You didn't tell your Marines this story?" I asked a smiling James Thomas before I continued with, "They probably think you actually *like* listening to Kelly Clarkson!"

James took his cue and said, "Okay, here it is. Captain Chontosh"— a highly decorated Marine and a Navy Cross recipient from the initial push—"was my class adviser at IOC [infantry officer course]. He is a Rochester guy like me and Lieutenant Daly, so I like to think he gave me special attention, only I don't mean in a good way.

"So my group of lieutenants is sitting around listening to me give an operations order in the crushing heat of the Mojave Desert on an August day. Chontosh, with a look of disgust, is evaluating me." James paused for a second, spitting out a massive wad of dip.

"I get into the Fire Support Plan, talking about my time line for tank, air, and artillery fires. I didn't get very far. Chontosh jumps up and rips into me hard-core. Once he's satisfied that he made his point and that everyone understands how fucking stupid I am, he looks at us all and says, 'Combined arms and Kelly Clarkson.' Everybody is lost, clueless to the connection. Chontosh then goes off on a tangent about the capabilities of combined-arms assets: tanks, Cobra gunships, artillery, mortars. You name it, he was saying what it could do.

"Then he says, 'Since you been gone,' three times real quick, punching his fist into his hand each time. He follows it up with 'Tank main gun! Mark-19! J-DAM!' using the same mannerisms; punching his fist into his hand. The guy is shouting at us now. Screaming about how combined arms is contagious like Kelly Clarkson's songs and that the rhythm of her music is like the pulse of combat. He even says that the structure of a song is similar to the four phases of combat. The lyrics are the unknown; anything can happen during your movement from the line of departure to phase line one. You can get ambushed, take a casualty, get lost, whatever. But the chorus is the constant. You always know what to do at phase line one because it is preplanned, just like the chorus is repetitive. Once actions for that phase line are complete, it's back to the lyrics during the movement to phase line two. Then he orders us to drop our blouses, and we follow him on a deathly quick four-mile run. He PT'd us into the dirt. Only then did we execute the live-fire exercise."

Another dramatic pause, then he concluded with, "That's why we listen to Kelly Clarkson."

The group of Marines continued to joke into the early-morning hours. Even though I had heard that story a million times before, I went to sleep that night thinking about the pulse of combat.

For whatever reason, I was genuinely excited during that day's engagement. I didn't only surprise my enemy, but I also watched thousands of bullets fly through the air at him. The sensory overload made me another person. Maybe it was the fact that I knew exactly where the insurgent was, as well as who was shooting and why. Whatever the reason, my mind was no longer in fear of the intense nature of battle as it had been during Lima 2. Instead it was focused, trying to anticipate the flow of events. I decided that it was this mental state that Chontosh had described as the pulse of combat.

The following day was uneventful. Not a single shot was fired in anger. In response to the lull, each platoon, except Rage 3, which would act as a reserve, planned to execute its own raids in the surrounding areas. Rage 1 was going to head south into the vicinity of the fortified network of fighting positions they had discovered during our last stay. Rage 2 decided to clear the structures between building 17 and the abandoned COP, which the insurgents had turned into their own position.

Rage 2 stepped off first. Lieutenant Thomas led the patrol with Corporal Davila's squad. I sat in the COC with Captain Smith and monitored their progress. The first few buildings were empty, but twenty minutes into the patrol James Thomas came over the net and said, "Rage COC, this is Rage 2 Actual; we are going to need EOD. There's two large cylindrical containers with wires running to them on the second floor of building 4, patrol sector Golf 4. We also found mortar rounds in rice bags on the first floor. In the courtyard there are a few circular targets drawn on the exterior wall with corresponding bullet holes. Next to the targets is a visual depiction of how to shoot down helicopters. Marlo is trying to translate the script around the drawings right now, over," said Lieutenant Thomas.

I was intrigued by his find and went straight to the map. Finally, it dawned on me that Qatana wasn't simply the capital of the Islamic State of Iraq; it was an urban training facility for its fighters.

Not even 200 meters to the south, on the other side of Racetrack, was the rifle range and the large cache we had discovered during Hue City I. Farther south, directions dictating a safe path through Qatana's streets were drawn on the walls, allowing new and most likely foreign (Iraqis refer to out-of-towners as "foreign") fighters to maneuver around our positions. Even the IED that struck Lieutenant Thomas's radio operator was within 300 meters of the site, the Arabic script on the wall above it warning the locals of its presence. I wondered how many American lives would have been saved if we all spoke the same language as our enemies and could read the graffiti in front of our faces.

Lieutenant Thomas began to head back with the patrol. He was trying to find the easiest route for EOD to make it to the building.

About halfway back, he halted the unit. A round container was partially buried underneath a pile of rocks. It rested against the side of the building they had just been inside. The platoon commander called up Sergeant Sempert and sent him to investigate the device.

"LT! Back 'em up! Back the fuck up!" shouted Sempert. Lieutenant Thomas quickly did as the sergeant commanded, staring at the flustered Marine, who was cutting every wire running in the direction of the rock pile. Sempert grabbed a copper wire and tugged on it. The opposite end revealed itself, connected to the cylindrical tank atop the pile. Later, the combat engineer would explain that he was almost on top of the device when he spotted what appeared to be mortar rounds beneath the rocks.

The quick-acting Sempert had disarmed the IED. It was a good thing he did. There weren't only mortar rounds underneath the rocks, but the cylindrical tank was also stuffed with a hundred pounds of explosives. If an insurgent had set off the IED with the squad on top of it, the result would have been devastating. We made another request for EOD to come to our position.

When EOD arrived an hour later, Captain Smith released Rage 1 for their raid. Rage 6, who had probably slept only five hours in the last three days, succumbed to his drowsiness soon afterward. I decided to let him sleep and monitored Rage 1's progress with Lieutenant Thomas.

Rage 1 Actual, Lieutenant Shearburn, brought two squads out on the raid. First he scoured the network of fighting positions his men had largely destroyed a week earlier and found them in the same pathetic state as they had left them. Along the no-name street paralleling Dobber to the north, however, they found an Impala car, the back of which was reconfigured as a sniper's firing position. It was also on the same street where they had found the graffiti outlining the safe passage through Qatana.

Lieutenant Shearburn requested to destroy the car. I approved and looked over to Captain Smith to get his permission. Rage 6 was out. I thought about waking him but ultimately decided against it. I found it hard to fathom that he would disagree with the decision. I told Lieutenant Thomas to give Shearburn the green light to destroy the car. I didn't bother to tell Tarheel.

The Marines of Rage 1 dropped an incendiary grenade through the Impala's engine block. The resulting inferno lit up southern Qatana, and Shearburn quickly led his men back to their position.

An angry voice spewed out over the battalion net. "Rage 6, this is Tarheel 3!" said the battalion operations officer. I responded in Rage 6's absence.

"I'm looking at our UAV feed, and it looks like there is a huge fire in your sector. Did your patrol start that fire?" he asked.

I responded with an affirmative and gave him the specifics of the scenario. What I didn't ask him was why there was a Predator UAV flying over our positions without our knowledge. There was a litany of enemy fighting positions that we could have used the UAV to observe and recon before our raids left the safety of their defensive positions. Instead, our Marines left before its arrival and therefore increased the risk involved in the operation. I felt as if 1/6 was using the asset to spy on us, rather than to increase our combat efficiency.

"Rage FO, I want to speak to Rage 6. The car just exploded! This is unacceptable!" Tarheel 3 was on a tirade. I leaned over and apologized to a sleeping Captain Smith. Then I woke him up.

Rage 6 rolled his eyes after Lieutenant Thomas and I briefed him on the firestorm he was about to endure. He grabbed the radio hand-set and got on the net. Then Tarheel 3 berated our commander so that the entire battalion could hear. When he was done, Captain Smith got hold of Lieutenant Shearburn and yelled at him over the company net.

The entire time I awkwardly sat in my chair, wondering why so many people were upset that we had destroyed an insurgent vehicle. Rage Company was quickly becoming a dysfunctional family.

The following day was as uneventful as the previous had been. That night, though, our last full evening in Qatana, was different. It was one of my most unsettling experiences to date.

In the middle of a four-hour watch, I sat listening to the radio. Eakin was dozing off in the corner, but for whatever reason I was having no problems staying awake. Earlier in the shift, I had heard over the net that Weapons Company, 1/6 was going to run a route clearance mission along Michigan, between checkpoints 295 and 296. It was nothing out of the ordinary. Pathfinder had already cleared the route after dark, and the battalion usually executed similar missions every few days. The intent was to ensure that IEDs were not hastily emplaced after Pathfinder came through.

It started when I heard Weapons give Tarheel a radio check, stating that they had made it to checkpoint 295. I recognized the voice of the company commander as my executive officer from the Basic School (TBS). I considered him the best of my instructors.

Five minutes later his voice came over the net again. "Tarheel, this is Warrior; we have two MAMs lying in the reeds on the northwest side of the Michigan–Fire Station intersection. They have what appears to be a wire running from them to an object in the middle of the road. Request permission to engage, over," said the captain.

My former TBS instructor's request told me everything I needed to know about 1/6, Tarheel. They were the dysfunctional family.

There was no reason to ask for permission to shoot two insurgents. Maybe on your first day out or during your first firefight, somebody might say something like that, but these Marines had been here for five months. Everybody knew that the area around the IED was deserted. Every building in the surrounding blocks was incredibly scarred by the war, and the men were lying directly in front of the building that 1/6 had hit with the GMLR only days earlier. The only things that lived there were IEDs.

This wasn't the captain's first deployment, either. His question was a result of the command climate. Rage 6, Captain Smith, didn't really care whether Tarheel 3 berated him on the net; the guy didn't write his fitness report and therefore couldn't affect his career.

For the organic 1/6 units, however, Tarheel was the man. The battalion staff approved their awards and coordinated their chow, ammo, and mail. They assigned the companies their sectors, missions, and collateral duties. Basically, the Marines of 1/6 owed their daily existence to their battalion staff. In a bureaucratic sense, it was logical that the captain would ask for permission to shoot; he had probably heard the conversation between Rage 6 and Tarheel 3 the previous night and wanted to avoid such an event. It couldn't cause any harm letting the battalion know before you opened fire, could it?

Yes, it could. The other side of this coin is the guy behind the desk on the other end of the radio. He isn't sitting in an M1114 with the engine running. He doesn't see two guys lying in a small puddle between four-foot-high weeds. He doesn't realize how obvious the wire running to the plainly visible IED is. By asking him permission, the captain, my former instructor, was forcing the desk jockey, Tarheel 3, to second-guess his judgment. Tarheel 3 had no choice! The Marine on the scene was asking for his opinion.

It was a horrible opinion.

"Warrior 6, this is Tarheel 3; have one of your Marines fire an M203 illumination round over the two men in order to confirm they are in fact hostile, over," said the operations officer.

Warrior 6 responded with "Roger."

I sat in my chair, dumbfounded. I must have said something out loud because Eakin immediately woke up. "What is it, sir?" he asked me.

I didn't say anything.

An explosion shook Qatana. It wasn't very big, but then again it didn't have to be. In order to fire the illumination round, a Marine had to get out of his vehicle. In relation to the blast of an IED, he might as well have been naked. I continued to listen to the radio. Weapons Company was requesting that a recovery vehicle come tow the M1114 humvee that was damaged in the blast.

I handed the radio handset to Eakin. I couldn't bear to listen to any more stupidity. It was the final significant event in Qatana. In a few short days, Rage Company was back at Camp Ramadi.

January 9, 2007

Captain Smith was furious. He stormed into the southern entrance of the headquarters tent and barked at the XO to get all of the lieutenants into the room. Rage 6 then kicked out all of the junior Marines in the tent. With the XO gone, I grabbed my small camp stool and took a seat next to Captain Smith. A stack of photographs was in his hand.

Rage 6 handed me the photographs and didn't say a word. I began to peruse the PowerPoint display of digital pictures. The first was of Albin's carving in the Ice Palace. "America, fuck yeah!" was imprinted on the white wall. "Found by Comanche in building 76" was written next to arrows that pointed to the carving. I continued to flip through the pages in disbelief. Drawing after drawing of stick figures and stupid caricatures were painting a picture of a company out of control. Then I got to the end. The photograph, from building 17, showed a life-size mural depicting what could only be explained as pornographic material. The artist was clearly talented, but the graphic scene he drew did not do his abilities justice.

I handed the photographs back to Captain Smith. The other lieutenants arrived and sat across from us. Lieutenant Shearburn picked up the stack first and chuckled when he got to the last picture, portraying the porno. This small gesture riled Captain Smith, who fidgeted in his chair, saving his comments until all of the officers had seen the photos. The pile went down the line to Jahelka and Thomas. Then James Thomas passed them back over to Lieutenant Grubb, who had taken a seat next to Shearburn.

Grubb started off the conversation when he saw the last picture. "That was my platoon, sir. I know there is no justification, but I thought battalion was going to destroy building 17 after we left, so I didn't make them cover it," he said.

Captain Smith nodded in acknowledgment of Grubb's remarks. Then he tried to remain calm. "I just got my ass handed to me by the 1/6 battalion commander and the brigade. The worst thing is they were right. I saw Albin drawing his little sketch of the Team America theme song; no big deal. However, what it spiraled into without my knowledge is despicable," said Captain Smith, who began to raise his voice slightly.

"What if CNN or MSNBC had that last picture? What would the headlines say or show? Better yet, what about the insurgents? We all know this is a propaganda war, a war of information. You cannot win that war by showing the Iraqi people cocks, with USA tattooed all over them, sliding under veils! It is a fucking disgrace of this company, the Corps, and, most important, our nation. Frankly, I don't know what to do," continued Captain Smith. He was visibly disappointed.

A momentary silence hung over the group. Shearburn was the first to break it. "Sir, they are just pictures and random drawings. Marines are going to do stuff like that. We can't—"

Captain Smith interrupted him mid-sentence. "Bullshit! You will not tolerate this behavior, and if you do I'll find somebody to take your place," he said, angrily glaring at Rage 1 Actual.

At that moment, Cullen Shearburn gave in to his frustration, which had been building up for weeks. On almost every mission, he had received some sort of verbal "counseling" from Captain Smith. Whether it was for destroying insurgent vehicles without permission or not giving advance warning for controlled detonations, Rage 6's correcting was always about the professional conduct of his platoon. There was a sense, however, that Rage 1 was getting an unfair share of criticism.

Now Shearburn was going to respond. He questioned Captain Smith's integrity, the core of every Marine officer. "Come on, sir; you were laughing with us about that picture earlier today. Remember, when Lieutenant Grubb and I were looking at his computer, you came through the door, we all laughed about that picture on his computer,"

Shearburn continued. Captain Smith's face was covered in bewilderment. I didn't know whom to believe.

"Are you calling me a liar?" asked an infuriated Rage 6. Shearburn responded with about ten words, the gist of which was yes. In Cullen's mind, enough was enough; he wasn't going to let Captain Smith get away with any more hypocrisy.

The two men went back and forth. I couldn't bear to listen to it. Instead I focused on the fact that 1/6 had turned us into a dysfunctional family. Shearburn was our most tactically capable platoon commander. Without question, he led the strongest platoon. Now he was the rebellious firstborn, quarrelling with our incensed father. To say the least, I was concerned.

Like poison, their argument was about to contaminate the company.

After the horrific heated exchange, Captain Smith stood up. "Inform your men that the entire 15th MEU is being extended. The new out-date for Ramadi is 15 February." Then he walked out of the tent, heading to chow with the XO and the senior SNCOs.

Twenty minutes later, I went to chow by myself. Once through the line of soldiers and contractors, I found an isolated spot within earshot of a TV and sat down at the wooden table constructed of plywood and two-by-fours. President Bush was on the screen, announcing to the United States his new strategy for the war in Iraq, the so-called surge. After a few seconds, I ceased to pay attention. The surge in Ramadi had begun long ago. What the president was saying wasn't new to me; it was simply an affirmation of why the MEU was being extended.

I began to focus on my food and hardly noticed when a Marine sat down across the table from me. It was Jason Mann.

"Come on, Daly, I know you have some friends," he said, taking note of the fact I was sitting alone.

"No thanks to your battalion," I responded. We proceeded to engage in small talk for a few minutes, then I asked him if he thought Operation Hue City had achieved any success in AO Tarheel.

"Depends on your definition of success," he replied. "The majority of our fighting, as you know, has shifted to the eastern fringe of the AO. That huge cache you guys found and the establishment of COPs Firecracker and Qatana have relieved the pressure on Sheikh Sattar's tribe. You know who he is, right, the leader of Sahawa al Anbar [SAA] and Thawar Al Anbar [TAA]?"

"Yeah, I've heard of him." I said.

In September, Sheikh Sattar Abdul al-Rishawi, an ex-insurgent sympathizer, declared an Awakening of Anbar's tribes against Al Qaeda in Iraq and vowed to defeat the extremists. Ever since the AQI parade on October 18, his fighters had gone into covert mode. He was conducting an Iraqi-style insurgency against the current Ramadi government, the ISI. One intel report described members of the TAA bursting into a local mosque and executing two dozen members of AQI while they prayed. Their success, however, was limited to two or three of these types of operations, and AQI was holding their own.

"Well," Jason said, "Sattar claims to have captured the leader of AQI in Ramadi, Thamir Hamid Nahar." I remembered the name from Major Mayberry's in-brief.

Jason kept speaking. "I think this is evidence that if Operation Squeeze Play continues to contest AQI neighborhoods, like we have in Qatana, then these TAA guys will be able to move in and hit AQI where they hide. Their knowledge of AQI's structure and leadership is invaluable."

"Well, Jason, Sattar was probably one of them until that firefight between 1920s and AQI a year ago. You really think Sattar would be better for Ramadi than AQI?" I asked.

"Tom, what is your detainee internment rate? Ten percent? And how many locals provide you with information after you barge into their homes? Ten percent? Think about it: Sattar, or men like him, is the answer. He can give us credibility with the locals and neighboring tribes. His spies are actually capable of infiltrating the al Qaeda network and exploiting detainees. Plus, you know he is a winner. The dude has his own TV channel and wears American sunglasses." Jason was looking at his watch and trying to wrap up the conversation.

"Gonna miss the convoy back to Hurricane Point?" I said.

"Yeah, if I don't hurry up. Seriously, though, when it comes to the good of Ramadi, I don't pretend to think that Sattar is the best choice. However, the first thing we need to do is to get these people to stop killing one another. He can do that."

Jason stood and picked up his tray. "Sorry about the rant. Send my best to your brother," he said. Then he trotted for the door. Jason had me convinced; the Awakening was the answer for Ramadi.

It was also the last time I saw Jason Mann. On July 17, 2008, in Afghanistan, the Corps lost one of its best officers. More important, his wife lost her husband; his daughter, her father.

I lost a friend.

PART THREE

1st Battalion, 9th Infantry

9

SILENCE THE DOGS

January 12, 2007

Craig Trotter and I walked along a gravel road in Camp Ramadi's tent city. Double-stacked HESCO barriers surrounded the white tents that had been our home for the last two months. Under a setting sun, we made it to the row of Porta-John toilets along the path. I swung open the door to the closest one, revealing an exhibition of graffiti complemented by ridiculous caricatures.

Most of them were harmless, the usual Chuck Norris joke or something from boot camp. The fresher ink on the cold plastic walls wasn't so mundane, though. The Marines had taken to referring to Captain Smith as "CS," and the Porta-Johns were now their disgruntled sounding boards displaying hateful rhetoric against this acronym.

I exited the makeshift bathroom and kicked at some of the gravel rocks while I waited for Trotter to finish up. "XO, you think Captain Smith knows that he is CS?" I asked, still thinking about the graffiti.

"Daly, he's not an idiot," said Trotter. "He might sound like one sometimes, but he's pretty smart for a guy who majored in forestry science." Then he exited the stall and hesitated.

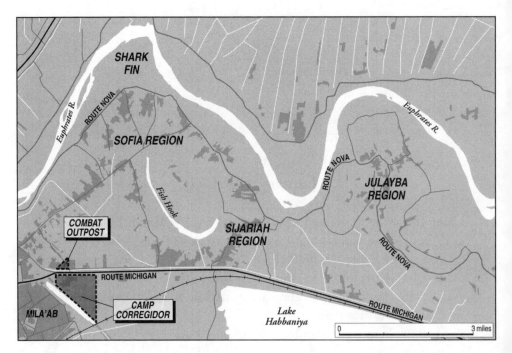

Area of Operations Manchu: 1/9 Infantry's area of operations in eastern Ramadi.

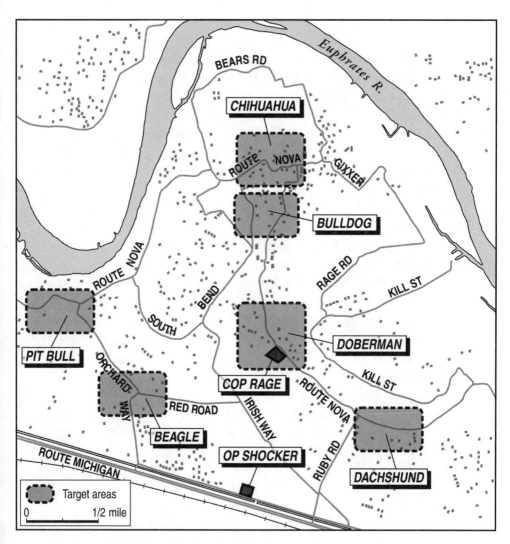

Operation Churubusco: The battalion's target areas during Churubusco.

"These stupid-ass jokes are a reflection on us, the lieutenants, not on him. Too many fuckers venting in front of their Marines." The XO was now in the street, buttoning his trousers.

I nodded in response.

Personally, I understood what was being said in the jokes. Rage Company's deployment had been extended. Morale was low. The Marines were bitter because they would spend another month and a half in Ramadi. Thoughts of reuniting with friends and family were being delayed, replaced with the consideration that luck only lasts so long and eventually bullets find their mark.

The men needed someone to blame, so they turned to the bearer of the bad news. It didn't help that Captain Smith's slow, monotone voice was easily interpreted as arrogant and condescending. The perception from the younger Marines was, however, a false perception. I could easily overlook it.

Professionally, I saw this writing on the wall in the same light that the XO did: as a reflection of Rage Company's leadership. We, the lieutenants, were not doing a good-enough job of ensuring that criticism flowed up the chain of command, rather than down.

"You ready for this?" I asked Trotter.

He was still deep in thought. Such an attitude from the XO was rare. He usually spoke before he thought. "What do you mean?" he asked. "You scared about the convoy through 295 and 296 or moving out to suburbia in Julayba? I hear there are going to be some desperate house-wives out there to meet us."

"Never mind, asshole. But I meant the convoy."

"Come on, Daly, I know you watch that shit," said the XO. "You *are* married. Plus, I have you all figured out. You don't talk unless there is something to say, and you are content with silence. We have more in common than you think."

"Well, if I am so easy to read, what am I thinking right now?" It was a rhetorical question that the XO decided to answer.

"Based on the look you're giving me . . . you think I'm an asshole."

"Right on."

We shared a laugh and walked to our waiting Marines. After running through the usual pre-mission checks, the convoy departed Camp Ramadi.

Three hours later, after waiting for Pathfinder to clear Michigan, our vehicles pulled into Camp Corregidor, safe and sound. Most considered it an uneventful convoy. Nobody was hurt, and we traded only a few hundred rounds of ammo with a group of insurgents around checkpoint 296.

In the dark landscape of Corregidor, headquarters platoon dismounted the trucks and set up shop in a two-story cinder-block building. The north side of the structure became our parking lot. A hundred meters south was 1/9's battalion headquarters. We selected a dusty, empty room for the company's command post. It had one crucial comfort item: a fifty-inch television. The Marines set up their standard-issue green cots and went to bed.

January 13, 2007

Unlike at Camp Ramadi, you had to wear your Kevlar helmet and body armor everywhere you went at Camp Corregidor. The base was constantly being mortared. I had to put on my gear to walk next door to the battalion command post. Between the two structures were three Porta-Johns. They served as the only toilets for a few hundred men and were cleaned every other week. Unfortunately for us, the three stalls actually required cleaning every three or four days. One was overflowing as I went past.

Inside the adjacent building, two dozen soldiers and Marines milled about 1/9 infantry's headquarters. I headed up the dusty stairs to the second floor and went straight into the briefing room. I figured it was better to show up early for the confirmation brief and get a chair, rather than arrive at the last possible moment and stand for three hours. As a lieutenant, I found a spot in the cheap seats, two dozen black solitary chairs. Opposing them were three elongated tables positioned in the shape of a U. On the wall behind the U hung a mural of 1/9's area of operations. The map was so large, you could read the building numbers and the patrol sectors for every structure. The command was taking advantage of their extensive wall space.

Over the next twenty minutes, I watched the representatives of each unit come into the room. The laundry list of characters represented the broad scope of our next mission: Operation Churubusco. There was an Iraqi army battalion commander, a platoon of Navy SEALS, Rage Company, military working dogs, tactical human-intelligence teams, a psychological operations team, Baker and Dog Company 1/9 INF, EOD, and a squad reinforced with infantrymen from 3rd Battalion, 2nd Marines. The room was quickly filled by the leadership of each unit.

The battalion commander for 1/9 INF, Lieutenant Colonel Chuck Ferry, gave the mission brief. He began by allowing each of the unit commanders sitting at the U to introduce himself. Then he started to speak. "Manchus, the shaping phases of Operation Squeeze Play are over. We have one major neighborhood in Ramadi left to clear, the Mila'ab, which is in the process of being barricaded. The insurgents obviously know what is coming. In anticipation of their fleeing from the city, we are going to hit Julayba, an eastern suburb of Ramadi."

The lieutenant colonel paused and allowed the translator to repeat his words for the Iraqis. Then he turned around and began to brief off a PowerPoint presentation: "The Julayba area of greater Ar-Ramadi has become a safe haven and a C2 node for AQ operatives in the Al Anbar Province of Iraq. From this remote rural community, AQ has facilitated, planned, and supplied insurgent operations in neighboring cities and throughout the country. Recent operations, lack of a coalition presence, and the emergence of Thawar Al Anbar have made Julayba the only viable safe haven in the Ramadi-Fallujah corridor for AQ." The colonel spoke very smoothly, and the badges on his shoulder identified his background as an operator, a Ranger.

"Since the AQ attack on the Abu Soda tribe on the twenty-fifth of November, support for coalition forces has dramatically changed. Tribal support continues to grow with the development of the Sofia Reconstruction Counsel and Sheikh Sattar's meeting with the leaders of the eastern tribes. If we successfully isolate AQ in the Mila'ab and deny them the ability to launch coordinated assaults out of Julayba, then their ability to influence the eastern tribes will be minimal. Without this AQ threat, I believe the locals will support their tribal leadership in renouncing AQ." I made a note of the battle of Sofia. I needed the details from the intelligence officer.

The lieutenant colonel continued, "Here is my intent for Churubusco:

1. Isolate AO Julayba to prevent escape of insurgents during first seventy-two hours of operations.
2. Kill/capture the Hanush Network with a series of targeted raids.
3. Maintain the ability to rapidly attack emerging targets.
4. Find and recruit the tribal sheikhs.

    5. Conduct Search and Attack to clear routes, control key terrain, collect HUMINT [human intelligence], and recon for a permanent COP.

    6. Build a COP to sustain long-term control of Julayba."

I wrote down each of the tasks. During the briefing of intent, I couldn't help but notice the difference between Churubusco and our previous missions. We weren't simply clearing a district. The colonel's tasks specifically stated that we were to find and recruit the tribal sheikhs. Rage Company was being ordered to engage the local populace and no longer treat them as neutral observers.

"We are currently in the initial phase of Churubusco: the reception of Rage Company," Lieutenant Colonel Ferry said. "The second phase will commence on 17 January. On that night three separate raid forces [RF] will enter Julayba, each clearing their respective objective areas." He went through the task organization for the mission. Raid force 1 was the SEALs and Baker 1/9. They would amphibiously insert in the northern portion of Julayba, utilizing DSU riverine patrol craft. Rage Company was the second RF, and Dog Company 1/9, which would also assume operational control of Lieutenant Jahelka's Rage 3, was the third. Each raid force had its own attachments, including Apache and Cobra gunships, a platoon of Iraqi army soldiers, interpreters, and so on. For heavy support, there would be a company of Bradley fighting vehicles and another of Abrams tanks.

The next slide was a map of Julayba. The prominent geographical feature of the area was the Euphrates River; the northern boundary of Julayba, it cut the region into the shape of an ancient shark tooth with soft, rounded edges. Using a laser pointer, Lieutenant Colonel Ferry continued: "For this phase there are six objective areas: Chihuahua, Dachshund, Doberman, Bulldog, Pit Bull, and Beagle. RF 1 is responsible for Chihuahua and Bulldog; RF 2, Doberman and Dachshund; RF 3, Pit Bull and Beagle. The S2 [intel section.] has identified five potential river crossing points: Frog, Newt, Salamander, Komodo, and Cotton Mouth. In order to successfully isolate the region, all units are authorized to destroy any boat near these points. Next slide."

The colonel went through a few slides, highlighting the main roads and names of local tribes, as well as the locations for known schools and mosques. Then he went over the four targeted high-value individuals (HVI). "Hamid Ali Hamadi is the current head of AQI in Ramadi. AIF propaganda says he has left the area, but his wife and children still live on the western edge of Julayba, near the intersection of Route Nova and Orchard Way. Hamadi is well versed in the planning and coordination of IED, VBIED, and direct-fire attacks. He facilitates the movement of foreign fighters within the region, and his stated goal is to control or destroy the government of Ramadi." Hamadi was one of our standard targets. Every battalion had him on their list of active terrorists.

"Daham Hanush Hamid is the emir of AQI's legal court within Ramadi. A former nationalist turned extremist, he passes judgment on local nationals in accordance with his interpretation of Sharia law. His personal wealth allows him to finance and coordinate attacks through-out the Euphrates River Valley between Habbaniyah and Ramadi. His four sons all lead their own insurgent cells that are capable of mortar, rocket, sniper, IED, and direct-fire attacks against coalition forces. The Marines to our east, 3/2, have received the brunt of the Hanush network's attacks and believe the family is based out of Julayba." The picture accompanying the slide showed Hanush in a black suit and a tie. He resembled a middle-aged businessman.

"Ali Hamid Mutar, aka Ali Siyagah, is a Wahhabi religious leader. His network is financed through Saudi Arabia and provides him with the money to recruit suicide bombers, as well as to afford the logistical assets to preach at a large number of Anbar's mosques. Siyagah is also Daham Hanush's personal religious adviser. Our intel assessments placed Siyagah and a small security detachment in Julayba preaching at the Albu Musa mosque two days ago." Siyagah was a new target. He was also the first terrorist I'd heard of who was actively preaching to the populace.

"Hatim Hussain Ali Sa'id is the only known sheikh in Julayba. He has close ties to multiple IED cells and uses his tribal influence to recruit for AQI. Hatim also houses and facilitates the movement of foreign fighters for Umar Daham Hanush. Hatim has three sons: Marwan, Wissam, and Muthana. Marwan runs a construction company that provides significant funding to AQI through its business. We have no information on the other two sons."

The colonel paused to drink from his glass of water. I looked at Hatim's picture projected against the wall. There was a bit of irony in the fact that we were ordered to find and recruit the local sheikhs after we arrested the only known one. I foresaw dozens of Iraqis claiming to be sheikhs and wanting to fill the power vacuum we would create.

The rest of the brief served as an opportunity for the representatives to coordinate their unit's actions. I met up with the battalion intelligence officer, Lieutenant Hopper. I asked him about the battle for Sofia.

He was more than happy to provide a summary. "The Abu Soda tribal area was a historic point-of-origin site for mortar attacks against Corregidor and the Combat Outpost [a small facility housing 1/9 INF units across Corregidor on the northern side of Michigan]. Our response was usually two or three rounds of 155mm artillery from Camp Ramadi. The result of our response was the destruction of the Abu Soda's crops and fields. Their leader, Sheikh Jassim, pressured us for a long time to stop firing the counter-fire missions into his fields. Obviously, we told him to stop the mortar attacks." Lieutenant Hopper was distracted for a moment while he answered a soldier's question.

"Sorry about that. I have nine companies to support and three soldiers who work for me. To be honest, it's a bit much. So Jassim agrees to stop the mortar attacks. He orders his tribesmen to set up checkpoints along Route Nova and Apple, as well as on some of the secondary access roads into his territory. He doesn't order his men to fight al Qaeda, just to tell them to go away and use a different place. Fertile ground is hard to come by in a desert. After about a week of these checkpoints, mortar attacks against Combat Outpost and Corregidor stopped. Then AQ, either Mullah Qahttan or Daham Hanush, orders the destruction of the Abu Soda tribe. A couple hundred AQI fighters, mostly tribesmen from Julayba supporting Hanush's cells of well-trained insurgents, invade Jassim's territory. Intense fighting results, and we get a satellite call from Jassim pleading for assistance. We threw a bunch of AKs, 7.62 ammo, and food in the back of some five-tons and drove it out there to Jassim. With the extra weapons and the support of a few Apache helicopters, his men repulsed the al Qaeda attack." Hopper rushed the last few sentences. Lieutenant Colonel Ferry was motioning for his presence.

I left the brief and went to chow with some of the platoon commanders. I was surprised by the variety and amount of food available at the base. It was almost the same as at Camp Ramadi, just on a smaller scale. After all, Camp Ramadi housed roughly six thousand soldiers, while Corregidor supported only a thousand. I shared the hundred-meter walk back to the company command post with Lieutenant Thomas. An entire platoon of Iraqi army soldiers was going to execute Churubusco with his men.

"You have an interpreter for the Iraqis?" I asked.

"Yeah, but I put Sergeant Karras in charge of them. I basically told him that he was the Iraqi platoon commander," replied James.

"Have fun, you freak; I'll be sitting here twiddling my thumbs," I said.

I thought about how I would be stuck at Corregidor during Churubusco's execution. The XO and I were going to act as the company's quick reaction force (QRF), commanding a convoy of armored humvees that would react to scenarios as needed. It was a job nobody wanted: pure boredom. If you did get called out, it was usually because someone was killed or wounded. Then you immediately regretted thinking about how you wished the job wasn't so damn boring. Plus, IEDs target vehicles more than they do dismounted infantry. Being a member of the QRF was a mental triad of boredom, danger, and regret: a wonderful combination for any man's psyche.

"Tom, I've got eighty-eight guys going into this raid. That's about the same number of soldiers operating out of COP Falcon or Grant," said James.

"So?" I wasn't sure what he was getting at.

"So . . . there is an army captain I am in charge of, a Marine lieutenant who is senior to me, and an Iraqi army lieutenant. Not to mention the tanks and helicopters in support." I sensed the optimism in his voice and realized that he wasn't unsure of how to handle the situation. He was excited.

"Hey, man"—there was more giddiness in James's voice—"I think you left before he said this, but Lieutenant Colonel Ferry wants all of our squads to be outfitted with one suppressed rifle."

"What the hell for?"

"He wants to maintain the element of surprise. He thinks suppressed weapons will allow us to silence the local dogs without anyone noticing we are there." James was chuckling as he finished.

"Sounds like some Ranger shit to me," I said as we parted ways. James headed to his platoon's barracks, while I went to the command post.

I thought that shooting the dogs was an absurd idea. With helicopters, tanks, Bradley fighting vehicles, and a few hundred heavily laden American infantrymen, the colonel was worried about the local dogs compromising the element of surprise. Plus, one raid force would have ended up shooting at another when the dogs ran between our separate groups. Hell, if we had told our Marines to silence the dogs, they would have used fixed bayonets and saved the ammunition. No need for suppressed rifles.

I did, however, like where the colonel's mind was. He wasn't going to let anything prevent us from capturing the enemy. In fact, "silence the dogs" became something of a motto for Rage Company's officers before the mission. We said it to one another as a greeting, a joke, and mostly as a threat to our enemies. In our minds, the dog wasn't a four-legged animal, it was al Qaeda. And al Qaeda would be silenced.

2000, January 16, 2007

The convoy of seven-tons drove down Route Michigan with a tank-and-Bradley escort. Lieutenant Thomas watched the turrets of the armored vehicles spin from side to side, scanning the darkness with their high-powered night optics. The vehicles traveled 6 kilometers to his insertion point and began to unload his men—a motley collection of Iraqi soldiers, U.S. Marines, military working dogs, and a human-intelligence team. As they dismounted the vehicles, the platoon commander arrayed his raid force in a defensive posture. Dozens of wild dogs were barking at the intruders, and 1/9's battalion commander's orders to maintain the element of surprise were already unrealistic. Maybe the suppressed rifle wasn't that bad of an idea.

Lieutenant Thomas surveyed the ground. The terrain to his immediate front was open and relatively flat. Two hundred meters east was a lone gas station. In the opposite direction and at the same distance were the outskirts of an Iraqi village. A few lights illuminated the dozen walled homes. His objective, however, was 800 meters north, across the open, flat terrain. There the platoon commander hoped to find Sheikh Hatim, his sons, and a suitable position to establish as Combat Outpost Rage.

"Sir, can you tell the trucks not to leave yet?" asked Davila. His voice was coming over the intrasquad radio.

Lieutenant Thomas directed his radio operator to relay the request on the convoy net. He didn't get a response.

"I'm not getting them. What do you need, Davila?" replied Thomas.

The trucks began to execute a three-point turn on Michigan.

"Shit, sir, we left our rockets on the seven-tons," stated Davila. Fury gripped James Thomas. Thoughts of his infantrymen being ambushed by fortified machine gun positions flashed in his mind. Without anti-tank rockets, it would be a nightmarish scenario.

He thought about yelling at Davila, but he could see the squad leader taking action. A column of Marines, Davila's entire squad to be precise, was running onto Michigan. They flagged down the seven-tons like hitchhikers a few miles from a prison.

To the dismay of Lieutenant Thomas, the vehicles behaved like passersby in the prison scenario. The first two seven-tons swerved around the men, ignoring the pleas.

The third stopped. It took Davila's Marines a few moments to secure their misplaced rockets. Then Rage 2 began its movement to objective Doberman.

Minutes into the tactical movement, Lieutenant Thomas began to appreciate the geographic features of Julayba. In this suburban, agricultural-based region, his men could properly maneuver, machine guns could fire at their max effective range, and sophisticated night optics could spot the enemy 1,000 meters out, rather than two buildings away. The fields and the dispersed populace also offered the opportunity to use supporting arms: mortars, artillery, and close air support were readily available.

Although the infinite ambush points of Ramadi's urban sprawl were missing, they were replaced by a less deadly and more annoying nuisance: hundreds of wild dogs. As the Marines approached the first street they would cross, Irish Way, packs of dogs heckled the raid force. Multiple Marines requested permission from their platoon commander to shoot the dogs. James Thomas said no. That was before a massive white husky went after the highly trained German shepherd military working dog. Without permission to kill the wolflike beast, Corporal Davila threw a smoke canister at the animal. The dog immediately bit onto the canister and stepped away from the group.

Unfortunately for the animal, the canister had a delayed fuse. When the smoke grenade "popped," sparks shot from its mouth. They were followed by a loud whimper and a cloud of smoke that outlined the path the dog took away from the Marines. Lieutenant Thomas figured the dog wasn't coming back.

The point element began to cross the linear danger area that was Irish Way. The far side was a small tree line. Once the first squad crossed and set up security, another squad established a blocking position along the road. The Marines laid out a spike strip and used barrels and other debris littering the side of the road to stop all north-south traffic. Then they continued their movement to the objective.

Walking under the tall palm trees, the German shepherd was attacked again. James Thomas recognized it as the same white dog. Enough was enough. He shot the animal. Like in an Alfred Hitchcock movie, the dog struggled back into the shadows it had come from.

A few hundred meters through the palm trees, the raid force entered an orchard. Orderly columns of fruit trees lined the area. Beyond them was a steep incline. The change in height was only about 10 meters, but in a mainly flat landscape it was advantageous terrain. More important, there was a solitary building on the higher ground overlooking the orchard and the palm trees. It was a commanding presence, accompanied by a dirt path that led to the structure from Irish Way. The path was clearly a secondary access point because Lieutenant Thomas knew, from his map, that Route Nova ran along the front of the structure. The building became James Thomas's primary location for COP Rage.

The raid force continued north toward Route Nova and approached the paved road 200 meters east of the large building. A single row of homes rested between the troops and the road. On the far side of Nova was the southern end of objective Doberman. From the cover of the tree line, James Thomas spot-checked his position against his map.

"Sir, Bradford has eyes on the Hatim target house. It has the large water tank on top of it," said Corporal Davila via the intrasquad radio.

About a quarter mile east, the sounds of Rage 1 and Rage 4 using shotguns to breach doors inside objective Dachshund filled the night. The near-simultaneous raiding of Julayba was beginning.

James Thomas confirmed that all elements were set. Then his Marines emerged from the tree line, crossed through two backyards, and stormed across Route Nova. Davila's men kicked down the door to Sheikh Hatim's house.

Inside, the squad of shouting Marines cleared the structure. The military-age males were consolidated into one room. Lieutenant Thomas removed the target package from his drop pouch and matched faces with two of the sitting men. Sheikh Hatim and his son Marwan were in Rage 2's custody. The men were blindfolded and flexi-cuffed.

With the primary objective, Sheikh Hatim, secured, James Thomas turned his attention to the secondary task. "Sergeant Karras, take the IA platoon and check out the house that overlooks our avenue of approach. I want to know if it is capable of housing the company," said Lieutenant Thomas over the radio.

"You want me to send the detainees over there, too, sir?" asked Corporal Davila. He was standing next to his platoon commander.

"No, I want to search the objective area as fast as possible. Let's go."

Davila's men exited the house. Above, helicopters hovered in the dark sky; armored vehicles stood by along Route Michigan, and six separate units were raiding their respective objectives. Faced with such a large air-ground task force, the local al Qaeda militants offered no resistance during the night.

0100, January 17, 2007

"Manchu, this is Rage Mobile, requesting permission to depart Camp Corregidor. Seven victors, twenty packs," I said into the radio headset. I was impressed with the communication system inside my vehicle. I could talk internally to the driver and the turret gunner merely by speaking into the microphone, rather than having to yell over the roaring engine. To communicate over the humvee's radios, I simply pressed a switch and spoke into the same microphone. It was much more convenient than holding the handset to your ear for hours on end.

The battalion cleared my resupply convoy to leave the camp.

"Lieutenant Daly, what time is Gunny Bishop leaving in the morning?" asked First Sergeant Carlson. Rage 8 was bored with sitting around and found a seat in the back of my humvee.

"Around 0700. His convoy is going to focus on our guys in the south. This one is more focused on the soldiers in the northern area of Julayba," I said.

We drove onto Michigan and headed east. I took the convoy slowly, only about ten miles per hour. Pathfinder, which was clearing our route, was ahead of us and going the same speed. I decided that I would stay between 400 and 800 meters behind them. If I stayed too close on Michigan, my less-armored vehicles would be easy targets for any lurking insurgents. Pathfinder's white light would negate the darkness of my convoy, which drove by infrared light. But I had to stay as close as possible because once we started to make stops to drop off supplies, Pathfinder would get ahead of me. It didn't take insurgents very long to emplace IEDs after Pathfinder went past.

The first landmark on the way to Julayba was two connected concrete arcs that towered over the road. Before the war, this had been some sort of checkpoint; unoccupied booths stood on both the east and the west side. More important, the arches signaled that you were entering the Sijariah region. It was a region, like Julayba, dominated by al Qaeda. Insurgent RPG and machine gun teams used the landmark to time their attacks against coalition convoys. They would emerge once they spotted you passing through the arch and would fire a few RPG shots or count down their IED initiation sequence, based on whatever speed they estimated you were going.

My first trip through the arches was uneventful.

Past the arches, the terrain on the southern side of Michigan was open. A handful of houses were spread out over a few hundred meters, and most lay a significant distance from the road, 200 to 300 meters at a minimum. On the northern side, it was village after village. Each of the tribal enclaves was connected by an access road that ran parallel to Michigan no more than 50 meters away. The Marines in my vehicle commented on the impressive Arab architecture lining the access road. Clearly, the region had been well off under Saddam. My turret gunners spent most of their time scanning the northern side of the road.

"Gentlemen, you are now entering Julayba," I said to the other men in my truck. The convoy approached the first intersection in our new home: Orchard Way and Michigan. A tank sat atop the median, turret oriented north along Orchard Way. The right side of Michigan turned into a giant berm of sand that stood about twenty feet high. Beyond the berm, south of Michigan, was Lake Habbaniya. It provided the berm's purpose: to prevent flooding if the water level of the lake ever rose too high.

We drove a few more minutes and hit the intersection with Ruby Road. There was another tank on Michigan, with its turret oriented along Ruby. The M1114 humvee turned left off Michigan and immediately swerved around a fallen telephone pole. The turret spun to the left to cover an open field as we passed the X-shaped intersection with Irish Way. It was the same field that James Thomas had crossed hours earlier. There was a mosque on the right, followed by our first drop point: the Nasaf Marketplace. It wasn't much of a drop, just a case of water for Rage 1 and Rage 4. I was, however, surprised by the small size of the marketplace. It was the only one in Julayba, but there were only a dozen stalls that I could see.

After dropping the water, the convoy made a left onto Route Nova. Nova was a significant road in the brigade's battle space. It was the only route that went from Ramadi to Fallujah that was open to civilian traffic. In Ramadi, it ran along the southern banks of the Euphrates and was not controlled in the same manner as Michigan. It was a mostly uncontested road, meaning that the coalition did not exercise any control over it. In Julayba, Nova ran through all of the major tribal areas. During our mission brief, Captain Smith had identified it as the key route to influence.

Along Nova, the houses were built a few meters from the road. Their close proximity made me more attentive. The turret gunner even had to deal with low-lying power lines. I wondered how they hadn't been snapped down by Pathfinder's larger vehicles.

About 400 meters after we turned onto Nova, the houses stopped on the left. There was an open field, accompanied by an orchard and palm trees. I noticed that Nova was raised up higher than the field but was level with the houses on the right.

"Rage 2's position is in that mansion on the left," said my turret gunner. We didn't make a stop. Gunny Bishop was bringing his convoy there in a few hours.

It was another 500 meters north on Nova before we made our next stop. A soldier was crouched along the berm that Nova had been built on top of, waving an infrared strobe. He directed our vehicles where to drop the chow, the water, and the batteries. Then a dozen soldiers emerged from a house and began to ferry the supplies inside.

In the thirty minutes it took the dozen men to move the supplies, I lost visual contact with Pathfinder. Once we began moving again, the convoy drove much faster than before, twenty miles per hour.

I was now in the heart of Julayba. We passed mosques, schools, and hundreds of homes. In fact, in the area there were twice the number of actual homes than there were on the map. Since 2004, Julayba had apparently experienced a construction boom. I wasn't that surprised. Ramadi and Fallujah weren't exactly hospitable, and there had never been an American presence in Julayba. It was a likely choice for the urban areas' refugees. I wondered whether the houses had been built by Marwan's construction company.

The extra houses did make it difficult for me to match the terrain I saw with that on my map. It was a good thing I had the Blue Force Tracker navigation system working in my vehicle because I was confused when we hit the Nova-Gixxer intersection. I thought it would be a clear T-shaped intersection, based on my map, but in reality it was more of a veer left to stay on Nova. Closely packed houses surrounded the area.

We made the left, and the road narrowed slightly. Potholes were everywhere. I recognized some as blast craters. I scanned the northern side of the road. After two small houses, there was an open space. It was one house's front yard and another's backyard. Two palm trees sat in the middle. As I went to look away, a shadow appeared. It was the frame of a small boy, no more than four or five years old. He emerged from behind one of the trees and stared at my convoy. I couldn't make out the color of his clothes, but they appeared to be in the same style as the stereotypical insurgent black pajamas. He was definitely wearing a ski mask. In that moment I froze. I did not say a word. I watched the shadow jump over a small irrigation ditch, so narrow a man could have stepped over it, and disappear behind the second tree.

Again, I thought about saying something. But it was only a boy, and he didn't have a weapon. If I had said something, my Marines would have been on edge. On first sight, that four-year-old would have been killed. And for what, wearing a ski mask?

But I also knew that insurgents used young boys. Their fingers were just as capable of setting off IEDs. Plus, we didn't suspect them. My Marines were in danger, and I purposely did not warn them. All for the life of some boy I would never meet, never know.

Like many people in a predicament, I ignored reality. I told myself the child was not real, that my eyes were playing tricks on me. It was 0230 in the morning, and there was no way a kid was running along the street. The convoy drove on.

Not even 100 meters away, we drove into an area with a few lit street lights. They obviously illuminated my convoy and forced me to raise my NVGs. My vehicle passed through without incident.

"Rage Mobile, seven-ton one; our turret gunner lost his NVGs," said a vehicle commander on the convoy net. I immediately halted the convoy. I turned around and looked at First Sergeant Carlson. He recognized that I was looking for his input.

"We gotta look for them, sir. If the hajji find it and kill a soldier or a Marine because they got 'em . . . that's fucked up on us," he said, then he keyed the convoy net. "Seven-ton one, Rage 8; did he just lose them right now or what?"

"Roger 8, when we entered the lighted area, he flipped them up, they got caught on a power line or something and came off his Kevlar," replied the vehicle.

I thought about the first sergeant's advice and agreed with him. We had a duty, a moral responsibility to our fellow American to at least look for the NVGs—no matter how dangerous it might be.

The first sergeant and I got out of the truck and walked back into the light. We passed seven-ton one, and an angry Rage 8 had words with the lance corporal whose NVGs were missing. Then we began to search the side of the road. First Sergeant Carlson took the north, while I was opposite on the south. The entire time I thought about the little boy blowing me up with an IED.

We made it all the way to the last vehicle without finding the NVGs. Then first sergeant got on the last humvee's radio and spoke with seven-ton one. He confirmed that they had searched the back of their truck. Seven-ton one said they had, but a minute later they claimed to have found the NVGs atop the canvas liner that covered the bed.

I was so mad, I laughed. When I passed seven-ton one on the way to my truck, it was my turn for some choice words with the crew.

The convoy began to move again. I increased our speed to thirty miles per hour and caught up to Pathfinder at the Nova–Orchard Way intersection. They were dismantling an IED when we pulled up behind them. Once finished, though, they went at a snail's pace back to Corregidor. We followed.

I encountered Pathfinder's commander in 1/9's headquarters. The lieutenant told me they had found three IEDs, two right after the intersection of Gixxer-Nova and one at Nova–Orchard Way. I was horrified by his information. He was saying that there were two IEDs in the same area where the boy had been. Not only was the boy real, but if Pathfinder had missed one of the IEDs, he probably would have blown me or one of my guys high into the sky.

I awkwardly went back to our company command post. The majority of the Marines were in front of the building, smoking and talking about searching for NVGs. I sat down with them and refused a few offers to smoke.

"I might have been seeing shit, but did anyone see a young boy wearing a ski mask around Gixxer-Nova?" I asked during a lull in their conversations.

Most of the Marines scoffed at the thought and made jokes about it. The one corpsman on our convoy, who was the turret gunner in the vehicle behind mine, just stared at me, his mouth slightly open.

"Look, Doc Beaton, I don't need a psych eval or anything. I was just wondering . . . ," I said. There were a few more jokes, but Beaton's face didn't change. Seconds later he said, "I saw him, too."

0600, January 17, 2007

James Thomas rolled onto his back and stared up at the sky. The sun was slowly rising, and he was ready to sleep, not to wake up.

The platoon commander rolled back onto his chest and continued scanning the Ruby-Nova intersection. His reinforced squad was spread out over the surrounding rooftops and was securing, by observation, the surrounding roads. After the first resupply convoy, Captain Smith anticipated insurgents emplacing IEDs along Route Nova. In the last few hours of darkness, he ordered Lieutenant Thomas to establish an over-watch on the intersection. It would place American eyes along every foot of asphalt that Gunny Bishop's convoy was about to cover.

"Rage 2, this is Rage 1, over."

Lieutenant Thomas grabbed his handset. "Send it, one," he said.

"My squad is set up over here. We have eyes on the route, over," said Lieutenant Shearburn. Rage 1 was ready to relieve Rage 2's position. Shortly, they would receive the convoy. Then Gunny Bishop would head to Rage 2, the bulk of which was located at the mansion.

James Thomas ordered Sergeant Kastner to take his men off the rooftops and consolidate on the southern side of Nova. They were going to walk behind the row of houses that followed the southern side of the road back to the rest of Rage 2 and the Iraqi army platoon. The Marines would be in defilade, moving parallel to Nova at the base of the road's berm.

In the damp, cool air, Kastner's Marines got into formation. The alert and weary group began to walk at a slow pace in the early morning light, their bodies still frozen from hours of no movement. It wasn't a very long walk. After passing a dozen Iraqi homes, the large defensible position occupied by the rest of the platoon was visible.

With 200 meters left, the row of houses stopped. The terrain opened up with a field that led to the entrance of the mansion's long half-circle dirt driveway. The point element was moving up the berm and onto the driveway when AK fire erupted from the opposite side of Nova. Lieutenant Thomas, the second-to-last man in the formation, immediately crouched behind the berm. He watched Kastner lead the point element of the squad into the house.

The ricocheting of bullets against the asphalt above forced the platoon commander to crouch lower. He stepped away from the road, improving his view of the houses opposite him. In seconds, James Thomas identified two insurgent firing positions.

He fired roughly twenty rounds at the two muzzle flashes and got back down against the berm. Dozens of bullets zipped over his head.

The platoon commander noticed that no one was firing from the roof of the mansion. He knew Davila's or Holloway's men were up there, but not a single round of suppressive fire was going down-range.

"Davila, Holloway! Why isn't anyone shooting from the roof?!" he yelled into his radio. There was no immediate response.

The rear section of the formation began to move in tandem toward the house, some suppressing the muzzle flashes as the others moved. Their efforts paid off; everyone made it back. James Thomas was the last one through the home's massive double doors.

Mounds of dirt were spread across the tile floor. Inside Rage Company's future COP, the Iraqi army platoon sat in the front two rooms. Most of them were relaxing without their body armor on. The soldiers hardly noticed the Marines entering and didn't seem to care that their allies had just been ambushed. James Thomas ignored the Iraqis and went straight into the foyer. He didn't have to open the second set of double doors; they were propped open.

The platoon commander sprinted up the wide staircase in front of him and turned right at the top, going up another five stairs. For a moment he was standing along the foyer's rotunda, which, like the staircase, did not have a railing. Because of this fact, not many noticed the large dome above the foyer—nobody wanted to experience the fall that might accompany a few missteps as you looked up.

Entering the house's northern wing, Lieutenant Thomas opened the first door on his left. The wooden staircase in front of him led to the roof and the Marines who had not provided suppressive fire to cover his movement back into the house.

"What the fuck!" James identified Corporal Bradford, his expert rocket-man, standing among the group on the roof. "You fuckers couldn't cover us on the way back? No rockets, not even a SAW or M16 burst?"

"Sir, we can't see them. We could shoot randomly, but we don't have positive identification of hostile intent from any of those buildings," replied Bradford.

The group ducked low as a few rounds sailed overhead. A couple impacted against the house.

"You do now." James Thomas pointed out the two houses he had previously exchanged fire with. Two of the Marines from 3/2 fired multiple HEDP grenades from their M203s. The point-detonating 40mm grenades slammed into the insurgent firing positions.

"Sir, the convoy is coming to our position!" yelled Corporal Davila. He was standing on the wooden stairs. His head was only a few feet above ground level, sticking out from the hole in the center of the roof that provided access.

James Thomas sprinted downstairs. He rounded up half a dozen smoke grenades and went out in front of the mansion. With the Marines on the roof covering him, he threw the grenades across Nova to the north. The white cloud of smoke covered the heavily exposed flank that was nothing but open farmland. If the insurgents were going to engage the convoy, they would have to shoot through or from the houses directly across the street. The Marines on the roof would easily suppress such an endeavor.

The convoy sped down Nova. Gunny Bishop quickly oriented the gun trucks in a defensive posture around the perimeter of the large dirt front yard. Within minutes, pallets of chow and water were dropped a few feet from the mansion's front door.

On the roof Corporal Jimmy Pickett recognized that the smoke screen was wearing thin, so he took out a purple canister. He pulled the pin and stepped back to throw it. Unfortunately, he bumped into Corporal Holloway as he let it fly. The canister hit the retaining wall and fell down toward the convoy below. Mid-flight the grenade popped, letting off the first few puffs of purple smoke. Instead of hitting the ground, it bounced off Gunny Bishop and landed in the pile of plastic water battles he stood over.

An irate gunnery sergeant was quickly sprayed with a cloud of purple smoke, tinting his uniform this dark color. "Are you kidding? Are you fucking kidding?" he yelled up to the roof.

Somebody responded with, "Hey, it's Barney!"

1300, January 17, 2007

"Rage 2, this is Rage 6; stand by for time-sensitive target, over."

"Standing by, go ahead, Six."

"In the vicinity of grid 538 017, battalion has identified four or five MAMs loading bongo trucks with miscellaneous weapons removed from the ground. I want you to action. Rage 4 will provide over-watch from the northern side of the field," said Captain Smith.

It took James Thomas five minutes to get two of his squads briefed and out the door. He left Combat Outpost Rage; Captain Smith had made the official decision hours earlier, with Davila's squad leading, followed by Kastner. Holloway stayed at the COP with the Iraqis.

The tactical column moved into the open fields to the northeast of COP Rage. The target was 150 meters north of Rage Road and 400 meters west of the intersection of Gixxer-Rage. It was a 1,000-meter movement over irrigation ditches and farmland. Dispersed trees and shrubs offered minimal cover.

As James Thomas neared the grid, he identified the freshly dug-up earth from a hundred meters out. The insurgents were nowhere to be found. The Marines carefully approached the cache site, and James Thomas set up one of the squads as security. He oriented them to the south to cover the houses along Rage Road within the Albu Bali tribal area.

"Rage 6, Rage 2, I am at the cache site. No sign of the owners or the bongo trucks—break—I have two large-caliber artillery shells stuffed with explosives, multiple improvised rocket launchers, garbage bags of explosive material, and a few welded stands that could be used to mount IRLs [improvised rocket launchers] or as firing platforms, over," said Lieutenant Thomas.

Three or four solitary rifle shots crackled in the distance. None of the rounds had been fired at Lieutenant Thomas's men.

"Stand by, Two, we are getting an update from battalion," said Captain Smith. James Thomas decided to change his radio's channel to battalion's and listen in.

Rage 4 was receiving accurate harassing fire from 1,000 meters to the east. The origin was a small collection of homes, sort of a family compound on the northeast side of Gixxer-Rage. Then Manchu 6, the battalion commander, came on the net. He told Captain Smith that he had just received information that the family compound was the hideout of Ali Siyagah's driver and security detail. Siyagah was potentially there.

Lieutenant Thomas flipped back to the company frequency. Within moments, Captain Smith ordered him to move into an over-watch position covering the compound. If necessary, Lieutenant Thomas was to support, by fire, Captain Smith and Rage 4's isolation and subsequent clear of the houses.

The two squads of Rage 2 Marines moved east toward the compound. They stopped at a large house about 500 meters shy of the new objective. Inside was a young Iraqi couple. The woman offered Lieutenant Thomas and his men food. They politely refused. The group of Marines headed straight for the roof.

"I think this is a good spot, sir. We can cover both the cache site and the compound from here," said Corporal Davila.

The platoon commander agreed. He moved to the north side of the roof and looked out at Rage 4. Accompanied by Captain Smith and a small headquarters element, Rage 4 was beginning to enter the field. Harassing fire from the insurgents continued. Multiple gunshots targeting Rage 4 rang out. Lieutenant Thomas and his men could not identify their origin. Nearly 400 meters from the compound, the Marines crossing the field took cover in an irrigation canal. The isolation of the objective was almost complete. Rage 4 covered the northern and western approaches to the compound, while Rage 2 cut off the south. To the east was the Euphrates River, only about a hundred meters wide; the insurgents would have to swim or find a canoe to escape.

To James Thomas, it seemed as if they were taking the last option. Two Apache gunships appeared from the southeast. The battalion must have spotted the insurgents crossing the river because the helicopters fired a few hundred rounds from their chain guns in that direction.

"Manchu 6, this is Rage 6, objective is isolated. I have one platoon in a support by fire, with a second as maneuver. Requesting permission to action the objective, over," said Captain Smith on the battalion net.

"Negative, Rage 6, maintain isolation. A section of tanks and Bradleys will approach from Rage Road to maneuver on the objective, over," replied Manchu 6. The tanks and the Bradleys were Manchu 6's personal security detail. Lieutenant Colonel Ferry was doing something I had never seen a battalion commander do: lead his men into battle.

Unfortunately, the colonel's good intentions had a serious drawback. Captain Smith and Rage 4 sat exposed in the field for five hours, waiting for the tanks and Manchu 6 to show up. Any insurgents who were on the objective were long gone by the time the colonel and his cavalry took down the houses. Because the target was initially deemed time-sensitive, Lieutenant Thomas and his men left COP Rage without their night-vision devices. By wasting five hours so that he could assault the objective personally, the colonel had forced some of his subordinates to walk in the dark without the NVGs' technological advantage.

The Marines did, however, get a good meal out of the colonel's time wasting. James Thomas was able to accept the woman of the house's offer of food, and the Marines enjoyed authentic Iraqi cuisine: bread, vegetables, and goat meat, with cups of chai tea to wash it down.

January 25, 2007

In the battalion's command post, I let out a loud sneeze at the top of the stairs. The second floor of 1/9's CP was the only place that still held dust to irritate my sinuses. Everywhere else was mud. Then I pushed aside the flimsy plywood door to the Tactical Operations Center (TOC) as if it was weightless. I took off my Kevlar and noticed that the TOC was unusually quiet. Captain Clark was the watch officer. He immediately recognized me as I came around the corner of the plywood wall on my left, which separated incoming personnel from the five television screens and half-dozen computer monitors in the room.

"Rage Mobile, good to see you. How is Julayba going?" he asked.

"Just wonderful. There's enough excitement for everyone out there." I forced a smile. I was tired and wanted to get my convoy out to COP Rage as soon as possible.

For the last twenty-four hours, I had been finishing up the paper-work on the company's dozen detainees from Churubusco. It was a frustrating process; the human-intelligence soldiers stationed at Camp Corregidor didn't even make a visit. Without them, we couldn't ask the detainees anything more than their names or where they lived. When I found the sergeant first class in charge of the soldiers, he told me not to worry about it; the ARDF would interrogate them. His answer wasn't just bullshit, but because I wasn't an intelligence officer by trade, I didn't have access to the interrogation summaries. Plus, the ARDF, when it was full, would question only those detainees who had significant evidence or reporting against them. If the detained individual was unknown, the overworked interrogator would provide the three thirty-minute sessions and recommend him for release. The bureaucracy of our detainee process benefited both innocent and guilty Iraqis. I couldn't stand it.

Sensing my lack of sincerity, Captain Clark got to the point. "There are twenty-five Kit Carson Scouts, for lack of a better term, over at Camp Ranger waiting for you to pick them up. How many of your seven-ton trucks do you have here?"

"Two, sir, but I will fit them into one; the second is full of ammo, chow, a refrigerator, and four hundred Wag-Bags." There were a few dozen Marines squeezing cheeks, awaiting the arrival of the Wag-Bags at the COP.

"Wow, that's a lot of shit. How long does that last you?" The tone of sarcasm in his voice told me he was referring to the Wag-Bags.

"A couple of days. With all the shooting out there, the Wag-Bags get some use." I reflected on my own experience of calming pre-mission nerves with a relaxing sit on a plastic stand.

"If you would, Lieutenant Daly, stop your convoy out front of Camp Ranger, and I will have the scouts waiting for you. There is a major in charge of the Military Transition Team at the camp, and he will link up with you on Michigan," said Captain Clark.

"No problem, sir. Do you have any idea what these scouts want to do?" I asked.

"They are concerned citizens. The Iraqi army has given them the chocolate chip desert uniform and body armor. All I know is that they want to help. I am pretty sure Captain Smith got a packet of information on them, including a proposed mission against al Qaeda targets in Julayba."

My mind was screaming. I was his intelligence officer, and he hadn't given me a heads-up on this? There must have been a good reason, or maybe the information was worthless.

"Roger, sir; my convoy is ready to go with six vehicles, twenty-one packs. I will inform you when link-up is complete," I said.

"Rage Mobile, you are good to stage on Michigan. I will let Camp Ranger know you will be there in ten minutes. See you around."

I glanced around the different stations in the TOC and thought about being a watch officer. The captain read my mind. "One day you will be sitting here, too," he said. It was no secret that being a watch officer was a miserable job. I was certain that Captain Clark would have traded his for mine at the first opportunity. I swore to myself that I would never be reduced to his position.

As I walked out of the TOC, I opened the wooden door by leaning my shoulder into it. I slid my flak jacket on with my arms at the same time. With all of the gear on my legs, I somehow skipped down the dusty stairs and straight into my M1114. I started to think about why I should be in a good mood. I had showered, albeit in freezing water, shaved, and was looking forward to seeing what these scouts had to offer. *Lawrence of Arabia* was a damn good movie, and I felt as if I was going to have a similar opportunity. I climbed into the front seat and slid on my headset. It took a few attempts to shut the armored door.

"What is it this time, sir?" Corporal Joseph Jones asked. He was manning the 240G machine gun and wondered why I had kept him out in the dark and cold for an extra ten minutes.

I pressed the intervehicle communication button and shouted, "No prisoners!" It was the only line I remembered from the movie *Lawrence of Arabia.*

"I knew it. I knew one day Lieutenant Daly was going to walk out of that building just straight-up crazy," Jones said, exchanging a few laughs with my driver, Corporal Jason Sperry.

"Rage Mobile Collective, this is Mobile Actual, roger up in convoy order," I said on the convoy net. All vehicles responded.

"All stations, we will stop in front of Camp Ranger. Seven-ton one, you are going to pick up twenty-five Iraqis who want to help us. We will be bringing them to COP Rage. Convoy is moving," I said, fastening my NVGs to my Kevlar.

Sperry revved the engine, and my humvee roared through Corregidor's gate. An interesting trip to COP Rage was beginning.

10

THE SCOUTS

January 25, 2007

"Sir, those guys all have guns," said my driver, his voice filled with concern. I didn't respond to his statement; instead, I pushed open the armored door to the M1114. I stepped out into the street; the convoy of seven-ton trucks and humvees pulled up behind my vehicle and came to a halt. I headed toward the group of Iraqis on the far side of Route Michigan.

After passing through downtown Ramadi, Michigan became a two-lane road in either direction. The small median that stood a foot above the ground was hardly noticeable, destroyed by the weight and the tracks of armored vehicles driving over it for the last three years.

I stumbled over the broken concrete as I crossed the road. The dust kicked up by my seven trucks blew over the group of waiting men. I hoped it would blind the concerned citizens to the reality that each of the machine guns atop my vehicles was oriented in their direction. All of my Marines were keenly aware that the group was not supposed to be armed.

Looking for the American adviser, I scanned the stationary Iraqis through my NVGs. The silent group appeared to be in formation. One of them, a tall figure out front, was smoking. A Kalashnikov hung over

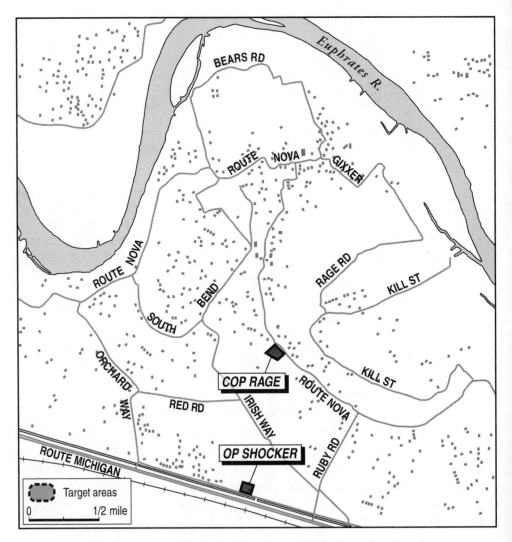

Area of Operations Rage: Rage Company's area of operations after Churubusco.

his chest. The rest of the group carried similar weapons. Most of the men each also held what appeared to be a small sack or blanket to combat the low-forty-degree weather.

An extra set of hands appeared around the tall leader, and I quickly spotted the American on the opposite side of the towering but skinny Iraqi. I walked directly in front of the group and took the opportunity to stare at each face as I strolled past, knowing that from their point of view, I was nothing more than a shadow floating through the dark night.

Collectively, the Iraqis were old. Every face was worn with wrinkles and lines. None was younger than thirty. It dawned on me that they were Saddamists, Iraqi veterans experienced through decades of conflict. I would come to find out that their perspectives were an even mix: half were officers; the rest, senior enlisted. Some had fought in the Iran-Iraq War; most, in the Gulf War. Nearly all of them were the soldiers who put down the Kurdish and Shi'a uprisings in the 1990s and the Ba'athists whom the United States faced in March and April 2003. Now they were forsaking their goals as nationalist insurgents to assist their notorious enemy in facing a greater threat to their social structure: the danger from al Qaeda.

I stopped between the smoking Iraqi and the one American. "Major, sir, Lieutenant Daly," I said, extending my hand to the adviser. He shook it and introduced himself. Then he turned to the Iraqi, whom he referred to as "general," and introduced me. The two of us exchanged greetings in simple English.

"General, you and your men can get on this truck," I said, pointing at the vehicle behind me. The seven-ton was stationary opposite the group on the far side of the road. The senior Iraqi barked orders at one of his men, and the disciplined formation broke ranks and moved toward the vehicle.

As the Iraqis went past, the American major leaned over and spoke softly. "Lieutenant, treat this guy like an American general," he said. "Do not make him ride with his men." The simple words would become the most important advice I ever received in Iraq.

I spotted the general counting his men as they climbed onto the seven-ton. "Sir, I have a seat for you in my truck," I told him.

"Okay, Daly," he replied. He directed one of his men to take over counting. Then the general moved next to me at the front of the seven-ton and yanked a small laminated card from his left breast pocket. He gave it to me.

I pulled back part of the infrared lens covering the headlight and read the piece of plastic paper, roughly the size of a Community Chest card from the game Monopoly.

"This is to certify that _____ is a member of Thawar Al Anbar." Below, it continued, "courtesy of 3rd Battalion, 2nd Marines." I looked up at the general. His broad smile revealed the immaculate trimming job on his thick, black mustache. The card was his offer of cooperation. He informed me that all of his men had the same card. Although I understood how dangerous it was for the general and his men to carry such an item, it was not going to be enough to convince my fellow Marines to trust him. Twenty-five random Iraqis, all of them armed and none screened or vetted, were not going to be welcomed by many at COP Rage.

We walked together to the head of the convoy. I opened the door to the seat directly behind me for the general. He was immediately captivated by the map of the surrounding area displayed on the monitor next to my green chair. I didn't hear his questions about the map; my thoughts were hovering around the fact that the truck behind the Iraqis, seven-ton two, did not have a machine gun. I put my headset on and keyed the radio.

"All victors, this is Mobile Actual; stand by for change in convoy order. Gun truck 3, I want you to move between the seven-tons to—" I paused, thinking that the general might understand English more than he was letting on and would take offense to my orders of moving a machine gun to cover his men. I didn't want him to know my thoughts about the twenty-five Iraqis possibly assisting in a complex ambush of our convoy. "To better protect our cargo. Acknowledge receipt," I said, finishing the radio transmission. Once the vehicles were in order, we began another trip to COP Rage. As the convoy went through the arches, the general pointed toward the north, the Sijariah crossing, and stated, "Al Qaeda neighborhood." I pretended to be surprised by his information.

When my vehicle turned onto Ruby Road, it immediately halted. A column of tanks and Pathfinder vehicles were at a stop, occupying the hard-packed dirt path. Their pause in route clearance meant that they had found something.

"Daly, there is IED near mosque," said the general. "You should move on this road." The general pointed to the left window of the vehicle. He was referring to Irish Way.

I could not follow his advice, because in our push into Julayba, Pathfinder had never cleared Irish Way. The engineers had focused on the Ruby–Nova–Orchard Way loop that followed the region's perimeter. Irish Way was a risk I did not have to take. The general might know the area better than I did, but I was willing to wait and follow Pathfinder.

The tank in front of us began to spin its turret. In seconds it stopped, the 120mm cannon pointed directly at my vehicle.

"Convoy on Ruby Road, this is Warlord Blue 1, identify yourself, over," said a voice on the battalion net.

The Marine manning my truck's turret flashed his middle finger at the tank. I, too, was upset. For the last ten minutes I had been the only voice on the radio, passing my convoy's location to battalion. Only moments earlier, I had stated that the convoy was turning onto Ruby Road. The tankers were probably sleeping and spooked by our presence. Their actions, however, gave me an excuse not to respond to the general's advice.

"Warlord, this is Rage Mobile, convoy is en route to COP Rage. Recommend you orient your turret to an exposed flank, over," I said. The tankers moved their turret and informed us of a pending controlled detonation 100 meters north on Ruby. I assumed that Pathfinder had found the IED outside the mosque. After the blast, the convoy moved agonizingly slowly through the Nasaf Marketplace and along the dimly lit Route Nova to COP Rage. The snail's pace allowed the general plenty of time to give me his version of an intelligence update on the local area. I was impressed.

Albin's head rested on the gray metallic table. He intently monitored the radio but also listened to the discussion that I, Captain Smith, and all four of the platoon commanders were having.

"All right, I know each of you is wondering who the hell these random Iraqis are who just showed up, so here is what I know." Captain Smith began to read an official Iraqi government document that had been translated into English. "This guy, the general, I think he is General Faris. Under Saddam, he was a high-ranking Ba'athist and considered a war hero. He created the Saddam Fedayeen and worked with Uday. Now he is the commanding general for the First Iraqi Army Division."

Something didn't seem right to me about Captain Smith's assessment. He continued on, saying that the men with the general were not Iraqi soldiers but local nationals who lived in the area. During Operation Churubusco, they got together and went to Habbaniya, a thirty-minute drive east. Once there, they offered their services to the Marines of 3/2, saying they wanted to help the Marines in Julayba. Two days later they were here.

As I followed Captain Smith's summary, it was apparent to me that the general was not Faris. Faris commanded thousands of soldiers. We had a hard enough time convincing Iraqi captains to patrol with their men, and now an Iraqi major general was here to work with a company of Marines? Analyzing the scenario, I found it unlikely that Faris would leave his post to command twenty-four locals in a small raid against al Qaeda. He had a division to run.

"Who gave them the weapons?" asked Jahelka. He was sitting on the COC's couch with Shearburn.

"The Iraqi army," I responded.

"Sir, yesterday we would have shot these twenty-five armed Iraqis if we happened to cross paths. Now the fuckers are in our COP, scoping out our positions, our troop strength, and the layout of our perimeter," said Shearburn. His thoughts led to Captain Smith and the other platoon commanders drawing up boundaries the Iraqis must follow: no scouts on the roof, no scouts outside.

While they discussed what the scouts could and couldn't do, I flipped through the document Captain Smith had previously been looking at. It was an order from the commander of Iraqi Ground Forces, Lieutenant General Majeed, directing the formation of an Anbar Support Committee. On the second page, it listed nine tasks approved by Prime Minister Nouri al-Maliki to be executed by General Faris. The tasks outlined the basis of a relationship between the Iraqi government and what I knew as the TAA; they called it the Anbar Salvation Council.

I continued to flip through the pages, amazed that I was looking at something that showed the Shia government's willingness to work with Ba'athist insurgents. I breezed through the rest of the pages: a list of names approving appointments of Sunnis within TAA to official military posts, another list containing fifty targets in Julayba, and a series of maps detailing how the targets should be attacked. I went back to the beginning, unsure whether I was reading it correctly.

Then the platoon commanders and Captain Smith decided to disarm the scouts. I was perplexed that they would consider such an action.

"We don't need to take away their weapons," I said. This was immediately followed by comments from the platoon commanders, each sung to the tune of, "Yes, we do!"

"If you take them, whatever trust that exists between our groups will vanish," I said.

"And you trust these guys?" replied Shearburn. "How could you ask us to trust them? None of us know their agenda."

Shearburn was capitalizing on my poor command of the English language. *Trust* was the wrong word. I meant *common ground*. I had blown the opportunity to change opinions. Captain Smith had made up his mind.

"We will wait until morning to take away the weapons. Shearburn, ensure that the sergeant of the guard posts a watch on the scouts' door," said Captain Smith.

I was struck by the amount of fear in the room and what it was causing us to do. In my hands was a document that portrayed the scouts as an opportunity. But Rage 6 and the platoon commanders didn't pay much attention to it, due to the source. It was an example of our bias against everything Iraqi, commonly referred to as "hajji." In a sense, it was a continuation of our predeployment perspective—a perspective that envisioned our unit fighting Saddamists, not working alongside them.

I thought about trying to remake my point. The last thing I wanted to do, though, was isolate my voice. Plus, Captain Smith had already considered the options and drawn a conclusion. I accepted that the discussion of how we would treat the scouts was over.

"Daly, go get the general. I want to see his plan," said Rage 6.

"So, what was Uday like, Faris?" asked Captain Smith. The general didn't understand. He wasn't Faris and probably didn't know Uday very well. Captain Smith didn't care. He continued to press the subject saying that he knew the general was Faris, that he was Fedayeen, and so on.

I saw it as a dangerous line of questioning. We were supposed to be discussing the raid that would be executed in less than twenty-four hours. Instead, the last hour was spent asking the general questions about the Fedayeen, Saddam, Uday, and Qusay. Rather than discussing our common purpose in the mission, the conversation focused on the differences of the past.

Eventually, Captain Smith asked the general about his plan.

"They did not show it to you?" replied the general, continuing with, "I was told they translated it into English."

From Captain Smith's expressions, I could tell he and I were thinking the same thing: that's your plan—a list of fifty targets and a map of where they are? Captain Smith explained to the general that we needed more detail. He described the coordination that was required for helicopters, tanks, and other assets to be used properly.

The general was caught off guard. "There is no time for that now. We have to leave in one hour," he said.

Captain Smith laughed. "The mission is tomorrow night," he said. Our two groups were clearly not on the same page.

The general turned to our interpreter, Jack, and let fly a few short bursts of Arabic that were accompanied by a successive chopping motion with his hands. The interpreter spoke English about as well as the general did, so we didn't even bother to let him translate.

"General." It was the first time Captain Smith referred to the senior Iraqi's status. "I do not have all of my men and equipment. The mission must be tomorrow." Two out of the three squads for Rage 1 and Rage 3 were occupying platoon patrol bases roughly 1,000 meters from the COP. Their lieutenants took the other as an escort to the COP to execute mission planning. Rage 4 was due to arrive that night after a few days' rest.

"Smith, understand my men live here. They have been gone three days. Wives and neighbors expect them to be home yesterday. How would they explain their absence? If we wait to do the mission, everyone will know it was them that helped the Americans."

Captain Smith leaned back in his chair. He went to stretch his long arms into the air, but his right forearm knocked his spit bottle off the desk. It flew a few inches past Albin's resting head. The crashing of the plastic bottle was followed by the proverbial "Fuck!" as a saliva-and-tobacco mix seeped onto the floor. A quick-acting Albin grabbed some paper towels out of the desk and began to wipe it up. Captain Smith leaned over and tried to clean what he had created, but Albin insisted. Accepting the rebuke, Rage 6 returned to the conversation.

"The timing of the mission is nonnegotiable. It will be tomorrow night," said Captain Smith, who paused and looked around the room. There was no response from the general. After making eye contact with each of the platoon commanders, Rage 6 asked, "How do we want to do this? . . . Daly, what's the total number of scouts?"

"Twenty-five, including the general, sir," I said.

"And we are going to have two squads from Rage 2, 3, and 4. So that would be six four-man teams, one for each squad, and the general will go with headquarters. Will your squads be comfortable with that?" said Captain Smith. He directed the question at Lieutenants Thomas, Jahelka, and Grubb. Each of them nodded in agreement but did not comment.

"Shearburn, operating from your patrol base, you will be the company's reserve," continued Captain Smith.

Shearburn looked annoyed. He wasn't used to being a reserve. Rage 1 was always the main effort. He didn't question the order; instead, he recommended that his patrol base, recently named OP Jack Bauer in honor of the 24 character, be made into a permanent fighting position. Captain Smith said he would think about it and returned his attention to the near fight.

"Now, each of these teams of scouts needs a leader. General, do you have six men you can depend on?" asked Captain Smith.

The general was confused by the question. "I am the leader, and I have more than six men," he said. It literally took a notepad and a few sketches of the structure Captain Smith was proposing to get him to understand—although once he did, he informed us of some crucial facts. The general already had cells of fighters in each of the neighborhoods who not only knew everything about the local subtribe but were actually members of the tribe. The leaders of these cells were already here.

With this information, Captain Smith took out his map, which had the fifty targets labeled on it, and identified six objective areas—one for each squad. He showed the areas to the general and asked him to marry up each of his leaders with one of the objective areas. At the same time, we assigned one of our squads to the same objective. Then the general went and got his chosen men.

The six scouts came into the room and sat at a few empty chairs or stood around the map. The general did not introduce them, and Captain Smith had to ask who was for which objective. As the scout for each objective was revealed, he was introduced to the platoon commander he would work with. The two men shook hands, but the scouts did not speak. After the first three behaved in such a manner, Captain Smith was becoming agitated.

"Well, what are their names?" he asked the general.

"They do not want to tell you; your men may say it in front of the people," the general responded.

"Not their real names. I want to know their aliases, their fake names."

As the general translated what Captain Smith wanted, the tension eased out of the room. The scouts began to smile and joke with one another. Two even argued over who was going to be "Abu Ali." The general resolved the dispute. There was another round of introductions, followed by the details of the plan.

Unlike on previous missions, where we left as soon as it was dark, the scouts advised that we wait until midnight. They said at that point, the terrorists would have decided nothing was happening and would have gone to bed. Once under their blankets, they would be too lazy to run when we showed up. We took their advice.

At midnight, Lieutenant Jahelka would take two squads from Rage 3 and hit the two western objective areas in Julayba. The majority of his targets were along Orchard Way in the vicinity of the Al Risala mosque. Rage 4, Lieutenant Grubb, took the central objective areas that followed along Route Nova to the north. Captain Smith and I would move with Lieutenant Thomas and Rage 2 to the northeast. Their targets rested near the Albu Musa mosque. In another striking contrast to our previous missions, it took Captain Smith only thirty minutes to come up with and brief the plan. The abbreviated process was a result of the meshing of our planning style with the scouts'. They knew where the targets were and would have simply walked to them. We usually took a day to coordinate aerial and tank assets, as well as brief our superior and adjacent units. The result was the banditry I had envisioned outside the headquarters of 1-37 Armor two months earlier. There weren't going to be any tanks, helicopters, or Pathfinders on this mission, just the scouts and our infantrymen.

An hour of conversation between the scouts and their Marine counterparts solidified the working relationship. The general left with his leaders to discuss the mission with the rest of the scouts. Soon after their departure, the COC began to empty. With only a few lance corporals in the room, I took the opportunity to indirectly revisit the issue of taking away the scouts' weapons with Captain Smith. "What if they say no?" I asked him.

"They probably will. But come on, FO, I read the same packet of information as you. We will do whatever it takes to execute this mission," he replied. I realized that Captain Smith saw the scouts as the same opportunity that I did. Though how he was going to handle taking away their weapons the next morning was still uncertain in my mind.

The general came back into the room and proceeded to engage in an hour of small talk with Captain Smith. I was surprised to hear his stories of recent travels to Amman, Kuwait, and Dubai. How such traveling was possible in Iraq was beyond my comprehension. After some banter by both sides, I continued to follow the advice I had received earlier from the adviser and provided the general with a cot in the senior enlisted and officer quarters. The few individuals who were awake in the room were not too happy but didn't offer any more discord than muttering, "Is that a fucking Iraqi?"

After I told a few individuals that the general could sleep in the room, everyone returned his attention to the small pillow on his cot. The hand-sewn camouflage cushions had been provided by Craig Trotter's mother at Christmastime. They were greatly appreciated by every Marine in the company. Uncle Sam didn't issue pillows. On that particular evening, the anticipation of what was going to happen the next day occupied the remaining thoughts I had. Thanks to my pillow, they were short thoughts. Within minutes, I was asleep.

"What the fuck!" shouted the XO. I rolled over in my cot and stared at his shadowy frame in the doorway. The high-intensity light from fluorescent bulbs entering the room forced me to squint and raise a hand to my eyes.

The XO took a few steps into the room and pointed at the general, who was awkwardly sitting up in his cot, unsure of what was happening. "What makes you think you are sleeping in here, motherfucker?! Get out! You hear me? Get out! That's the company gunny's cot!" shouted Lieutenant Trotter.

I sat in shock that Trotter would scream at the general. I looked over at our Iraqi ally. "Mister, what you say? Me? Go?" said the general. He inserted a few Arabic sentences to add to the confusion. I finally awoke from my slumber and stopped the XO.

"Trotter, I brought him in here and gave him the cot," I said. "He's a general, man; we don't need to make him sleep with the other Iraqis."

The XO turned and focused his attention toward me. "So you would make Gunny Bishop sleep with the Iraqis instead? Besides, he isn't a general; he is an ex-general, a Ba'athist," said an angry Trotter, who made a relevant point regarding the gunnery sergeant's sleeping arrangements.

"It's my fault, "I said. "I didn't realize Gunny Bishop was staying here tonight, instead of at Camp Corregidor like usual. He can have my cot; I have a shift as watch officer in a few minutes anyways," I was willing to give up my cot if it got the XO out of the room.

It worked; the disgruntled XO replied, "Whatever," and left. I was aghast at the scenario. My first thought was that Trotter had destroyed any chance of a working relationship between us and Thawar Al Anbar. Then I realized that Trotter had provided me with a unique opportunity.

I hopped out of my cot and pulled out my laptop case, which had been underneath me.

"Why you let him speak to you and me that way, Daly?" asked the general. I sat down next to him on his cot and turned on the laptop.

"General, he is number two in command after Captain Smith," I replied. The general understood rank structure and nodded.

"So what are you, Daly, number three?" he asked.

I looked at the general and smiled. "I am the intelligence officer." Then I seized on one of Captain Smith's mistakes from earlier. "I know you are not General Faris," I said.

His usual broad smile that didn't reveal teeth overcame his face, and I knew I had his attention. I returned to the laptop and opened a folder of pictures from Hawaii and San Diego. I double-clicked on the first one, and the skyline of San Diego appeared on the screen. The general stared at the picture, as I explained that I had taken the photo while leaving San Diego's harbor back in September. After a moment, I continued on to the next image. It was a view of Honolulu from a few miles offshore. The city's towering skyscrapers were silhouetted by a combination of the lush green hills of Oahu's interior and a clear blue Pacific horizon.

As the general focused on the screen, I gauged his reaction to each photo. His eyes were glued to the computer, but a sense of confusion occupied his facial expressions. I went to the next picture. A series of images of my wife and me at the Turtle Bay resort on Oahu's North Shore took over the screen. The general agreed with me that Aimee was in fact beautiful. It was at that point that he stopped the procession of pictures.

"Why do you show me this, Daly?" he asked. I was waiting for this question and almost out of pictures.

"Because you and I want the same thing," I responded. "We both have families, and our dreams of their future do not include war and destruction but hope and success." I knew I was being cliché or overly serious, but I wasn't speaking to an ordinary Iraqi. The general was a significant member of the Ba'ath Party, a man of influence in the Saddam regime. The events of the last three years, during which he saw the destruction of everything he and his predecessors had built, were undoubtedly in his mind. After listening to him describe the more modern Arab cities of Dubai and Kuwait, I wanted to evoke his thoughts that together we could lay the groundwork for such a transformation in Iraq. I knew it was a shot in the dark, but I figured why not try?

The general was silent for a few moments, probably searching for how to express himself in English. "Two years ago, my brother killed an al Qaeda man in Sofia," he said. "Daly, he was one of the most powerful men in my tribe, but the strength of al Qaeda forced him into exile in Jordan. Now, for the safety of my wife, my daughters, we will remove the terrorists. Then I will signal the return of my brother, the sheikh of the Fahadawi tribe." He glanced toward the ceiling and muttered something in Arabic. Then he went on to tell me how much I would like Dubai, and he swore that one day Julayba would be a tourist attraction with its own amusement park.

I didn't respond to his comments, but instead I closed the laptop, returning the room to the near-pitch-black status that had been interrupted by Trotter.

"General, you should go back to sleep. Tomorrow will be a long night," I said, thinking it was a good point to end the conversation on.

"Yes, yes, Daly," he said.

I stood up from his cot and headed toward the door. The plywood creaked when I pulled on the handle, and the bright light of the COP's foyer illuminated the windowless room.

"I like you, Daly," said the general as I went through the door frame.

I was unsure of how to respond. Somehow I forced out, "I like you, too," with a straight face and walked into the blinding light. Of course, one of the Marines sleeping on the rotunda overlooking the foyer heard my comment and called me out on it.

"Sir, that's probably the gayest thing I've heard in Iraq," he said.

"Don't get any ideas, Corporal," I replied.

I went down the staircase and stood four hours of watch. I took note of the fact that absolutely nothing happened and I was doing everything in my power to not fall asleep. Half a dozen cans of Rip It energy drink were my only relief. I decided that leaving at midnight just might catch some militants asleep in their beds. Al Qaeda didn't have Rip Its.

Two steps behind Captain Smith and the general, I entered the five-hundred-square-foot room where the scouts were staying. Most of the men were sleeping under their blankets, with their heads toward three of the rectangular-shaped room's walls. They naturally formed a half-circle for the general to address them from. I stood against the far, unoccupied wall with my arms crossed, disappointedly looking at the Iraqis, who were about to have their only sense of security snatched from their hands.

Earlier that morning, Captain Smith had informed the general of his decision. I was surprised when the general offered no real resistance to the idea. Based on his acquiescence, the other officers of Rage thought that maybe the scouts wouldn't make a fuss over the issue of being disarmed. I knew, however, that the general was picking his battles. Like me, he did not want to create tension. His best bargaining tool would be when his men refused to go on the mission without the weapons.

From the center of the dim room, the general began to speak.

It went down as I thought. The general uttered two, maybe three sentences. Then his men began to shout at Captain Smith. For a moment, I feared for our lives. The twenty-four scouts were pumping fists and rifles, while shouting in Arabic. Captain Smith and I were both unarmed, with nothing more than the clothes on our backs to protect us from the immense stopping power of a 7.62mm bullet. My mind anticipated what I would do if one of the scouts started shooting.

The general's booming voice filled the room. The scouts went silent. It was an example of the respect they held for the general's tribal status.

Jack, the interpreter, came through the door. In the second that it was open, I made eye contact with the sergeant of the guard, who had a few Marines behind him. Their presence put me at ease, but I motioned for them to stay outside the door. I figured armed Americans would only increase tension.

"Jack-O." Captain Smith spotted the interpreter as he came into the room. "Come over here and tell me what these clowns are saying."

The general was going around the room and getting opinions from each of his men. Most of them responded with "*La*," Arabic for no. From the responses, I assumed that he had asked them whether they would go on the mission without their weapons. Halfway through the group, one of the scouts gave a short speech. Jack translated. "The Americans not trust us. The area is very dangerous, and we already know they cannot protect us. Maybe they and the Iraqi army want to kill us," said Jack on behalf of the scout.

Most of the scouts agreed with the man. Some did not. Captain Smith interrupted the process, telling Jack to say, "We must build trust between us. This will help my men focus on our common enemy, al Qaeda."

There was a temporary silence in the room while the group thought about al Qaeda. The four or five ardent naysayers dismissed Captain Smith with their hands. The process of individual reactions continued.

Rage 6 was visibly frustrated. He turned his back on the group and headed for the door. "Well, I'd say that fucking went well," he muttered as he passed me. I didn't have to hear the sarcasm in his voice. It was written all over his face.

I was now the only American in the room. Jack left the general's side and took a spot next to me against the wall. Together, we listened to the last few scouts disagree with the general about the weapons. "Daly, they all want to go home," said Jack when they were done.

I felt that I had to do something.

The general turned and headed for the door. I stopped him. "May I speak to your men?" I asked.

"Of course, Daly."

I walked to the center of the group. A few of the men were now sitting on their blankets, while the majority still stood. I began by introducing myself. After Jack's easy translation, the general added in a few words. I wasn't sure what he said, but I was sure it was giving me credibility. When he was done, I received a few nods from the majority of the scouts. I chose my next words carefully, aiming for the same purpose as the sentences just uttered by the general.

"I will speak to Captain Smith about letting you take your weapons on the mission," I said.

I had no intention of actually speaking to Captain Smith. But based on our previous discussions regarding the opportunity the scouts represented, I knew he was going to let them take the rifles. If the Iraqis thought I had something to do with his change of heart, they might start to come to me with their requests. Then I hoped to figure out which scouts held critical information that could be useful.

"If you need anything while you are here, you can ask me," Jack translated.

Then I turned my focus to al Qaeda. I said a few sentences that focused on their brutality and crimes against locals. I got carried away, though, and ended with a line about the extremism of al Qaeda and how we could return Iraq to its secular status.

The scouts' faces soured. I had assumed that they were all secular. It was poor form on my part, because I had ignored the fact that for the last three years these men had fought against me with a mutual understanding between themselves and al Qaeda. The general went into damage control on my behalf. When he finished, his men were arguing with one another. Chaos had taken over, and I knew I had no future as a motivational speaker.

"Daly, they are hungry. Do you have food for them?" asked the general.

"Of course. Give me a few minutes." I left and grabbed a case of Otis Spunkmeyer muffins and another of twenty-ounce Gatorades. I was disappointed that I hadn't realized that the scouts were not being fed. When they first arrived, Captain Smith ordered the Iraqi army soldiers to provide them with food. This order ignored the fact that the relationship between the Shia Iraqi army and the armed Sunni, ex-Saddamist scouts wasn't based on common interests or beliefs. The obvious result was the neglecting of the twenty-five volunteers.

When I returned, the scouts drank the Gatorade but weren't very interested in the muffins. I guess the preservatives were an acquired taste. I thought about leaving the room, but Abu Ali, one of the general's appointed leaders, approached me. He wanted to see the pictures I had shown the general the night before. Within five minutes, I had 75 percent of the local Iraqis in a semicircle around my laptop screen.

The group wasn't very interested in the first few pictures of San Diego or Honolulu, but when a picture of my wife appeared, they all commented to one another in hushed voices. It dawned on me that the general had told them of the beauty of my wife, and it was probably this fact that had earned me a few nods from the crowd earlier.

"Daly, she have sister?" asked one of the scouts. I knew what he was getting at: an arranged marriage.

"Yes, she does."

"You let me marry her, no? We be brothers, then!" he continued.

"She is very expensive," I said. "But that is for her father to decide." The scouts collectively agreed when Jack translated. I flipped through the remaining pictures. At the end, the men thanked me for showing them. I left somewhat confident that the mission was going to happen.

Around midday, Captain Smith and I went for round two with the scouts. The purpose was to announce that we were going to allow them to keep their weapons. We assumed that such a decision would unite our two groups.

So Captain Smith was caught off guard when, after he announced his decision, the scouts still refused to go on the mission. We had miscalculated their primary concern. It wasn't being able to carry their weapons into the fight. Instead, the majority believed that by their executing the mission and not being able to quickly return home, al Qaeda would figure out who was assisting the Americans. The fear instilled by al Qaeda's murder-and-intimidation campaign was evident on their faces.

I felt like a new toy had been snatched from my hands before I could play with it. I watched Captain Smith, who was looking at the floor, and waited for him to tell the scouts that the trucks would bring them back to Camp Ranger. We couldn't force the group to fight alongside us. Rage 6 was silent for a solid thirty seconds.

"Jack, tell them that the trucks are not coming."

"Sir?" replied the interpreter.

"There are no trucks. Headquarters had to divert them to another unit in Ramadi. They are stuck here for the night and might as well do the mission as planned," said Captain Smith.

It was a bald-faced lie. I didn't know how many would buy it. Then the general asked how many would go on the mission anyway. Four raised their hands. As it sank in that those four men would execute the mission and therefore cast suspicion on the entire lot, because none of them would be home the following morning, more hands began to go up. Soon we had 100 percent participation. As soon as they all agreed to go, we immediately left the room before they could change their minds.

I went into the COC with Captain Smith. I let out a few laughs once the door was closed. "Sir, that was the most obvious lie I have ever heard. The damn trucks are sitting outside!" I said.

"It worked because they can't speak English and don't realize that I am a horrible liar. Plus, they aren't allowed outside and will never see the trucks," he said.

"So long as Gunny Bishop is out of here before midnight," I replied.

"Good point. Go get that fucker."

Eakin pushed the barbed wire off the path with the muzzle of his M16. Albin and I slowly moved through the gap, and another Marine from Rage 2 traded spots with Eakin. Behind us, the ten-foot concrete barriers that protected COP Rage stood in the darkness. It was the first time I had been outside their protection and not in a vehicle.

The formation walked up the slight berm that held Route Nova above and crossed the asphalt road. We immediately went down the far side and within 100 meters were moving through the rich farmland that encompassed half of Julayba's acreage. The open terrain served as a natural north-south boundary between the Albu Musa and Albu Bali tribal villages that sat on the eastern side of Julayba. This boundary was more of an obstacle for the enemy than it was for us. For us, it provided a clear insertion route into the two pro–al Qaeda villages and prevented them from assisting each other during an attack by coalition forces. Isolating the two tribes was much easier for it.

Our presence alerted the natural sentries that watched over the region. A dozen wild dogs barked in the night. Some were close; most were distant, but to the area's insurgents their ruckus was evidence that something was afoot.

We crossed into a farm that resembled something out of a Vietnam War movie. I stepped down into an irrigation ditch. The soft dirt rose up around my boots, and I struggled to get up the opposite side. After clearing the obstacle, I turned around and offered Eakin and then the general my hand in assistance. Moving through the grass field, we were in a heavily exposed position. Irrigation canals ran parallel to our direction of movement. The accompanying palm trees and shrubs that lined the canals provided excellent cover and concealment. They ensured that a small group of men could tactically move through the adjoining fields without our knowledge. I scanned the numerous potential ambush points with urgency.

A massive explosion rang out over the farmland. I dropped to a knee and rotated in its general direction. The blast was loud but distant. Its origin and flash of light were probably a mile to the southeast.

"Eakin, anything on the company net?"

"Negative. Must be 3/2, sir."

I agreed with him. Before we had left, the Marines on our eastern boundary informed us of a Pathfinder mission in their AO that would cross into Julayba. It was a standard method to blur the tactical boundaries for our enemies. The result was Pathfinder hitting a massive IED in the Albu Bali tribal area.

I gripped my rifle tighter, and we moved another thousand meters through the open fields. The column halted about 300 meters south of a cluster of buildings that formed the outlying perimeter of the greater Albu Musa tribal village. A team of scouts was at the front of the formation scoping out the homes, undoubtedly getting their bearings after trudging through the fields in the pitch blackness. Navigation was easier for us; we wore NVGs. The scouts sported black ski masks.

The leader of the four-man team, Abu Tiba, ran back to the command element. Captain Smith, Lieutenant Thomas, the general, and I were crouched behind a cluster of small shrubs and palm trees. Three cows tied to old wooden poles grazed 100 meters away. Abu Tiba knelt next to the general and relayed his knowledge of the local area.

"This house is the legal court of the ISI. Ali Siyagah lives here," said the general. He pointed to the center house of the three. Captain Smith exchanged a look of "Sure it is" with Lieutenant Thomas and me; capturing Ali Siyagah couldn't possibly be this easy.

Lieutenant Thomas got on the PRR and directed his platoon. Corporal Davila's squad would clear the structure after Holloway's established an inner and outer cordon. We watched from behind the palm trees as the Marines moved into position. Davila personally went through the building's front door, followed by his squad. The command element was less than a minute behind him.

I went up two stairs onto the home's porch and through the front door. By the time I was inside, Davila's men had cleared the one-floor building and were separating the women and the children from the men. Abu Tiba picked out the man of the house, his son, and his teenage grandson to be brought into the foyer. None of the three matched the description of Ali Siyagah. Captain Smith and I commented to each other on this fact. Abu Tiba noticed our demeanor and explained that we were at the wrong house. A sense of doubt regarding the effectiveness of the scouts began to build in my mind. The Marines prepared to leave.

As they did, I was struck by what the four-man team of scouts was doing. One of them was in the room with the women and the children. He stood in front of the terrified group of civilians, lecturing them. I tried to walk into the room, but the general stopped me.

"Daly, he is telling them what they need to know," he said. Then he tried to close the door. My first thought was that our scouts were about to beat the locals. I stuck my foot in the door and pushed against it with my hand. "I am going to listen and watch from out here," I said. The general acquiesced and opened the door. The family was in the corner on the opposite side of the room and could not see me. I shouted for Jack to come over. Before he got there and began translating, all I could discern was "Thawar Al Anbar," over and over.

Once Jack arrived, he explained to me what was happening. "Lieutenant, it is propaganda. He says Thawar Al Anbar is the real power, that they declare jihad against al Qaeda, that they will kill the terrorists, and so on," relayed Jack. At the end of the speech, the scout removed a piece of paper from his jacket. I waited for him to leave the room and asked him to show one of the pages to me. Jack explained that it said, essentially verbatim, what the scout had just discussed.

"Jack-O, get in here!" yelled Captain Smith from the front of the house. I went with the interpreter to the foyer. Abu Tiba was harshly questioning the home's only military-age male. The chubby Iraqi receiving the brunt of questioning was sweating, even though the temperature hovered in the mid-forties. Abu Tiba noticed that the general was in the room. He quickly ordered the three males of the house to turn around and face the wall. Then the masked scout approached the general and whispered to him. In turn, the general leaned over to me and said, "This man can bring us to Ali Siyagah's house." I doubted whether it was true. Captain Smith had begun to look uncomfortable. No longer were the scouts directing our movement, but a random local was going to lead us. It seemed like an obvious trap, but Captain Smith rolled the dice. The squat, fearful Iraqi would lead us.

We left the house, and Abu Tiba, along with the chubby Iraqi, went to the front of the formation. We crossed over more farmland, moving through half a dozen irrigation canals. We approached another cluster of houses and came across a canal that was full of water. The chubby Iraqi moved south, away from the houses, and led us to a stone dam that controlled the flow of water. I was nervous that such an obvious crossing point, the only place where you don't get your feet wet, would have an IED or something protecting it. But the scouts went across without hesitation, and we followed.

After crossing, we headed back to the north, moving through a small orchard of fruit trees. The column of Marines walked past another group of grazing cows and resting sheep. After a few hundred meters, we were looking at a small village. The chubby Iraqi led us through overgrown brush and tightly packed trees between the two southernmost homes. He halted us at a dirt path that ran from the southern house to what I thought was Gixxer to the north.

Abu Tiba ran back to the general, who was with me. The chubby Iraqi accompanied him. When the random Iraqi got to us, I could see that he was petrified. Clearly, he did not want to go anywhere near the home that we were now looking at.

"Smith, can you leave men to guard him here?" the general asked Rage 6. Lieutenant Thomas agreed to leave a team of Marines with the Iraqi.

The process of cordoning off the house and the subsequent clearing followed in the same format as the first. When I neared the home with the general, the other scouts went insane. Before we even made it inside the house, they became agitated.

"These are Ali Siyagah's cars!" said the general, pointing at the two vehicles under the one-story home's carport. Holloway's team of scouts immediately joined Abu Tiba's in assaulting the vehicles. They began to break the windows and the glass with the butts of their rifles. Captain Smith ordered them to stop.

"Why?! We must send a message!" said Abu Tiba.

Captain Smith responded by making the sound of an explosion and demonstrating it with his hands. The scouts got the idea, but one of them decided to break off a side mirror regardless. They wanted the personal satisfaction.

We entered the house, which was split by a long central hallway. In the second room on the left, eight men were kneeling on the concrete floor. They were enjoying a comfortable conversation with Davila's Marines. Then the scouts, with their black ski masks, entered the room. I watched the demeanor of each man on the floor rapidly change. Eyes grew wide. Mouths dropped.

Without asking any questions, Abu Tiba began to angrily address each man by name. He moved to an older teenager who sat only a few yards from me. He kicked the kid in the leg and pulled his hair. The scout looked at me and said the kid's name over and over. I was about to tell him to stop, and then I realized I wasn't hearing the name for the first time. Pulling out my list of terrorists of Julayba, I realized that the kid was Ali Siyagah's personal driver.

"Davila, bag and tag this guy," I said, pointing at the kid for the squad leader.

Abu Tiba went around the room. The driver and other young boys on the floor began to cry. The poor bastards knew the game was up. Two more of the men, who looked like they should have been in college, were Ali Siyagah's bodyguards. I was amazed that these terrorists were openly admitting who they were to the scouts. Ali Siyagah, however, was not in the house. His loyal bodyguards and driver explained that he had fled across the river after Operation Churubusco.

Abu Tiba questioned all of the men but decided to take only four. He said the other four were locals who had been forced into perform-ing small tasks for al Qaeda. As in the previous house, the women and the children, as well as the four males who stayed behind, received the propaganda speech from Abu Tiba.

I walked out of the house. Sergeant Sempert and a few of the scouts were pushing the parked vehicles down the dirt path, away from the house. Somebody informed the scouts that Sempert was an engineer because once the cars were far enough away, they all began to mimic Captain Smith's previous gesture of an explosion. Sempert was initially amused but quickly grew annoyed.

Before the explosion, I headed back to the team guarding the chubby Iraqi who had led us to the house. When I got there, a scout was ques-tioning him.

"Hello, Daly," said the scout. I was surprised that he spoke English.

"Are we going to let him go?" I asked, recognizing the scout as the leader of the team with Holloway's squad.

"No, no," he replied. "He led us here because he knows very much about the terrorists because he is one. You must blindfold him so the others don't think he worked with us. It is dangerous for his family."

"Uh . . . okay," I responded. I went back to the house and asked the general the same question about releasing the chubby kid, and he gave me the same response. Holloway bagged and tagged him.

Davila's squad finished up with the processing and a detailed search of the home. When we were ready to go, Holloway's squad removed the family from the home and brought them 200 meters north to their neighbors. We wanted them to be as far away from the exploding cars as possible. From their agonizing sobs, the family seemed to think they were about to be executed.

Sempert set the charges and began a short countdown. The two cars were destroyed in simultaneous blasts shortly thereafter. The thundering noise produced shrieks from the women. It looked like one had fainted, but I quickly decided that she was faking. A Marine helped her to her feet. Then she and the rest of the family walked back to the house.

The platoon was now in the vicinity of Gixxer, somewhere south of the Albu Musa mosque. We had hit only two houses and held five detainees. I wondered how the other squads were faring.

"Sir."

"What is it, Eakin?" I asked.

"Battalion wants to know if we started the fires all over Julayba," he said. I informed Rage 6 that the battalion was asking questions about fires being set across our area of operations. We were responsible for two: the burning remains of a couple Chevy Impalas. The other squads were probably setting their own. At least, it seemed that way; 1/9 INF was saying that they counted five separate fires from their UAV feed.

I snatched the handset from Eakin and listened to 1/9's operations officer order Captain Smith to stop destroying private property without permission. Watching Abu Tiba coordinate with his scouts and a Marine team leader which houses needed to be hit, I heard the OPSO tell Captain Smith to "get your act together." Rage 6 didn't respond over the radio but chose his present company to express his thoughts.

"Fucking watch officers," he said.

I took the opportunity to correct him. "You mean battle captains," I said, referring to the proper terminology for the army's desk jockeys. Watch-O was the Marine Corps version.

"Shut up, FO."

Davila's and Holloway's squads split up, each led by their respective team of scouts. In a few hours, they cleared each target building within their objective areas. It was an unusual experience. The scouts led the platoons, based on their knowledge of the terrain, not on the best tactical route. On multiple occasions, we walked along the same road or alley, back and forth, searching for an al Qaeda's home. The third time around, the scout would recognize the residence and direct the Marines to clear it. The result was a growing trail of detainees.

Around 0400, Rage 2 was finishing up with their assigned targets. We headed west toward the intersection of Gixxer and Route Nova to assist Rage 4. Lieutenant Grubb had the most targets and the largest objective area.

We cleared a string of houses and hit the fourth one in a row. It was unusual because no one was detained in the first three, and most of the homes we searched were spread out, never consecutive. When Davila's squad made it into the fourth, Abu Tiba informed him, through Jack, not to bother with the clear. The squad was standing in Abu Tiba's house, and he wanted some tea. He said we had cleared the previous three homes to make it look like we were searching for someone, rather than making a visit. Although it was a tactical waste of time, I found the event somewhat comical. The humor allowed me to join Abu Tiba in a cup of tea.

At the end of the break, we continued. With every house we entered, the night began to lose darkness. Soon I found myself half a mile away from COP Rage, standing in an alleyway fully illuminated by a rising sun. I was highly uncomfortable with the idea of having to drag the detainees back in the light of day. Al Qaeda was awakening on that particular morning to some bad news. If they knew we were still roaming the streets, they were going to try to find us.

Captain Smith emerged from the last house we had cleared, with the scouts in tow. The general was begging him to continue the search for a few targets. Rage 6 didn't see any reason to. There were twenty detainees from the platoons, and Rage 3 was already back at the COP. He ordered Rage 2 and Rage 4 to the COP by the fastest route. The result was forty Marines and a dozen ski-mask-clad Iraqis walking down the middle of Route Nova. With the knowledge that six IEDs had been detonated along this stretch of Nova in the previous week, I wasn't very happy about the route. I scanned the dirt more than usual. The scouts, on the other hand, conversed with one another and ignored their surroundings. They seemed to think there was nothing to fear. They were right. We made it back to the COP.

"Abu Ali was awesome," said Lieutenant Jahelka. His comment was followed by stories from lieutenants Thomas and Grubb to the same effect. Three of the scouts were gaining notoriety among the platoon commanders: Abu Ali, Abu Tiba, and Salim.

The XO was less enthused. "Which one of you dingleberries is taking my place?" he asked. Trotter had been serving as the watch officer for the last eight hours and wasn't involved in the mission. Boredom had overpowered his mind. Lieutenant Thomas took his post.

Captain Smith came into the COC, after rising from two hours of rest that followed the mission. He informed the group that the scouts were not going home yet. Rage 6 was going to use the same lie as before. Then that night he would take a smaller group to hit the dozen targets not yet actioned due to the lack of darkness.

"You think they are going to buy that truck story again, sir?" asked Jahelka.

"Maybe."

Maybe was good enough. The scouts might not have bought the story, but some of them executed the second mission and helped detain seven individuals. I stayed at the COP. The amount of paperwork required for the first twenty was overwhelming. To make matters worse, our one THT (tactical human-intelligence team) soldier refused to question the detainees. When I pressed him, his response was, "I can't force them to say anything." The nineteen-year-old specialist was a far cry from Sergeant Champion. The lack of initiative by this soldier sparked a bolder thought in my mind.

For the entire day, the general tried to get access to the detainees. Technically, I was not allowed to question the detainees, so I obviously declined his requests. But it was clear from working with the scouts that they would be capable of gathering significant information if given the opportunity. I remembered Sheikh Hatim, his son, and the other HVIs captured during Operation Churubusco and how they hadn't been questioned by THT either. I brought it up in the form of a pointed question to Captain Smith when he returned from the second mission.

"Sir, what if the scouts question the detainees under my supervision?" I asked.

Twenty minutes later, I had convinced Captain Smith that it was a good idea.

11

Running Out of Luck

0700, January 27, 2007

I walked out of the mansion's big red front door. What had been an Iraqi's home just a week earlier now resembled a fortress. Hundreds of concrete barriers formed a perimeter around COP Rage's two structures: the mansion and an unfinished house next to it. Thousands of sandbags lined the mansion's walls, roof, and windows. The empty shell of a house next door offered no such protection. The only additions to its exterior were a few sheets of white cloth that covered the windows, preventing distant observers from seeing inside.

The fortification of COP Rage, which began when Sergeant Karras kicked down the mansion's door, was continuous. A few hundred more sandbags were piled on the ground in front of me, awaiting their final resting place. This was in addition to the camouflage netting that covered the four wooden, sandbagged fighting positions on the roof and the two similar towers that stood over the compound's two entrances. One gate was at the northeast corner of the compound, connecting to Route Nova; the second opened to the dirt-path access road that James Thomas had passed during Operation Churbusco. Both of them were blocked by vehicles and numerous strands of barbed wire.

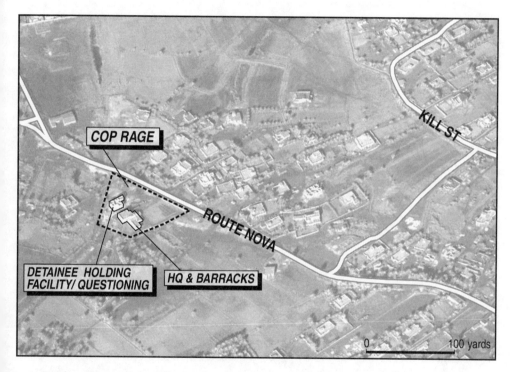

Combat Outpost Rage: The Combat Outpost Rage and the immediate terrain around it.

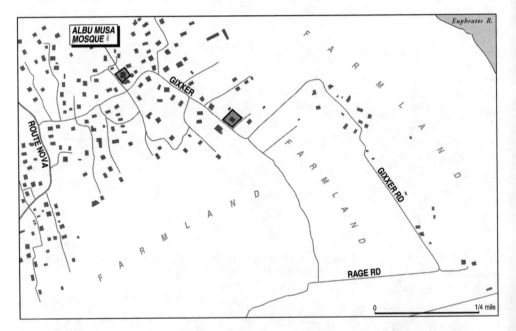

Ambushed: The open field where Rage 1 was ambushed in early February 2007.

The defensive materials arrived from Camp Ramadi in daily convoys led by Lieutenant Trotter. Every night the XO drove through checkpoints 295 and 296. His trucks usually got shot up, but it was never anything serious. After one convoy, Trotter was supervising the unloading of the logistical vehicles carrying the company's supplies. He watched as two female soldiers hopped out of their large truck and began talking about getting lit up by insurgent rifle fire at 296. "No, they didn't!" said one of the women. I could see that the mere sound of a woman discussing the danger of combat made Trotter uneasy. I went down the three steps of the mansion's front rotunda. The men walking behind me were thinking of ways to make the twenty-seven detainees sitting in the empty building next door uncomfortable. As I went through the COP's parking lot, the size of two football fields, I could hear the general and his men discussing their plans in Arabic. Thirty minutes earlier, I had informed them they would be allowed to question the detainees. Now they were strategizing. The scouts had done this before. A few even admitted to being interrogators in Saddam's army.

I walked into the tan cinder-block building. There were no doors and no glass in the windows. Only the central foyer had a real floor; the floors of rest of the surrounding rooms mostly consisted of broken pieces of concrete or rocks. On the first floor, three rooms faced the south, each opening to the foyer and isolated from the other neighboring rooms. On the northern side, a spiraling staircase rose to the second floor, which had no roof and was to be used only for firing positions in dire circumstances. Facing the parking lot out front was another large, elongated room full of plywood and two-by-fours. It adjoined a narrow hallway that led to an opening where a front door should have been, the same hallway the ski-mask-clad scouts and I had walked through.

I met the two Marines standing guard duty in the foyer and gave them an update on what was about to happen. The twenty-seven detainees were currently sitting in one room, each blindfolded and flexi-cuffed. Each of them had an index card draped around his neck with a number on it. The numbers went, logically, from one to twenty-seven and were written in both English and Arabic. The scouts would go into the room, identify which Iraqis they wanted to question, and place them in the middle of the three rooms. Then, one at a time, each detainee would enter the remaining empty room of the three that faced south. Roughly ten scouts would be waiting for him.

The general asked me to have the guards "play games" with the men who waited to be questioned. It took a translation from Jack until I realized that the general wanted to find out about the detainees' personalities. One of the scouts would watch the games, nothing more than boot camp gimmicks of "get up, get down" scenarios. The scout would take note of the men who did what the guards said, essentially those who tried to please us, with the idea that they would be more likely to talk. This would also distract the waiting detainees, potentially allowing the individual being questioned to feel more at ease that no one would hear what he was saying.

I took a seat among a bunch of jagged rocks in the room where the questioning would be conducted. The scouts took about ten minutes to figure out who would be questioned first: they chose about a third of the twenty-seven detainees. In the middle room, the two Marines yelled at the detainees to stand up. Obviously, not many of the Iraqis understood English. Most of them remained sitting. So, the guards had to help them to their feet. Once all were standing, the guards yelled at them to get down. Again, the process of having to assist some of the men repeated itself. In the middle of the confusion, one scout snatched the first man to be questioned. It was Ali Siyagah's driver.

They led the man into the empty room and pushed him into the far corner. The general sat down on my left. Jack, the interpreter, followed him seconds later on my right. The general held a black leather case with gold Arabic script lining the top flap. A map of Iraq was emblazoned on the cover. The general opened it and started to review a few pages inside. They appeared to be diagrams of various insurgent networks. The other scouts distracted me from looking at the pages, which I couldn't read anyway. The questioning began.

The detainee was encircled by six or seven scouts, all of them leaning only inches from his face. One scout fired off questions. I could tell that he repeated the question when he got an answer he didn't like. An older scout, with graying hair and a beard, took copious notes on a yellow pad. Sometimes he asked questions for clarification. The rest of the scouts simply listened. When the detainee said something they knew was false, the quiet men would lean over and tell the lead interrogator what they knew. The quiet men were the locals, the neighbors of the detainee, and knew everything about the man. For good reason they didn't ask any questions. The detainee might have recognized their voices, placing the lives of the scouts and their families in danger.

I continued to sit on the jagged rocks, fascinated by the process. I could hear the Marines in the other room having fun by playing their own version of Simon says with the detainees. As the general had anticipated, most of the younger detainees were competing for the Marines' attention. Whoever did first what the Marines said, received shouts of praise. Most of the older detainees ignored the guards and still had to be manually picked up or sat down. In the room where I sat, Siyagah's driver was blabbing on about something. I assumed it was good, because the scout with the yellow pad was writing furiously.

Then Abu Ali, who was one of the silent scouts, left the room. He sort of stormed off, which I found somewhat surprising. The lead interrogator began to repeat the same question over and over. He raised his right hand high above his head. I thought he was stretching or something. I was wrong. In one fell swoop the open palm went from high to low, smacking the detainee squarely on the side of the face. The sound of palm meeting skin was so loud, I could feel the stinging on my own cheek.

I looked at the general, whom I had specifically told not to let his men hit or manhandle the detainees. I was about to tell him to stop the questioning. The scouts were clearly not capable of containing their hatred for al Qaeda. But I noticed that the general wasn't looking back at me; his eyes were searching the face of someone standing behind me who was the real decision maker. I turned around and spotted Captain Smith. As I did, Abu Ali walked back into the room with a green garden hose. Before I could ask him why he had such an object, he leaned over to Jack and whispered in Arabic.

"Daly, can he hit the detainee with the hose? It won't leave any marks or bruises," relayed Jack. It was the worst possible timing. I didn't know how long Captain Smith had been standing behind me, but if he had just walked in, it would've looked as if I was complicit in the beating of our detainees. I motioned for Abu Ali to lean in closer to me. "Hell, no," I said. I laughed ever so slightly and smiled at Abu Ali, attempting to minimize the effect of my denying his request. Then Captain Smith spoke up in a hushed tone: "General, if he hits him again, you are done."

The general nodded in agreement. He got up and walked over to the lead questioner, the same scout who had hit the detainee. He grabbed his hand and waved it around so the other scouts saw what he was doing. Then he shook his head no. The group acknowledged the general's directive and continued questioning. Captain Smith went back to the COC.

An hour later, we were on the third man. To me, someone who had no idea what was being said, the previous two detainees had done a lot of talking. Jack informed me every time the detainee admitted to doing something wrong. The first man said he had personally conducted or was complicit in the murder of local civilians. The second guy admitted to planting IEDs and killing an Iraqi general. Each of the events was accompanied by the date the event took place. I decided that later I would try to get the scouts to let me have the yellow pad of paper. The information written on it was worth translating.

The questioning was interrupted by a shrieking blast. The sound of shrapnel ricocheting off the COP's concrete perimeter wall startled me. I jumped up off the floor, realizing that it was an incoming mortar round. The general and the scouts seemed oblivious to the explosion. They continued their questioning without interruption. I figured, as former insurgents, that they had been on the receiving end of countless mortar and artillery rounds, not to mention American close air support and helicopter missiles. They weren't going to be threatened by only one incoming round.

I, on the other hand, did feel threatened, very threatened. I moved to the room's only window. It faced southwest, directly toward the sound of the blast. Peeling back the white cloth that covered the gaping hole, I spotted the dissipating smoke. It was only 50 meters outside the perimeter wall, no more than 100 meters away. For an observer, it was almost a perfect initial round. All the insurgents had to do was adjust 100 meters to their technical-firing data and drop in a few rounds, and COP Rage would have been blown apart.

A minute later, a second blast struck to the northwest. It was the same deal as the first, just outside the concrete wall. This time, the scouts paused to look at one another. A couple picked their helmets up off the ground and put them on. Then they continued questioning. I grabbed Jack and moved into the central foyer. It was the only interior room, meaning that its walls did not connect to the structure's exterior and had no windows. It was the safest place from incoming shrapnel.

The moment I began to sit down, the building was shaken by the concussion of another round. The explosion was deafening, only a few meters outside the nonexistent door. I listened to the 120mm mortar round's twisted iron shrapnel fly through the air, impacting the COP's generator and vehicles. It even flew through the hallway that led into the building, pinging off the narrow walls opposite each other. The round landed directly in the center of the COP. If the enemy dropped a few more with the same data on the weapon system, we would be in trouble. Fortunately, it was the last incoming round.

The scouts responded to the danger by returning to the original room that contained the majority of the detainees. They snatched a young man, probably in his late teens, and dragged him out into the foyer. They threw the boy at my feet and told me he was a member of the mortar team that was firing at us. Then the two questioning scouts heckled him for the rest of the detainees to hear. They spouted off the names of the boy's family and friends. They even rattled off the names of the other members of his mortar cell. It was sort of a morale crusher for the detainees, who had probably taken satisfaction in knowing their comrades were dropping mortar rounds all around us. The scouts were informing them that their one advantage over the Americans was no longer in play. The shadow of anonymity surrounding the local militants was thrust into the light. Instead, the insurgents would now wonder who was helping the Americans. For the first time I felt that my deployment to Ramadi might mean something; I might leave with some sort of accomplishment. I think the general read my mind.

"They will fight you much harder," he whispered into my ear, motioning toward the sky with his finger. "This is only the beginning; they will respond. All of the people know what we have done." I couldn't possibly have known the truth of which the general spoke.

For the rest of the day, I watched the scouts question the detainees. It was fascinating but also mind-numbing. I knew that the information being obtained had to be captured, but Jack wasn't very capable of speaking proper English, let alone writing it. So, during piss and chow breaks, I showed the dozen other scouts, who were relaxing inside the COP, how to write out sworn statements against each of the detainees. They were not enthused about having to fill out the bureaucratic paperwork of the Americans, but none of them complained after I explained that any detainee who didn't have two statements against him would be released.

In the early evening, the company staff discussed how to proceed with the scouts. Some of the men wanted to continue working with us, but all of them wanted to go home first. They said that going home was the best way to stay anonymous, and once they gathered new information on al Qaeda they would return. I wasn't so sure. There was, however, a carrot dangling in front of the scouts. Captain Smith had decided to begin a formal request to build an Iraqi police station in Julayba. The proposal, which took about six months to be approved, would be sent to the prime minister of Iraq's office. That office would have the final say on how many police would be authorized and what their pay would be. I thought the idea might be premature. But if the scouts did come back, they would get to decide who would fill the positions at the station. They would essentially provide us with their nominee for police chief, as well as the other officers. If none of them came back, somebody else would fill the position, maybe someone from a rival tribe.

After the discussion, I loaded up the twenty-seven detainees into the back of one seven-ton and the twenty-five scouts in another. Standing in the darkness of the COP's parking lot, the general told me that he would not come back to Julayba. He had work elsewhere to finish. I knew what he meant; he hadn't exactly being shown the respect deserving of a general. To add insult to injury, I replied by making him sit in the back of the seven-ton. With the large number of detainees and armed Iraqis, all of the humvee seats were filled by Americans for extra security. The prospects of future cooperation with the Iraqis seemed rather dim.

2300, January 27, 2007

"Rage 6, this is Manchu 3, over." The battalion operations officer was on the net. Lance Corporal Eakin, who was radio watch in COP Rage's COC, gave the handset to Captain Smith. After exchanging a few greetings, the operations officer got to the point.

"Rage 6, we need you to recover the vehicle you found at Hamadi's house last night. We want to run a few forensic tests and try to collect DNA, over," said Manchu 3. Captain Smith was beside himself. The night before this, Rage 6 had refused the same order; now he was being told to do it again.

"Negative, Three, I'm not going to have my Marines driving an Iraqi vehicle on uncleared roads, over," said Captain Smith. The two men exchanged a few more radio transmissions. Then Manchu 3 informed Rage 6 that it was an order, directed by higher headquarters. Captain

Smith took a moment to weigh his options. He could refuse, but to do so would cost enormous social capital. Such an action would likely result in greater micromanagement from the battalion. After making a decision, he got back on the radio. "Manchu 3, my Marines will secure the vehicle, but you get Pathfinder out here to pick it up, over."

The operations officer wasn't happy with the answer, but he knew it was acceptable. In a few hours, Pathfinder was clearing the intersection where Hamadi's house was located. As a compromise, the battalion had added an extra vehicle to Pathfinder's convoy to tow the car to Corregidor.

Captain Smith moved to the map and found the closest unit to Hamadi's house. It was Corporal Seth Collard's 3rd Squad, 3rd Platoon strongpointing just north of the Irish Way–South Bend intersection. Captain Smith passed the mission on to Lieutenant Jahelka. A few minutes after midnight, the squad was moving toward the target.

Corporal Collard planned to head directly west, almost as the crow flies, to the home. The platoon sergeant, Staff Sergeant Crippen, accompanied the patrol. Neither man was at all enthused about the mission. Both knew that Sergeant Ahlquist had requested to destroy the vehicle the night before and was denied. They also knew Captain Smith had refused to recover the vehicle during that same incident. Plus, nobody likes to visit the same place twice, especially on consecutive nights and at roughly the same time as the last visit.

After leaving the house that was their strongpoint, the Marines zigzagged through the alleyways and the dirt paths on the northern side of the bowl shape made by South Bend. The area was dark. Not many houses were running generators, and only a few distant bulbs flickered. The patrol passed through the village and came to an open field. The point element was now about to cross South Bend about 200 meters south of its intersection with Nova.

"Corporal, I got something. Looks like an IED at the intersection with Nova about ten meters off the road," said Lance Corporal Duvall over the radio. Collard immediately spotted the object. It appeared to be a small rock pile next to an empty car. The squad leader put his Marines in a defensive posture and moved closer to get a better look. He shined his PEQ-2 laser at the object. The infrared light illuminated command wire running from a tube above the rock pile and into the field on his right. Collard knew the tube wasn't an IED; it was an improvised rocket launcher (IRL). The launcher was oriented south along South Bend, at his entire squad.

Collard acted quickly. There weren't any combat engineers with the squad, so both he and Staff Sergeant Crippen moved to the command wire. They cut it with a leatherman. What was left of the wire ran out into the field. Opposite the open space was a tree line, sort of a palm grove. At both the northern and the southern side of the grove was a single house. The wire seemed to run toward the southern house, about 200 meters away.

"Staff Sergeant, I think we should investigate this, look for the triggerman," said Collard. Crippen agreed and after he passed it over the radio, so did Rage 6, who gave the patrol permission to deviate from the original task.

Corporal Collard put his squad into a wedge formation. Duvall's team took point, accompanied by Crippen. Lance Corporal Anthony Melia's team was on the left, Lance Corporal Jackie Clinton's on the right. The formation moved slowly through the field, with Collard at the center of the group. A helicopter flew overhead and got a radio check with Collard's platoon commander, Lieutenant Jahelka. The aerial gunship had an hour of playtime with the battalion, and Collard's squad was the only patrol out at the moment.

The slow progress of the squad became slower. Staff Sergeant Crippen and Duvall were finding all sorts of command wire running through the field. The formation's movement slowed down every time they ducked over and cut another wire. Collard noticed that Melia's team was moving too far up; they were almost online with Duvall's stationary Marines. Such things happen on patrol, and Melia probably would have adjusted once the group began to move again, but Collard was demanding. He wasn't going to accept the risk of exposing his left flank for a few seconds.

"Melia, back the hell up; maintain dispersion," said the squad leader into his PRR, the intrasquad radio. Melia quickly moved his team back a few meters. Lance Corporal Melia was one of the youngest team leaders in the company. Unlike most Marines, Melia arrived to the battalion as a lance corporal, the result of superior performance in boot camp and SOI, the School of Infantry. Such performance was noticed by his current leadership, and Collard held Melia to a high standard for good reason—Melia had already been selected to be a squad leader on the next deployment. Such a selection was made by the collaboration of Lieutenant Jahelka, Staff Sergeant Crippen, and the platoon's squad leaders. Basically, Melia was on the fast track because he was a damn good Marine, although Collard never would have told him as much.

In Collard's mind, his responsibility was to treat Melia like the rest of his team leaders, which included nitpicking his positioning on patrol.

Crippen and Duvall got up off the ground after cutting another wire. The patrol began to move again. It was less than a hundred meters to the house, and the palm tree line was directly in front of them. The Marines were about to find out that four Iraqis, two separate two-man machine gun teams, were watching them. The IRL was sort of a decoy for the enemy, channeling the Marines directly toward the ambush position. The four insurgents waited for the Marines to get close, probably too close. They didn't maximize the amount of suppression they could have achieved if they had opened fire a little sooner. Regardless, with the Marines about 70 meters away, the two machine guns opened fire.

Dozens of incoming 7.62mm rounds sent every Marine into the dirt. Collard hit the ground so hard, the battery cap to his NVGs came off, momentarily thrusting him into total darkness. While Collard fumbled with the cap, his patrol's three squad automatic weapons began to battle the insurgents for fire superiority. Hundreds of tracers flew through the night. Collard requested the company QRF from his platoon commander.

The squad leader then asked whether the helicopter could identify the insurgent position. The eyes above said no, the enemy was too close; opposing forces could not be distinguished from friendly. Corporal Collard shouted at his men, "Stay down!" then he stood up and sprinted toward Duvall's team, closer to the ambush point. He shined his PEQ-2 laser at the enemy position and let off a few rounds. The laser shining at the insurgent position didn't matter; the helo said the enemy was still too close.

The enemy's withering fire negated the fact that the American infantrymen outnumbered them three to one. Collard thought about buddy-rushing through the objective, with one man suppressing while his partner closed on the insurgents by three or four steps, but the incoming fire was too great. Stranded in a field of reeds and grass, each Marine desperately searched for micro-terrain between magazine changes.

"Collard! We got one down; he's urgent!" shouted the squad's corpsman. Machine gun bursts were still raking the squad, but the number of outgoing 5.56mm rounds greatly outnumbered the incoming 7.62mm. The squad had gained fire superiority.

One of the insurgent machine guns ceased firing. Some of Duvall's Marines could hear the enemy trying to execute, unsuccessfully, a magazine reload on their weapon system. With only one operational machine gun and hundreds of incoming bullets, the insurgents withdrew.

Collard was about to order his men to pursue, but his corpsman stole his train of thought. "Melia is down! I barely have a pulse!"

The squad leader had a decision to make. One of his men was dying, and the culprits were getting away. The problem was, he couldn't safely evacuate the casualty and pursue the enemy at the same time. It would require at least a team of Marines to move Melia back to South Bend and link up with the QRF. That left less than ten men to go after the enemy. If the Marines were caught by another ambush, the unit could be wiped out.

Collard's greatest fear wasn't death, however; it was that someone could kill one of his Marines and get away with it. In the awkward silence during the calm that immediately follows every firefight, Seth Collard made up his mind. "Staff Sergeant, take Melia's team and link up with the QRF at South Bend. I'm taking the rest of the squad onward to that southernmost house."

In the decisiveness of the moment, Collard realized he wasn't going to see Melia. He watched from 50 meters away as the remaining members of the fire team picked up their leader and began moving toward South Bend. Collard sensed that Melia wasn't going to make it. His body was motionless. There were no cries of pain, none of the drama associated with a living gunshot wound. Instead, Melia was at peace. Collard would later find out that a round had sliced into Melia's NVGs and through the lower portion of his helmet. The young Marine had been instantly killed by a single gunshot to the head.

The helicopter above offered to assist with the casualty. The gunship said it could land and pick up the potentially living Melia. Lieutenant Jahlka asked how he could do that; there were only two seats on an attack helicopter, and both were for the pilots. "My navigator will get out and stay with you; the casualty will take his seat," said the pilot. It was a truly heroic gesture that would have put Melia in a hospital in roughly fifteen minutes. But Melia didn't have a pulse.

"Collard, he's, uh, he's KIA, man," said the corpsman via PRR. Collard asked whether he was sure. The corpsman said Melia never had a pulse; he realized when the gunfire stopped that he was feeling his own.

Then Crippen asked Collard whether he had any body bags.

"Staff Sergeant, I don't . . . ," said Collard. Crippen already knew as much. He specifically didn't make his squad leaders carry body bags on patrol: too much bad karma. It wasn't an unusual thing. The leadership of the company had a diverse collection of rituals to maintain its current streak of two and a half months in Ramadi with no KIAs: James Thomas and I smoked before patrol, Holloway carried shrapnel that had nearly killed him in his previous deployment, and Crippen didn't carry body bags, just to name a few. No one could predict when our luck was going to run out.

Collard informed Lieutenant Jahelka not to have the helicopter land. The casualty was KIA and no longer urgent. Melia's status was changed to routine.

With the two elements moving in opposite directions, the QRF showed up. Luckily, instead of the humvees of the company QRF, it was a section of BFVs and an M113 ambulance from the battalion. The lead vehicle pulled through the Nova–South Bend intersection and turned right to scan the tree line with its optics. As it did, it set off an IED on the right side of the road. The blast sent Collard and his men back into the dirt. Fortunately for the BFV, it was a smaller IED. To the heavily armored vehicle's crew, it was nothing more than a loud noise.

Following the momentary pause in movement, Collard and his men sprinted into their target house. There was nothing suspicious inside, and Collard went straight to the roof. Looking out into the darkness, he realized that the enemy might get away. He leaned against the roof's retaining wall and listened to the radio. The net was clogged with traffic. The helicopter above was on the four insurgents' trail, and Lieutenant Grubb was leaving COP Rage with two squads to hunt them down. On the northern side of the tree line, Collard spotted the infrared strobes belonging to a squad of Marines moving south toward him. It was Ahlquist's squad. The Marines were going to effectively trap the four insurgents. Collard's team blocked the south, Ahlquist the north, and the BFVs from the QRF the west. The four insurgents split into two groups and headed east, right into Lieutenant Grubb. When the Iraqis realized they were trapped, they hid in two separate houses. Grubb sent one of his squads to each house and detained every military-age male he found.

A sense of relief overcame Collard. Grubb's boys got the fuckers, he thought. He looked back at the M113 turning around on South Bend. The squad leader watched the vehicle drive out of sight through his

NVGs. Inside was the company's first KIA. From that point on, every patrol carried body bags.

The next day I made it back to Camp Corregidor, after dropping off the detainees at Camp Ramadi's detention facility. I found Captain Smith inside the battalion command post. He was furious at Manchu 3. He even gave the battalion commander an earful about the legality of the battalion staff's issuing him orders when he was the on-scene commander. The decision to recover the vehicle should have been his call, not battalion's. By the end of the one-way conversation, Captain Smith had attained leverage. From that point on, the battalion would let Rage Company do as it pleased in Julayba.

0700, February 1, 2007

The sun was rising. Warming in the heat of its rays sat Cullen Shearburn and the Marines of his second squad. The group of men manned a rooftop on the eastern side of Julayba a few hundred meters north of the village where Manchu 6 had personally hunted for Ali Siyagah's driver two weeks earlier. Surrounding the roof were another dozen buildings, most of them smaller and less defensible than the one where Shearburn sat.

Collectively, the Marines of Rage 1 were tired. The day after Melia was killed, their rest period at OP Trotter, a small base down the road from Corregidor, was canceled. Captain Smith was swapping them out with Rage 3, so that the members of Melia's platoon could give him a proper farewell. When Shearburn arrived at COP Melia, renamed for the fallen Marine, Captain Smith tasked him with executing a seven-day patrol to the north, through the Albu Musa tribal area. That was as much direction as the platoon commander received; the details of what would happen on the patrol would be up to him.

Since the night of January 28, Rage 1's Marines had been conducting cache sweeps and strongpointing for short periods of rest. During that time, the Marines were shot at every day. Sometimes it was a five-minute burst of automatic rifle fire or an inaccurate RPG flying overhead; on other occasions, it was hours of harassing sniper fire. Whenever Shearburn's men identified the enemy positions and responded with their own rifles, however, the enemy broke contact. So far, the insurgents were not willing to stand and fight the Americans. The lieutenant and his men didn't know it, but today was going to be different.

A section of Apache helicopters flew overhead. They were continuing the battalion's mission of sealing off Julayba, screening the Euphrates River for any sort of canoe or boat to destroy. The lead helicopter flew low over Shearburn's roof, about fifty feet above him. The aircraft proceeded north along the riverbank when the Marines on the roof heard the swooshing sound of an RPG shot. They all looked at the black aircraft. The air burst from the rocket-propelled grenade was 3 meters from the tail rotor, close enough to rattle the pilot but not to cause any significant damage.

Shearburn visually traced the smoke trail to the northwest. It was only a few hundred meters away. The lead helo's wingman did the same, except that he maneuvered his aircraft and spotted the culprit. He told the Marines that the shot had come from a blue bongo truck that was egressing south along Gixxer. He informed them that he had no shot. The area was too urban and required clearance from the brigade, a process that would have ensured that the enemy would get away. Plus, the helicopters had only another five minutes on station before they had to leave and refuel. Unfortunately for the occupants of the blue bongo truck, they were driving straight into Shearburn's view.

The platoon commander looked out over the field to the west of his building. The open farmland was more than a square kilometer in size, and the mansion he was staying in dominated the entire area. Through his scope, he sighted in on Gixxer, the spot where it emerged from the urban area and intersected with a no-name trail that ran through the field. Moments later, the bongo truck appeared. Five men were in the vehicle, two in the front and three in the back. Most of them were clearly armed with automatic weapons. The patient Marines waited for the mini-pickup truck to get to the middle of the field, about 400 meters away. Then they opened up with hundreds of rounds of 5.56mm bullets.

The vehicle stopped. Under fire, two of the insurgents crawled out of the truck and into an orchard on the far side of the field. The other three were either dead inside or sprawled out on the ground next to the blue pockmarked truck. The Marines ceased firing.

Cullen Shearburn informed Captain Smith of the event. Then he received orders from his commander for that day's mission: conduct a sweep along the banks of the Euphrates for weapons caches. He took two squads, Corporal Adam Brown's first squad and Corporal Scott Guinn's third. Corporal Dustin Anderson's second stayed at the current location, maintaining observation over the disabled vehicle. The platoon commander quickly briefed his squad leaders on the sweep. Brown's squad would search along the riverbank, while Guinn provided over-watch in the line of houses that ran parallel to the river. As Brown's Marines progressed in searching the riverbank, Guinn's Marines would keep pace by bounding from house to house. It allowed the Marines to search not only the riverbank but also the houses Guinn would occupy. At about 0800, the Marines left for the patrol.

The two squads maneuvered northeast through the small village they had cleared the night before, passing the house that contained multiple Saddam-era camouflage uniforms, ski masks, a couple of AKs, and potential IED-making material. The night before when they had searched it, Shearburn wanted to detain the men living there. He was denied by Rage COC. Technically, nothing the men possessed was illegal. So, Shearburn burned the clothes and other flammable items. He left the AKs. He remembered this last fact as his men moved past.

Once through the village, the Marines began the sweep portion of the patrol. They moved methodically for hours, searching the concrete blocks that contained water pumps for Julayba's fields and clearing the homes closest to the river. Their efforts were slightly rewarded. The two squads discovered two small pieces of ordnance, which they blew in place. Later in the day, they found a target range in a cluster of palm trees. There were metallic firing platforms welded together and three small metal targets to accompany them. The targets were scarred with bullet holes and also put together via metalworking. All of the items were buried under piles of the surrounding trees' palm leaves. The Marines destroyed everything.

At 1400, Lieutenant Shearburn consolidated the two squads and ended the cache sweep. They began moving south, back toward Corporal Anderson's squad, which was still stationary inside the village they had come from. Five minutes into the movement, Captain Smith radioed Lieutenant Shearburn. He said that Rage 1 needed to do a detailed sensitive sight exploitation (SSE) on the disabled bongo truck. The platoon commander did not like the idea. Hours had passed since his men had shot up the vehicle and two of the occupants got away. Now they and their friends were probably waiting for the Marines to expose themselves by moving out into the open field to search the vehicle. For this reason, Shearburn had avoided doing an SSE earlier. Now Captain Smith was ordering him to do it. The platoon commander lodged his protest. "Rage 6, this is Rage 1, I have no good way to get to the vehicle. Recommend we at least wait until night, over."

Captain Smith denied his request. The two men went back and forth again with the same outcome, at the end of which Shearburn replied, "Sir, there are three bodies, a few AKs, an RPG launcher, and a shot-up truck . . . what else do you want to know?"

"No, you need to do the detailed SSE, Rage 1; let me know when you are done," said Captain Smith.

The lieutenant decided that he had protested to the fullest extent possible. In between a few Iraqi houses, he pulled out his map and looked for the best way to get to the vehicle. There was no easy tactical answer. Every option ended with some of his Marines entering the field exposed. It was simply too large an area for the forty-one members of Rage 1 to secure. The best thing he could do was establish mutually supporting positions that would protect whoever moved out across the exposed space.

Shearburn continued to stare at his map, identifying key terrain. The field had a rectangular shape. The northern and eastern sides were formed by Gixxer and the houses north and east of the road. Anderson's squad was set up in a small village on the eastern side. The southern edge was Rage Road, an east-west route that represented the northern edge of the Albu Bali tribal area. The western edge was more than 1,000 meters away. About 400 meters northwest from where Anderson was on the eastern side, however, Gixxer emerged from the urban area to the north. That's where the bongo truck had left Gixxer, following a dirt path south into the field. A few hundred meters down the path was its final resting place. Where the bongo truck had left the pavement, Gixxer made a ninety-degree turn east and headed toward Anderson.

Shearburn decided that he had to control the intersection of Gixxer and the dirt road the bongo truck was on. So he sent Guinn's squad to the village on the northeast corner and set them up in two different over-watch positions. Guinn's closest team to the intersection would be three houses east. While Guinn moved, Shearburn led Brown's squad to Gixxer on the northern side of the field, between Guinn's and Anderson's squads. Once there, he left one of Brown's fire teams to man yet another over-watch position, while the nine remaining men in the squad got ready to search the truck. Before leaving the house, Lieutenant Shearburn had a very bad feeling.

Then he and eight other men crossed over Gixxer and onto the dark earthen farmland. The group moved in a right oblique, maximizing firepower to the right and the front. Dead ahead was the bongo truck, with the tree line of the orchard behind it. Slightly to the right, at a forty-five-degree angle, was the intersection that Guinn overlooked. Three cows lazily grazed between the Marines and that intersection. Each of the nine men maintained enormous dispersion, roughly ten meters between every Marine. Lieutenant Shearburn was in the center, scanning the distant orchard and the village on its right and north.

The squad minus drew closer to the vehicle and farther out into the open field. The ambush Shearburn knew was coming began with a pouf of smoke from the orchard. It was just shy of the intersection and the two opposing villages on either side of the road. Guinn was in the village closest to Shearburn. No Marines were in the village on the opposite side of the road.

The platoon commander immediately knew what was happening. A rocket had been fired at him. He screamed at his men to get down. The weapon exploded significantly short of the exposed group. The detonation was followed by dozens of bullets that zipped around the Marines. A hundred thoughts entered Cullen's mind. Were there any casualties? Could he identify the ambush point? Did the over-watch positions have a clear line of fire on the enemy? The thoughts didn't stop. Instead of lying prone for cover, Cullen was on one knee. He looked around the field to build his understanding of the situation, somehow impervious to the bullets impacting around him. It wasn't that he couldn't feel the dirt kicking up onto his feet and hitting the inside of his thigh or hear the high-velocity bullets fly past his head; it was that he knew his job was to plan his platoon's response—something he could not accomplish by lying in the dirt and simply returning fire. He needed situational awareness.

"The orchard! Suppress the orchard," he directed his squad leaders. Outgoing M203 rounds began to impact on and above the enemy positions. Shearburn recognized that the insurgents were in a deep and well-entrenched irrigation canal. The M203s' accuracy stunned the lieutenant, but he was more surprised that the 40mm grenades didn't reduce the volume of fire produced by the enemy.

"Anderson! I want continuous fire on the hundred meters from that intersection south along the orchard!"

Anderson's squad had the majority of the platoon's light machine guns, the M249 SAW. In seconds, the Marines established fire superiority. The ambush was still in its opening minute.

Shearburn looked around the field. Dirt was being kicked up around every man. Shearburn finally got down into the prone position, lying behind a mound of dirt no more than four inches off the ground. Sighting in on the enemy positions, he let off a few rounds. Then a bullet crashed into the dirt pile he lay behind, spraying his face with cold, fertile soil. Shit. He peered at the other eight men in the field. All of them had found their own piece of micro-terrain, their own rock of Gibraltar. Three were hiding behind the now-deceased cows. Staff Sergeants Todd Colwell's and Jerry Eagle's voices were also audible, directing the Marines surrounding them to different targets.

Lying in the dirt, Shearburn looked back at Anderson's building. The SAWs on his roof were laying down a withering base of fire. Yet somehow, the insurgents continued to pour it on the nine men in the field. The platoon commander realized that the enemy was choosing to stand and fight, unlike in previous engagements. If the insurgents didn't withdraw, it would be only a matter of time before the Marines in the field were picked off. Rage 1 needed help; they needed the company QRF. Cullen grabbed his handset. He could hear Captain Smith calling for him on the other end, wanting to know what the hell was going on.

"Rage 6, Rage 1, I am currently engaged by a squad-size element. I am heavily exposed and am requesting the QRF to assist via Rage Road, over," said Shearburn.

"Do you have any casualties?" replied Captain Smith.

"Not to my knowledge . . ."

There was a momentary pause in the radio transmission. Around Shearburn, bullets continued to hit everything except his body.

"Rage 1, you are on your own. The roads are not clear, and I can't risk the vehicles."

Cullen was irate. Risk was inherent in everything he and his men did. Now Rage 6 was keeping the QRF from coming to Cullen's assistance. Without responding, Cullen returned his attention to the firefight.

Two RPGs, fired seconds apart, flew at Corporal Anderson's position from the orchard. Both were horrible shots and didn't impact anywhere near the Marines, but they did tell Cullen one thing: the enemy was desperate to silence Anderson's SAWs. The Marines responded by firing two of their own shoulder-fired rockets into the orchard, blasting apart chunks of palm trees and earth.

The lieutenant engaged muzzle flashes in the tree line. Then he looked for Guinn. Instead, he spotted movement. A couple of black shadows were heading through the alleyways near Guinn's position. The lieutenant personally shifted his rifle fire and accurately engaged the black-clad men. One crumpled to the ground. The enemy responded by trying to cover their comrades. Another RPG flew at the Marines in the field, and two 57mm IRLs fired from a homemade, welded-together stand) went at Anderson. The lieutenant didn't see where they landed; he was busy hugging the earth.

After the impacts, he lifted his head and reengaged the enemy in the orchard. Moments later, there was an eruption from the houses directly next to Guinn and on the northeast corner of the intersection he over-looked. Lieutenant Shearburn turned his head ninety degrees to the right and saw a PKM medium machine gun spewing bullets along the axis of the nine men in the field. Fuck. It was a textbook L-shaped ambush, with a machine gun at the base of the L. He was outflanked, and the PKM had enfilading fires on his men. In minutes, if the PKM was still in action, they would all be dead.

Shearburn grabbed his handset and again called for the QRF. Captain Smith repeated that the risk to the vehicles was too great. It was the last radio transmission between the COC and Rage 1 during the firefight.

The Marines in the field clung to the dirt. They were no longer able to effectively engage the enemy. Corporal Guinn recognized the severity of the scenario and began to suppress the PKM from his two positions. The engagement was close; only one house separated the opposing forces. Guinn's actions caught the insurgents off guard and placed the PKM team in a dilemma: which group of Americans should they engage?

The corporal identified that the enemy didn't realize he was there and followed up his suppression with an even bolder tactic. He sent one of his fire teams, led by Lance Corporal Christopher Carter, directly at the enemy fighters. The four men rushed as two-man buddy pairs and outflanked the enemy. The PKM team and the other insurgents in the village, who probably outnumbered the four Marines, withdrew under the pressure.

No longer caught by the L-shape ambush, the Marines in the field and the remaining over-watch positions pounded the orchard. M203 grenades, shoulder-fired rockets, and continuous SAW and rifle fire filled the palm trees and the irrigation canal. The enemy fired off another IRL. Then their machine guns ceased firing. Anderson's men could see from their elevated position that small groups of insurgents were egressing out of the orchard to the west. The enemy didn't have a chance. The Marines nailed a few with their SAWs.

Still under sporadic small-arms fire, the Marines in the field seized the opportunity to get out of their exposed position. With the insurgents breaking contact, they might be inclined to drop a few mortar rounds into the field. If accurate, the shrapnel would have been devastating to the nine Marines.

The left side of the line, closest to the bongo truck and the orchard, began to "banana peel" back toward the house where Brown's one fire team was. In two-man teams, the Marines took turns bounding and suppressing. Halfway back, Shearburn passed one of his Marines facedown down in the mud. He was motionless. The fear of that moment suspended time, scarring the lieutenant. Cullen thought one of his men was dead. He leaned out to touch the man, only to see the Marine turn his head and look up. "I'm good, sir, just shooting." It was Lance Corporal Craig Jahner, one of the platoon's combat engineers.

"Well, come on, get back," said the lieutenant. It was Jahner's turn to move. The first elements of the formation began to reenter the house. When Shearburn got close enough, he stopped and waited for the rest of his men to get inside. Once they all crossed the threshold that was Route Gixxer, he made his way toward the door.

A few feet from it, Cullen heard a loud thunk, a sound similar to that of a mortar being fired. He pushed the Marine in front of him in the direction of one of the house's pillars. Then he dove behind a pillar on the other side. The platoon commander was barely behind the column before there was a thunderous explosion 25 meters away. After Cullen regained his senses and ensured that everyone was okay, he realized it wasn't a mortar blast. The short amount of time between firing and impact meant that it was another IRL from the orchard: the enemy's final, parting shot of the firefight.

The two sides continued to exchange periodic bursts of fire. Miraculously, there were no casualties on the American side. Inside the house, the platoon commander went up to the roof and got the standard updates from his squad leaders, the most important of which was the ammo report. He learned that the platoon as a whole was down to 30 percent ammunition, had no M203 grenades, and had only half of its SMAW rockets remaining. A silent, uneasy calm lay over the Julayba skyline.

Cullen looked around at the other men on the roof who had entered the field with him. The necessary purging of fear that's required after such an event was taking place. Each man was coming to terms with the near-death experience in his own way. Some took off all of their gear. A few ate, some hugged each other; another high-fived the guys around him. Cullen reached under his shirt and pulled out the Saint Christopher medal his parents had given him. They had told him that his grandfather wore one during World War II and it worked. Now it protected Cullen. It wasn't the only religious symbol the lieutenant carried; the soldier's prayer card was in his left breast pocket. He pulled it out and read the prayer, given to Charlemagne by Pope Gregory.

A couple of months earlier, when the company first arrived in Ramadi, Shearburn had asked his parents to send enough of the prayer cards for his entire platoon. After a mission brief, the platoon commander set the cards down on a table and told his men to each take one. If religion wasn't their thing or they didn't want one, that was fine. There was no pressure; the cards stayed on the table indefinitely for the men to take as they pleased. Eventually, the cards disappeared.

After reading the prayer, Lieutenant Shearburn looked at the other men on the roof again. Most of them were doing the same thing he was, reading the card. Individually, the men took as long as they needed. Then, with the night beginning, they headed inside. Each man had to pass Shearburn to do so; he was sitting next to the doorway that led to the stairs. A few of his men expressed their thoughts on the way down. "Fucking-A, sir, this shit works," said one, holding the prayer card in his hand. Another told Shearburn he would never take it off his body.

A minute later, the lieutenant's calm moment on the roof was interrupted by Rage 6 on the radio. "So, were you able to do a detailed SSE on the vehicle?" asked Captain Smith. There were plenty of things the platoon commander wanted to say, but he kept it simple: "Negative."

The absurd question planted an idea in Shearburn's mind. He decided to do a detailed search of the irrigation canal that night. After waiting for it to get darker, he briefed up Anderson and his squad. Then the Marines left the safety of the house and moved out of the village, heading north. The squad's fire teams bounded in the darkness, each one covering its assigned sector of fire perfectly during the movement.

Shearburn avoided Gixxer. Earlier, he had noticed a large, six-foot wall that lined the road between him and the orchard. Gaping holes were visible in the cinder blocks. The lieutenant feared that it may have been where the enemy stuffed the wall with a shape charge or other explosives, a standard tactic.

The Marines stayed a few hundred meters north of Gixxer as it ran east-west. Once they got to the village that Guinn had been in earlier and Gixxer turned north, they crossed. The group was now in the village that Lance Corporal Carter had outflanked the PKM in. Within minutes, they entered the orchard. The lieutenant leaned against the cold ground and looked out at the field he had nearly died in earlier. He could not fathom how the enemy hadn't hit him or any of his men.

Anderson and his squad searched the dry canal. The men were amazed at how detailed the enemy's recovering of items was. There were no shell casings from expended ammunition, no bodies, only the visible impacts from the Americans. It was impressive. Cullen knew that the insurgents collected shell casings to stuff inside anti-personnel IEDs and suicide vests, but this was ridiculous.

Farther down the canal, the Marines found two IRL stands. Over the next hour, they uncovered a total of two IEDs: an acetylene torch canister set up as a bomb, and a propane canister stuffed with PE4. There were also signs of the casualties the Marines had inflicted. An empty chest rig, pieces of clothing, and a face wrap were strewn about, probably ripped off a wounded man. Cullen decided that he needed to search the canal in the light of day. It offered substantial cover and provided a clear view of the surrounding farmland. Something had to be there.

The IEDs hadn't been hooked into an initiation device yet, so Staff Sergeant Eagle blew them where they were found. Then the squad headed back to the rest of the platoon at the strongpoint they had come from. As they left, a few of the men noticed white wire hanging in multiple trees.

0200, February 2, 2007

At the platoon strongpoint, Lieutenant Shearburn was arguing with Captain Smith about how to resupply his platoon. Rage 6 wanted the lieutenant to send a squad of his Marines back to the COP to collect the necessary chow, water, and ammunition. Then they would carry the platoon's worth of supplies back to their strongpoint. It would have been about a 5,000-meter movement. Cullen's problem wasn't that his men would carry such a heavy burden so far. It was that they would make the movement low on ammo, with the prospects of enemy contact high. Pathfinder was even coming to Julayba to clear the roads that night; why couldn't Captain Smith task them with clearing a route to his men?

The radio stalemate eventually ended when Lieutenant Grubb offered to meet the squad from Rage 1 halfway. Hours later, the resupply was complete.

With a new stockpile of ammunition, Shearburn decided that he would press the issue with the enemy. The villages and the urban area north of the field were clearly hostile. The streets were always deserted during the day, and the people were overly fearful when the Marines entered their homes. He decided to shift his strongpoint to the mansion that Guinn had occupied during the ambush. Using it as an over-watch, he would take Brown's squad to the orchard and search it in the morning.

At 0500, Guinn's squad left with Lieutenant Shearburn to reoccupy the sprawling compound he had been in earlier. Once on the roof, the lieutenant knew he had to control the structure. It dominated the surrounding neighborhood and every key route that connected the Albu Musa and Albu Bali tribal areas. Cullen was unaware that he was establishing his platoon in the heart of al Qaeda's command-and-control network for the Ramadi-Fallujah corridor.

The remaining two squads left the former strongpoint, one at a time, and headed for the new position. The Marines renamed the house OP Rebel. Anderson's squad went on rest. Guinn's set up security. At the first sign of light, Brown left with the platoon commander for the orchard.

Moving through the deep ditch, the Marines immediately discovered what the white wire was for. Shovels were hanging beneath the wires in the tree. In the earth, small culverts had been dug beneath the trees that contained hanging wires. After the Marines removed a few shovels-full of dirt, the standard white rice bag or plastic barrel was revealed. The rice bags and the plastic containers protected the contents of the small holes: insurgent weaponry. The next hour of digging revealed the following: five U.S. style 155mm rounds, one Soviet Bangalore, seven 60mm mortar rounds, two 82mm mortar rounds, one 5" IRL, one 5" rocket, one 57mm rocket, thirteen pounds of an unknown explosive, seventy-nine mortar fuses, ten mortar boosters, twenty Draganov rounds, six phone base stations, twelve Soviet-style red/green star clusters, five hundred feet of wire, four motorcycle batteries, a steel cutting saw, various assortment of tools, and a pile of clothes with black masks.

Staff Sergeant Eagle supervised the inventorying of the items. Once the list was compiled and the cache contents consolidated, he prepared the site to blow the items in place. Shearburn asked Captain Smith for permission to detonate the explosives. He was denied. Per the ROE, EOD had to supervise. To Rage 1, it was more bullshit. EOD would take hours to show up, reinventory, and then blow the cache. The last thing Cullen wanted to do was sit in the orchard longer than he had to.

Yet he had no choice. For the next two hours, the Marines sat in the orchard awaiting EOD. Finally, they got a call on the radio. "Rage 1, this is Rage 6; EOD and Rage Mobile are at the intersection of Gixxer and Nova. I want you to patrol the route along Gixxer they are going to take, sweeping it for IEDs."

Cullen was confused. EOD drove a mine-resistant ambush-protected vehicle. Why on earth did his commander want him to sweep the street with his dismounted infantrymen? The platoon commander voiced his concerns. Still, he received the same order from Captain Smith. Livid at the order, he executed it anyway.

The men painfully patrolled down Gixxer until it intersected with Nova. Somewhere in the neighborhood, an insurgent was furious with himself for not setting an IED on Gixxer. A dozen Marines were walking down the street in the light of day. It was probably the easiest target an insurgent could wish for. Luckily for the Marines, there were no blasts.

Inside the COC, we could all feel the tension between Rage 1 and Rage 6. Until that point, Captain Smith had been making tough decisions. I could see the movement of the QRF during the previous day's engagement both ways. Yes, the roads were dangerous and there were plenty of triple- and quadruple-stack IEDs being found in Julayba, the detonation of which would send a humvee flying through the sky. But Captain Smith had given in to battalion's demand to do a detailed SSE sooner rather than later. If he wasn't going to send the QRF in case of an emergency, he could have told battalion to pound sand. The SSE would wait until dark. Obviously, that's not how it went down.

Waiting for EOD that day wasn't even a choice for Rage 6. We told battalion about the cache as soon as Shearburn found it. Once battalion knew it existed, they expected us to use EOD to destroy it, in accordance with MNF-W ROE. To do otherwise would be violating an order set in place by a three-star general. We had violated the rule before, but Captain Smith was going to follow it this time.

With that said, those of us in the COC did not understand why Captain Smith wanted Shearburn to patrol Gixxer for IEDs. It wasn't the only time he would give such an order. A few days later, he made Lieutenant Thomas do the same thing. When I finally grew the balls to ask him why, he told me that dismounted Marines will spot the IEDs before the vehicles do. They are slower, more attentive.

I didn't agree. Between Captain Smith and me, it was a difference of tactical thought. For Lieutenant Shearburn, it was dangerous.

The dismounted patrol linked up with the four-vehicle convoy at the intersection. The senior EOD engineer opened the door to his vehicle as Cullen came close.

"Is that road clear?" asked the engineer.

"It is now."

The engineer was perplexed. He asked Lieutenant Shearburn why he was clearing the road for armored vehicles. Cullen ignored the question.

The patrol turned around and went back to the orchard the way they came, only this time armored vehicles were between the columns of men on either side of the road. When they finally arrived at the orchard, EOD began to reinventory the cache's contents. Lieutenant Shearburn and Staff Sergeant Eagle watched in boredom as their numbers were slowly confirmed.

Cullen heard one of his Marines yelling at the turret gunners on Rage Mobile's three humvees. It was Corporal Chris Barnes. Apparently, the gunners had all been seated in their turrets—no scanning, no aggressive posture. Each was motionless and waiting to react. Barnes clearly didn't appreciate the lack of a defensive posture. Shearburn returned his focus to the inventory.

The boredom dragged on. Then it ended. The sound of an incoming rocket screeched toward the Marines. It was followed by an explosion. Shearburn ran toward the rocket. It had been fired north on Gixxer, down the axis of the road, targeting the vehicles of Rage Mobile. One of the turret gunners pointed toward the orchard, yelling at Shearburn that the rocket had careened away from the trucks at the last second.

The lieutenant looked over and spotted Corporal Barnes. The Marine was staggering, eyes glazed over. His tan trousers were quickly turning red. The squad's corpsmen rushed to the scene and cut away Barnes's trousers to see the extent of the injury. All along the Marine's right side, from the small of his back down his legs, there was blood. Shearburn called in the Medevac. Within half an hour, Barnes was at 1/9 Infantry's aid station. There he received good news: the wounds were superficial and shrapnel had not penetrated any of his major organs.

EOD eventually blew the cache, and Lieutenant Shearburn headed back to OP Rebel. There he, his platoon sergeant, and Staff Sergeant Eagle planned their defense of the OP. Over the next five days and four nights, the enemy would test the obstacle plan they came up with. The Marines were not alone in the neighborhood; only a few meters separated the opposing forces. Somehow, all of the Marines of Rage 1 would live to tell of the small-unit fighting that took place.

Every day and night brought another encounter. In the silence of one night, a team of insurgents crept in close and threw a grenade at a rooftop sentry. The grenade bounced just short of the top of the house and detonated below. Another night the enemy set off a trip flare outside the COP. The flare illuminated multiple shadows in the orchard, which the Marines cut down with automatic rifle fire. The shadowlike insurgents removed any bodies before the arrival of the squad that Shearburn sent to conduct SSE. On a separate night, the enemy engaged the OP in a short but intense firefight. The two sides were in opposing buildings. As on the previous night, a team of insurgents maneuvered into another trip flare. Again, the Marines shot at the shadows but never found any bodies, not even blood.

When Lieutenant Shearburn's seven-day patrol finally ended, he recommended to Captain Smith that they make OP Rebel permanent. The enemy wanted the Marines gone for a reason, and Cullen did not want to give them the satisfaction of withdrawing. For the moment, his recommendation was ignored. Rage 1 was ordered back to COP Melia. The Albu Musa tribal area reverted to its uncontested status. Control returned to al Qaeda.

Captain John Smith speaks with members of the scout-led militia during the Julayba uprising.

From the left, Abu Tiba, Captain Smith, and Double A during a mission.

Members of the scout-led militia wounded in a mortar attack on their makeshift command post during the Julayba uprising.

Iraqi militia in an F-350 during the Julayba uprising.

The militia's version of Pathfinder. The Iraqi holding the shovel dug up the region's IEDs. He was also the individual who put them in the ground.

An Apache attack helicopter in action above Julayba.

Lieutenants Thomas Daly (standing) and James Thomas with the leadership of the scouts.

Lieutenant Thomas Daly outside COP Rage.

Lieutenant Thomas Daly and the general.

The citizens of Julayba protest the detention of a local on the northern edge of COP Rage.

Sergeant Dimitrios Karras on patrol in Julayba.

A 500lb JDAM air-strike silences an insurgent position along Red Road.

Sergeant Clinton Ahlquist on patrol in Julayba.

Captain Smith poses with Abu Ali and the general during the tactical questioning of detainees.

A tactical cache found by Rage 2 in the Albu Bali tribal area.

The militia gathers for the first Iraqi led operation in Julayba.

Lieutenant Thomas and Captain Smith with two of the scouts outside COP Rage.

An IED found by a patrol of Marines from Rage 2. Luckily the explosives weren't connected to an initiation device yet.

The cache found underneath fishing net in building 88 off Orchard Way.

Lieutenant James Thomas inspects an RPG launcher found hanging in a tree.

Lieutenant Thomas holds the empty tube to a SA-7 surface to air missile.

Marines from Rage 1 stand over a cache of weapons delivered by the scout-led militia.

Staff Sergeant Eagle and another Marine prepare to detonate a weapons cache.

From the left, Lance Corporal Craig Jahner, Staff Sergeant Jerry Eagle, and Corporal Dustin Anderson in Julayba.

The leadership of Rage 1. From the left, Staff Sergeant Todd Colwell, Lieutenant Cullen Shearburn, and Staff Sergeant Jerry Eagle.

12

DEADLY GAMES

February 5, 2007

The company staff gathered inside COP Melia's COC. The plan of rotating platoons in and out of sector was starting to take shape. Lieutenant Thomas and Rage 2 were about to go on rest back at Corregidor, returning from a four-day platoon-size operation that saw them clear the banks of the Euphrates along the western side of Julayba. Rage 3 was headed out, tasked with doing a similar sweep on the eastern side.

I sat at my laptop next to the radio watch. Near the computer was a pile of SanDisk memory cards containing photos of the numerous small tactical caches that James Thomas and his men had found. The pictures showed bags of explosives buried in dirt along the river, metallic IRL stands, sniping platforms with corresponding welding equipment, and the usual mortar rounds, accompanied by larger-caliber artillery rounds. While I put all of the information together to pass to battalion, the platoon commanders chatted behind me. "Every time I went close to the river, I got shot at," said Lieutenant Thomas. He was sitting next to Jahelka on the COC's brown and yellow couch.

"Anything sustained?" asked Jahelka.

"Only during the day; at night, it was always just a few shots of harassing fire."

Captain Smith came into the room. He reviewed the tasks he had previously given Jahelka: sweep for caches along the eastern side of Julayba near the Euphrates, then establish a patrol base northwest of the Gixxer-Nova intersection. The patrol base would be about 3,000 meters from the cache sweep. From that position, Rage 3 would spend the next few days patrolling the surrounding area. They would take the place of Lieutenant Shearburn's Marines. Instead of swapping positions with Rage 1, Captain Smith was shifting the focus of Jahelka's men to the tribal area on the northwestern side of Julayba. He wanted to see the response Jahelka received from the locals.

An hour later, Rage 3 left. The platoon moved to a house between the Albu Musa and Albu Bali tribal areas and strongpointed. There they waited for the day to end before they began their sweep for caches.

Richard Jahelka looked out at the almond-shaped piece of land jutting off the eastern edge of Julayba. It was the perfect spot for an insurgent cache: not too far of a canoe trip from the other side and relatively isolated. The terrain was perfectly flat and open, meaning the enemy could easily keep an eye on whatever was hidden there. With dusk enveloping the landscape, the platoon of Marines moved onto the open ground.

The lieutenant directed his squad leaders over the PRR. "Collard, put your squad in the building and take up an over-watch position. Ahlquist and Conley, let's start around the building, doing a wagon-wheel in the immediate area." The building Collard headed to was the only one on the awkwardly shaped peninsula.

Richard Jahelka moved through the knee-high reeds with Ahlquist's squad. Dusk was quickly turning into night, but you could still make out shapes on the far side of the river with the naked eye. Jahelka used the remaining light to get a solid grasp of his surroundings and relate their positioning to the terrain on his map. In particular, Lieutenant Jahelka noticed the standard small cinder-block structures that housed the irrigation canal's water pumps. Opposite his men were half a dozen of them, and the platoon commander was aware of how easily the structures could be turned into fortified fighting positions. He wasn't the only one to notice; feeling this same insecurity, each of the infantrymen alternated his focus between the ground around him and the other side of the river. All of the Marines were aware that coalition forces did not have a strong presence on the opposite bank.

Based on the stories from Rage 2's sweep to the west, none of the Marines were surprised when the first single shot flew at them from the far side of the river. It was followed by three or four more: standard harassing fire. Half of the Marines didn't even get down or seek cover. Instead, they sighted in on the far banks and tried to identify the shooter's position. They couldn't; no one returned fire.

"Rage 3 Collective, get down and take cover. We will resume our cache sweep once it gets darker," said Lieutenant Jahelka. Each of the squads went stationary and assumed a purely defensive posture. Jahelka decided to use the darkness to his advantage. The current intelligence assessment stated that the local insurgents were not night-vision capable. They were not known to use the devices to coordinate or execute their attacks within the surrounding area. It was the main reason the coalition conducted almost all of its operations in Ramadi under the protection of darkness.

The Marines sat for no more than ten minutes. At that point, it was pitch-black. Conley's and Ahlquist's squads resumed the cache sweep. Inside the lone building, almost all of Collard's men were oriented toward the far side of the river; it was the primary threat.

In the ten minutes that it took to get pitch-black, a dozen insurgents had occupied multiple fighting positions across the river. Somehow they saw the Marines stand up and resume their movement. All at once, the other side of the river exploded. Four machine gun positions and multiple Kalashnikovs opened fire.

Unlike the Marines' reactions to the previous potshots, every man dove into the hard-packed mud around him. Jahelka blamed himself, realizing that in order to get the protection of darkness, he had sacrificed the most valuable battlefield asset: time.

Dozens of rounds zipped past Jahelka. They smacked the dirt, cut down the surrounding reeds, and pinged off the building behind him. The platoon commander looked across the river. Each of the machine gun bursts appeared to be coming from a well-fortified bunker. It had to be the concrete structures that housed the irrigation canal's pumps. How had they occupied those positions without Jahelka or his men seeing them? It was possible they had been there before Jahelka arrived, but it didn't matter. Jahelka was dealing with a group of well-trained fighters. Their machine guns maintained a withering fire on his men, but each gun fired for only a few seconds. They knew not to overheat their barrels and to limit the amount of time that they gave away their exact locations via muzzle flashes. The platoon's six PEQ-2 lasers searched the dancing flashes of light, each one trying to identify targets for their fellow Marines. The *thunk* of outgoing M203 grenades responded to the enemy.

Jahelka analyzed his position. Ahlquist's men were the only ones effectively returning fire. Collard was being heavily suppressed inside the building, which made sense: the building was probably the only thing the enemy machine gun teams could make out in the dark. Then he realized Conley's squad was behind the building. "Conley, get up here," said Jahelka, pausing his transmission. He looked at Ahlquist's right flank and saw that it was nothing but sand, almost like a beach. The left offered the slight protection of hard mud and more reeds. "Take up a position on Ahlquist's left flank, the northern side."

The platoon commander grabbed his radio handset. He could hear Rage 6 yelling for him on the other end of the net. "Rage 6, Rage 3, I'm dealing with numerous machine guns and small arms, requesting supporting arms . . . CAS, mortars, whatever is most responsive, over," said the platoon commander.

"Negative, Three, cease fire . . . I say again . . . cease fire. Battalion says you are shooting at Iraqi police. Pop-up illum."

Jahelka was shocked at Captain Smith's response. Through his NVGs, he could clearly see the Iraqi police station. It was a building across the river with an infrared strobe flashing on its roof. It was at least 300 meters south of the enemy positions. He knew he wasn't shooting at IPs.

A foot stepped in the mud next to Jahelka's face. The platoon commander looked up and saw Sergeant Ahlquist standing, seemingly oblivious to the bullets whizzing all around him. "Hey, Ahlquist, you aren't supervising a rifle range. Get down!" shouted Jahelka.

The sergeant looked at his lieutenant with disgust and took a knee. "Cool-Guy, where's my rockets!" bellowed Ahlquist. The added firepower of Conley's squad joined the fracas as they came online. An entire platoon of Marines was firing their weapons at the cyclic rate. Thinking about the forthcoming antitank rockets to be fired from the shoulder of Lance Corporal Couoh Galvan, Jahelka almost ordered his Marines to cease fire. But he knew he couldn't. His men had the right to self-defense, and whoever was shooting at them was doing it deliberately.

He also knew he couldn't shoot off an illumination flare. To turn night into light would negate his one advantage and expose his men to the sights of the enemy's weapons as the men lay helplessly in the reeds and the mud of the flat terrain.

"Rage 6, Rage 3, negative on cease firing, negative on illum. These are not IPs, over," said the platoon commander, trying to refuse Captain Smith's order in as professional a tone as possible. The blast of an outgoing SMAW rocket made the last portion of the transmission almost inaudible.

Back inside COP Rage, Captain Smith was in an impossible scenario. The battalion was shouting at him to cease fire, saying that he was shooting at Iraqi police. His platoon commander had refused the order. Captain Smith thought that the only way to resolve the issue was through the illumination flare. Yet he didn't know the tactical ramifications of using the flying candle. He wasn't pinned down in an open field, listening to bullets fly past his head with darkness as his only protection.

Again, Captain Smith ordered Jahelka to use the illumination flare.

Again, Jahelka refused.

Rage 6 became irate—not at his platoon commander but at the situation. I turned to the map, plotting possible grids and extracting an azimuth to the target for a mortar fire mission. The battalion was too busy telling us to cease fire, rather than accepting our declaration of a TIC (troops in contact), the ramification of which was no air support. Once in a TIC, the brigade and division headquarters would surge any available air assets to that unit. Without the TIC, our scenario dictated the use of the 120mm mortars of 1/9 Infantry; they would be most responsive.

Captain Smith grabbed the handset to the COC's secondary radio. He changed the frequency to the army unit across the river to our north. Within seconds, the army company commander confirmed that the unit Jahelka was engaging in fact was hostile. Anger overcame every man in the COC. Minutes earlier, they had told us the shooters were IPs. Now they had figured it out and didn't bother to tell anyone. Captain Smith switched back to the battalion net. He picked up the handset and directed his frustration at 1/9's battle captain—the same individual who was still ordering us to have Jahelka cease fire. The battle captain realized his mistake and cleared us for supporting arms.

The machine gun fire was relentless. Numerous M203 grenades had smacked the concrete bunkers, but still the enemy fought. That is, all but one bunker, the one that Cool-Guy decimated with a shoulder-fired rocket. Sergeant Ahlquist was assisting the lance corporal with reloading and preparing the next rocket.

"Rage 3, this is Rage 6!"

Jahelka wondered whether he was going to be ordered to shoot an illumination flare again. "Send it, Six . . ."

"You are cleared for mortars!"

Jahelka sent the fire mission without looking at his map. "Roger, adjust fire, grid 543 028, over."

Then Cool-Guy fired another rocket. To the cheers of forty Marines, it smacked another machine gun position. The other two machine guns, as well as the teams of individual insurgents, picked up their rate of fire. If they had known what was coming, they would have withdrawn.

The two sides exchanged another minute of hostilities. Then Jahelka spotted the adjusting round. It landed between the opposing forces, sending a geyser of water straight into the air just short of the opposing riverbank. It was online with its target: the dancing muzzle flashes of a dozen enemy fighters.

"Direction 6350, add 100, fire for effect, over!"

The enemy continued firing, seemingly oblivious of the first mortar round. Maybe they mistook it for a M203 grenade or an inaccurate SMAW shot; whatever the reason, they were still fighting a minute later when twelve 120mm mortar rounds exploded around them. Each of the shrieking shells momentarily lit up the night and shook the dark, muddy earth.

"Right 50, repeat, over!"

Jahelka decided to send another barrage, aimed at the last bunker, which had barely been missed by the first. Another twelve concussions flashed in the night. The firefight was over.

The lieutenant began to check on his men. Conley's and Ahlquist's squads were unscathed, but Collard wasn't answering the PRR. The platoon commander moved back to the building that Collard was fighting from. The walls were covered with bullet holes.

Jahelka jogged to a window. His boots crushed multiple pieces of glass as he drew near. One of the Marines heard him coming. "Can we get the fuck out of here, sir?" asked the prone Marine. He quickly discovered that Collard's men were fine and somehow Rage 3 had escaped the ambush without any serious injury.

On the far side of the river, the army sent two Bradley fighting vehicles to do a battle-damage assessment. They found the bodies of six enemy fighters. I relayed the information to the 120mm gun-line. As an artilleryman, I knew there was nothing more satisfying to a gun-rock than knowing the results of your work.

February 8, 2007

The Iraqi scouts returned. Gunny Bishop brought the men who had decided to come back on his nightly resupply to COP Melia. Only three of the original scouts walked through the COP's double doors: Abu Ali, Abu Tiba, and Salim. Two new faces accompanied the three.

Captain Smith and I met the group in the foyer. Abu Ali was genuinely excited. He professed to Captain Smith that he would help us until al Qaeda was defeated or he no longer drew breath. Hate consumed his eyes as he described how insurgents had brutally murdered his brother in front of their family, forcing his nephews, nieces, and sister-in-law to watch as his brother's head was severed. Such an execution was ordered because Abu Ali's brother would not swear allegiance to al Qaeda's leadership. He was a secular insurgent caught in the insurgency's internal fighting. Captain Smith promised to assist Abu Ali in his quest for revenge.

Then we were introduced to the new men. The first was Colonel Mohammed. He had been a career infantry officer in Saddam's army and was the scouts' nominee to be Julayba's chief of police. The older veteran's Middle Eastern complexion sharply contrasted with his graying hair. In the general's absence, he was the new leader of the scouts. The colonel refused the option of using a pseudonym.

The other man was my equivalent. As soon as he came through the doors, he addressed me by name and said that the general had told him to work with me. We were the same size: five-seven with an athletic build. Another former Saddam guy, he had expertise as an intelligence officer. He also spoke decent English. I laughed when he said he wanted to be called Abu Ali, wondering who the hell this character was who inspired so many Iraqi nationalists. I explained that we already had an Abu Ali, but we would call him "Double-A."

The room we had used to isolate the twenty-five scouts during the last stint had been turned into the COP's kitchen and mess hall, so we moved the Sunni Iraqis to the room directly across from the Shia Iraqi army soldiers. After watching the veracity with which the scouts had questioned the detainees roughly ten days earlier, the Shia soldiers were more trusting of the Sunni tribesmen. By putting them in such close proximity, we hoped to expedite the process of their finding common ground.

An hour later, the colonel updated the company staff on his latest information about Julayba. He identified the region's key intersections and asked Captain Smith to establish checkpoints at each of them. Rage 6 shot down the request. It was the key difference in tactical thought between us and the Iraqis. They wanted to establish fixed positions to hold ground. To us, that just made more stationary targets for the insurgents to plan against. Marines are fanatical followers of maneuver warfare. If we wasted our combat power manning fixed positions, we would face the same scenario that 1/6 had in Qatana. Instead of bringing one hundred Marines out on a mission, we would be able to muster only twenty.

The colonel accepted Captain Smith's rebuttal. Then Rage 6 asked whether the scouts could conduct operations on their own, without our assistance. They said yes, but with only about ten to twenty men. It was also very dangerous. If one of them was killed or captured, al Qaeda would be able to hunt them down. "Then why can the Albu Obaid IPs do it?" asked Captain Smith.

I recognized where he was going with the question. The Obaid was a subtribe north of Julayba on the other side of the Euphrates. The only reason we'd ever heard of them was because on February 3, their tribesmen had found more than three hundred 82mm mortar rounds in a cache that also included rockets, artillery shells, numerous types of explosives, and other miscellaneous items. The cache was only a couple hundred meters north of the position used by the enemy to ambush Jahelka a few days earlier. Captain Smith was hoping to strike a chord of competitiveness between the various Sunni tribes.

"The leaders of the Obaid are protected by American tanks and Bradleys," replied Abu Ali. "It is not as dangerous for them."

"Do you know them?" asked Captain Smith. The scouts smiled. They all knew the Obaidi leadership. It was another Saddam-era connection. The revelation led to a discussion about getting the Obaid tribe to help in Julayba. We wanted to know whether it was possible for them to cross the Euphrates. Abu Ali and Colonel Mohammed both said they would pursue the question with their connections across the river. The two men personally knew the Obaid's police chief and head sheikh.

The conversation turned to more immediate issues. The next night, the five scouts would escort multiple squads of Marines in a smaller version of our first mission. Colonel Mohammed and I stayed at the COP and prepared the paperwork. Personally, I wasn't interested in spending another eighty-two hours awake as I had during and after the first mission. This time I slept on the COC's couch throughout the mission's execution. The radio watch woke me every time we had a new detainee, so that I could relay the names on to battalion and run them in the Multi-National Corps Iraq database of known insurgents.

When the squads returned, I immediately began the questioning. Six of the detainees were older teenagers. Most of them were students of another detainee, a fat teacher who was suspected of recruiting students from his classroom to assist al Qaeda. They all lived in the Albu Musa tribal area. According to Double-A, one of the young men was the teacher's son. In the son's pocket was a brown mask, a Seneao phone, and a twelve-round magazine full of 9mm ammunition. With some prodding, the kid admitted that the phone was set up to detonate an IED near Nova-Gixxer and that he had thrown his 9mm pistol out the window as the Marines entered his house.

While questioning another young man, I quickly realized that he had been beaten. The corpsman lifted his dark blue man-dress, revealing dozens of bruises. Dried blood was caked in his hair. I asked the young man what had happened. He said that a few days earlier, members of Thawar Al Anbar came into his house and beat him for working with al Qaeda. He denied being a militant but admitted that insurgents had forced him to watch attacks on coalition forces. It sounded like a training program. He said the insurgents would come to his house at night and take him out on missions. They would set up overlooking an IED and wait for us to hit it. When we did, he said the explosions were thrilling and that the insurgents were pressuring him to set one off himself. I asked him and the kid with the phone if they would write out a statement, just to say they weren't militants but that al Qaeda was trying to force them into its ranks. Both said they would like to, but they couldn't. They were illiterate.

I found it to be rather convenient; was it widespread knowledge that a videotaped confession was inadmissible in Iraqi court? All the boys had to do was deny what they had told me when they made it to the Ar Ramadi Regional Detention Facility, and they would most likely be released.

The questioning was over at about 0500. Back in the COC, I asked Colonel Mohammed and Double-A whether they knew who had beaten the boy. The two men unnervingly smiled. "I was there when it happened," said Double-A. "We must teach him a lesson. We brought him to you because we know he went out with al Qaeda after we got to him."

It led to a conversation in which I tried to explain why they could not beat local citizens and expect anything to change. Then I shifted to a more trivial matter.

"Why did you target these kids and the teacher?" I asked. The scouts had decided which houses we went to, and they never told us who we were going after. I knew that they shared only a small amount of the information they possessed about al Qaeda, and I couldn't fathom why they went after low-level operatives. They obviously knew where the leadership of al Qaeda lived in the same neighborhood.

"Pressure; these are their future soldiers," said Double-A. "They take the place of the others when we capture them. If the leaders have no fighters, they will get them from somewhere and will make people angry. The people will resist. Then when we capture the leaders, there will be less people to take their place." I found his answer interesting but ultimately unconvincing. I figured the scouts were still trying to negotiate with some of the moderates in the Albu Musa and Albu Bali tribes to join them.

The colonel was trying to stay awake on the couch. He didn't speak English, and there was no interpreter. I told the two Iraqis to go to bed. The next day, February 11, I led a convoy with the scouts and the detainees to Corregidor. Twenty minutes after I had passed OP Squirrel on Irish Way, al Qaeda responded to our latest mission with the scouts.

A young man driving a blue bongo truck with flashing lights and a white flag turned off Ruby Road and onto Irish Way. While passing OP Squirrel, he careened his bongo truck, with a refrigerator stuffed full of explosives on its bed, off the road and into the concertina wire ten meters outside the OP. Luckily for the Marines, the truck's tires were caught among the concertina, and the explosives detonated in the driveway. The ensuing blast was so powerful, it knocked Lieutenant Shearburn and his platoon sergeant to the ground inside COP Melia, half a mile away.

At the time, Corporal Guinn's squad was in the building. Following the blast, some of his men were trapped inside OP Squirrel's rooms. The frames of the doors shifted and turned the doors into an extension of the walls. The house's carport collapsed. Five Marines were wounded, most of them knocked unconscious. From Corregidor, six and a half miles away, I heard the ensuing chaos over the radio. Then I spotted the mushroom cloud as I got out of my humvee. It was a huge explosion that would have been disastrous if the bongo truck had made it all the way to the building.

I wondered whether the suicide bomber had been a boy recruited by the detained teacher. Frequent violence was terrorizing Julayba.

February 17, 2007

Sergeant Karras shined the blinding beam of his Surefire flashlight into the eyes of the Iraqi. It was the only light in the crowded room. A dozen other faces were distorted by darkness. The sergeant looked over at the scout's informant. The informant was flexi-cuffed and blindfolded. Well, at least the people in the house *thought* he was blindfolded. The goggles over his eyes weren't actually blacked out. Thirty minutes earlier, the Marines of Rage 2 had been led to the informant's house in the Albu Musa tribal area by Abu Ali and the scouts. They pretended to detain the man. Then he led the group to the houses where al Qaeda's leader-ship was staying. Now he was nodding yes or shaking his head no when the Marines shined their flashlights into the faces of the home's occupants. This time the informant nodded yes.

Karras shoved the man toward two junior Marines. One of the home's other occupants approached the sergeant. In English, he pleaded with Karras not to arrest the man. "If you leave him, I will tell you where there is an IED near here," said the Iraqi, who had already been passed by the informant.

Sergeant Karras immediately responded, "Okay, where is the IED?"

The man described the Nova-Gixxer intersection. On the southeast side, he said, there was a bomb. "Thank you," said Karras, who had no intention of releasing the other man. He responded to the information by shining his flashlight's blinding beam in the pleading man's eyes and looked back at the informant. For a second time, the informant nodded to not detain the man. Karras did as the informant recommended. The Marines finished with the rest of the home's occupants. Then they continued on their search.

The informant went from house to house in the area immediately surrounding the Albu Musa mosque. Karras and the rest of the Marines noticed the trend. Every home around the mosque was being searched. Some had every man inside cuffed, blindfolded, and dragged into the street. With a few hours until sunrise, the short targeted raid ended. Lieutenant Thomas led Davila's and Holloway's squads back to Combat Outpost Melia and turned in the detainees. On the way back, the informant was released and sent back to his home.

At the COP, James Thomas handed the eighteen Iraqi men over to me. In the pitch blackness of our detainee holding facility, I took photographs of each man. Before I took the photo, I would introduce myself and inform the individual that he was suspected of being a member of al Qaeda. So, I was used to hearing a complaint or a declaration of innocence. That night, however, detainee number seventeen glared at me in defiance. I sensed an unusual arrogance in his attitude.

"*Ismak*," I said, asking for his name. The movement of the Iraqi's mouth showcased his trimmed beard. Somehow I didn't recognize the words. Maybe it was his accent or the fact I knew him only by his nickname. Maybe I was stuck in a routine. Whatever the reason, I didn't know that I was inches away from al Qaeda's regional commander. He was number two on Al Anbar Province's HVI list. Most Americans knew him as Mullah Qahttan. He controlled AQI's operations in Ramadi, Fallujah, and dozens of other cities across Anbar. His men beheaded people at the wave of his hand and employed children as suicide bombers.

I went to the next guy, ignorant of the previous fact. In twenty hours, I would find out that a gray-fleece-and-tan turtleneck covered up Multi-National Forces West's HVI number two's true being: evil. Then he would no longer be just another dude.

After taking the photographs, I headed back into the COP. I had to beg Abu Ali to write out sworn statements against the detainees before he left. It took a Snickers bar to convince him. He breezed through the paperwork in an hour. Then he and the handful of other scouts returned home. They called Colonel Mohammed, who was staying at the COP semipermanently, on a satellite phone and informed him that they had arrived safely.

The following evening, I took the detainees to Corregidor. I left the still undiscovered Mullah Qahttan and the other Iraqis under the supervision of Lance Corporal Albin and a few other Marines. In my absence, they shuffled the men through the standard medical screening. I went across the street to the battalion headquarters.

On the second floor, the room housing the staff was empty, so I headed across the hall to the Tactical Operations Center. I walked in at an opportune time. On the larger center flat screen of six, three insurgents were running for their lives. Their body heat displayed them as three white images floating across the screen. The men were in the urban jungle of east Ramadi, climbing over walls and between homes. The visual feed was being provided by an Apache helicopter.

"Clear to use a Maverick," said the radio operator a few feet from me. His voice was followed by a small explosion on screen. It missed the three running men by about 20 meters. One of the men fell, probably from shrapnel. Of the remaining two, one stopped and looked back; the other kept chugging down the deserted street.

The night-shift intelligence clerk saw me standing in the corner. He walked toward me and whispered. I didn't take my eyes off the screen. "They set off an IED on 1/6 and ran into our area of operations. So now we get to kill 'em," he said.

The guy who stopped to look back at his friend started to run away again. Another missile hit close by but missed the two. The pilot asked whether he was clear to continue hunting the two men or if he needed clearance for every missile. "You are clear to fire as you choose," replied the battle captain.

The next missile hit on the screen. It was only 5 meters or so from the first guy. Somehow, he ran through the flash of light and continued running. The men in the TOC declared him a lucky fucker. Then, without any further blasts, the man stopped running and crumpled on the ground. The adrenaline propelling him through the previous blast must have worn out. The injuries that accompanied the explosion overcame him.

The remaining insurgent must have been pretty good friends with the guy. He picked up his buddy and moved into an abandoned lot between two houses. There he leaned against the lot's surrounding wall next to his comrade. I could only imagine what words were being exchanged. Another Maverick struck in the street outside. The blast was absorbed by the wall that the Iraqis hid behind. Then the surviving

Iraqi's survival instinct set in. His white heat image started to search doors for shelter. They were all locked.

He climbed a wall and sprinted down an adjoining alleyway. At the end he climbed another wall, crossed an alley, and traversed over the opposite wall. The Apache was waiting for him to make such a mistake. The final wall he climbed led into an empty lot. The image of his body had no sooner dropped from the wall than the lot disappeared in a flash of white light. The three men were dead. Cheers sounded throughout the TOC.

Sympathy tugged at my mind. Yes, this man was an insurgent. He had detonated an IED on Marines I knew. Hell, I had probably fought him on and around Christmas. Still, I felt sorry for the man. I could appreciate what he had just done. The desk jockeys had no clue. Where they saw him climb a wall without hesitation, they assumed that they could do it, too. These soldiers in the TOC never left the wire. They didn't know that at the top of almost every wall is a collection of shredded glass and metal, the likes of which will cut to the bones in your hands.

I began to look at my fellow Americans with a sense of disgust. These guys never got shot at. They couldn't possibly fathom being chased by an Apache helicopter, knowing that you can't hide. It took some serious balls for that dude to stop in the street and contemplate going back for his friend. Not to mention that he carried a dying comrade to safety behind a wall. I decided that the dude was as badass as it gets. Now a couple of pimple-faced nineteen-year-olds were cracking jokes about his final moments. To them, it was a game, nothing more. Somewhere deep inside my hatred for al Qaeda, I appreciated this one man's display of valor.

"Daly, snap out of it, man!" said the battle captain. Apparently, he had been trying to get my attention for a few moments. I sat down in an executive chair next to him. He knew I was there to find out when the next convoy was heading to Camp Ramadi. I intended to fall in with a seven-ton and transport my detainees under their protection. The captain explained that a convoy was leaving in an hour and that he wanted me to go specifically with that one. I objected; the detainees probably weren't finished with their screening. The captain didn't care, though.

A new lieutenant straight from the states was leading the convoy. The soldiers he led weren't the usual convoy guys, either. They were infantrymen who had been switched to running convoys because of a lack of manpower. None of them had ever driven through Ramadi, and the captain asked whether I would go in the first humvee to make sure they didn't get lost. I responded with a less than enthused "Sure." Then I headed to the convoy staging area on Corregidor. Usually, it was called the dust bowl. In the rainy season, the name changed to the mud bowl.

I spotted the convoy's humvees and supply vehicles right away. A few soldiers pointed me in the direction of the lieutenant, and I caught him in the middle of his convoy brief. The brand-new second lieutenant spoke in a rigid tone and was a little nervous. Everyone knew it was his first convoy. He was also in a tough situation. These weren't his soldiers; he hadn't trained them and probably didn't know any of them either. The bigger lieutenant, probably a football player, finished up his brief.

Before he told the soldiers to get on their vehicles, the platoon sergeant, who was the assistant convoy commander, mentioned to the group that a seven-ton was going to join the convoy on Michigan. The larger senior enlisted soldier, a non–football player sergeant first class, explained to the soldiers where the seven-ton would be in the convoy. He finished the formal portion of the brief and covered the areas missed by the new lieutenant. Then the two leaders took questions from the group.

"How soon are we leaving, sir?" asked one of the soldiers. I was baffled by the lieutenant's response.

"As soon as possible. We don't want to get stuck behind Pathfinder, and they are already staged as well."

I almost shouted at the butter-bar, but I opted not to embarrass him in front of his men. The convoy was driving through checkpoints 295 and 296. Historically, they were two of the most dangerous intersections in all of Iraq. I looked at the muscular lieutenant joking with his fat sergeant first class. The idiot had no idea where he was going. It reminded me of a story Craig Trotter had told me only hours earlier.

On the afternoon of February 16, 2007, Craig Trotter had found a friend. His name was "Bird Dog," and he happened to be the command sergeant major for 1/9 Infantry. The two men liked each other because they were both assholes. Each held a billet that demanded authoritativeness, and both excelled in their duties.

Two months earlier, during a short three-day 1/9 Infantry, I had my own run-in with Bird Dog. At the time I was the QRF commander and was on my way to set up security along the operation's critical re-supply route. Bird Dog decided he was going to take his own convoy out to check up on the troops. When I showed Bird Dog where Rage Company's forward command post was on a map, he told me I was "a no-good fucking lieutenant who couldn't navigate between your cock and your balls." I laughed, knowing that such sergeant major language translates into "I was told they are somewhere else." Then we argued over where the COC really was. Of course, I was right and the sergeant major was wrong, which resulted in his vehicle hitting a small IED while he drove aimlessly, checking on the troops. Nobody was hurt, and I enjoyed the satisfaction of looking him in the eye as his busted-up M1114 hummer was towed past my vehicle. In Bird Dog fashion, he flipped me the bird.

Inside Bird Dog's office that day, Trotter and the sergeant major were exchanging a few hunting stories. Their jovial conversation was inter-rupted by the battalion communications chief.

"LT sir, one of your Marines is dead," he said. "They got his lifeless body sprawled out in front of your building." Trotter could see from the soldier's pale face that he was serious.

Rage Company's XO flew out of Bird Dog's office and down the stairs of the battalion command post. Lieutenant Trotter didn't know what to think. Rage Company was the only Marine unit at Corregidor, but there weren't any convoys out. No incoming mortar blasts. How the fuck could one of his Marines be dead in front of the company CP?

At the base of the stairs, Trotter ran straight through the front door, passing a couple of soldiers who were mumbling about what they had just seen. Outside, he moved past the concrete blast walls and stopped in the dusty street. He turned to the right and saw the dead Marine lying in front of an M1114. Trotter could see the gore, brain tissue, and other pieces of flesh, and he was 50 meters away.

The XO sprinted toward the fallen Marine. He had no idea why there were three M1114s, one of them with a fucked-up roof, in front of the CP. Anger overcame him.

"What the fuck are you bastards looking at?" he screamed at the crowd of onlooking soldiers. "If you ain't going to help, go the fuck away!" shouted Trotter. The junior soldiers took the enraged officer's advice and walked away.

Then the XO spotted a few Marines standing around with their backs
to him. His mind was about to explode. How could his boys leave one
of their own, with half a head, lying in the street for all to see? Trotter
thought about tackling the dazed men. He looked back at the fallen
Marine they were ignoring, now only a few feet away. He didn't recognize the face.

The XO stopped running. The two Marines turned around, and
Lieutenant Trotter didn't recognize them either. A sense of relief overcame him. None of his men were dead. The relief was immediately
replaced by regret. On the ground next to him was someone's husband,
a father of two.

Corporal Dean Cugliotta and a few Marines from headquarters platoon ran out the front of the brown cinder-block building that was
the company CP.

"XO, sir," said Cugliotta, now standing next to Trotter, "they are
3/6 guys, supposed to be replacing 3/2 in Habbaniya. They drove their
entire head shed through checkpoint 296 and got hit."

Corporal "Coogs" knew checkpoint 296 rather well himself. In 2004,
back when 2/4 drove the streets of Ramadi in unarmored humvees,
he had been riding shotgun in a convoy through the checkpoint. An
incoming RPG flew through his plastic door, past his face, and decapi-
tated the driver. The grenade failed to detonate, sparing Cugliotta his
life. But the driver's foot was stuck on the gas pedal, and the humvee
slammed into the concrete wall that surrounded the Saddam mosque.
Coogs survived with a concussion and multiple broken bones. Now it
was 2007, and he was back in Ramadi driving through the same intersection every few days.

"They drove through 296 now, in the middle of the day?" said Trotter.

"Yeah, we spotted them when they pulled up. They asked where
medical was. Sergeant Sperry [promoted from corporal] put the two
wounded in one of our high-back humvees and brought them to the
battalion aid station. The driver for that truck, the one the dead guy
was in, he was hurt so bad he couldn't stop the vehicle. One of our guys
had to hop in and hit the brakes."

"Well, do you know who is in charge?" said Trotter. Cugliotta shook
his head.

"Uh, their battalion commander, XO, sergeant major, and a bunch of
other brass went with Sergeant Sperry. That guy on the ground is their
operations officer," said Coogs.

Then Cugliotta walked away from Trotter and helped the other Marines put a body bag over the fallen captain. Lieutenant Trotter walked toward one of the Marines from the convoy. He noticed that the guy was the same rank, a first lieutenant. When Trotter got closer, he realized that the other lieutenant was mumbling to himself.

"Hey, man, you need anything?" asked Trotter.

"I . . . my boss is dead . . . my guys are all wounded . . . I don't have a scratch on me," said the lieutenant. Trotter tried to ask him a few simple questions. Nothing registered with the dazed man. Craig Trotter grabbed his peer just below the shoulders. Inches separated their faces.

"Dude, your trucks are blocking the gate and need to be moved. My boys will take care of your boss. Why don't you head over to medical and check up on your guys?" said Trotter.

The other lieutenant regained his focus. "Yeah, I need to go check on my guys," he said. Then he headed across the street to the Combat Outpost. The truck that had been hit stayed behind.

Trotter sat down on a concrete barrier and stared at the vehicle. He was pissed. Who the fuck would drive their entire battalion leadership through checkpoint 296 in broad daylight? Not to mention that they didn't know where the nearest aid station was. How could such a large group of officers be so careless? What Trotter didn't know was that 3/6 had arrived in Iraq ten days earlier. Plus, they were stationed out of Habbaniya. Nobody they transitioned with had ever driven through 296. To them, it was just another intersection on a map.

A couple of EOD soldiers showed up. They began to do an analysis of the blast hole and the shrapnel in the vehicle. What they found shocked Trotter. The shrapnel was from an 82mm mortar round. The angle indicated that it had been fired directly at the vehicle, not in the conventional indirect method. The insurgents had somehow turned a mortar tube into a cannon. From an elevated position, they had fired this homemade contraption and hit a moving target. Pretty impressive for a bunch of dudes in black pajamas.

Now I stared at another lieutenant who was willing to make a similar mistake. I was enraged not only by his carelessness but also because I was beginning to realize how easy it was for the enemy to take advantage of new, inexperienced units.

After a few more questions, the soldiers began to disperse and head for their vehicles. As they did, I couldn't help but think that Pathfinder cleared the IEDs for us, so what was the point in their existence if we didn't wait for them to go out? Once most of the soldiers were gone, I introduced myself to the other lieutenant.

After we'd learned each other's names, he started to ask me where I was from. I ignored the personal question.

"What the hell are you leaving before Pathfinder for?" I asked.

"They are slow and drive with white lights; we would be sitting targets if—"

"Listen to me, you boot-ass mother . . . Pathfinder will save your and your boys' lives." The other lieutenant's eyes grew wide, shocked that another officer would speak to him in such a manner. "Don't be in such a rush to get your men killed."

The sergeant first class opened his mouth, saying something about how if Pathfinder found an IED, we would be stuck stationary on Michigan for the enemy to light us up. I didn't bother to look at the man. "You got a map?" I asked the lieutenant.

"My Blue Force Tracker . . . I don't have a . . ."

I picked up three rocks from the ground and laid them on the hood of the humvee. They formed a straight line. Then I professionally asked the sergeant first class to go away. When it was just the two of us, I started.

"Corregidor, checkpoint 296, then 295, in the order we will hit them," I said, pointing at each rock. "Now, this is a similar principle to displacing your machine gun teams in a firefight: you echelon them."

"Right, separate their movement by time, keeping continuous fire on the enemy, but I don't see—"

"It is a different relationship; the enemy now is the road, not a man, and you don't want continuous fire but continuous observation after Pathfinder clears it," I said.

The concept wasn't sinking in.

"Listen, Pathfinder clears the route every night for a reason. The enemy is constantly low crawling to the side of Michigan and pushing new IEDs out there," I said. The other lieutenant started to look nervous.

"I'm not following what you want me to do," he said.

"Stage your convoy on Michigan outside Corregidor," I said, pointing at the rock that was Corregidor. "Then get on the battalion net and listen for Pathfinder's radio check saying they cleared checkpoint 296.

Then switch over to 1/6's battalion net and listen for when they reach checkpoint 295. When they get there, you leave. This will ensure that only about twenty minutes have elapsed since they cleared the major intersections. And after 295, if you get stopped it doesn't matter; the tribes in that area are neutral."

"All right, that makes sense," he said.

I told him I needed one of his soldiers to ride shotgun in my seven-ton and take my place so I could ride in his lead humvee. Then I headed back across Michigan to get my detainees. Albin was finishing up with the paperwork when I arrived. Luckily, he knew what he was doing; I didn't have time to review any of it.

After maneuvering the truck to its position in the convoy, I headed to the lead vehicle. Pathfinder's massive vehicles crawled down Michigan toward Ramadi as I walked. Their large mine-resistant ambush-protected vehicles made our convoy look like a column of ants.

At the first humvee, I was surprised when neither the sergeant first class nor the lieutenant was in the vehicle. Instead, there was an ancient staff sergeant with wrinkled features and graying hair. He and the other two soldiers in his crew were on edge. It was their first 296 experience. But unlike the lieutenant, they had been here awhile and knew what 296 entailed. The soldiers' determined faces made me wonder what I had looked like before I drove through the checkpoint for the first time. I remembered Trotter's comment about the desperate housewives. For him to crack such a corny joke meant one thing. I had been just as on edge as these men were now.

I got in the humvee behind the staff sergeant on the passenger side. We sat in the dark for ten minutes before I noticed that the Blue Force Tracker (BFT) screen was blacked out. I assumed that he had the screen in blackout mode, but over time I became curious. I pulled out my flashlight and shined it on the switch that provided power to the computer monitor and the Dagger GPS. The stream of white light indicated that the digital mapping system was not turned on.

"LT, what are you doing?" asked the staff sergeant. He was shocked that I would turn on my flashlight inside his vehicle.

"Why isn't your BFT on?"

Though we sat next to each other, we spoke over the M1114 intra-vehicle communication system.

"That crap? It doesn't even work half the time, and we don't even have to turn off Michigan; it's a straight shot," he said. I didn't know what to say. Checkpoint 296 was anything but a straight shot. Scores of Americans hadn't died at the damn place because it was easy to navigate. I was in his vehicle for a reason. I leaned over and flicked the power switch.

"What the hell, LT? It's going to light up my entire truck." The statement revealed the staff sergeant's true ignorance.

"You can black out the screen," I replied.

We waited on the side of the road, 20 meters from the wall surrounding Corregidor. Just before the BFT was powered up, a flash of light and a concussion shook the distance. It was checkpoint 296. Pathfinder was doing their job. One less IED for us to deal with.

I wondered, with me in the lead vehicle, whether the now-detonated IED would have killed me or some of the other men in the vehicle. I was glad I had stopped the other lieutenant from leaving before the engineers. But I also became extremely nervous. I prayed for Pathfinder to hurry up and get to checkpoint 295. The sooner they did, the less time the insurgents had to reseed any blast holes.

Twenty minutes later, with the BFT blacked out, we sped toward the city. We passed the Y in the road leading north to Entry Control Point Eight. The buildings started to get bigger and closer together. On the left was the Mila'ab District; to the right, OP Hotel and the industrial area. Two hundred meters after that, we entered 296.

To some people, the word *checkpoint* elicits thoughts of a stationary roadblock manned by a few soldiers. In the modern era, however, the military term *checkpoint* isn't referring to a red-and-white pole that blocks your convoy's movement. Nobody is going to be there to check your ID. Instead, it is a prominent and easily identifiable point on a map that is used to relay a convoy's progress over the radio. Unlike its usage in previous conflicts, the word doesn't denote any form of control over the terrain.

Our vehicle came to a halt just short of the first Y in the road. "Which way, Staff Sergeant?" said the driver.

The older soldier took a few seconds to stare at either path. At the junction of the Y and separating the two routes was the checkpoint's always-identifiable water tower. Behind it was the Saddam mosque. The convoy commander, the new lieutenant, asked over the radio why the convoy was coming to a halt. The staff sergeant turned his head halfway back to me. "Sir?" he said.

"Left, south of the water tower," I replied. This was the easy direction through the checkpoint. If the staff sergeant had turned on his BFT, he would have easily been able to see this for himself.

The vehicle roared past the water tower. Then it came to a screeching halt only meters from the Saddam mosque.

"This can't be the right way!" declared the driver.

"It's blocked off, LT, can you see it?"

"That's the way, Staff Sergeant," I replied. I sat up in my seat, trying to see past the BFT's monitor. Eventually, I could see out of the windshield. Sure enough, Michigan was blocked off by a wall of concrete barriers where it intersected with Y-road. I started to second-guess myself and looked out the window. This was the right way, but the barriers were clearly visible. I realized what was happening, or rather what wasn't happening: cross-boundary coordination. The barriers were in 1/6's AO. Tarheel was probably redrawing their barrier plan for the upcoming Mila'ab offensive and hadn't informed 1/9 of the changes. Now I, the guy who was supposed to know where to go, was confused.

"Cut across the median and check out the other way," said the staff sergeant.

Before the driver started to move the vehicle, I interrupted. "At least tell the rest of the convoy to hold its position before you start searching for the right route," I said. "We don't need ten vehicles doing a three-point turn in the middle of 296."

The staff sergeant took my advice. The other vehicles stayed on the path that was usually used. We skipped over the median and roared over the ground between the water tower and the Saddam mosque. It wasn't a very safe thing to do, but Michigan was barricaded. At least that was what I perceived.

The M1114's massive tires dropped back down on the other side of the large median. The vehicle was now oriented down the road north of the mosque. Unlike the south side, the road was clear and the engine groaned as the truck accelerated.

"Stop!" I shouted into the headset.

The vehicle halted. Nobody said anything.

"Turn on the BFT," I ordered.

The staff sergeant hesitated. I lunged forward and did it myself. The screen confirmed what my eyes recognized. It was Racetrack in the opposite direction.

"Turn around and go back."

"It was barricaded, LT," said the driver.

"Trust me; go back," I said. The staff sergeant reached to turn off the BFT. I'd had enough of the games. I wasn't driving one more inch down an unclear route. "Leave it on," I said. The words were accompanied by my left hand on his shoulder.

The vehicle sped in reverse. Then it jumped the median and went back to our previous position. The BFT put us back on Michigan. It was the only way.

"Tell the convoy to follow us," I said.

The staff sergeant did as I asked, and we roared past the mosque and into the intersection with Y-road. The usual M1 Abrams tank was manning its vehicular OP. Our speed began to decrease as we drew closer to the concrete barriers. All four of us in the truck realized the obvious at the same time. The barriers weren't continuous. Somebody had set out a serpentine farther than usual to slow traffic on Michigan in front of OP Horea. I felt stupid.

After Fire Station Road, the Government Center, and checkpoint 295, the convoy was essentially over. We made it to Camp Ramadi without a shot fired.

At the Ar Ramadi Regional Detention Facility, I had left Albin in charge of turning in the detainees. When I got back, he informed me that Mullah Qahttan was in our custody. I didn't know what to say. It was a huge development. Capturing a living al Qaeda regional commander changed our momentum. After our first mission with the scouts, morale had plummeted. Firefights, rockets, and mortars were a daily threat. We suffered our first KIA. The deployment was extended by another month. Only a handful of scouts came back for a second mission.

All of this was negated when we captured Mullah Qahttan. Senior levels of command took note of Rage Company's effort. They even got fully behind Captain Smith's plan to transition the scouts into a police force. Somehow, we all sensed that it wasn't going to be our last tangible success.

Personally, I was pumped that we got the Mullah but felt like an idiot because I hadn't even known. The next morning we followed Pathfinder back to Corregidor. I was anxious to relay the news to the scouts. Surely, such a success would propel their guerrilla movement. They were officially a force to be reckoned with in Julayba.

13

BY WAY OF DECEPTION

February 20, 2007

Richard Jahelka was wrapping up his usual morning routine, checking on each of his squads via the platoon radio. He sat inside Rage Company's newest static position, Observation Post Shocker. The building was huge. It also offered natural protection. The open fields surrounding the house, along with its concrete wall, were very defensible, and the roof overlooked Route Michigan. This latter fact gave OP Shocker its purpose: ensure that 1,000 meters in both directions on Michigan remained clear of IEDs.

On that morning Lieutenant Jahelka was uneasy. His platoon, Rage 3, was spread out over three separate and not mutually supporting positions. Before Captain Smith had taken over the OP, he had informed all of the platoon commanders that the company's next objective was to clear the area surrounding the Risala mosque on Orchard Way. It was the next step in the strategy Captain Smith was employing. The platoons were systematically surging into various sectors of Julayba. In doing so, they effectively identified the ones controlled by al Qaeda. The Albu Musa and Albu Bali tribal areas in the east were confirmed as hostile. The tribes north and west of the Gixxer-Nova intersection were seemingly neutral.

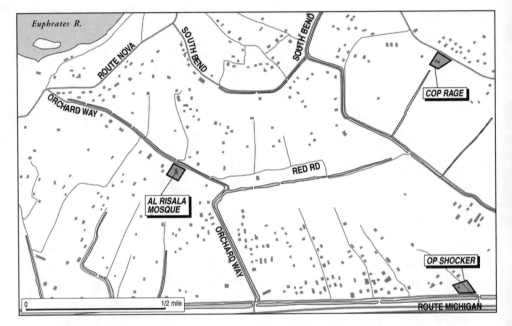

The Risala Takedown: The scene of multiple skirmishes in late February 2007 and a region with a historically strong al Qaeda presence.

Risala was different. Everyone knew it was bad without going there. The intersection of Orchard Way and Michigan was a notorious IED hot spot. Abu Musab al-Zarqawi, the now-deceased leader of AQI, had been known to preach at Risala. A few intel reports even said that the current head of AQI, Abu Ayyub al-Masri, had preached there in the past. To Captain Smith, the area was infected, and the staff dubbed his plan to cure the contaminated region the "Risala Takedown."

During this takedown, Rage 6 was going to surge elements from two platoons into the area known as the Sijariah crossing, where, on the map, the Euphrates dips low and almost touches the Nova–Orchard Way intersection. To isolate the area, the respective platoons would establish checkpoints at Orchard Way's northern and southern intersections: Nova and Michigan. This would effectively cut off any vehicular escape. Then the Marines would sweep the area for HVIs who were known to live in the area.

To set up the Risala Takedown, Captain Smith had ordered Jahelka to position two of his squads in over-watch of the company's quickest route to the area. The squads had moved into position during the previous night. Conley's second squad was overlooking the intersection of Red Road–Irish Way, while Ahlquist's watched Red Road–Orchard Way. It was the route the QRF would take from COP Melia in the event of a sustained firefight. At the moment, the roads in the vicinity of Risala were not clear. Pathfinder had not made a visit in almost two weeks.

Lieutenant Jahelka finished checking up on his squads. He tried to relax but found his attempt fruitless. A few solitary gunshots rang out. They came from the vicinity of the Risala mosque. Sergeant Ahlquist's squad was closest to the area. Rather than soliciting information, Lieutenant Jahelka waited for his squad leader to report the situation to him. Moments later, the platoon commander was informed by the sergeant that one of his Marines had been shot.

On the roof of the home that was now Sergeant Ahlquist's fighting position, Lance Corporal Cody Hadden had been shot in the upper torso. A 7.62mm bullet had struck above his small arms–protective insert (SAPI plate) on the right side. The injury was sustained while Hadden sat exposed, maintaining a watchful eye to the north of the squad's position. Unlike in Qatana, there was no ballistic glass to protect the Marines on the building's roof.

Blood was splattered against the gray cinder-block wall. The other Marines on the roof immediately rushed to their comrade's assistance.

The event put Ahlquist in a dangerous situation. Hadden was wounded and required immediate care, but the injury was not currently life-threatening. It didn't merit the QRF's driving on uncleared roads to get to his position. Under the circumstances, the safest option for the QRF was for Ahlquist to physically escort the casualty to the nearest cleared intersection. The sergeant instantly directed his team leaders on his course of action. He would lead two fire teams to the intersection of Orchard Way and Michigan. There, about 600 meters away, Rage Mobile would pick up Hadden. Then Ahlquist would head back to his position, where his other four-man fire team remained. All of this would take place with enemy snipers still lurking in the distance.

At OP Shocker, Lieutenant Jahelka approved Ahlquist's plan, then headed for a humvee. The platoon commander was going to link up with Ahlquist at the casevac point. Next, he would assess the situation and attempt to flush out the sniper team that shot Hadden.

Racing down Route Michigan, the M1114 humvees and the M113 ambulance that were Rage Mobile blew past OP Shocker. A minute later, Jahelka's lone humvee followed behind them. Over the radio, he could hear Ahlquist communicating with the convoy ahead. One of the squad's fire teams had secured the intersection, and Ahlquist was in the process of personally placing Hadden into the back of the M113. Jahelka was only a few hundred meters from the convoy.

Ahlquist started to say something on the radio, then an explosion rocked the intersection. Static filled the frequency. Smoke began to rise. Jahelka's humvee pulled up behind Rage Mobile. The convoy's humvees were unleashing 40mm grenades and .50 caliber rounds on something. Captain Smith, who heard the explosion back at COP Melia, was shouting for Ahlquist on the radio. There was no answer.

Jahelka ripped off his headset and dismounted the humvee. He sprinted toward the intersection. In the smoke-filled aftermath of the explosion, the platoon commander came upon one of his Marines in shock. It was recently promoted Corporal Aranez, whose torso was covered with blood. A thousand emotions flew through Jahelka's mind.

"What's the situation, Corporal?!" shouted Jahelka. Aranez mumbled something. With the machine guns firing only meters away, nothing was audible. Jahelka got as close as possible to his Marine and repeated the question.

"Sergeant Ahlquist is dead," replied Aranez.

Jahelka looked beyond the corporal and into the hazy intersection. He spotted the broken body of his most capable Marine.

After Ahlquist had placed Hadden in the ambulance, he turned and walked back toward his men surrounding the intersection. With Aranez behind him, Ahlquist stepped on an IED that he had narrowly missed on his way to the ambulance. Directionally, the blast shot into the sky, sparing the Marines around the intersection but concentrating its force on the sergeant.

The event ended the life of the battalion's strongest squad leader. Before the deployment, Ahlquist had earned the title of battalion color-sergeant, and his command presence would have been a problem for any officer less capable than Jahelka. Now, the squad stared out at their lifeless leader. The Marines were collectively in shock.

For a moment, the platoon commander was in a similar state. Then he remembered the look Ahlquist had given him during the firefight along the Euphrates. It was that somewhat condescending glare Ahlquist gave in response to being ordered to take cover that drove Jahelka's thought process. He knew how Ahlquist would have taken control of his squad, and it wasn't by focusing on the death of a Marine; it was by decisively attacking the enemy.

Jahelka seized control of the situation. He directed the Marines of Rage Mobile to gather Ahlquist's remains. Then the platoon commander led his infantrymen back to the remaining fire team. After Jahelka had a short radio conversation with Captain Smith, the decision was made to begin the Risala Takedown now, rather than under the cover of darkness. Lieutenant Thomas's Rage 2 and the platoon of Iraqi army soldiers in support of Rage Company both surged into the Sijariah corridor.

As the additional combat power arrived, harassing sniper fire continued. The accurate rifle fire was consistently coming from the villages to the west of the Risala mosque. Roughly 500 meters of open fields and sporadic palm groves separated the Marines and the teams of insurgent snipers. After a few hours, the Marines began to recognize the buildings that were consistently used by the enemy. Using the homes to the south and the north of the open fields, elements of Rage 2 and the Iraqi army platoon bounded closer to the insurgents. Late in the afternoon and only a few hundred meters from the enemy's positions, the insurgents withdrew in the face of the closing coalition forces. One two-person team ran away in plain view of the Iraqi army soldiers. Later, the *jundi* (Arabic for "soldier") would explain that they were certain one of the snipers was a woman. The myth of a female Chechen sniper spread through the company like a highly contagious virus.

Dusk settled on the landscape without any other casualties. Night began with Rage Company in control of the Sijariah corridor.

Early into the evening, Lieutenant Jahelka headed back to OP Shocker to get an update on the company's plan from Captain Smith. After a short meeting, Rage 6 told Jahelka that he was going to pull Rage 3 out of sector and replace them with Rage 2 and the platoon of Iraqi soldiers. Lieutenant Thomas's men would even take up the same position where Hadden had been shot that day. Jahelka objected to letting Rage 2 occupy the same position. Without ballistic glass, the roof was too exposed, and insurgent snipers were clearly capable of taking advantage of the situation.

Richard Jahelka couldn't persuade Captain Smith. In Rage 6's eyes, the building was key terrain and had to be controlled. Rage 2 would occupy it.

The platoon commander accepted his company commander's decision. Then he left the room and went straight to his platoon sergeant, Staff Sergeant Crippen. Together, the two men cannibalized some of the ballistic glass protecting OP Shocker and moved it to Rage 2's future location. A few hours before daylight, Lieutenant Thomas's men took over. One of them stood post in the exact spot where Hadden had been shot. Blood was still smeared all over the wall.

As the sun rose, Lieutenant Jahelka was just as nervous as he had been the day before. As events had played out twenty-four hours earlier, this morning was exactly the same. A solitary gunshot, and the Marine manning Hadden's post went down. This time it was Lance Corporal Carillo Soto. He was hit in the upper torso after spotting the sniper's movement and coming out from behind the ballistic glass to fire his weapon. A hidden enemy covered his day's previous work with fresh blood.

Again, the Marines evacuated the casualty via Orchard Way and Michigan. This time there was no blast; nobody stepped on an IED.

Anger gripped lieutenants Thomas and Jahelka. Together, their platoons conducted a clearance in zone looking for the sniper. Instead of focusing on finding the shooter, however, they also questioned the occupants of every house they entered. After hours of aggressive patrolling, their efforts paid off. Multiple citizens provided a rough location of the sniper's home: north of the mosque. They said he drove a blue bongo truck and had no family. Unfortunately, none of these informants knew where the sniper kept his rifle. The Marines would have to catch him in the act in order to find him. The infantrymen returned to their static positions and waited for night.

While darkness approached, Lieutenant Jahelka decided to act. He didn't ask for permission from his company commander; he didn't even notify anyone other than Lieutenant Thomas of his plan. Instead, he directed eight of his most seasoned noncommissioned officers to go light, removing any gear that was bulky or had the potential to bang together. Jahelka personally checked each man. Once he was satisfied that they could maneuver silently, the nine men left their position near the Orchard Way–Michigan intersection.

They patrolled directly into the thick palm grove to the west and followed it north. In the shrubbery of the grove, they halted just shy of the Risala mosque. The objective was 100 meters away: a large house that was somewhat destroyed and 50 meters from the mosque. Jahelka knew that the remaining windows in the building were a type of stained glass and reflected outward. He was going to set up a position behind those windows and wait for the sniper to appear. The bait was already set. Lieutenant Thomas and his men were still in the same house where Hadden and Carillo Soto had been shot. Richard Jahelka prayed that the sniper would appear for a third time.

The Marines moved to the house. Their noise discipline was impeccable. No one made a sound.

Once inside the empty building, Jahelka placed each Marine, mapping out all of the men's respective sectors of fire in his mind. Because of the need to stay hidden, there was no way the Marines would cover every approach to the house. Agonizingly, seven of the patrol's nine men were used to cover all possible entry and exit points. That left only two men to go to the roof and visually observe for the sniper. The lieutenant went above.

With one of his riflemen behind him, Richard Jahelka crawled onto the roof. Conveniently, debris piles were scattered around the broken structure. Jahelka found a position on the northern side and made himself comfortable. Lying on remnants of concrete and wood, with an old rug/blanket over the top, he waited.

Slowly, the cold air sunk into his skin. Watching the silent black skyline dulled his senses. An hour passed. Roosters began their morning calls. The sun appeared, casting shadows across the landscape. A slight fog rose from the earth. Villagers began to emerge from their homes.

Most were conducting their morning routines. None of them looked toward the Marines' position. The patrol remained undetected.

Jahelka waited. Time passed. There was no sign of a sniper, no shots at Rage 2's position. The lieutenant continued to watch his sector.

A man in his mid-twenties walked out the back of his home. Wearing a brown sweatshirt, he stretched his arms toward the sky and awkwardly looked around the open fields in front of him. Then he looked directly at Jahelka.

The lieutenant realized that he was sighting in through his scope. The man was at least 300 meters away; there was no way he could actually see Jahelka, could he?

The Iraqi looked away. After another stretch, he turned around and walked back to the door. Then, still standing in the doorway, he started to reach for something inside. Jahelka looked at the side of the house; there was a blue bongo truck. His senses peaked. Blue was the same color of truck that the sniper drove.

Jahelka thought about it for a moment. Almost every bongo truck he had ever seen was blue. It probably didn't mean much. He continued to watch the man. Two minutes later, the Iraqi turned around and walked back outside. In his right hand was what appeared to be an elongated object covered with cloth.

No fucking way, thought Jahelka. It had to be a rifle. He put the reticle pattern at the base of the Iraqi's head. The thought of firing entered his mind. But what if it wasn't a rifle?

The man walked toward the truck. Jahelka had to make a decision. This could be the sniper who had shot Hadden, who was responsible for the situation that killed Sergeant Ahlquist, and who had shot Carillo Soto. Now Jahelka hesitated. The power to take another man's life rested in that single moment.

The Iraqi opened the driver's side door. He raised the object in his right hand. The cloth fell away to reveal a scoped rifle. The sniper got into the truck and closed the door.

Adrenalin pumped through the lieutenant's body. He knew his duty.

Jahelka calmly inhaled. He placed his reticle pattern on the enemy's head. A second into his exhalation, he softly depressed the trigger of his M16A4 service rifle. The bullet seemed to take an eternity to reach its target. But when it did, it struck the Iraqi cleanly in the neck.

The insurgent fumbled with the door. He eventually got it open and stumbled out. Still clutching the door, the dying man looked around for his attacker. That's when Richard Jahelka's second shot finished the job, impacting the sniper's head. The body collapsed into the grass next to the truck. Now, as in life, the sniper was hidden from the Marines' view.

The patrol broke down its position. The objective was no longer to kill the sniper. Instead, it was to retrieve his tool, his rifle.

The nine men exited the heavily damaged building. The locals were going nuts. Women were shouting. Men ran into the streets. Jahelka had to move fast. The enemy would quickly react to his small band of lightly armed Marines.

They covered the 300 meters to the bongo truck at a moderate trot. What they found was shocking. Blood was everywhere, but the body was gone. There was no rifle in the cab. In the time that it had taken Jahelka to get off the roof and out the door, the enemy had retrieved their fallen comrade and his weapon.

Jahelka ordered his men to quickly search the immediate houses. They were full of nothing but frightened civilians. He thought about doing a detailed search. There was more shouting outside from the locals. It wasn't worth it. The Marines were overextended and in a bad neighborhood. Time was not Lieutenant Jahelka's friend. They returned to the previous night's position. By way of deception, one insurgent sniper was dead.

Later that day, Lieutenant Jahelka's Marines patrolled out of the Sijariah corridor and toward OP Shocker. They were replaced by the Marines of Rage 2 and the Iraqi *jundi*, in the execution of the Risala Takedown. On the way back to Shocker, however, Jahelka's men discovered a significant IED on the roof of a house they had occupied. The house was a few hundred meters east of the Orchard Way–Red Road intersection and on the north side. The two squads of Jahelka's men took shelter along the southern side of the road, roughly 200 meters from the sprawling mansion complex they had evicted. In the confusion of the evacuation, one of the Marines thought he had left an SMAW rocket on the roof.

Within minutes, Jahelka's men began to receive fire from the house they had left and from others in the surrounding area. The intensity of the firefight quickly escalated to a sustained exchange of machine gun and rifle fire. Inside the COC at COP Melia, we immediately declared TIC and received approval for a GMLR. We would also receive a section of F/A-18s fifteen minutes later, in case they were needed. I excitedly tried to observe the incoming GMLR strike from the COP's roof with Lieutenant Shearburn. We stared in the direction of the firefight and maintained a countdown to the rocket's impact. When time-on-target arrived, there was a faint dud in the opposite direction and no mushroom cloud.

I immediately recognized what had happened. Unlike the rest of the Marines on the roof, I didn't look for the actual impact. There was only one thing that mattered to me: the GMLR had missed. It was the first time ever in Iraq. I looked to the sky, wondering, Why me? For months, I had spoken incessantly of the impressive capability of rocket artillery. Now—the only chance I would ever get to observe one in combat—the expensive and innovative warhead had landed God knows where. I gave up my selfish thoughts and focused on the fact that Jahelka was still taking fire from the enemy.

The battalion pulled the F/A-18s out of their holding pattern. To the cheers of dozens of American infantrymen, the Marine fighter pilots dropped two 500-pound JDAM warheads on the mansion complex. The blasts ended the firefight.

For the rest of the afternoon, Rage 2 swept the Risala area for caches. They succeeded in finding a number with fewer contents. There were the usual mortar rounds, a Katuysha rocket, and, most important, a clinic with sophisticated medical equipment. The clinic had only one operating table, but the bloodied bandages and well-stocked shelves of antibiotics and painkillers showcased its use as a makeshift insurgent hospital. Risala was clearly an insurgent base of operations.

During the last two hours of daylight on the twenty-second, Lieutenant Jahelka and his men conducted a battle-damage assessment for the earlier air strike. They were also trying to confirm that the missing SMAW rocket was in fact in the house destroyed by the air strike. Unfortunately, after a detailed search, there was no sign of the munition. The fact that it wasn't found raised doubt as to where and when it had been lost. Under questioning, the Marine responsible for the rocket quickly declared that he was unsure of where he had left it. Out of due diligence, Jahelka and his men spent the night searching the houses they had occupied in the last two days, trying to find the SMAW. Captain Smith also tasked them with finding the blast crater of the GMLR, an order relayed to us by battalion and originating from the division level.

Jahelka never found either of the rockets. Yet James Thomas was searching for the SMAW rocket as well. The platoon commander and a squad of

Marines from Rage 2 were occupying the house on the northwest corner of the Orchard Way–Michigan intersection. It was the same building that Jahelka's men had occupied a day earlier and was a potential location for where the rocket had been left behind.

When Lieutenant Thomas took over the position, Jahelka informed him where the occupants of the house were now living. It was across the street. Every day the men who owned the house would come over and offer the Marines tea and one of their goats. The Iraqis were really trying to check on a cache of weapons hidden in the residential complex's garage. For the last few days, they had been content in the fact that the American's hadn't found it. But thanks to the missing rocket, James Thomas revisited the garage.

Most of the small concrete structure was taken up by a huge table, roughly twenty feet by twenty feet. On the table were hundreds, if not thousands, of pounds of fishing net. The maze of webbing was piled up to the roof, a distance of about six feet. Due to the table's weight, fifty-five-gallon drums were used as the table's legs. Previously, the owners had explained that they were fishermen during Anbar's warmer months. Their stated profession hadn't sent up any red flags; Lake Habbaniya was less than a mile away.

Looking at the net, the lieutenant thought, Maybe some Iraqi hid the rocket in here. He walked up to the table. The top half of a fifty-five-gallon drum was exposed. James shined his Surefire light down into the dark hole. At the bottom was an old, worn ammo can. He looked closer. It wasn't just any ammo can; it was U.S. style for a 240G. The thought of how the Iraqis had gotten the can infuriated James Thomas. Was it taken off a burning humvee? A dead Marine? For forty-five minutes, he ripped the fishing net off the table. With only a quarter of it on the floor, he could see the shapes of shipping crates, at least half a dozen of them. The lieutenant's anger faded, replaced with a sense of satisfaction. The Iraqis who lived here were going to rot in prison.

After getting some more bodies to help remove the net, the Marines revealed the cache. Still in their packing grease and shipping crates were two RPG launchers with one day/night sight and binoculars, fifteen RPG-7s, two NR4 RPGs, six antipersonnel OG-7 RPGs, twenty RPG boosters, a hundred mortar boosters, two PKM machine guns w/two barrels, two G3 assault rifles with nine magazines, five thousand 7.62 3 39mm armor-piercing (AP) ammo (for an AK), five thousand 7.62 3 54mm AP ammo (for a Dragonov), ten thousand 7.62 3 51mm AP ammo

(U.S. style), and miscellaneous accessories and IED-making material. The Marines neatly aligned and set up the weaponry on display.

Then they headed to the house next door. Instead of going on a rampage, Lieutenant Thomas had a better idea. They offered all of the men at the house chai. In all, there were four adult males. The neighbors were an older gentlemen and his younger son. The owners were another father-son pair, but both were much fatter than the average Iraqi. In line with the lieutenant's desire, the Iraqis accepted the offer of chai and followed the Marines back to their house.

As soon as everyone was inside the front door, Corporal Clark Davidson slammed it shut. James Thomas was purposely standing next to the owner of the house, the middle-aged fat man. He was also at the head of the group. Everyone watched as James hip-tossed the Iraqi to the floor. Then he flexi-cuffed the fat, stunned man. When he was done, he stood up, pinning the man to the floor with his boot, and looked back at the others. Three scared Iraqis and a cluster of pleased Marines couldn't believe what they had seen.

"Well? Take those fuckers down!" shouted James.

His Marines did as ordered but not nearly as harshly as their platoon commander had. Each of the Iraqis asked, "Why, mister?" The Marines provided no immediate response, but eventually they brought the Iraqis one at a time to the garage. When the old Iraqi saw the dozens of weapons on display, he spit his dentures at the Marine escorting him, Corporal William Downum. The hatred covered up by offers of tea and goats was now obvious. Both sides knew the other's true feelings.

After being delivered to the ARDF, the men who lived to the north (the neighbors) quickly blamed the cache of weapons on the two fat men. The response of the two accused men shocked the interrogators and us. They didn't deny owning the cache but instead said that the neighbors to the north were the ones responsible for planning and coordinating the suicide car bombing of OP Squirrel not even two weeks earlier. In turn, the neighbors responded by saying that the owners of the cache were also the individuals who had planted the IED that killed Sergeant Ahlquist.

Three months later, the owner of the house with the cache, an al Qaeda emir, according to intel, was handed a sentence of death by hanging from the Iraqi government. I do not know if the government went through with the punishment.

Ultimately, Rage 2 didn't find the missing SMAW rocket. Instead, they captured an al Qaeda emir, the fat man James Thomas had hip-tossed. He wasn't anywhere near the ranking of Mullah Qahttan, but he was a battalion-level target.

Over the next few days, the sporadic firefights in the Sijariah corridor continued. The insurgent snipers were becoming increasingly effective. Under the pressure of constant and accurate harassing fire, most units would withdraw from the contested territory. To the insurgents, Rage Company was no different from its predecessors. By February 26, all coalition troops would move out of Sijariah.

Yet our withdrawal was for different reasons than most. There was deception associated with the tactic. We wanted the insurgents to fill the void we would create. Two nights after our planned withdrawal, 150 tribal allies from north of the Euphrates would cross the river in Julayba's northwest corner. Once in Julayba, they would move to a pre-determined link-up point with our scouts. Then the militia would break into three groups and hunt down the region's al Qaeda militants by themselves. It would be our first test of the scouts' ability to become a real military force.

February 24, 2007

Staff Sergeant Jerry Eagle was upset. As the company's senior combat engineer, he had the right to advise Captain Smith on all things pertaining to explosives. But the issue that troubled him had nothing to do with engineering. Instead, Eagle was dwelling on the fact that the company had not been conducting presence patrols around COP Melia. In his mind, the Risala Takedown was receiving too much of the company's focus, at the expense of security in our own backyard.

The native of White Lake, Michigan, wasn't the only concerned Marine. For the last thirty minutes, on the COC's dirty-looking couch, he had been discussing this lack of patrols with the leadership of COP Melia's new security platoon: Lieutenant Shearburn and Staff Sergeant Colwell. The three men were quickly in agreement on the need to execute more localized patrols.

The trio was surprised when Captain Smith initially rebuffed their proposal. After discussing the matter, however, Rage 6 eventually agreed to allow a squad-size patrol. He gave them one condition: do not enter the heart of the Albu Bali tribal area, everything north of Kill Street. With that one restriction they decided to head east along Nova, search the Nasaf Marketplace, and patrol to AO Rage's easternmost boundary. They would head back following generally the same route.

Lieutenant Shearburn assigned Corporal Anderson's squad to the patrol, and Staff Sergeant Eagle volunteered to go in support. As Shearburn briefed Anderson, Eagle went to get his gear. With eight 27-round magazines, two fragmentation grenades, a smoke grenade, a .45 pistol, fifteen pounds of C-4 in a demo bag, the always-useful duct tape, an M-4 and an M-14 rifle, and an insane amount of water, the staff sergeant was ready for anything. Add in the body armor, the Kevlar helmet, and the radio, and the weight he carried was in the triple digits. It was a lot of shit for a five-foot-six guy to carry. Then again, Jerry Eagle was deceptively strong.

Once he was ready, he met Anderson's squad in the foyer. Lance Corporal Jahner, one of Eagle's subordinate combat engineers, and the company's senior line corpsman, Doc Del Castillo, would also be attached to Anderson's squad for the patrol. It was around midday when they finally left.

Staff Sergeant Eagle and Lance Corporal Jahner exited the COP with Corporal Anderson's first fire team. The squad left via the COP's main gate onto Nova and headed southeast toward the Nasaf Marketplace, which surrounded the intersection of Nova–Ruby Road. The Marines stayed in the defilade provided by the berm on Nova's south side. It was the same protection that James Thomas and his men had hidden behind a month earlier. In buddy pairs, the heavily armed men bounded between the houses paralleling Nova. After 1,000 meters of alert patrolling, they came upon the somewhat functional market. It was one of the only places that we knew about where Iraqis could purchase food.

Civilian traffic was minimal. As Staff Sergeant Eagle crossed Ruby Road, however, he noticed multiple Iraqis glaring at him and his men from the north. The combat engineer knew they were up to no good. He wasn't the only Marine to notice. The patrol's squad leader, Corporal Anderson, also made a mental note of the group and the small pickup truck they hung around.

The Marines didn't head after the suspicious men. To do so would have led them farther north and deeper into the Albu Bali tribal enclave. Without visible evidence to arrest the men on, the best course of action was to continue on their original heading—directly east.

After passing the last few houses of the village, the Marines entered rural agricultural terrain. The squad formation was generally exposed. Open fields stretched for about 300 meters to the north, while sporadic clusters of houses dotted the landscape to the south. The blond-haired, blue-eyed Eagle was keenly aware of his surroundings. The dark-brown earth was crisscrossed with dozens of irrigation ditches and plenty of vegetation. The staff sergeant anticipated finding his enemy hidden behind every possible position that offered cover and concealment.

After they had patrolled about 1,000 meters farther down Nova, the squad veered off the road and searched the open ground to the north for tactical caches and IEDs. When they found nothing, they continued heading east. Then, near the turnaround point, they spotted an IRL that wasn't completely set up. Eagle recognized a lone small building, nothing more than a shack, not far from the IRL. He guessed that it was the hide-spot that would be used to initiate or time the IRL's launch.

Eagle relayed to Anderson that he wanted to search the shack, and the squad leader agreed. The Marines slowly patrolled to the IRL. On arrival, Eagle successfully dismantled and loaded it into his pack. Then they headed for the shack. Inside, they found an air compressor and random IED-making material.

Anderson requested from the COC that they be allowed to detonate the items in place. Shearburn gave him the green light. Minutes later, after Eagle added the IRL to the pile of IED material and set a charge of C4, the small shack ceased to exist. With the items successfully destroyed, the squad began to head back to the COP. They executed the movement in a V-sweep, with Staff Sergeant Eagle at the base of the V, using his metal detector. They didn't get very far. Minutes in, half a dozen sporadic sniper shots rang out from the north. The rifle fire originated on the opposite side of the field that they had previously searched.

Instantly, the Marines gave up the V-sweep and took cover on Nova's south side. Just as Nova was bermed around the COP and the Nasaf Marketplace, it was bermed on the southern side as well. The raised road offered the crouching Marines about three feet of defilade.

The squad continued west toward the Nasaf Marketplace and its surrounding village. About midway through the 1,000 meter movement the insurgents opened fire again from the north. The shots missed high. Aware of the sniper threat, the Marines bounded along the base of the road. Eagle could hear Lance Corporal Jeffrey Foy, the squad's radio operator, trying to explain what was happening to the COC. There seemed to be confusion in Foy's voice, and Eagle decided to take the handset and do the explaining himself. After he did, Lieutenant Shearburn informed the staff sergeant that the QRF was getting on their vehicles. If things got out of hand they would be readily available.

The shooting ceased. An even mix of fear and excitement seemed to grip each Marine. They all sensed what was coming. The patrol was nearing the Nassaf Marketplace, the same place where the group of young Iraqis had stared them down earlier. It was most likely this group of men that was paralleling the Marines along Kill Street to the north and harassing them with inaccurate rifle fire. Now the Marines knew they were about to be predictable. It was no secret the patrol had to cross Ruby Road to make it back to the COP. If the insurgents wanted a fight, they would be waiting in the village.

Staff Sergeant Eagle was at the front of the formation. When they came to the outskirts of the village, Eagle approached a fence. He cut a hole through it with his wire cutters. Immediately after he ducked under the cut wire, he encountered a large, mud-filled ditch. In a full combat load, he jumped over the crevice and made it to the far side. Slowly, the Marines followed behind. Once the squad was almost entirely across, they heard a fit of expletives from the rear of the formation. Doc Del Castillo had rolled his ankle jumping over the ditch. It was a pretty serious sprain. Lance Corporal Alexander Torres, a big muscular kid who was one of Anderson's riflemen, had to help the corpsman limp onward.

In two-man teams, the squad entered the village 50 meters south of Nova. It was deserted. The Marines intently navigated between the two rows of houses until they reached the major danger area on their return to COP Melia—the crossing of Ruby Road. Maintaining their two-man buddy pairs, the first team crossed. Staff Sergeant Eagle went with them. They made it to the opposite side unimpeded. From the corner of a house, Eagle sighted through his scope to the north, looking for targets. The first buddy pair of the second fire team crossed. Then it was Torres and Doc's turn.

They made it a few steps out into the road. All at once, ten different AK variant weapons opened fire from the north. Eagle instinctively looked into the street at his exposed brothers. Dozens of bullets were tearing through the sky between him and the two men. The urgency in their faces said the obvious. They weren't going to make it.

Torres got hit. The high-velocity round spun his body 180 degrees. His athletic frame crumpled in the road. Unable to stand by himself, Del Castillo also went down.

Panic encompassed the scene. By now, the Marines were matching the intensity of the insurgents' rifle fire. They also shouted to one another on opposite sides of the street. Eagle executed a magazine change. As he did, he cursed his enemy. They were smart and patient fuckers. Not only did they engage the slow-moving target, but they also waited for the squad's combat power to be split by the road. Four Marines were still on the far side of Ruby, and at some point they had to cross.

Eagle finished the magazine change and continued firing. In the corner of his eye, he saw Doc Del Castillo help a dazed Torres to his feet. Somehow, the two made it out of the street without further injury. The men went straight into a small house, joining a few members of the first fire team who had already found shelter inside.

The insurgent fire tapered off. The Marines continued to suppress at a sustained rate. Corporal Anderson ordered the rest of the Marines into the small house. He and Staff Sergeant Jerry Eagle took turns firing at the enemy and shouting to Lance Corporal Mitchell Janicki, who had his three men on the roof of a house across Ruby.

Once Janicki was ready to cross, Anderson ordered two Marines with the M249 SAW to come out of the house and provide covering fire. Lance Corporal Jahner and Private First Class Kevin Convery sprinted out the door. They immediately took up positions oriented on the now-quiet insurgents. With their light machine guns, they suppressed the enemy's previous positions. Two Marines crossed. They were challenged by only a handful of inaccurate insurgent shots.

The process repeated itself. All of the Marines were now on the western side of Ruby Road. Anderson ordered the patrol into the small house. Torres and Del Castillo needed a casevac.

Eagle entered. He expected the worst for Torres. Instead, he found one of the luckiest Marines in the company. Torres had been hit but not cleanly. The bullet had slammed the side of his SAPI plate, punching into the Kevlar along the plate's width, not on the surface. The width was only half an inch. The bullet had missed the soft tissue on the side of his upper torso by centimeters. But the side of the body armor wasn't where the bullet's trajectory stopped. It deflected off the Kevlar and into Torres's right bicep. Somehow, it didn't break the skin and only left a massive bruise.

Regardless of his luck, Torres was having a hard time breathing, and Del Castillo could hardly move. The squad still needed the casevac. Del Castillo personally called it in to the COC. He was dumbfounded when Captain Smith denied the request.

When the firefight began, both Lieutenant Shearburn and I were in the COC. Cullen was doing a solid job of tracking what was happening, but Lance Corporal Foy, Anderson's radio operator, could not give us an accurate location to their position. He thought the patrol was still east of Ruby Road.

At this opportune moment of immense confusion, Captain Smith walked into the COC. He took over the radio from Shearburn and tried to take control. The problem was that we knew the logical next step and he didn't. We should have pushed the M1 Abrams tank at the intersection of Ruby and Michigan north to Nova-Ruby. It took Captain Smith two to three potentially crucial minutes to come to the same conclusion. During that time, he denied any request, including the one for the casevac. He didn't know Torres had been shot and thought it was only Del Castillo with a sprained ankle who required medical attention. Cullen Shearburn responded by shouting at Captain Smith to let him speak to his men. It was a frustrating moment.

To save the potentially crucial minutes, Captain Smith should have built his situational awareness before taking the radio. In the grand scheme of things, it is a seemingly inconsequential behavior to dissect, but for the Marines of Rage 1 this event made them lose confidence in Rage 6. Word spread among the lance corporals, inaccurately, that Captain Smith was trying to get them killed. In their minds, he was denying the casevac to protect the lives of the Marines in headquarters platoon (the Marines manning the QRF). In reality, he was trying to gather more information before pushing out the QRF. The result was a significant drop in morale.

After Corporal Anderson's patrol loaded Torres and Del Castillo into the M113 ambulance, they continued to the COP on foot. Instead of heading directly to the base, they stopped to search the surrounding buildings. On the roof of one, the Marines found four chiseled holes in the retaining wall: standard insurgent spider holes. Each of them was oriented toward COP Melia. We were being watched.

Again, Staff Sergeant Eagle was upset at the lack of presence patrols. They would have prevented the enemy from being comfortable enough to get this close. The insurgent doesn't know what you're doing when you enter a house. Maybe the person is giving you information. Maybe he isn't. Either way, the insurgent knows he is no longer the only influence on the population. He becomes more subtle, more deceptive. In turn, the people do not see him as much. The insurgent's threat of terror, which is the basis of his influence, is no longer the only thought in the population's mind. People become more receptive to your patrols and your requests for information. Truly, just showing up is 80 percent of winning. No one is more aware of this fact than an insurgent.

February 28, 2007

Double-A casually sat on the COC's couch. He wore the same clothes I always saw him in, a black turtleneck sweater and blue jeans. An olive-drab tactical vest was draped over the sweater. Multiple AK magazines filled its slender green pouches.

"You come out on the mission with us, Daly? I take you to my house and show you my family," said my Iraqi counterpart.

I continued to stare at the map on the floor between us. I was trying to get an idea of the mission's target locations. Double-A had circled half of the map, saying that's where the scouts and their tribal allies would search. There was no rhyme or reason to the circling. I gave up on trying to understand it.

"I'm sorry, Double-A, but this is an Iraqi-only mission. No American interference," I replied. "The people must see that you are in charge."

Double-A gave me his usual genuine grin. "But you, Sheikh Smith, Thomas, you are all famous. The people will want to meet you," he said.

I tried not to laugh. Double-A was a master of exaggeration. For a second time, I politely refused to go on the mission with him. Unless I wanted to be the only American wandering in the dark with a mob of Iraqi citizens, I was staying at COP Melia.

Captain Smith came into the room. Lieutenant Thomas followed him a few seconds later. Both men were in full battle-rattle, ready to go. Out in the foyer, Corporal Davila's squad was staging for movement.

"You ready, Double-A?" asked Captain Smith.

The Iraqi nodded, and together the three men walked out of the room. A minute later, they left COP Melia with Davila's squad. The group of three scouts and the squad of Marines patrolled to a house roughly 1,200 meters to the northwest. Once there, the Marines set up security and nervously waited. More than a hundred members of a tribal militia were heading to their position.

Through their NVGs, the Marines spotted the locals roughly 500 meters away. The supposedly allied Iraqis were a ragtag bunch. Most were dressed in Adidas tracksuits and ski masks. To Lieutenant Thomas, it looked like an army of insurgents was coming to kill him and his men. The platoon commander agonizingly watched as the heavily armed locals walked inside the home's exterior wall.

Abu Ali and the other scouts waited for the militia outside. They exchanged hugs and greetings with the first group of tribal fighters that entered. Then Captain Smith and Lieutenant Thomas headed outside to meet the leader of the militia, Sheikh Jabbar. Jabbar was probably the youngest sheikh any of the Marines had ever met. His position was based on merit; the fighters accompanying him were some of the first to oppose al Qaeda.

After exchanging introductions, Jabbar professed his commitment to destroying al Qaeda. Captain Smith welcomed his assistance and stressed that it was Jabbar's role to help our scouts take control and not to exact revenge over old tribal rivalries. While it was impossible for us to distinguish between the two (al Qaeda's support was drawn along tribal lines), we were wary that Jabbar may simply have been trying to expand his influence south of the Euphrates. The conversation ended with Jabbar declaring that his men would not beat any of the prisoners they took. He also agreed to return, along with his militia, within two days, to the northern side of the river.

As Captain Smith and Jabbar spoke, Lieutenant Thomas watched the militiamen. After entering the compound, the clusters of Iraqis quickly formed three platoon-size formations. Clearly, the tracksuits and the lack of uniformity in their appearance hid the military training of the group.

Each formation would be led by a two- or three-man team of our scouts. The planned execution of the mission was very similar to our first with the scouts: the western side of Julayba, from Sijariah to the tip of the shark tooth, was broken into thirds. All of the groups would look for militants in one of those thirds. Before Double-A left COP Melia, he explained to me how they planned to search for al Qaeda members. He and the militia would approach the suspected militants' homes in small groups, knock on the doors, then ask the occupants whether they wanted to go fight the Americans. In their black ski masks and standard insurgent garb, Double-A and the militia were very believable as members of al Qaeda. Obviously, how the occupant replied would determine how Double-A and the militia proceeded.

I was shocked by the simplicity of the scouts' approach. It was uniquely deceptive but also required almost no planning. The teams of scouts knew which houses they were responsible for and simply needed Jabbar's manpower to perform the mission. The greatest concern between the scouts and us was how the militia would respond if al Qaeda fought back. The two worst options were that the scouts would be killed and/or compromised or that the militia would destroy an entire tribal village.

The only way to mitigate the risk was to provide each militiaman and each scout with an infrared device. Then we would be capable of tracking their progress via UAV or other aircraft. If a significant firefight did develop, we would have the ability to intervene.

With the militia and the scouts in formation, the squad of Marines distributed infrared chem-lights to each man. Because none of the Iraqis could see the infrared light that was produced, they desperately wanted to ensure that these were working. After they each received one, most of the Iraqis double-checked with the Marine who had cracked and given them the chem-light to see that it was emitting IR light. Many of these men, ex-insurgents, had been on the receiving end of American airpower before. They did not want to be accidentally targeted.

After all of the Iraqis were outfitted with IR, the Marines nervously headed back to the COP. Three months earlier, the same squad had been ambushed in southern Ramadi on their first standard patrol. Now they were patrolling away from 150 heavily armed, insurgent-looking Iraqis. James Thomas was very aware of the difference. The tactical methods were at the opposite ends of the spectrum of war. Rage Company was no longer a conventional military unit. Instead, it was facilitating the use of a purely guerrilla force against its guerrilla enemies.

The Marines returned, covering the 1,200 meters without incident. I met Lieutenant Thomas in the COP's foyer. He proceeded to describe the surreal feeling of standing among so many men whom weeks ago he had considered enemies. For the rest of the night, we sat in the COC listening to relays of live feeds from UAVs or what various Apache pilots were seeing. They all saw the same thing: dozens of IR lights wandering through the region's villages.

At 0300, the first team of scouts returned to COP Melia. Only a handful of militiamen accompanied them. They informed us that a blue pickup truck was going to ferry their prisoners to us and not to shoot at it. We confirmed the route it would take and informed our rooftop positions not to engage. We also had an Apache identify the truck long before it got close to the COP.

Twenty minutes later, the truck was heading toward us. In compliance with the request we had given the scouts, the truck stopped 50 meters shy of the main gate on Nova. Then, over the PRR, one of the Marines on the roof relayed what he was seeing to his platoon commander, Lieutenant Thomas.

"Hey, sir, they are beating the shit out of the guys in the back of that truck," said the Marine.

The words sparked something in James. He stood up in the COC, threw on his gear, and headed for the door. "Where are you going?" I asked.

"They are beating the detainees" was his only response. Then he ran outside. I didn't know what to do. Should I follow him? Should I order someone else to escort him? I realized I was wasting time thinking about it. I reached back into the COC and grabbed my gear, then put it on as I headed for the door.

By the time I made it outside, James was already at the truck. He had run outside the COP by himself and ordered thirty armed militiamen to refrain from beating the detainees. From the steps of the front door, I could see James grabbing what appeared to be baseball bats out of the militiamen's hands.

Three Marines rushed out of the COP's door, passing me. Shit, what kind of friend was I? How long had I been standing there? Five, ten seconds . . . that's five or ten seconds longer than James was out there by himself. I followed the three Marines to the main gate. By the time we got there, James was walking in the middle of a crowd of bound Iraqis and militiamen. The latter were spewing insults at the bound men.

Quickly, the team of Iraqi soldiers and the Marines we had identified to take custody of the detainees showed up at the gate as well.

It took a few hours, but we slowly searched and transferred the detainees to the partially built house that was our holding facility. Half of them were visibly beaten. One had a ruptured eardrum. Another's nose was bloodied. The majority flinched in pain every time we touched them. In the usual fashion, I took pictures of the men, but I also sent a corpsman over to screen the group for any urgent injuries. None were life-threatening.

Midway through my taking the photos, Double-A came out to meet me in the holding area. He explained that some of the detainees had bragged in such detail of crimes against some of the militiamen's families that the militia, at times, became uncontrollable. Double-A's words sparked an ominous thought in my mind—how many detainees had been summarily executed?

I finished taking the pictures and headed to the COC with Double-A. We went through the men's photos, and he provided me with details of why they'd been detained. From the Risala area, there were two brothers who answered the knock on the door by saying they were the best snipers in all of Julayba. Before they were beaten, they told the scouts that they had been fighting the Americans in the area for the last week. I purposely shared this information only with Captain Smith. I didn't want to tempt our own men with the idea of exacting revenge.

As we went through the photos, Double-A identified spies, propagandists, and more members of direct-action cells—all of them offering the militia assistance against the Americans. By the end of the night, there were fifteen detainees in all. While fifteen was a significant number, I didn't feel it wasn't nearly enough for the scope of the operation. I felt that the scouts or the militia might be holding other detainees, but Double-A was smart enough to not admit it.

We were walking a fine line. Not only was the paperwork nearly doubled (because the detainees had been beaten), but I also had to explain the situation to military intelligence (MI) at the ARDF a few days later. Although they accepted all of the detainees, the information we provided on their backgrounds was not taken seriously. MI felt that the scouts had tortured them to get the information. I couldn't necessarily prove otherwise. Heading back to Julayba, I was worried. If the citizens saw us as being openly brutal, then we might lose their confidence in the same way that al Qaeda had.

In the first ten days of March, however, attacks against the company dropped dramatically. Our patrols were generally uncontested. Calm spread over Julayba. The problem was that the citizens didn't seem calm.

The enemy was adapting. When we caught them off guard with the first scout-led mission in January, they responded by attacking us, the Americans. During the month of February, small-unit combat was a daily occurrence in Julayba. Two of our Marines were killed, and a handful of others were wounded. Now the militants understood the real threat. It wasn't only a few locals helping the Americans; we were now capable of raising a large guerrilla force against them.

The insurgents recognized the need for action. Instead of engaging Marines, they were going after the root of the problem. They wanted the identities of our scouts.

14

A Dog's Dying Bite

1130, March 11, 2007

"Wake up! Wake up, Daly!" I opened my eyes to Jack's concerned face. It had been only three hours since I got off watch, and I heard no shooting, no explosions. What could possibly make the tan complexion of my Arab interpreter as white as a ghost?

My sympathy for his fear made me forget where I was. I shot straight up in my bed and smacked my forehead hard against the wooden bunk above. Jack ignored my succession of four-letter words and tried to tell me what was going on. The only thing I could make out from his rambling was that a woman was crying in front of the COP, and Trotter was busy on the radio. I looked beside me and saw Captain Smith out like a rock in his rack. Every day that went by seemed to turn Rage 6 into more of a zombie, so I wasn't surprised that Trotter would ask Jack to wake me, rather than Captain Smith.

The Arab interpreter hustled out the door of the dimly lit room. I couldn't fathom why it was so urgent, but I still skipped putting on my socks and boots. Instead, I walked out of the room in sandals, wearing my body armor, helmet, and rifle. I even neglected my blouse, opting for the

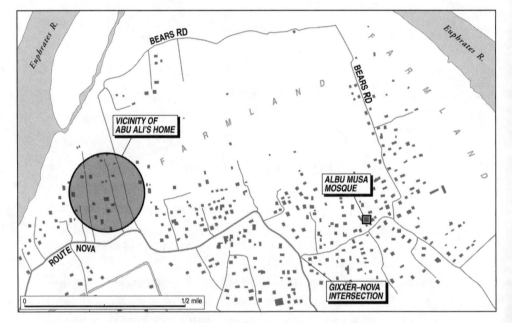

The Upsrising: On March 11, 2007, al Queda tried to murder Abu Ali at his home. What actually transpired was something remarkable.

tan T-shirt that wasn't standard Marine Corps issue. I didn't exactly look like officer material.

I found Jack waiting for me in the COC. Sure enough, Trotter was on the radio. Between transmissions, he explained to me that there was a woman out front crying about something, but he was stuck on the radio with battalion. I grabbed a couple of Marines and Iraqi army soldiers for security, then I went outside.

As soon as I went around the interior concrete barricade, I spotted the sergeant of the guard (SOG). He and another Marine were watching a woman in the standard black garb and headdress. She was not wearing a veil. The middle-aged woman was flanked by three men, each holding a makeshift white flag. I headed toward the group.

The woman and her three compatriots were standing along Route Nova on the northern edge of COP Melia. Thanks to the berm that raised Nova, it was the only spot where the concrete barriers dipped down low and the asphalt was actually higher than the barriers. It made the scenario slightly awkward: the woman and her friends were yelling down to us, while we looked up at them.

I walked alongside the SOG and told him he could go back inside. No reason to create a crowd with extra bodies standing around. Then I told Jack to figure out what the grieving woman wanted. When the SOG was gone, the woman went hysterical. I figured she was repeating the act she had put on for the out-of-sight SOG. Jack was having a hard time understanding her, and one of the men began to speak on her behalf. Jack translated as he went: "Al Qaeda came to her house this morning. They dragged her husband into the front yard, saying he is one of the men helping the Americans. Then they beat him while she and their children watched. When they were done, they drove away with him in a black car."

The woman's plight was not unusual. What *was* unusual was that she had come to us for help, in broad daylight.

"What is her husband's name?" I said to Jack. He relayed my question. The woman pulled out a picture and said, "Kasim," a dozen times.

The enormity of the situation struck me. I didn't know who Kasim was, but if al Qaeda did in fact have one of the scouts, they would torture him until he revealed who the others were. That meant all of our scouts were in danger and had to be warned. I needed the woman's picture to show Colonel Mohammed. Then, for the second time, I thought about how unusual it was for her to come to us for help. Maybe it was a trick; maybe one of the men was a suicide bomber.

"Jack, have the men raise their shirts," I said. Each one did as asked. No one had a bomb strapped to his chest. Jack directed the group to meet us down the road at the COP's Nova entrance. I had the Iraqi soldiers search each man just to be sure nothing was hidden. Again, each of them was clean. I offered to let the local citizens come inside the gate, not out of hospitality but so that I didn't have to stand exposed in the street to talk to them. They refused. Al Qaeda was probably watching, and they did not want to walk inside and immediately become "collaborators."

I took the picture of Kasim. Like most of the scouts, he was a middle-aged man. In the picture, he sat Indian-style in his front yard. Three bushes were behind him. I didn't recognize his face, but I no longer doubted his wife's story. She was now only an arm's length away, sobbing in fear and anxiety. The idea of losing a lifetime of memories had consumed her. I glanced back down at the picture. This man was everything to her, literally. I thought about one of my Arabic culture classes in college, Woman in Arab Fiction and Film. Almost every book I had read in that class was about Arab widows and the negative ramifications associated with such a status. There was no life insurance for this woman to rely on, no functioning government. At her advanced age, the prospects for having a good life in a tribal society were minimal. She would most likely sell herself into marriage, as a second or third wife, for less money than I made in a month.

I sent one of the Marines inside to wake Captain Smith. He would have some decisions to make. Then the woman told us she knew where the insurgents had taken her husband. She turned and pointed into the Albu Bali tribal area, which was across the street. She said Kasim was at the Kurtabah School, no more than 300 meters away. I told Jack to start grilling her on the details. He gave me a synopsis: "They came to her house an hour ago, five or six men with masks in two black cars. She didn't recognize them. Kasim is innocent; he does not help the Americans and does not fight."

Then why would she come to us for help? I interrupted Jack's synopsis and asked where she lived. The woman pointed northwest, in the same direction as Abu Ali and the friendlier tribes of Julayba. The situation was starting to become clearer. Al Qaeda was picking up random locals in the neutral tribal areas to torture them for information on the scouts. That was how desperate al Qaeda had become to know who our scouts were.

I headed back to the COC with Jack. The Iraqi soldiers stayed outside to talk with the woman and the men. Inside the COC was a groggy Captain Smith, accompanied by lieutenants Trotter and Shearburn. Out in the foyer, two of Shearburn's squads were getting their gear together.

I gave Captain Smith a summary of everything I had heard outside. It was slightly more detailed than the update he had received from the Marine who woke him. When I finished, it was obvious that Captain Smith and Shearburn felt uneasy about going to the Kurtabah School. There was no way we could tell whether the woman was being truthful, and she could be setting us up for an ambush. After all, the Albu Bali tribal area was openly hostile.

As Rage 6 debated sending out Shearburn, Colonel Mohammed came into the COC. He had a worried expression on his face and a satellite phone in his hand. He began speaking to Jack faster than I thought was possible. At one point, I thought he was going to hit Jack with the phone.

When the colonel had finished, Jack turned to me and the other confused Americans. "Kasim is Abu Ali's relative.[1] The colonel just got a call from Abu Ali on his phone. Kasim knows Abu Ali is a scout; we must find him if we can."

The new information told Captain Smith what needed to be done. Lieutenant Shearburn grabbed his Kevlar and moved into the foyer. He quickly briefed his squad leaders on the situation and left the COP at a slow trot. As he did, he passed the grieving woman and the three men, who still sat at the COP's entrance. The two separate groups looked at each other, both knowing that Cullen Shearburn and his Marines were the only chance that anyone would see Kasim again.

I sat on the COC's couch and listened to events unfold. It took Shearburn only a few minutes to get to the school. "Rage 6, this is Rage 1, there is nobody here. The school is empty—break—we did see three black Opels speed away from the area as we got close, over."

Jack translated for Colonel Mohammed what Shearburn had said. Then the colonel left with his phone, probably to inform the other scouts that Kasim was being moved in three black Opels. After a few

---

1. To protect Abu Ali's identity, I have refrained from inserting his relationship to Kasim.

minutes, the COC was bombarded by radio traffic from other units. The Marines to the east, soldiers to the north, and our parent battalion all called over the radio to inform us that al Qaeda had kidnapped one of the locals. Other Iraqi tribes, friends of the scouts, were concerned for their welfare. It was the first time that I realized the far-reaching capability of the scouts' network—a network built by the man whom we had treated so poorly that he wouldn't return to Julayba: the general.

Colonel Mohammed came back into the room. He had received a call from one of his spies, the same one who had led us to Mullah Qahttan. The man had spotted the three Opels pulling into the Albu Musa mosque. He claimed to have personally seen Kasim being moved into the building.

Getting to the Albu Musa mosque was harder than gaining access to the Kurtabah School. The mosque was almost 2,000 meters away, in the middle of a very hostile neighborhood. The roads leading to it were not clear, and the closest friendly unit was Lieutenant Grubb's Rage 4, located about 500 meters west of the Gixxer-Nova intersection. Captain Smith requested intelligence, surveillance, and reconnaissance assets from the battalion. The request went up to brigade and was partially denied. Anything available was already in use by a higher-priority unit. We would, however, get a section of Apache helicopters in two hours. I thought that by then, Kasim would probably be dead.

We didn't like it, but none of us were surprised by the brigade's decision. Understandably, searching for kidnapped locals wasn't one of the commander's critical information requirements; he needed his UAVs and helicopters to protect his men.

Denied in his request, Captain Smith pondered moving Grubb's platoon. He needed to get eyes on the situation. Before he made up his mind, the Marines to the east gave us another call on the radio. The general was in their COC and had described to them the importance of the situation. They informed us that one of their Predator UAVs was entering our area of operations, and they would relay what they saw. Captain Smith thanked them for their generosity.

We sent the UAV to the Albu Musa mosque first. It spotted a few individuals armed with Kalashnikovs but nothing we considered unusual. The three black Opels, which we all expected to see parked next to one another, were not there. Then Rage 6 sent the UAV west into the neutral tribal area and waited for the next transmission. A couple of minutes later, the Marine on the other end gave us a grid to what they were looking at. I quickly plotted it on the map. It was very close to where I believed Abu Ali's house was. "We got a white sedan and a black sedan parked out front. About ten armed men are finishing off and doing some sort of search on half a dozen bodies in the front yard. The men are getting in the vehicles; you want us to follow them?"

"Yes," said Captain Smith.

No one in the room spoke. We knew al Qaeda had ended the scouts' anonymity and was going to exact their revenge. Captain Smith broke the silence and told Colonel Mohammed to go call Abu Ali. Mohammed did as asked and headed outside to get reception. Then Rage 6 got on the company net. He quickly gave Lieutenant Grubb a brief on the situation and ordered him to get to the Gixxer-Nova intersection as soon as possible. We needed to shut down the main transportation routes between the opposing tribes and buy the rest of the scouts time—time for us to inform them of the danger they faced.

The Marines to the east continued to relay what they saw on the UAV feed. The white and black sedans headed straight for the Gixxer-Nova intersection. There wasn't a chance that Grubb's dismounted infantrymen would beat them to it. Colonel Mohammed came back into the room. Abu Ali was not answering his phone. Then the colonel left to call the rest of the scouts.

The white sedan barreled into a group of pedestrians at the Gixxer-Nova intersection. According to the Marine watching the UAV feed, it was obviously intentional. The result was one lifeless body on the side of the road. I wondered whether it was a scout or one of their spies. My heart sank; we were powerless to help them.

The two vehicles full of armed men continued east on Gixxer at a high rate of speed. They turned north onto Bears Road and surprised everyone when they flew past the Albu Musa mosque without stopping. Instead, they drove through the heart of the Albu Musa tribal area. The colonel came back in. Abu Tiba had answered his phone and informed the colonel that Kasim's headless body had been dumped near the Gixxer-Nova intersection. The information helped explain why the vehicle had not stopped at the mosque. The militants had extracted all they could out of Kasim; now they were hitting the targets he had given them.

The battalion called on the radio. The Apaches were coming early. They would be on-station in ten minutes. I hoped the two rampaging sedans would still be driving around when the attack helicopters showed up. Then we would be able to end their killing spree with a few well-aimed missiles.

There was another transmission via the UAV relay. Like the previous one, it began with a grid to the event. I plotted it at a random house along Bears Road. "The two sedans stopped outside a house. A few armed individuals came out the front door. Then some of the guys in the cars started shooting, while others got out. The individual standing outside the front door threw a grenade at the cars. It's hard to tell, but it looked like one of the men caught it and threw it back; either way, the grenade exploded on the guy standing outside the front door. Then the men in the sedans searched the house. We could see muzzle flashes coming from the windows while they were inside. They got back in the cars and are now moving north on Bears Road."

All of us in the room looked at one another. Who was it who had just gotten whacked? None of us thought it was possible for any of the scouts to live in the Albu Musa tribal area. It was too hostile. Maybe the house belonged to one of their spies. But still, why would they come out the front door to meet the enemy? Uncertainty filled the COC. The UAV was out of flight time. Our only source of information flew back to Camp Taqqaddum. We patiently waited for the section of Apaches to show up. They did moments later.

"Rage COC, this is Attack 17; what can I do for you, sir?"

Captain Smith grabbed the handset and gave the helicopter section leader a situation update. He instructed the attack helicopters to look for the white and black sedans along Bears Road, heading north toward the Euphrates. It took a few minutes, but the helicopter eventually found a white sedan heading west along Bears Road, back toward the neutral tribal area. The black sedan was no longer with the vehicle, but the pilot described it in the exact same fashion that the UAV relay had. I didn't think anyone doubted that it was the same vehicle.

I waited for Captain Smith to give the order. It was the perfect time to destroy the sedan. The portion of Bears Road it was driving on was sparsely populated and mostly farmland. The risk of collateral damage was low. I thought the priority was to prevent the vehicle from getting back to the neutral tribes, where the majority of the scouts lived. Now was the time to strike.

The pilot informed Captain Smith that he had a clear shot at the vehicle. To my dismay, Captain Smith told the helicopter not to fire. I could tell that he was not convinced that the white sedan we were now following was the same one as earlier. Captain Smith was the only man in the room who felt that way. Everyone else wanted the car blown into pieces. The vehicle reentered the neutral villages, placing it in the middle of a populated area. It then pulled onto a few dirt roads and finally into a driveway. The helicopter identified five potentially armed men getting out of the car and heading into a mansion that occupied the land. The two Apaches circled overhead for the next few minutes, and nothing happened. No muzzle flashes, no signs of violence.

We got a grid location from the helicopters and plotted the mansion on the map. To us, it was just another random house. There was no prior reporting on the location. For the next thirty minutes, Captain Smith directed the Apaches through the Albu Musa tribal area, searching for the white and black sedans. We never found them. I was convinced that the white sedan at the mansion was the one we were looking for.

A few minutes after the Apaches left, Colonel Mohammed burst into the COC yet again. Abu Ali was alive and on the phone. Captain Smith grabbed Jack and went outside to listen to the conversation. I stayed in the COC with the rest of the lieutenants. At first, I was relieved that Abu Ali had escaped the clutches of the militants hunting him. That was before Captain Smith returned with Abu Ali's details of what had happened that day.

When Kasim had been kidnapped, Abu Ali was one of the first to find out. He knew that al Qaeda would torture Kasim until they got whatever information they needed from him. Instead of running away or hiding, Abu Ali set up a surprise for his enemies in the form of an ambush at his house. Using the dozen fighters who had already crossed the Euphrates to prepare for the oncoming mission, Abu Ali laid in wait. When al Qaeda showed up, he killed them as soon as they exited their cars, the white and black sedans.

But that wasn't where Abu Ali stopped. He followed up his successful ambush with an aggressive assault. He drove to the Gixxer-Nova inter-section and ran over the group of al Qaeda lookouts who had dumped Kasim's body. Then he went for the leadership of the group. He knew where al Qaeda's regional commander, Safa Daham Hanush, lived, and the al Qaeda vehicles he and his masked men were now driving would ensure that they enjoyed safe passage through the Albu Musa tribal area. So they drove past the mosque and stopped in front of Safa's house. Safa even walked out the front door, thinking that his fighters were returning with Abu Ali's head. Instead, it was Abu Ali who emerged from the vehicle. He killed Safa and his bodyguards. Then he returned to the neutral tribal area.

As Captain Smith spoke, I sat in shock. Single-handedly, Abu Ali had somehow turned an impossible scenario into a victory. Even more shocking was the fact that if the decision had been up to me, I would have ordered the attack helicopters to kill Abu Ali without hesitation. If I had done such a thing, everything that subsequently happened would never have materialized.

That night, at the behest of Captain Smith, Abu Ali came to COP Melia. We all knew the scout's anonymity was over. Captain Smith wanted to formulate a plan to maintain the initiative, and there were many options. The one we went with, though, was the one presented by Colonel Mohammed and Abu Ali. The next day they would use the tribal Iraqi police to the north of the river, the same men who had helped in the previous Iraqi-only mission, to root out the small number of al Qaeda cells and spies in the neutral areas. Then they would recruit the neutral sheikhs to assist them in attacking the Albu Bali and Albu Musa tribes—an alliance they felt they could easily secure by emphasizing the brutal murder of Kasim.

It was a bold plan, and, collectively, the Marines of Rage Company liked it. There would be no American involvement. Iraqis would execute, supervise, and coordinate the entire mission. Not Iraqi soldiers but, literally, normal Iraqi civilians. Butchers, shepherds, farmers, and man-dress makers were going to wield weapons against one another. I sat down at my laptop and began to chronicle the day's events. The battalion needed to know what was happening.

That night, while Abu Ali told us his version of exchanging grenade throws with Safa, a hundred tribal fighters crossed the Euphrates just north of the Sijariah crossing. The tribes of Julayba were about to go to war.

1200, March 14, 2007

The sounds of multiple intense firefights engulfed the skyline. The fighting had raged for a full forty-eight hours, and we had no idea who was winning. From the roof of the COP, dozens of tribal fighting positions were easily visible. Each was a collection of men in masks, cloth head wraps, and the standard man-dresses. The scary thing was that they all had RPGs, medium machine guns, and various AK-style weapons. We were unsure of where the weapons and the ammunition to sustain the fighting had come from, but wherever it was, it was a large pile. It had to be; the fighting was continuous.

I put on my combat gear and headed outside to sit in the fresh air and the sunlight. To avoid the large group of Marines smoking on the back side of the COP, I headed out front and sat on the front stairs that led up to the double doors.

A perfectly clear blue sky greeted me as I relaxed on the steps. The days were getting warmer. The temperature was reaching into the seventies, and for the first time I had begun to feel hot on a daily basis. Soaking in the gorgeous weather, I thought about how miserable my existence was. For months, I had spent most of my waking moments hiding in buildings and shunning the light of day. I reminded myself that in a couple of weeks, it would all be over. Soon I would be on a ship sailing back to the States.

My thoughts were interrupted by the rude reality of where I was. The successive thumping of large-caliber shells leaving a mortar tube sounded over the horizon. I hustled into the COP for shelter. The sound was loud enough for me to identify that the mortar tubes were close, within a few hundred meters. It meant they were the enemy's. The only coalition mortar systems in Julayba had been put away in the COP's makeshift armory.

Shouts of "Incoming!" sounded through the COP. I stood in the foyer and patiently awaited the forthcoming concussions of close explosions. They arrived about thirty seconds later: three of them, each separated by about five seconds. I was surprised by their weakness and realized that the COP was not the target. I went back outside and looked north along Nova. Three pillars of smoke rose from the ground about 500 meters away, just off the road. The insurgents were targeting the Mohammara School, the location chosen by the tribes as the future Julayba Iraqi Police Station. The school was located directly between the two pro–al Qaeda tribes, making it a key launching point for our friendly tribes to assault the others from. Earlier in the day, you could see dozens of scout-led fighters moving about the complex; now there was rising smoke.

A blue bongo truck sped down Nova toward the COP. From a few hundred meters away, I could see that the bed was full of people. It could mean only one thing: casualties. I looked back into the COP. The SOG spotted the same thing from the roof and was already assembling Rage 1's corpsmen. Some of them were assisting lieutenants Trotter and Shearburn in setting up one of the front rooms as a makeshift aid station.

Captain Smith exited the COP and stood beside me on the stairs. He mentioned that it was convenient timing for the enemy; Colonel Mohammed had left the COP that morning to go to the school and conduct a planning meeting with the rest of the scouts. The scouts' entire leadership was at the school. A team of Marines and Iraqi soldiers rushed past us and toward the gate. Captain Smith yelled at the hustling Marines to search the vehicles and their occupants before letting them in.

The vehicle arrived at the gate and honked at the Marines and the Iraqi soldiers to get out of the way. Shouting developed between the two groups as the Marines tried to search the truck. I didn't see the point. Colonel Mohammed was clearly visible. He had taken to wearing his crisply pressed military fatigues in the last few days and was sitting in the front seat. We all knew who he was. Captain Smith, though, was furious when the Marines let him pass without doing a detailed search. I was relieved. Our allies were bleeding out in the back of that vehicle.

With the Marines yielding, the truck accelerated the final 50 meters to the interior concrete wall, only a few strides from where I stood.

I immediately heard the cries and moaning of injured men. Their comrades began to unload them, and the first two were carried toward me. The sight of the aftermath of when flesh meets flying shrapnel was horrific. I got to experience the view from up close when the two men were dropped off at the base of the stairs. The uninjured Iraqis begged me to help them, communicating through hand motions and Arabic I didn't understand.

At first, I didn't know what to do. I stared at the abdominal wound of one man and then at the shoulder wound of the other. The injuries required urgent attention, and four sets of eyes were staring at me for help. For some reason, I was still stuck on the fact that the Iraqis were bringing their wounded to our doorstep. For years, these men had fought us. It was a hatred that brewed for over a decade. Now they were pleading with me, an American, in broad daylight for help. I turned around and led the men into the aid station. Within minutes, the room was filled with slightly more than a dozen wounded and a contingent of feverishly working corpsmen and Marines.

Captain Smith maintained his vigilant focus. He was busy kicking out the uninjured Iraqis and had set up a security post to ensure that none of them went past the second set of double doors leading into the foyer. At the time I could not fathom his thought process, but I did know it was necessary. The confusion of a mass casualty event was the perfect time for a suicide bomber to strike. Not to mention that in Julayba's tribal society, friend and foe shifted with the wind. It made for a very dramatic lifestyle.

In the next few minutes, I watched our corpsman perform nothing short of a miracle. With the most rudimentary equipment and untrained Marines as assistants, they stabilized each of the casualties for transport. In less than thirty minutes, Rage Mobile had left the COP, carrying the wounded Iraqis to Corregidor's surgical/triage unit. Of the six urgent-surgical casualties, one lost his life. That left five living men whom the Iraqis had delivered to us with the expectation that they would die. The event showcased the incredible competence of our corpsmen. Such proficiency in saving lives cemented our relationship with not only the scouts but also the populace. Five husbands and fathers who weren't expected to come home did. It also improved the morale of our growing militia. Combat is a much easier enterprise to engage in when you know that modern health care is less than an hour away.

Once things began to settle down at the COP, Captain Smith decided to do a foot patrol to the Mohammara School. It was meant to be a show of support for the friendly militia. Lieutenant Shearburn didn't like the idea. He objected on the grounds that the situation was too fluid, with too many randomly armed men, and the Marines couldn't distinguish friend from foe. Not to mention that we had already treated their wounded. In his mind, we had shown our support.

As the two men spoke, heavy exchanges of machine gun fire sounded in the distance.

Then Captain Smith disagreed. He saw the event as an opportunity. To him, it was the perfect time for the United States to show that we had picked sides in the fight and to display our commitment to al Qaeda's destruction. He ordered Shearburn to assemble a patrol.

The Marines left the COP, then followed Nova north while staying on the western side. Because Nova was raised three feet higher than the surrounding fields, any al Qaeda observers in the Albu Musa or Albu

Bali areas would not be able to clearly engage the unit. There was also a Bradley fighting vehicle, courtesy of the battalion, that paralleled the formation on Nova. Its turret was oriented east at the enemy-controlled villages.

The patrol made it to the school. The majority of the original scouts were there, as well as at least fifty heavily armed locals. Captain Smith met Colonel Mohammed in what was probably the former school's main administrative office. The scouts had turned it into an operations center. A basic map was on the wall, and half a dozen men with hand-held Motorola radios were getting real-time updates from the front lines. Colonel Mohammed informed Captain Smith that his fighters had a foothold in the insurgent-controlled tribal areas. He claimed to have almost a thousand men under his control.

Captain Smith responded to the colonel by asking him to gather any available men in the room. Rage 6 wished to address the growing citizen militia.

About thirty Iraqis assembled. John Smith wasn't the most inspiring public speaker, but the tone of the speech he was about to give was much different than the first time he had addressed some of these men two months earlier. In late January, we had viewed one another without confidence or trust. Now we were on the cusp of defeating al Qaeda. So, as Captain Smith spoke, his dry monotone voice probably bored the Marines around him; however, the Iraqis didn't hear Captain Smith. They heard our interpreter, Jack, whose conviction in our fast-approaching success inspired their commitment to our mutual objective. The pacification of not only Julayba, but the capital of the Islamic State of Iraq, was days away. Hope and optimism filled the room.

The meeting ended with handshakes, hugs, and requests from the militia for more rifles and ammunition. We promised to do our best to answer the request. Then something symbolic happened. The Iraqis declared Captain Smith the "Sheikh of Julayba." Coming from your average villager, such a title wouldn't mean much. Yet the room was not full of average villagers. The respective leaders of every subtribe in Julayba, as well as Sheikh Jabbar from north of the river, were in the room.

Captain Smith recognized what was happening. The Iraqis had just made him the region's "kingmaker." He quickly praised the work of the ever-competent Colonel Mohammed and asked the tribes to support him in the war against al Qaeda. Julayba's chain of command was established.

Then, as the group dispersed, Captain Smith asked Colonel Mohammed to bring his three best drivers to the COP right after sunset. When the colonel asked for more details, Captain Smith simply told him it was a surprise.

The Marines left the school, following the exact route they had arrived on. Halfway back to the COP, Lieutenant Shearburn's concerns materialized. From the Albu Bali tribal area, a team of insurgents fired a Katuysha rocket at the Bradley fighting vehicle patrolling on Nova. It missed the Bradley and screamed over the Marines' heads, then slammed into a house. The casualties were quickly brought to the COP. A young twenty-something mother suffered a serious shrapnel wound to the shoulder. She ended up losing her arm. Her son, seven or eight, had his nose cleanly removed from his face. It wasn't a life-threatening injury, but I expected him to be very scared. Instead, he smiled at me. An arm and a nose were the price paid by two Iraqis so that we could show our support for the militia. The fighting in eastern Julayba intensified.

As sunset approached, an ominous thing happened. While we were sitting in the COP's COC, OP Trotter came over the battalion net. OP Trotter was a secure army position next to Camp Corregidor where Rage 2 was garrisoned on rest. The voice requested an urgent casevac and followed it up with "One of the Marines shot himself or something."

The COC went silent, waiting for more information. Then our fears were confirmed. Lance Corporal Steven Chavez, twenty years old, had been killed by an accidental discharge of his shotgun. At that time, no one was sure about what happened. But later it became clear that another Marine had mistakenly set off the weapon. The event crushed morale. Chavez was one of the most-liked Marines in his platoon, full of life and vigor. It was taken away not by the enemy, but by his own brother, a fellow Marine. The needless loss of life ate away at our very existence. We fought and struggled for one another. What happened to Chavez was the exact opposite. Anger, sadness, and depression took over our minds. We tried to focus on something other than the emptiness and feelings of loss that consumed us.

Captain Smith left the COC with Colonel Mohammed and his three drivers. When he got to Corregidor, he showed the colonel his surprise: three brand-new F-350 Iraqi police trucks. To the Iraqis, they were the ultimate vehicle. Each one was painted blue and white, had blue sirens and a loudspeaker, and could transport a small army in the back. For the rest of that night, the Iraqis drove around the areas of Julayba under their control, flashing their sirens and declaring a jihad against al Qaeda via the loudspeakers. The fall of al Qaeda was almost complete.

After the excitement of that moment, Captain Smith began the preliminary investigation into the circumstances of Chavez's death. Our greater success had been soured by yet another incident with a shotgun.

March 16, 2007

For the first time, I awoke to silence—no gunfire, no explosions. Inside the COC, we all wondered whether it was simply a lull or if one of the tribes was victorious. From the COP's roof, we could see even more armed militiamen than usual. They were oriented in every direction, and we assumed they were friendly. No one was shooting at us. In fact, the most interesting part of the tribes' one hundred hours of violence was that no one had fired at the COP. With the Iraqis busy fighting one another, no one had bothered to mess with us.

I headed out to the foyer. An excited Double-A greeted me as I stretched at the base of the stairs. The scouts had another cache of weapons to hand over to us. For the last two days and on every day of the following week, they brought us piles of weaponry. In their fighting against the pro–al Qaeda tribes, they found antiaircraft guns, surface-to-air missiles (SA-7 and only spent casings), recoilless rifles, suicide vests, 120mm and 82mm mortar tubes with base-plates and accessories, dozens of mortar rounds, artillery rounds, rockets, grenades, rifles, machine guns, and a minimal amount of ammunition. I was always amused by the response I received after asking Double-A what the scouts hadn't turned over to us. He would smile and shake his finger but never offer any details.

I entered the COC. Inside, Lieutenant Trotter was dumbfounded. Colonel Mohammed was circling houses all over the map and declaring that each one was a friendly position. Trotter asked him to stop. There were at least seventy-five circles. He didn't want to take up the entire map with militia fighting positions.

The colonel headed to the kitchen for food. I sat on the couch. "Daly, help me figure this shit out. Captain Smith wants us to mark all friendly positions," said Trotter.

"Why? The dudes are everywhere; tracking their movement is almost impossible," I replied.

"Actually, it is impossible," continued Trotter, "but the mechanized infantry soldiers who are taking our place are coming out today. He wants to show them an updated map that accurately reflects our AO."

I stared at the map from the couch. Trotter probably thought I was contemplating a better way to depict the scouts' positions. I wasn't. The fact that someone was taking our place meant that my interaction with the scouts was ending. Soon they would be introduced to a different group of Americans. How would they react to one another? Were the soldiers going to disrespect them in the same manner we had early on? Would the movement lose momentum? Eventually, I stopped thinking about the unknown and helped Trotter with the map. In less than two weeks, I was going to leave Ramadi and was not at all confident in the capabilities of our replacements.

March 25, 2007

James Thomas stood on the front steps of the COP, a soiled and dirty red bandana slightly visible under his helmet. The sky was clear blue, and bright sun shone on the group. Thomas surveyed his men. Corporal Davila, a recently promoted Sergeant Holloway, Sergeant Karras, and a handful of other Marines stood in the parking lot. Next to them was the enlisted leadership of the soldiers who would take their places in Julayba.

None of the army officers were present. They didn't seem to be interested in patrolling, only in cleaning the COC. Their company commander had emptied every drawer, removed the furniture, and ordered his soldiers to sweep the dust and the sand out of the room. He didn't pay any attention to the fact that his soldiers were about to leave the wire for the first time in Julayba. Rage Company's staff found the army captain to be nothing less than absurdly clueless.

The patrol was ready. James Thomas made eye contact with Davila, who was 150 meters away. "All set, sir," said the corporal over his PRR.

"Roger, let's go," replied James.

The formation left the wire. In the back of every Marine's mind was the Heidbreder ambush months earlier. Each of them was aware of the irony in the fact that Rage 2 was executing the last two patrols that Rage Company would conduct in Iraq. The Marines saw it as a validation of their success, a stark contrast from the fighting that had engulfed Julayba weeks earlier.

On the other hand, the soldiers had just finished taking part in the clearing of the Mala'ab sector. They had been in Iraq for sixteen months. Their mind-set was still wrapped around the expectation of daily contact with the enemy. Each soldier's patrolling techniques showcased this uneasiness. The mechanized infantrymen bounded between buildings and intently scanned potential hide spots through their scopes. The Marines casually moved in a less threatening manner. Hide spots were scanned with eyes, while weapons remained oriented to the ground.

When the patrol came upon clusters of militia fighters, the soldiers were visibly nervous. The somewhat-complacent Marines waved to their allies. As the various groups passed close enough, Sergeant Karras would hand out American cigarettes. To the Iraqis, they were a delicacy. While Karras and the Iraqis interacted, Lieutenant Thomas could see that the soldiers were not comfortable.

The patrol continued on its route around the COP. Along Irish Way, they passed a group of militiamen and a young teenage boy manning a checkpoint. To show the Marines that the boy was a fighter, one of the militiamen gave the child his AK. The young kid pointed it at the Americans. Most of the Marines barely reacted. The soldiers, not knowing why the Marines were letting an Iraqi point a weapon at them, looked quizzically at their countrymen.

Sergeant Karras raised his rifle at the kid, only 100 meters away. He shook the muzzle up and down a few times as a gesture for the kid not to point the weapon at the patrol. The militiamen recognized their mistake. After snatching the weapon out of the kid's hands, they proceeded to beat him. They yelled, pushed, and kicked at the boy. Then they gave a thumbs-up to the American infantrymen. Attitudes toward the Marines had changed.

The patrol slowly moved back to the COP. Nothing exciting happened. They reentered friendly lines. The army company commander was busy rearranging furniture. A few of the Marines gave him blank stares.

"What time do you want to go on the night-patrol, sir?" asked Corporal Davila.

"Have them ready at 2000," said James.

Then the group headed to the chow hall. The leadership of Rage 2 and the enlisted soldiers used it as an opportunity to share war stories and review Julayba's most dangerous areas. After the discussions, the conversation turned to the night-patrol. Then the two senior soldiers, both sergeants first class, said something that haunted the Marine lieutenant.

"We can patrol a short distance outside the wire and sit in a house, LT," said one. The two soldiers exchanged looks, noticing James Thomas's silent, annoyed response.

"Hey, we obviously appreciate you guys doing the great job you did out here, fighting on a daily basis for months, but our captain won't have us leave the wire after you guys pull out. So we don't have to take any additional risks unless you want to, LT," continued the second.

James was still silent. The first sergeant to speak opened his mouth again. "Yeah, we'll go, LT, but we don't have to go far, you know what I mean?"

The Marine lieutenant was disappointed. He responded by telling the soldiers to meet him in the foyer at 2000. Then, when the time came and the group left on the patrol, he couldn't stop thinking about how the new American unit would change the region's dynamic.

On that patrol, Julayba's citizens met the Marines at the door, rather than hiding in a room and waiting for them to barge in. Interior lights were on; blinds were open. Families gathered in living rooms. A sense of normalcy that none of the Americans had previously seen in Iraq seemed to be taking place. The change tugged at James Thomas; would these soldiers allow this opportunity to founder?

On the way back to the COP, after six cups of sugar-laden chai, Lieutenant Thomas came to a realization. The incoming army unit, one that would exert no influence over the region, could be a blessing. By not engaging the populace, they would ensure that Colonel Mohammed and the scouts would have free rein. The men with the knowledge and the ability to exert control just might be in a better position to do so. To the Iraqis, it would appear that America was rewarding them with the power to govern themselves. Hopefully, other regions, tribes, and cities would recognize this and assist the United States in order to gain a similar power.

At least, that's how he hoped it would turn out.

The patrol made its way inside Combat Outpost Melia. Rage Company's deployment was over.

March 30, 2007

Two CH-53 helicopters swooped down onto the landing zone. A dim moonlight illuminated their frames on the ground. I clenched my jaw in anticipation. The wind from the aircrafts' rotational blades blasted the column of men I stood among. The ramp to the closest helicopter dropped. The crew chief exited, flagging us to him with an infrared device.

The column began to trot. Each of us carried more than a hundred pounds of gear, but I wasn't thinking about the weight. Instead, I was regretting what I was about to do. I was going to leave Ramadi.

The cool air of the beautiful spring night continued to pound into my body, propelled by the helicopters' whirring blades. A hundred meters to the ramp and the deployment was over. I felt more regret. Now was not the time to leave. The clearing of the Mila'ab was complete. In the Papa 10, the children who once hunted for American small-kill teams now searched for al Qaeda snipers. Every district was under coalition control. Insurgent attacks were nonexistent. After the dramatic turnaround in Julayba, I sensed what was coming.

Without militant interference, the tribes of Ramadi united. In the coming months, they would spread their influence across all of Al Anbar Province. On a larger scale, the rebirth of Iraq's Sunni population was about to take place. I wanted to be there when it happened.

My boots met the steel ramp. I entered the fuselage. We all took seats, weapons oriented to the floor. The ramp closed, and our helicopter began to take off. The moment it left the ground, I felt something change in my body. It was just as tangible as the rifle in my hands, but I have no idea what I was feeling. My first thought was that it was a reaction to knowing I was now safe or that I might not ever see Ramadi again. I had anticipated those emotions to be positive, however, and I was feeling anything but positive.

Instead, I felt like I was betraying a friend. The scouts had risked everything to help us. A little more than two months after accepting that help, we were leaving. Al Qaeda was on the run; now was the time to finish the job, not celebrate prematurely.

I looked around at the faces of my fellow Marines. Just about everyone was in a similar state of self-reflection. I wondered what they were thinking about. Did they know the importance of what they had just done? Did they or anyone in the United States know that the capital of al Qaeda's self-declared government had been secured by a combined force of American, Iraqi, and local militia? I knew the answer: no.

In many respects, the outcome of Rage Company's enterprise in Iraq was predetermined. During America's disastrous attempt at regime change, nothing but total failure was the logical outcome. Somehow, reporters and historians would explain away our success by saying that we hired Sunni insurgents to do the fighting for us. The spin would be that America was not responsible for the turnaround in violence during that spring. The thought angered me, but ultimately I didn't care. My greatest concerns were that our military would not learn the lessons of the counterinsurgency fight that had taken place in Ramadi. That Operation Squeeze Play would be forgotten. More important, though, I feared that men like Melia, Ahlquist, and Chavez would become nothing more than names on a wall. The true meaning and sacrifice that was their lives would remain hidden to those they had sacrificed so much for.

Hydraulic fluid from the aircraft dripped onto my groin pad and body armor. In the night's darkness, the fluid was jet-black. It pooled in two distinct spots, and I immediately recognized the symbolism. The color and texture of the fluid were, in the dark, the same as the blood of my fallen comrades. I looked up to find the source of the leak, waiting for the third and even more symbolic drop. It never came.

It didn't have to. I knew what had to happen. If the world was going to know of Melia's, Ahlquist's, and Chavez's sacrifice and the victory that forfeiture of life had achieved in Ramadi, someone had to tell them.

15

OPERATION SQUEEZE PLAY:
A SUMMARY

Part 1: The Situation

A. Purpose

On September 13, 2006, the 15th Marine Expeditionary Unit (MEU) sailed out of San Diego, California. Embarked on three naval warships were the members of Rage Company and their parent unit: 2nd Battalion, 4th Marines (2/4). The standard purpose of an MEU is to serve as America's rapid response force. At least two such units are continually deployed around the globe to protect American interests abroad. Our original orders were not to enter Iraq but to offload into Kuwait and stand by for any emergency that might arise in the Middle East.

On November 9, 2006, the 15th MEU was ordered into Al Anbar Province. General John Abizaid, the CINC U.S. Central Command, was transferring us to the operational control of Multi-National Corps-Iraq's commander, General George Casey. The use of the MEU was the result of a decision by Iraq's number two in command, General Raymond Odierno, and also received the blessing of Iraq's future commander General David Petraeus. Together, these two men had a plan to stabilize Baghdad, and it began by putting the pressure on al Qaeda's Sunni base of operations: Al Anbar Province.

B.   Strategy for Anbar

Once the decision to deploy the MEU in Iraq was announced, the junior officers of the battalion were immediately privy to a cascade of information, the most important of which was the plan for Operation Squeeze Play, what ended up being the shaping phase of the greater surge strategy. At the same time that Squeeze Play was being planned, Sheikh Sattar and his secular insurgents declared an "Awakening" against al Qaeda. It wasn't until Operation Squeeze Play was in full swing that they would overtly join America against al Qaeda.

Squeeze Play's planners chopped the MEU into three separate units. They sent the majority of the MEU—the command element, the artillery battery, the reconnaissance platoon, and the combat logistics battalion—to the western city of Rutbah. On arrival, the command element formed its own brigade/regimental area of operations: AO Bull-Rush. Before the creation of AO Bull-Rush, the entire region surrounding Rutbah fell to the responsibility of a single light-armored reconnaissance battalion. This battalion was spread out over hundreds of miles and exerted minimal control over Rutbah.

The second largest unit, the headquarters element of 2nd Battalion, 4th Marines and two subordinate infantry companies (Company G and Weapons), was sent to the Haditha Triad. The battalion's two remaining company-size units were sent to Ramadi.

If you were to plot these three cities (Rutbah, Haditha, and Ramadi) on a map, you would see their strategic importance. Only one highway runs west to Iraq's border with Jordan and southern Syria. It passes through Rutbah. The route to Anbar's other gateway, where the Euphrates River Valley flows into Syria, passes through the Haditha Triad. Heading east toward Baghdad, both of these routes intersect on the outskirts of Ramadi. Al Qaeda understood the three locations' strategic importance; large swaths of each city were under their control. Squeeze Play sought to contest these militant-controlled areas and hopefully divert the enemy's attention away from Baghdad. At a minimum, the insurgents would be forced to fight on multiple fronts.

C.   Executing Operation Squeeze Play

In the grand scheme, *Rage Company* was written from a narrow perspective. While it does capture the birth of the Awakening movement from a first-person point of view, it does not provide a larger context toward explaining how operational and strategic-level events shaped the Awakening. The following will help you grasp the root causes of the dramatic success that appeared seemingly overnight in Al Anbar Province during spring 2007.

Phase I: November 9, 2006–January 10, 2007

Rutbah: The 15th MEU Command Element and its subordinate units became operational in AO Bull-Rush at the end of November 2006. The initial focus was placed on securing the two major points of entry (POEs) on Iraq's western border with Syria and Jordan. Then they sought to bolster the regional Iraqi Highway Patrol. The center of Rutbah itself remained largely under al Qaeda's control.

Haditha Triad: When 2/4 arrived in the region, also at the end of November, there was a single Marine infantry battalion already on the ground and responsible for the entire triad. So, the adjoining units decided to use the Euphrates River as their boundary, with 2nd Battalion, 3rd Marines (2/3) occupying the towns on the western side (Haditha and Haqlaniyah), while 2/4 formed AO Bastard to the east in the town of Barwana.

The deployment for 2/4 began by taking control of Barwana. They did this by conducting a battalion-size assault and following it up with the construction of an earthen wall around the entire town. The populace of twenty thousand was essentially locked inside the wall, with all civilian traffic coming in and out subject to a search by the Marines. The constant barrage of insurgent attacks ceased almost immediately.

Ramadi: In Anbar's capital, the brigade received Company F (call sign Rage) and Company E, 2/4. Company E was immediately assigned to 1/9 Infantry, in order to help the undermanned army battalion occupy all of its required positions. Company F, or Rage Company as it is called in the book, was used as a brigade-level maneuver asset, a tactic I had never seen before. Instead of being assigned to a piece of land, we were moved from battalion to battalion, pushing the insurgents out of their safe havens and isolating them in the Mila'ab.

Phase II: January 11–April 1, 2007

At the end of Phase I, the Haditha Triad was under total coalition control. Ramadi was still contested, but the insurgents were being isolated in the Mila'ab and slowly pushed out of the city. The 1st Marine Division, in command of Anbar, shifted its focus to Rutbah, removing Company E from Ramadi and attaching them to AO Bull-Rush.

> **Rutbah:** In early January, a message between insurgent leaders was captured by coalition troops. Al Qaeda had declared Ramadi too dangerous and was seeking ways to relocate its base of operations. The message stated that the insurgents were going to move their weapons in a tractor trailer, through the desert, and attempt to reestablish themselves in Rutbah. At the time, the 15th MEU had not entered the city center itself, making Rutbah the last potential safe haven along al Qaeda's Syrian and Jordanian infiltration routes.
>
> Whether the insurgents actually shifted the bulk of their weaponry to Rutbah, I do not know. Either way, at the end of January, the 15th MEU assaulted Rutbah's city center and seized control of the city. Resistance to the coalition quickly dissipated.
>
> **Haditha Triad:** The arrival of 2/4 greatly reduced violence within the region. As a response, local sheikhs began to sign their men up for Iraqi police positions. Although sporadic attacks did occur, the repeated violence that had taken place before 2/4 arrived was effectively over. The Haditha Triad was pacified.
>
> **Ramadi:** In January, the city's insurgents were off balance. Isolated in the Mila'ab and unable to mount sustained resistance to the increased coalition presence, al Qaeda attempted to regroup. At some point, the terrorist group's regional commander, Mullah Qahttan, returned to the city, forsaking his mission of reigniting the insurgency in Fallujah.
>
> The decisive moment for the city of Ramadi was when Rage Company shifted out east to Julayba. When this took place, at the end of January 2007, the Sunni insurgency's two distinct factions (secular-nationalists and AQI Islamists) were placed in two very different positions. The secular groups were given an opportunity; al Qaeda was threatened. The evidence for this is clear on the secular side: Thawar Al Anbar moved openly

to assist Rage Company. But al Qaeda also subtly identified Julayba as its base of operations. In the first week after Rage Company arrived, IED attacks in Ramadi proper plummeted. In Julayba, they skyrocketed. For insurgents to shift their focus of effort and resources from the urban streets of Ramadi to a cluster of agricultural villages meant one thing: to them, Julayba was more important.

By our challenging al Qaeda in Julayba, the militant group's operations were severely disrupted. The leadership could no longer comfortably coordinate attacks; there was no rest-and-refit location for AQI foot soldiers. In less than two months, their regional commander was detained, along with more than one hundred followers, and a few dozen more were killed. The conditions for an uprising were set. The scouts, Abu Ali in particular, seized the moment in dramatic fashion.

The Lasting Success of Squeeze Play

The uprising that occurred in Julayba, a piece of what is commonly referred to as the Awakening, did not end in Ramadi. Instead, it spread like wildfire, scorching the al Qaeda network both east and west along the Euphrates River Valley. When it reached Baghdad, many critics thought it would falter, but it only grew more intense. Moving south to the Sunni Triangle and north into Diyala Province, countless Sunni sheikhs forcibly removed or killed al Qaeda's foreign leadership and reconciled their young men back into society.

Part of the reason for this momentum was the surge. All across Iraq, U.S. troops were entering cities, villages, and neighborhoods that historically had never had an American presence. By sending these additional troops into the same regions where the populace was dissatisfied with the brutal local al Qaeda government, America placed itself, for the first time, in a position to succeed in Iraq. We now had an opportunity to implement the key factor in defeating a guerrilla movement: finding common ground with the people of Iraq.

Part 2: Changing the Tide of the War

The following is a time line that I believe will help the reader understand where Operation Squeeze Play fits into a broader context of the

Iraq War's history. The time line begins when violence was at its peak, the summer of 2006.

Summer 2006: The U.S. president officially orders a review of military strategy in Iraq. In the city of Ramadi, soldiers of the 1st Brigade, 1st Armor Division begin to seize "combat outposts," turning Iraqi homes into American fortresses in the city's urban sprawl. The methods are what General David Petraeus refers to as "clear, hold, build."

September 2006: Sheikh Abdul Sattar al-Rishawi declares an Awakening of Anbar's tribes against al Qaeda from his home in Ramadi. His fighters begin a guerrilla campaign against the extremist movement.

October 18, 2006: Al Qaeda declares Ramadi the capital of the Islamic State of Iraq. Its fighters hold a parade 800 meters from Anbar's capital building and claim to have crushed Sattar's Awakening.

November 9, 2006: The 15th MEU is ordered into Al Anbar Province to execute Operation Squeeze Play. Almost 2,500 Marines are sent to the cities of Rutbah, Haditha, and Ramadi. The goal of the mission is to prepare the battlefield for the surge by denying al Qaeda its traditional stronghold.

December 2006–late January 2007: A series of coalition operations within Ramadi corners al Qaeda fighters in the city's Mila'ab neighborhood. The district is subsequently barricaded with massive concrete barriers.

January 10, 2007: President Bush announces the surge to America.

January 25, 2007: Awakening fighters approach U.S. Marines from the 15th MEU on the eastern outskirts of Ramadi, offering assistance against al Qaeda. The two units begin a campaign to rid the local area of al Qaeda's command-and-control network for Al Anbar Province.

January 2007: The 2nd Brigade, 82nd Airborne Division deploys to Baghdad. They are the first of the five surge brigades sent to stabilize the capital. The other brigades follow monthly throughout the spring.

February 2007: Operation Imposing Law begins in Baghdad; it is the first mission to use surge forces in Iraq's capital. In Ramadi, elements of 1st Battalion, 9th Infantry and the Iraqi army begin to assault the Mila'ab sector. After suffering five KIAs and fifty-two WIAs in five days, they halt the offensive and regroup. They eventually clear the entire sector with the assistance of 3rd Battalion, 6th Marines.

February 16, 2007: The House of Representatives passes a concurrent resolution stating, "Congress disapproves of the decision of President George W. Bush announced on January 10, 2007, to deploy more than 20,000 additional United States combat troops to Iraq."

March 11, 2007: After a series of joint raids between Awakening fighters and Marines east of Ramadi, who arrested 150 al Qaeda fighters, the extremist network begins a brutal campaign against local civilians. The violence backfires, sparking an open revolt against al Qaeda's terror that begins on this date.

April 2007: Violence in Ramadi abates, and the Awakening spreads.

June 16, 2007: Operation Phantom Thunder begins in and around Baghdad. Surge forces begin to enter former al Qaeda strongholds throughout the capital. Within months, the Anbar Awakening and surge forces in Baghdad drive al Qaeda from the Sunni villages south of Baghdad and Al Anbar Province. The terror group is eventually isolated in Diyala, north of Baghdad and Mosul.

Summer 2007: General Petraeus turns the Awakening into a permanent force, paying the fighters for their service with U.S. currency and calling them the "Sons of Iraq."

August 29, 2007: Shia cleric Moqtada al Sadr calls for his fighters to observe a six-month truce with U.S. and Iraqi forces. This call for a truce comes after the success of the Anbar Awakening and is a politically calculated move. This is not the first time Sadr declares a cease-fire to regroup (June 2004). The cleric understands that with cooperation between the Iraqi government and Sunni tribes, the focus of U.S. and Iraqi forces will shift to his militia. He is right.

Fall–Winter 2007: Violence in Baghdad drops dramatically. Surge and Iraqi forces, supported by secular Sunni militias, now occupy every major neighborhood and district except for Sadr City. In Ramadi, Iraqi forces begin to take over the combat outposts established by 1/1 AD. The Awakening begins to transition from a militia force to one that is capable of providing security to its citizens.

February 22, 2008: With Sadr's network of corrupt officials within Iraq's Ministry of Interior and Ministry of Health crumbling, he declares an extension to the cease-fire. The Iraqi government, empowered by the fact that Sunnis are no longer fighting them in large numbers, attempts to exploit the situation.

March 25, 2008: Iraqi forces launch an offensive against Sadr's militia in the country's third largest city, Basra. The fighting quickly spreads throughout southern Iraq, and the Iraqi army is initially repulsed by Sadr's fighters. A scene of Sadr's men celebrating over burning Iraqi vehicles, however, causes the militia's popularity with citizens to plummet. Iraq's prime minister, in a display of his determination, personally directs the operation in Basra. He also brings in thousands of reinforcements from an interesting place, Al Anbar Province. This would not have been possible without the cooperation of the Sunni tribes.

March 30, 2008: Sadr brokers a cease-fire from his hideout in Iran. The Iraqi government asserts military control over Basra the next day.

April 6, 2008: A joint U.S. and Iraqi offensive begins in Baghdad's Sadr City, a Mahdi Army stronghold. Heavy fighting rages in the Shia slum for weeks. The district is barricaded in the same manner as Ramadi's Mila'ab.

May 11, 2008: The Mahdi Army crumbles, unable to sustain prolonged fighting. Sadr declares a cease-fire yet again.

May 20, 2008: Coalition forces control all of Sadr City. For the first time, coalition-supported troops maintain a presence in all of Baghdad's nine districts.

The fall of Sadr City marked the end of the Mahdi Army. It was also the peak of the surge. Clearly, the additional combat power provided to General Petraeus by the surge shifted the tide in the Iraq conflict. Without the surge's additional troops, the United States would not have been in a position to exploit the opportunity given by the rise of the Awakening. Yet without Operation Squeeze Play, the shaping operation for the surge, the Awakening would not have happened in the manner it did. Success in Ramadi would not have been guaranteed, and the ability of the Awakening to spread beyond Anbar would have been jeopardized. Clearly, these events are not mutually exclusive.

In a greater context, we must ensure that the lessons of this reduction in violence are truly captured. The greatest obstacle to this is inaccurate information. After I left Iraq and was sailing toward Australia, I listened to CNN's Michael Ware (one of the best newsmen covering the Iraq conflict) explain the changing of the tide in Anbar as the United States paying thugs to secure the streets. This belief has led to an assumption that the United States can simply hire militias to do its fighting. Mr. Ware's statement is not completely correct, however. The streets of Julayba, Ramadi, and other villages across Anbar were secured before the fighters of the Awakening were ever paid. They fought first out of a determination to destroy al Qaeda. Our payments to them were to sustain our gains once they transitioned into a peacekeeping role. If the United States attempts to hire militia/guerrilla-style forces before it wins over the population, it will be repeating the mistakes of Afghanistan in the 1980s, an era when the country funded the efforts of Osama bin Laden.

This is only one of numerous lessons from Ramadi. Dozens more are threaded throughout *Rage Company*. Rather than continuing to list them in the style of a tactical manual, I have chosen to let the reader learn them in the same fashion I did: via experience. Challenge our decision making, our actions, and ultimately our results. In order to defeat the guerrilla threat of the future, we must understand how we won against Al Qaeda in Iraq in early 2007. Only then will we realize what the end-state in the "war on terror" looks like.

Index

Page numbers in italic indicate maps or photographs.